PROVING BRIBERY, FRAUD AND MONEY LAUNDERING IN INTERNATIONAL ARBITRATION

Over the past few decades, arbitration has become the number-one mechanism to settle international investment and commercial disputes. As a parallel development, the international legal framework to combat economic crime became much stronger within the fields of foreign public bribery, private bribery, fraud and money laundering. With frequent allegations of criminal conduct arising in international arbitration proceedings, it is crucially important to consider how such claims can be proven. This book analyses relevant case law involving alleged criminal conduct within international arbitration and addresses the most pressing issues regarding applicable criminal law and evidence. It is an essential resource for practising lawyers and academics active in the field of international investment and commercial arbitration.

KATHRIN BETZ completed her PhD thesis at the Chair of Professor Mark Pieth, Basel University, Switzerland, in 2016 (summa cum laude). As an academic assistant, her responsibilities included assisting the former Chairman of the OECD Working Group on Bribery. She coordinated the second edition of *The OECD Convention on Bribery* (2014) edited by Mark Pieth, Lucinda A. Low and Nicola Bonucci and published by Cambridge University Press.

PROVING BRIBERY, FRAUD AND MONEY LAUNDERING IN INTERNATIONAL ARBITRATION

On Applicable Criminal Law and Evidence

KATHRIN BETZ
University of Basel

CAMBRIDGE
UNIVERSITY PRESS

CAMBRIDGE
UNIVERSITY PRESS

University Printing House, Cambridge CB2 8BS, United Kingdom

One Liberty Plaza, 20th Floor, New York, NY 10006, USA

477 Williamstown Road, Port Melbourne, VIC 3207, Australia

314-321, 3rd Floor, Plot 3, Splendor Forum, Jasola District Centre, New Delhi-110025, India

79 Anson Road, #06-04/06, Singapore 079906

Cambridge University Press is part of the University of Cambridge.

It furthers the University's mission by disseminating knowledge in the pursuit of education, learning and research at the highest international levels of excellence.

www.cambridge.org
Information on this title: www.cambridge.org/9781108417846
DOI: 10.1017/9781108279260

First published 2017

A catalogue record for this publication is available from the British Library

Library of Congress Cataloging in Publication data
Names: Betz, Kathrin, 1982– author.
Title: Proving bribery, fraud, and money laundering in international arbitration : on applicable criminal law and evidence / Kathrin Betz, University of Basel.
Description: Cambridge [UK] ; New York : Cambridge University Press, 2017. | Includes bibliographical references and index.
Identifiers: LCCN 2017019175 | ISBN 9781108417846 (hardback : alk. paper)
Subjects: LCSH: Arbitration and award. | International commercial arbitration–Corrupt practices. | Bribery. | Fraud. | Money laundering. | Investments, Foreign (International law) | Criminal law. | Evidence, Criminal.
Classification: LCC K2400 .B53 2017 | DDC 345/.0263–dc23 LC record available at https://lccn.loc.gov/2017019175

ISBN 978-1-108-41784-6 Hardback

CONTENTS

ACKNOWLEDGEMENTS

My sincere thanks are due to Prof. Mark Pieth for supervising the PhD project on which this book is based. Working at his Chair at Basel University allowed me to dig deeply into a number of international arbitration cases, and exchanging views with him has been a constant source of motivation. I have learned a lot from him. Prof. Krista Nadakavukaren Schefer, my second supervisor, continuously supported the project and engaged in fruitful discussions, and Dr. Stephan Wilske was ready to act as an expert in the doctoral colloquium.

Professors Sabine Gless, Lukas Handschin, Anton K. Schnyder and Ingeborg Zerbes shared their perspectives on several aspects, for which I am most grateful. Kirstin Bentley proofed the final manuscript. The International Chamber of Commerce Institute of World Business Law generously gave me the opportunity to participate in their Annual Meeting on 'Addressing Issues of Corruption in Commercial and Investment Arbitration', allowing an insight into where things stand.

Last but not least, I would like to thank Kim Hughes and Rebecca Roberts of Cambridge University Press for their essential support.

TABLE OF ARBITRAL AWARDS

International Centre for Settlement of Investment Disputes (ICSID)

African Holding v. Democratic Republic of Congo, ICSID Case No. ARB/05/21, *African Holding Company of America, Inc. et Société Africaine de Construction au Congo SARL et La République Démocratique du Congo,* Sentence sur les déclinatoires de compétence et la recevabilité, 29 July 2008

Azpetrol v. Azerbaijan, ICSID Case No. ARB/06/15, *Azpetrol International Holdings B.V. et al. and The Republic of Azerbaijan,* Award, 8 September 2009

Bayindir v. Pakistan, ICSID Case No. ARB/03/29, *Bayindir Insaat Turizm Ticaret ve Sanayi A.Ş. v. Islamic Republic of Pakistan,* Award, 27 August 2009

Biwater Gauff v. Tanzania, ICSID Case No. ARB/05/22, *Biwater Gauff (Tanzania) Ltd. v. United Republic of Tanzania,* Award, 24 July 2008

David Minnotte and Robert Lewis v. Poland, ICSID Case No. ARB(AF)/10/1, *David Minnotte and Robert Lewis and Republic of Poland,* Award, 16 May 2014

EDF v. Romania, ICSID Case No. ARB/05/13, *EDF (Services) Limited and Romania,* Award, 8 October 2009

Enron v. Argentina, ICSID Case No. ARB/01/3, *Enron Corporation and Ponderosa Assets, L.P. v. The Argentine Republic,* Decision on Jurisdiction, 14 January 2004

Fraport v. Philippines I, ICSID Case No. ARB/03/25, *Fraport AG Frankfurt Airport Services Worldwide and The Republic of the Philippines,* Award, 16 August 2007

Fraport v. Philippines II, ICSID Case No. ARB/11/12, *Fraport AG Frankfurt Airport Services Worldwide and Republic of the Philippines,* Award, 10 December 2014

Getma v. Guinea, ICSID Case No. ARB/11/29, *Getma International, NCT Necotrans, Getma International Investissements, NCT Infrastructure & Logistique et La République de Guinée,* Sentence, 16 August 2016

Grynberg et al. v. Grenada, ICSID Case No. ARB/10/6, *Rachel S. Grynberg, Stephen M. Grynberg, Miriam Z. Grynberg, and RSM Production Corporation v. Grenada,* Award, 10 December 2010

Hamester v. Ghana, ICSID Case No. ARB/07/24, *Gustav F W Hamester GmbH & Co KG v. Republic of Ghana,* Award, 18 June 2010

Inceysa v. El Salvador, ICSID Case No. ARB/03/26, *Inceysa Vallisoletana, S.L. v. Republic of El Salvador,* Award, 2 August 2006

Libananco v. Turkey, ICSID Case No. ARB/06/8, *Libananco Holdings Co. Limited and Republic of Turkey,* Award, 2 September 2011

Metal-Tech v. Uzbekistan, ICSID Case No. ARB/10/3, *Metal-Tech Ltd. v. The Republic of Uzbekistan,* Award, 4 October 2013

Niko v. Bangladesh, ICSID Cases No. ARB/10/11 and ARB/10/18, *Niko Resources (Bangladesh) Ltd. and People's Republic of Bangladesh, Bangladesh Petroleum Exploration & Production Company Limited ('Bapex') and Bangladesh Oil Gas and Mineral Corporation ('Petrobangla'),* Decision on Jurisdiction, 19 August 2013

Phoenix v. Czech Republic, ICSID Case No. ARB/06/5, *Phoenix Action, Ltd. v. Czech Republic,* Award, 15 April 2009

Plama v. Bulgaria, ICSID Case No. ARB/03/24, *Plama Consortium Limited and Republic of Bulgaria,* Award, 27 August 2008

Quiborax v. Bolivia, ICSID Case No. ARB/06/2, *Quiborax S.A., Non Metallic Minerals S.A. and Allan Fosk Kaplún v. Plurinational State of Bolivia,* Decision on Provisional Measures, 26 February 2010

Rompetrol v. Romania, ICSID Case No. ARB/06/3, *The Rompetrol Group N.V. and Romania,* Award, 6 May 2013

RSM v. Grenada, ICSID Case No. ARB/05/14, *RSM Production Corporation and Grenada,* Award, 13 March 2009

RSM v. Grenada, Annulment Proceeding, ICSID Case No. ARB/05/14, *RSM Production Corporation and Grenada,* Decision on RSM Production Corporation's Application for a Preliminary Ruling of 29 October 2009, 7 December 2009

Saba Fakes v. Turkey, ICSID Case No. ARB/07/20, *Mr. Saba Fakes and Republic of Turkey,* Award, 14 July 2010

Salini v. Morocco, ICSID Case No. ARB/00/4, *Salini Costruttori S.P.A. and Italstrade S.P.A. v. Kingdom of Morocco,* Decision on Jurisdiction, 16 July 2001

Siag v. Egypt, ICSID Case No. ARB/05/15, *Waguih Elie George Siag and Clorinda Vecchi and The Arab Republic of Egypt,* Award, 1 June 2009

Siemens v. Argentina, ICSID Case No. ARB/02/8, *Siemens AG and The Argentine Republic, Award,* 6 February 2007

Sistem v. Kyrgyz Republic, ICSID Case No. ARB(AF)/06/1, *Sistem Mühendislik İnşaat Sanayi ve Ticaret A.Ş. and Kyrgyz Republic,* Award, 9 September 2009

Spentex v. Uzbekistan, ICSID Case No. ARB/13/26, *Spentex Netherlands B.V. and Republic of Uzbekistan,* Award, 27 December 2016

Tokios Tokelės v. Ukraine, ICSID Case No. ARB/02/18, Award, 26 July 2007

Tokios Tokelės v. Ukraine, ICSID Case No. ARB/02/18, Decision on Jurisdiction, 29 April 2004

TSA Spectrum v. Argentina, ICSID Case No. ARB/05/5, *TSA Spectrum de Argentina S.A. v. Argentine Republic,* Award, 19 December 2008

Wena v. Egypt, ICSID Case No. ARB/98/4, *Wena Hotels Limited v. Arab Republic of Egypt,* Award, 8 December 2000

World Duty Free v. Kenya, ICSID Case No. ARB/00/7, *World Duty Free Company Limited and The Republic of Kenya,* Award, 4 October 2006

Permanent Court of Arbitration (PCA)

Guyana v. *Suriname*, Award, 17 September 2007

Hulley Enterprises v. *Russia, Hulley Enterprises Limited (Cyprus)* and *The Russian Federation*, PCA Case No. AA 226, Final Award, 18 July 2014

Veteran Petroleum Limited v. *Russia, Veteran Petroleum Limited (Cyprus)* and *The Russian Federation*, PCA Case No. AA 228, Final Award, 18 July 2014

Yukos Universal Limited v. *Russia, Yukos Universal Limited (Isle of Man)* and *The Russian Federation*, PCA Case No. AA 227, Final Award, 18 July 2014

Agreement on Promotion, Protection and Guarantee of Investments among Member States of the Organisation of the Islamic Conference (OIC), Article 17

Al-Warraq v. Indonesia, Hesham Talaat M. Al-Warraq v. The Republic of Indonesia, Final Award, 15 December 2014

North American Free Trade Agreement (NAFTA), Chapter 11

Methanex v. *United States, Methanex Corporation* and *United States of America,* Final Award of the Tribunal on Jurisdiction and Merits, 3 August 2005

International Chamber of Commerce (ICC)

ICC Case No. 1110, Award; 10 *Arbitration International* (1994), 282

ICC Case No. 3344; 109 *Journal du droit international* (1982), 978

ICC Case No. 3913; summary published in Crivellaro 2003, 120

ICC Case No. 3916, Award; 111 *Journal du droit international* (1984), 930

ICC Case No. 4145, Interim Awards and Final Award of 1983, 1984 and 1986; *Yearbook Commercial Arbitration* XII (1987), 97 [cit. ICC Case No. 4145, Yearbook]; 112 *Journal du droit international* (1985), 985 [cit. ICC Case No. 4145, Journal]

ICC Case No. 5943, 123 *Journal du droit international* (1996), 1014

ICC Case No. 6248, Final Award, *Yearbook Commercial Arbitration* XIX (1994), 124

ICC Case No. 6320, Final Award, *Yearbook Commercial Arbitration* XX (1995), 62

ICC Case No. 6497, Final Award; *Yearbook Commercial Arbitration* XXIV (1999), 71

ICC Case No. 8891, Award; 127 *Journal du droit international* (2000), 1076

ICC Case No. 9333, Final Award; *Collection of ICC Arbitral Awards 2001–2007* (2009), 575 [cit. ICC Case No. 9333, Collection]; *ASA Bulletin* (2001), 757 [cit. ICC Case No. 9333, ASA Bulletin]; *ICC International Court of Arbitration Bulletin* (1999), 102 [cit. ICC Case No. 9333, ICC Bulletin]

ICC Case No. 11307, Final Award, *Yearbook Commercial Arbitration* XXXIII (2008), 24

ICC Case No. 12472, Final Award; 24 *ICC International Court of Arbitration Bulletin* (2013), Special Supplement, 'Tackling Corruption in Arbitration', 46

ICC Case No. 12732, Partial Award; 22 *ICC International Court of Arbitration Bulletin* (2011), 76

ICC Case No. 12990, Final Award; 24 *ICC International Court of Arbitration Bulletin* (2013), Special Supplement, 'Tackling Corruption in Arbitration', 52 [cit. ICC Case No. 12990, Bulletin]; also published (incorrectly numbered as ICC Case No. 12290) in *Collection of ICC Arbitral Awards 2008–2011* (2013), 831 [cit. ICC Case No. 12990, Collection]; 137 *Journal du droit international* (2010), 1406 [cit. ICC Case No. 12990, Journal]

ICC Case No. 13384, Final Award; 24 *ICC International Court of Arbitration Bulletin* (2013), Special Supplement, 'Tackling Corruption in Arbitration', 62

ICC Case No. 13515, Final Award; 24 *ICC International Court of Arbitration Bulletin* (2013), Special Supplement, 'Tackling Corruption in Arbitration', 66

ICC Case No. 13914, Final Award; 24 *ICC International Court of Arbitration Bulletin* (2013), Special Supplement, 'Tackling Corruption in Arbitration', 77

ICC Case No. 14470, Final Award; 24 *ICC International Court of Arbitration Bulletin* (2013), Special Supplement, 'Tackling Corruption in Arbitration', 90

ICC Case No. 14878, Final Award; 24 *ICC International Court of Arbitration Bulletin* (2013), Special Supplement, 'Tackling Corruption in Arbitration', 92

ICC Case No. 16090, Final Award, *ICC Dispute Resolution Bulletin* (2016), Issue 1, 147

Hilmarton v. *OTV*, ICC Case No. 5622, *Hilmarton Ltd.* v. *Omnium de Traitement et de Valorisation (OTV)*, Award of 19 August 1988; *Yearbook Commercial Arbitration* XIX (1994), 105 [cit. *Hilmarton* v. *OTV*, Yearbook]; *ASA Bulletin* (1993), 247

PIATCO v. *Republic of the Philippines*, ICC Case No. 12610/TE/MW/AVH/JEM/MLK, *Philippine International Air Terminals Co., Inc.* v. *The Government of the Republic of the Philippines*, Partial Award of 22 July 2010 (unpublished)

Westacre v. *Jugoimport*, ICC Case No. 7047, Final Award of 28 February 1994; *ASA Bulletin* (1995), 301 [cit. *Westacre* v. *Jugoimport*, Bulletin]; *Yearbook Commercial Arbitration* XXI (1996), 79 [cit. *Westacre* v. *Jugoimport*, Yearbook]

Westinghouse v. *National Power Corporation*, ICC Case No. 6401, *Westinghouse International Projects Company et al.* v. *National Power Corporation and the Republic of the Philippines*, Preliminary Award of 19 December 1991; 7(1) *Mealey's International Arbitration Report* (1992), B-1

X v. *Y* (2004 Geneva Award), ICC Case No. 12875/MS, Award of 16 August 2004 (unpublished)

Tribunal Arbitral du Sport/Court of Arbitration for Sport (TAS/CAS)

Adamu v. FIFA, Amos Adamu and Fédération Internationale de Football Association, CAS 2011/A/2426, Award, 24 February 2012

Ad Hoc Arbitral Awards

Oostergetel v. Slovak Republic, UNCITRAL ad hoc Arbitration, *Jan Oostergetel and Theodora Laurentius and The Slovak Republic,* Final Award, 23 April 2012

X v. Y (2004 Zurich Award), *ad hoc* arbitration, Partial Award of 19 October 2004, Zurich (unpublished)

X v. Y (2006 Zurich Award), *ad hoc* arbitration, Second Partial Award of 16 May 2006, Zurich (unpublished)

TABLE OF COURT CASES

France

*Appeals Courts (*Cour d'appel*)*

Paris Appeals Court, decision of 19 December 1991 (on *Hilmarton* v. *OTV*); *Rivista dell'arbitrato* (1992), 743

Société Labinal v. *Sociétés Mors et Westland Aerospace*, Paris Appeals Court, decision of 19 May 1993; *Revue de l'arbitrage* (1993), 645

Paris Appeals Court, decision 13/13278 of 17 February 2015 (on *Crédit Lyonnais* and *Bernard Tapie*)

Paris Appeals Court, decision 15/01650 of 21 February 2017 (on *Valeri Belokon* v. *Kyrgyz Republic*)

Versailles Appeals Court (on *Hilmarton* v. *OTV*); *Yearbook Commercial Arbitration* XXI (1996), 524

*Supreme Court (*Cour de Cassation*)*

Supreme Court (on *Hilmarton v. OTV*); *Yearbook Commercial Arbitration* XX (1995), 663

Supreme Court (on *Hilmarton v. OTV*); *Yearbook Commercial Arbitration* XXII (1997), 696

Switzerland

Cantonal Courts

Court of Justice of the Canton of Geneva, *Hilmarton* v. *OTV*; *Rivista dell'arbitrato* (1992), 735; *ASA Bulletin* (1993), 250

*Swiss Federal Supreme Court (*Bundesgericht*)*

BGE 76 II 33

BGE 95 II 37

BGE 118 II 199

BGE 118 II 353

BGE 118 IV 175

BGE 119 II 380 (on *Westinghouse* v. *National Power Corporation*)
BGE 120 II 155
BGE 126 III 249
BGE 129 III 320
BGE 131 I 272
BGE 131 IV 36
BGE 132 III 389
BGE 133 III 139
BGer of 17 April 1990 (on *Hilmarton* v. *OTV*); *Rivista dell'arbitrato* (1992), 739; *ASA Bulletin* (1993), 253
BGer of 30 December 1994 (on *Westacre* v. *Jugoimport*); *ASA Bulletin* (1995), 217
BGer of 28 January 1997 (on *Thomson CSF* v. *Frontier AG Bern et al.*); *ASA Bulletin* (1998), 118
BGer 4P.260/2000 of 2 March 2001; *ASA Bulletin* (2001), 531
BGer 4A_596/2008 of 6 October 2009 (on *Thales (formerly Thomson CSF)* v. *Frontier AG Bern et al.*); *ASA Bulletin* (2010), 318
BGer 4A_488/2011 of 18 June 2012
BGer 4A_538/2012 of 17 January 2013
BGer 4A_362/2013 of 27 March 2014
BGer 4A_448/2013 of 27 March 2014
BGer 4A_178/2014 of 11 June 2014

United Kingdom

High Court of Justice, Chancery Division

In re Dellow's Will Trusts [1964] 1 WLR 451

High Court of Justice, Queen's Bench Division

Archbolds (Freightage) Ltd v. S Spanglett Ltd [1961] 1 QBD 374
Hire-Purchase Furnishings Co. v. Richens (1887) 20 QBD 387
Westacre Investments Inc v. Jugoimport-SPDR Holding Co Ltd and Others [1998] 4 All ER 570 (QBD)

England and Wales Court of Appeal, Civil Division

Abner Soleimany v. Sion Soleimany [1999] 3 All ER 847
Hornal v. Neuberger Products Ltd [1957] 1 QB 247
R(N) v. Mental Health Review Tribunal (Northern Region) [2006] QB 468
Westacre Investments Inc v. Jugoimport-SPDR Holding Co Ltd and Others [1999] 3 All ER 864

House of Lords

Brown v. Rolls Royce Ltd [1960] 1 WLR 210
In re B (Children)(Fc) [2008] UKHL 35
In re H. and Others (Minors) [1996] AC 563
R. v. Sang [1980] AC 402
Secretary of State for the Home Department v. Rehman [2001] UKHL 47

United States

District Courts

RSM et al. v. *Fridman et al.*, Civ. No. 1:06-cv-11512-EJW (S.D. New York), Judgment, 19 February 2009
The Republic of the Philippines and National Power Corporation v. *Westinghouse Electric Corporation et al.*, Civ. No. 88-5150, Opinion of 4 February 1992 (D. New Jersey); 7(2) *Mealey's International Arbitration Report* (1992), A-1
US v. *Siemens AG* Cr. No. 1:08-cr-367-RJL (D. Columbia), Statement of Offense, 15 December 2008
US v. *Siemens SA (Argentina)*, Cr. No. 1:08-cr-368-RJL (D. Columbia), Statement of Offense, 15 December 2008

Supreme Court

Addington v. *Texas*, 441 US 418 (1979)
Mitsubishi Motors Corp. v. *Soler Chrysler-Plymouth, Inc.*, 473 US 614 (1985)
Precision Instrument Mfg. Co. v. *Automotive Co.*, 324 US 806 (1945)

European Court of Human Rights

Condron v. *United Kingdom*, European Court of Human Rights, Application no. 35718/97, Judgment, 2 May 2000
John Murray v. *United Kingdom*, European Court of Human Rights, Application no. 18731/91, Judgment, 8 February 1996
Saunders v. *United Kingdom*, European Court of Human Rights, Application no. 19187/91, Judgment, 17 December 1996

ABBREVIATIONS

AAA	American Arbitration Association
AC	Appeal Cases
AfDB	African Development Bank
All ER	All England Law Reports
AMLA	Swiss Anti-Money Laundering Act (Geldwäschereigesetz; GwG) (SR 955.0)
ASA	Association suisse de l'arbitrage (Swiss Arbitration Association)
BBl	Bundesblatt (Swiss Federal Gazette)
BGE	Bundesgerichtsentscheid (Swiss Federal Supreme Court decision, published)
BGer	Bundesgerichtsentscheid (Swiss Federal Supreme Court decision, unpublished)
BIT	bilateral investment treaty
CEO	Chief Executive Officer
CIETAC	China International Economic and Trade Arbitration Commission
CoE	Council of Europe
D.	District
DIAC	Dubai International Arbitration Centre
DIS	Deutsche Institution für Schiedsgerichtsbarkeit (German Institution of Arbitration)
DOJ	Department of Justice
EBRD	European Bank for Reconstruction and Development
ECHR	European Convention on Human Rights
EU	European Union
FATF	Financial Action Task Force
FCPA	Foreign Corrupt Practices Act (US)
HKIAC	Hong Kong International Arbitration Centre
IADB	Inter-American Development Bank
IBA	International Bar Association
ICC	International Chamber of Commerce
ICDR	International Centre for Dispute Resolution (the International Division of the American Arbitration Association)

ICJ	International Court of Justice
ICSID	International Centre for Settlement of Investment Disputes
IFFs	illicit financial flows
ILA	International Law Association
ILC	International Law Commission
J	Judge
LCIA	London Court of International Arbitration
LJ	Lord Justice of Appeal
MDB	multilateral development bank
MKAS	Международный коммерческий арбитражный суд (International Commercial Arbitration Court of the Russian Federation)
MoD	Ministry of Defence
MoJ	Ministry of Justice
NAFTA	North American Free Trade Agreement
NGO	non-governmental organisation
OECD	Organisation for Economic Co-operation and Development
OIC	Organisation of Islamic Cooperation (formerly: Organisation of the Islamic Conference)
OJ	Official Journal
OLAF	Office de Lutte Anti-Fraude (European Anti-Fraud Office)
PCA	Permanent Court of Arbitration
PDG	Président directeur général (chief executive officer)
POCA	Proceeds of Crime Act 2002 (UK)
QBD	Queen's Bench Division
SCC	Swiss Civil Code (Schweizerisches Zivilgesetzbuch; ZGB) (SR 210)
SCO	Swiss Code of Obligations (Obligationenrecht; OR) (SR 220)
SCPC	Swiss Civil Procedure Code (Schweizerische Zivilprozessordnung; ZPO) (SR 272)
SCrimC	Swiss Criminal Code (Schweizerisches Strafgesetzbuch; StGB) (SR 311.0)
SCrimPC	Swiss Criminal Procedure Code (Schweizerische Strafprozessordnung; StPO) (SR 312.0)
SD	Southern District
SIAC	Singapore International Arbitration Centre
SPILA	Swiss Private International Law Act (Bundesgesetz über das Internationale Privatrecht; IPRG) (SR 291)
SR	Systematische Rechtssammlung (Systematic Compilation of Swiss Federal Acts)
TAS/CAS	Tribunal Arbitral du Sport/Court of Arbitration for Sport
TI	Transparency International
UKHL	United Kingdom House of Lords
UNCAC	UN Convention against Corruption

UNCLOS	UN Convention on the Law of the Sea
UNCITRAL	UN Commission on International Trade Law
UNGA	UN General Assembly
VIAC	Vienna International Arbitral Centre
WGB	Working Group on Bribery (OECD)
WHO	World Health Organisation
WLR	Weekly Law Reports

PART I

Introduction

1

What Is at Stake?

Allegations of criminal conduct arising in disputes that are settled in international arbitration proceedings are not a new issue. In commercial arbitration, the landmark *Lagergren* case dates back to 1963,[1] and in investment arbitration, the well-known *World Duty Free* v. *Kenya* case was decided in 2006.[2] Arbitrators regularly have to deal with alleged transnational corruption and bribery, and allegations of fraud and money laundering equally come up. In a globalised economy, licit as well as illicit financial flows across borders are on the rise.

Over the past decades, international arbitration has become the number-one mechanism to settle international commercial and investment disputes[3] where large-scale economic interests may be at stake.[4] Independently of the rise of arbitration, another development took place: the international legal framework that criminalises public and private bribery, fraud and money laundering has become much stronger over the past twenty years. Transnational public policy plays an important role in arbitration nowadays, and allegations of criminal behaviour can have a decisive impact on the outcome of the proceedings.[5] Such allegations have the potential to serve as 'killer argument' in a case, giving one party a defence against all claims of the opposite party – if they are proven successfully. Therefore, the question how allegations of criminal conduct in international arbitration can be proven is highly relevant in practice.

[1] See discussion in Chapter 6. [2] See discussion in Chapter 5.

[3] For commercial arbitration: Born 2014, 93 et seq.; for ICSID arbitration: ICSID Annual Report 2014, 5.

[4] E.g. in *World Duty Free* v. *Kenya*, the former Kenyan Attorney-General pointed out that the claim in this case amounted to more than Kenya's budget at that time, emphasising that if the Claimant had succeeded, this might have halted the country's development and turned it into a failed state (Llamzon 2014, 117, 251).

[5] Cf. Pieth 2011, 1375 et seq.

May arbitral tribunals decide disputes involving alleged criminal conduct at all, or must state courts deal with such issues?[6] It is undisputed that the sanctioning of criminal behaviour is exclusively reserved to domestic state courts (or international criminal courts and tribunals).[7] However, this does not preclude arbitrators from applying criminal laws: '[I]nternational arbitral tribunals have no power to or interest in providing sentencing for criminal offences, while they may well have the power to assess the impact of criminal or other illegal activity on commercial transactions.'[8]

While domestic legislators could limit the possibilities of arbitration to assess the impact of criminal conduct on commercial transactions, this is not usually done.[9] With regard to Switzerland, the Federal Supreme Court held in 1992 that disputes involving matters of foreign mandatory law or public policy are not, in principle, exclusively reserved to state courts.[10] Today, it is established that any dispute of financial interest is arbitrable under chapter 12 of the Swiss Private International Law Act (SPILA), including disputes that in some way involve criminal conduct.[11] While opinions are not uniform in this regard,[12] the practice of arbitral

[6] Cf. Art. V 2. (a) New York Convention 1958. The question of arbitrability is not to be confused with the issue of separability of the arbitral clause (see discussion in Chapter 2 and in Chapter 10).

[7] Kurkela 2008, 282 (fn. 7); Mistelis 2009, 574 et seq.; on punitive damages: Mourre 2009, 220 et seq.

[8] Mistelis 2009, 575; see also Mourre 2009, 209 et seq.; Raeschke-Kessler 2004, 493; Srinivasan et al. 2014, 135 et seq.; and Voser 1996, 330 et seq. Different: Smit, who argues that arbitrators should be precluded from ruling on mandatory law issues (Smit 2011, 226).

[9] Cf. e.g. the US Supreme Court decision in *Mitsubishi Motors Corp.* v. *Soler Chrysler-Plymouth, Inc.*, 473 US 614 (1985), where the Court argued that a Japanese arbitral tribunal was competent to rule on alleged violations of the US Sherman Antitrust Act (Donovan and Greenawalt 2006, 14 et seq.; Mayer 1986, 279 et seq.); and the Paris Court of Appeals decision of 1993 that the arbitrability of a dispute was not precluded only because a rule of public policy was at stake (*Société Labinal* v. *Sociétés Mors et Westland Aerospace*; Mourre 2009, 216); cf. also Blackaby et al. 2015, 112 et seq., 586.

[10] BGE 118 II 353, 356 et seq.; Blessing 1997, 29 et seq.; Schnyder 1995, 297.

[11] Regarding corruption: Berger and Kellerhals 2015, 82; Kaufmann-Kohler and Rigozzi 2015, 102; Arfazadeh 2001, 681; in detail: Sayed 2001, 658 et seq.; on public procurement-related matters: Sayed 2004, 27 et seq.; cf. also BGE 119 II 380, 385.

[12] Smit argues that in order to ensure that arbitral tribunals apply mandatory law properly and consistently, such issues should be referred to a single judicial institution of the state whose mandatory law is applied: '[M]aterial issues of mandatory law are ruled non-arbitrable and are referred to a single domestic court.' (Smit 2011, 210). It remains open how practical such a solution would be, in particular with regard to the capacity of state courts in jurisdictions worldwide.

tribunals shows that those frequently decide on mandatory law issues, including matters of criminal law.

From a criminal law viewpoint, allegations of criminal conduct in international arbitration are not a mere morality issue. Bribery, fraud and money laundering are economic crimes. Committed on a large scale involving the abuse of public funds, they have a detrimental impact on national economies and the people's trust in public institutions. A state's assets are channelled away from the legitimate recipients – the people – into the pockets of a few powerful. This causes massive problems, as public funds (including aid money) disappear that would be needed for health, education and infrastructure projects. Reducing poverty and crime cannot succeed if the state's wealth is shovelled to offshore bank accounts or real estate, to the benefit of a few.[13]

The effects of corruption can also be perceived more directly: in public procurement, if a project is awarded – due to bribe payments or fraud during the bidding process – to a bidder whose performance is substandard, the work product will quite certainly not be 'state of the art' and, for instance, not fulfil essential safety standards.[14] The negative impact of bribery on fair competition is quite universally acknowledged.[15] For all these reasons, the international efforts to combat illicit financial flows[16] have been stepped up dramatically in the past decades, and most states nowadays criminalise bribery, fraud and money laundering in their domestic law. In short: if criminal conduct is alleged in international arbitration, it cannot be taken lightly anymore, or even disregarded, by arbitrators.[17]

In practice, when arbitral tribunals decide criminal law issues, difficult questions regarding the applicable law and evidence arise. Criminal law is mandatory and part of public law – it is not at the disposition of the parties – while in particular international commercial arbitration is private and autonomous from states, consensual and based on party autonomy.[18] The proceedings are in general confidential and closed to the public, which is disturbing if public interest issues such as corruption in relation to public procurement or to concessions to exploit natural

[13] E.g. Cockcroft 2014, 57 et seq.; Makinwa 2013, 301 et seq.; on the impact of corruption on sustainable development: Aidt 2011, 3 et seq.

[14] Cf. e.g. Wells 2014.

[15] See, e.g., Cremades and Cairns 2003a, 77.

[16] While no universally agreed definition of *illicit financial flows* (IFFs) exists yet, according to the World Bank, they are most commonly described as 'money illegally earned, transferred, or used that crosses borders'.

[17] Pieth 2011, 1380.

[18] Mourre 2009, 207.

resources are at stake.[19] In domestic legal systems, prosecutors must collect the evidence in criminal cases; in international arbitration, there is no public prosecutor. In principle, the parties produce the evidence. The merger of proceedings that are essentially based on party autonomy with substantive criminal law that falls into the domain of the authority of states raises touchy issues.

At some point, parties may agree to settle if circumstantial evidence indicates that criminal conduct is involved (and the arbitral proceedings become time-consuming and expensive)[20] – but what if they do not? How can parties successfully prove criminal conduct, and how can arbitrators distinguish real cases from unsubstantiated allegations?[21] How can arbitrators recognise that criminal conduct is involved, even if none of the parties alleges it (including sham arbitration)? Arbitrators are facing a genuine dilemma in such cases.

This book looks into the process of proving bribery, fraud and money laundering in international investment and commercial arbitration. The focus is, on the one hand, on the applicable criminal law: which substantive law applies if criminal conduct is alleged, and which law applies to procedure and evidence? On the other hand, selected issues of evidence are discussed: burden and standard of proof, adverse inferences, admissibility of evidence and the privilege against self-incrimination. The core of the text is an analysis of current practice of arbitral tribunals – in particular ICSID and ICC cases – when facing allegations of, or suspecting, criminal conduct. Through an inductive[22] approach, pertinent

[19] Rose 2014, 224 et seq. who points out that ICSID arbitration is more transparent than UNCITRAL or ICC arbitration. The new UNCITRAL Transparency Rules (UNCITRAL 2013b) should bring about a higher level of transparency.

[20] Cf. e.g. the *Azpetrol* v. *Azerbaijan* case (Llamzon 2014, 125 et seq., 200 et seq.; Rose 2014, 192 et seq.).

[21] Cf. the Separate Opinion of Professor Thomas Wälde in *International Thunderbird Gaming Corporation* v. *The United Mexican States* of December 2005 (at para. 20), where he argued that '[corruption] insinuations are now frequently employed by both claimant investors and respondent governments. They should be disregarded – explicitly and implicitly, except if properly and explicitly submitted to the tribunal, substantiated with a specific allegation of corruption and subject to proper legal and factual debate for the tribunal.'

[22] Not *deductive*: the starting point is not the content of the law, but the cases. See Hassemer 1990, 9 et seq. (on criminal law textbooks): '"Induktiv" *meint: Die Darstellung lässt sich nicht* ("deduktiv") *vom Inhalt des Gesetzes und der Auslegung leiten, die das Gesetz konkretisiert, um danach das Wissen für die Entscheidung von Fällen präsent zu haben; die Darstellung geht vielmehr vom (noch ungelösten) Fall aus und entwickelt an ihm Gesetzesinhalt und Gesetzesauslegung, die auf diesen Fall "passen".*'

questions on applicable criminal law and evidence are identified, followed by a critical assessment. The aim is to develop a decision tree for arbitrators on how they should proceed in such situations. Some passages of the text draw from Swiss and English law as examples for a continental and a common law system with modern arbitration legislation. Both are popular arbitration locations, and parties also like to choose the law of those two countries to apply.[23]

Numerous commentators have addressed alleged criminal conduct in international arbitration. In 2003 and 2014, Crivellaro collected the arbitration case law that deals with bribery and corruption.[24] The Collection of ICC Arbitral Awards of the International Chamber of Commerce (ICC) contains a number of cases that involve bribery and fraud.[25] In 2013, the ICC issued a Special Supplement with extracts of ICC cases involving bribery and corruption.[26] In 2004, Sayed published a comprehensive study on corruption in international trade and commercial arbitration;[27] and in 2014, Llamzon addressed corruption in international investment arbitration in a thorough study.[28] Many articles specifically deal with the topic of proving alleged bribery, fraud and money laundering, and their legal consequences, in international arbitration proceedings.[29] In general, those writings have a background in arbitration. The approach here is from a criminal law perspective.

The text is organised in five parts. After the Introduction, Part II presents the basic legal framework for international investment and

23 Born 2014, 144 et seq.

24 Crivellaro 2003, 119 et seq.; Crivellaro 2014; for a collection and summary of ICC case law: Martin 2003, 12 et seq.

25 The following cases discussed in this text are published in the Collection of ICC Arbitral Awards 1974–2011 (6 Volumes): ICC Cases No. 1110, 3916, 4145, 5622, 6248, 7047, 8891, 9333, 11307, 12290 and 14470.

26 24 *ICC International Court of Arbitration Bulletin* (2013), Special Supplement, 'Tackling Corruption in Arbitration', 39 et seq.

27 Sayed 2004. 28 Llamzon 2014.

29 See Bibliography; to name a few recent texts: Abdel Raouf 2009; Coşar 2015; Cremades 2005; Cremades and Cairns 2003; González García 2013; Hahn 2010; Haugeneder and Liebscher 2009; Hwang and Lim 2012; Karsten 2003; Kendra and Bonini 2014; Khvalei 2014; Kreindler 2010a; Kulick and Wendler 2010; Lamm, Greenwald and Young 2014; Lamm, Hellbeck and Khan 2015; Lamm, Pham and Moloo 2010; Lim 2013; Litwin 2013; Llamzon and Sinclair 2015; Martin 2003; McDougall 2005; Menaker 2010; Meshel 2013; Mills 2002; Mourre 2009; Nadeau-Séguin 2013; Nasarre 2013; Newcombe 2011; Partasides 2010; Philip 2003; Pieth 2011; Raeschke-Kessler 2004; Rose 2014; Sacerdoti 2009; Scherer 2002; Schill 2012; Schlabrendorff 2005; Srinivasan et al. 2014; Stacher 2011; Vincke 2014; Wilske and Fox 2011; Wilske and Obel 2013; Yackee 2012.

commercial arbitration, including the applicable substantive and procedural law. In addition, the forms and manifestations of criminal conduct that are the subject of this text are defined and discussed; and selected issues of evidence in common (English) law, in continental (Swiss) law and in arbitration are introduced. Part III analyses the current practice of international arbitral tribunals when they are confronted with alleged criminal behaviour, with a focus on ICSID and ICC cases. Part IV critically discusses issues of applicable criminal law and evidence that emerge from the case analysis. To round off the text, a brief look at the legal consequences of criminal conduct in investment and commercial arbitration is taken. Part V eventually summarises the results of the study, and draws a conclusion. The Annex is an attempt to draw up a decision tree for arbitrators on how they should proceed when they are confronted with allegations of, or suspect, criminal conduct.

PART II

Basics

International Arbitration, Crime and Evidence

2

Forms of International Arbitration

There exist a multitude of different forms of arbitration as a method for dispute resolution. Despite their differences, they are based upon the same concept:

> Disputants agree to submit their disputes to an individual whose judgment they are prepared to trust. Each puts its case to this decision maker, this private individual – in a word, this 'arbitrator'. He or she listens to the parties, considers the facts and the arguments, and makes a decision. That decision is final and binding on the parties – and it is final and binding because the parties have agreed that it should be, rather than because of the coercive power of any state.[1]

The topic of this text is international[2] (in contrast to domestic) investment and commercial arbitration. Where necessary, investment and commercial arbitration are discussed separately, with a focus on institutional arbitration.[3] *Ad hoc* arbitration[4] is briefly touched upon.

2.1 Investment Arbitration

Investment arbitration is a settlement mechanism for disputes arising out of foreign investment. Foreign investment can take different legal[5] forms, for instance: the formation of or participation in a company incorporated

1 Blackaby et al. 2015, 2.

2 A wide definition of 'international' is adopted here: 'An arbitration is considered to be "international" if . . . it involves parties of different nationalities, or it takes place in a country that is "foreign" to the parties, or it involves an international dispute' (Blackaby et al. 2015, 11; see also Art. 1(3) UNCITRAL 2006). For the ease of reading, the term 'international' is largely omitted in the following.

3 Institutional arbitration is 'administered by a specialist arbitral institution under its own rules of arbitration' (Redfern and Hunter 2004, 47).

4 *Ad hoc* arbitration is 'conducted pursuant to rules agreed by the parties themselves or laid down by the arbitral tribunal' (Redfern and Hunter 2004, 47).

5 The legal concept of investment is different from the economic concept: in economics, an investment is understood to be a process or activity and one distinguishes direct, portfolio

in the host state by the foreign investor (including shareholding);[6] a contract (concession, construction, leasing, services, management, licensing or purchase of real estate) between the investor and the host state (frequently, arbitral tribunals do not call the contract itself, but rather the capital contribution, an investment);[7] and loans or the purchase of bonds.[8] The parties to the dispute can be the investor and the host state, or (in rare cases) the home state and the host state.[9]

2.1.1 *General Remarks on the Legal Framework*

Investment arbitration is based on the consent of the parties. With regard to ICSID arbitration, the consent of the investor to this kind of dispute settlement will be expressed by its filing of a claim with the ICSID Secretariat. The consent of the host state, on the other hand, can be found in a contract with the investor (e.g. a concession contract); in a national law; or in a bi- or plurilateral investment treaty.[10] Until today, no multilateral investment treaty (with a wide range of participation) and no single international institution dealing with investment disputes exists. Instead, a complex web of bilateral investment treaties (BITs) and other trade agreements protects foreign investment.[11]

BITs are treaties concluded between states (as defined in Art. 2(1)(a) of the Vienna Convention),[12] and therefore governed by international law. Their purpose is the protection and stimulation of foreign investment: they are asymmetrical in the sense that they (deliberately) grant all rights to the foreign investors, while all obligations are on the host state.[13] From the point of view of public international law, a remarkable feature of BITs is that they, with few exceptions, confer upon investors (individuals and corporations) the right to directly arbitrate treaty violations before international tribunals, without the exhaustion of local remedies

and indirect investments (in detail: Grubenmann 2010, 40 et seq.; Yannaca-Small 2010, 243 et seq.).

[6] Grubenmann 2010, 36 et seq.; Schreuer et al. 2009, Art. 25 N 148 et seq.

[7] Grubenmann 2010, 37 et seq., 247.

[8] Schreuer et al. 2009, Art. 25 N 149.

[9] Nadakavukaren Schefer 2016, 430 et seq.

[10] Bjorklund 2011, 255; Nadakavukaren Schefer 2016, 466 et seq.; Peterson 2002, 10.

[11] Efforts to create multilateral mechanisms within the framework of the OECD or the WTO failed (Gazzini 2012, 100; Nadakavukaren Schefer 2016, 39 et seq.; Peterson 2002, 3). For advantages and disadvantages of the bilateral framework: Gazzini 2012, 102 et seq. Today, more than 3,000 international investment agreements exist (Nadakavukaren Schefer 2016, 1).

[12] VCLT 1969.

[13] Gazzini 2012, 106 et seq.

being necessary.[14] Today, BITs are the most important legal source for the settlement of investment disputes.[15] BITs usually contain an arbitration clause that allows investors based in one state party (the home state) to bring a claim against the other state party (the host state) government in front of an arbitral tribunal.[16]

2.1.2 ICSID

One possible avenue for institutionalised investment arbitration is the International Centre for Settlement of Investment Disputes (ICSID), which is part of the World Bank Group and located in Washington DC.[17] Investment arbitration that does not take place under the auspices of the ICSID will in many aspects be similar to commercial arbitration.

2.1.2.1 Jurisdiction

The ICSID is not an arbitral tribunal itself, but an administrative body offering detailed procedural rules and institutional support.[18] Jurisdiction[19] of the ICSID is regulated in Art. 25 of the Convention on the Settlement of Investment Disputes between States and Nationals of Other States ('ICSID Convention').[20] The arbitral tribunals determine their competence themselves.[21] There are requirements regarding the nature of the dispute (*ratione materiae*) as well as regarding the parties (*ratione personae*) for ICSID jurisdiction. The dispute 'must arise directly from an investment and . . . must be of a legal nature . . . [O]ne side must be a Contracting State and the other a national of another Contracting State.'[22]

A discussion of all requirements to establish ICSID jurisdiction under Art. 25 is beyond the scope of this text;[23] however, four topics that are

[14] Gazzini 2012, 108. See also Lauterpacht 2009, ix.

[15] On customary law and other sources of international investment law, see Hirsch 2011, 7 et seq.; Nadakavukaren Schefer 2016, 40 et seq.

[16] Nadakavukaren Schefer 2016, 36. On the inclusion of explicit anti-corruption clauses in BITs, see Mbiyavanga 2017.

[17] For a short introduction to ICSID, see Reed, Paulsson and Blackaby 2011, 1 et seq.

[18] Grubenmann 2010, 23 et seq.; Schreuer et al. 2009, Art. 1 N 3.

[19] The term 'jurisdiction' used in Art. 25 of the ICSID Convention is slightly misleading as the Centre only has administrative, not adjudicating functions (Schreuer et al. 2009, Art. 25 N 15 et seq.).

[20] ICSID 1965. As of June 2014, 150 states ratified the Convention (ICSID Annual Report 2014, 9 et seq.).

[21] Art. 41 ICSID 1965. [22] Schreuer et al. 2009, Art. 25 N 3.

[23] See Nadakavukaren Schefer 2016, 452 et seq.; Schreuer et al. 2009, Art. 25 N 14 et seq.

essential in the context of alleged criminal conduct are addressed below: the requirements *ratione personae*, the definition of the term 'investment', the legality requirement, and evidence at the level of jurisdiction.

ICSID Jurisdiction *Ratione Personae* Art. 25(1) of the ICSID Convention provides that one party to the dispute has to be a Contracting State (or any constituent subdivision or agency of a Contracting State), which means that by the time the ICSID proceedings are instituted, the state must have become party to the ICSID Convention.[24] As this is an absolute requirement, it is generally not possible for states which are not parties to the ICSID Convention to make *ad hoc* use of its procedures.[25] The other party to the dispute must be a national of another Contracting State. This can be a natural or legal person who has the nationality of a Contracting State (positive requirement) other than the state party to the dispute (negative requirement). Whether a state-owned company can be an investor in the sense of Art. 25(1) ICSID Convention should be decided not on the basis of its ownership, but on the basis of a functional test, i.e. whether the corporation is performing an essentially governmental function.[26] A request for ICSID arbitration can be filed either by the host state or by the investor (in practice, the request almost always comes from the investor).[27]

If one of the two parties to the dispute does not fulfil the requirements *ratione personae* of Art. 25(1) ICSID Convention, there is still the possibility to institute proceedings under the ICSID Additional Facility Rules. The ICSID Convention is not applicable in proceedings under the Additional Facility Rules.[28] If both parties to the dispute are not Contracting States to the ICSID Convention, they may still call upon the Chairman of the ICSID Administrative Council or the Secretary-General of the ICSID to appoint arbitrators. This is subject to an agreement between the parties; the Secretary-General is, however, not obliged to appoint arbitrators on an *ad hoc* basis.[29]

What Is an 'Investment'? The definition of the term 'investment' is a difficult, yet fundamental issue in ICSID dispute settlement. The ICSID

[24] Thirty days after a state's deposit of its instrument of ratification, acceptance or approval, the Convention enters into force for that state (Art. 68 ICSID 1965).
[25] Schreuer et al. 2009, Art. 25 N 213.
[26] Schreuer et al. 2009, Art. 25 N 270 et seq.
[27] Art. 36 ICSID 1965; Schreuer et al. 2009, Art. 36 N 9.
[28] Art. 3 ICSID 2006a.
[29] In detail: Schreuer et al. 2009, Art. 25 N 9 et seq., 227 et seq., 300 et seq.

Convention does not contain such a definition, although it is the centrepiece of the treaty. The drafting history of the Convention shows that there was quite some debate whether or not a definition should be included.[30] The benefit of not including one is that it is left open to the parties what classes of disputes they wish to bring to ICSID, and that the jurisdiction of the Centre also accommodates new and emerging forms of investment.[31]

The freedom is not entirely without limits, however. ICSID case law shows that tribunals often apply a dual test whether an investment is at stake in a concrete dispute ('double keyhole approach'): is the activity in question covered by the consent of the parties (subjective approach), and does it possess the typical characteristics of investment in the sense of the Convention (objective approach)?[32] The consent of the parties' can be expressed 'through a contract between the host State and the investor, through a provision in the host State's investment legislation that has been accepted by the investor, or through a clause in a treaty that has been accepted by the investor'.[33] The consent of the parties encompasses the definition of investment as it forms part of the contract, law, or treaty at stake.[34] Some ICSID tribunals rely exclusively on the parties' consent to accept that an investment is at stake in a certain dispute. However, in particular with regard to BITs, the parties' consent to the treaty definition of investment does not really say anything whether in the concrete case, the disputed transaction falls under this definition, and whether it is an investment in the sense of the ICSID Convention.[35]

Other tribunals therefore argue that the concept of investment has an objective meaning apart from what the parties to a dispute have agreed (also called the autonomous notion of investment). The activity must be an investment not only according to the terms of the contract, law or

30 Schreuer et al. 2009, Art. 25 N 113 et seq.

31 Rubins 2004, 323 et seq.; Schreuer et al. 2009, Art. 25 N 120 et seq.; Yannaca-Small 2010, 248.

32 Grubenmann 2010, 68 et seq.; Rubins 2004, 290; Schreuer et al. 2009, Art. 25 N 124; Yannaca-Small 2010, 249 et seq.

33 Schreuer et al. 2009, Art. 25 N 128.

34 For a more detailed account of the three options how consent may be expressed and the meaning of 'investment', see Grubenmann 2010, 68 et seq.; Rubins 2004, 291 et seq.; Schreuer et al. 2009, Art. 25 N 129 et seq. (for contracts relating to investment); N 134 et seq. (for national investment legislation); and N 139 et seq. (for a definition of investment in treaties).

35 For a detailed discussion, including case law: Grubenmann 2010, 70 et seq., 86 et seq. and Yannaca-Small 2010, 261 et seq.

treaty at stake but also for the purposes of the ICSID Convention. As the Convention does not define investment, arbitral tribunals had to be creative. Through case law, they developed criteria for the existence of an investment. ICSID tribunals dealt with this issue in different ways.[36] To cut a long story short: the so-called *Salini* test has gained normative impact.[37] According to that test, an operation should possess four objective characteristics to qualify as an investment in the sense of the ICSID Convention (the fifth characteristic of regularity of profit is supported by scholars, but not in case law):

- the project has a certain duration;
- there is an expectation of regular profit and return;
- both sides assume risk;
- the commitment is substantial and
- the operation is significant for the host state's development.[38]

However, those characteristics should not necessarily be understood as requirements for ICSID jurisdiction.[39] There is no uniform approach by tribunals to the elements of the *Salini* test.[40] It can be said, though, that if a certain activity is covered by the definition of investment in a BIT, contract or national law to which the parties consented, and it objectively meets at least some of the above listed typical characteristics of an investment, a tribunal will accept that the activity has passed the dual test for an investment and affirm its jurisdiction (provided, of course, that all other requirements of Art. 25 ICSID Convention are fulfilled).

In reality, ICSID tribunals are frequently confronted with investments that involve a complex web of legal forms and relationships and span over a period of several years. If a dispute arises, should the entire web be regarded as one investment, or should it be broken down into several investments? A number of older ICSID Awards dealt with this issue, and

36 For a detailed discussion, including case law: Grubenmann 2010, 88 et seq., 108 et seq.; Manciaux 2008; Rubins 2004, 300 et seq.; Schreuer et al. 2009, Art. 25 N 154 et seq.; Yannaca-Small 2010, 250 et seq.

37 For a critical view of the *Salini* test, see, e.g., *Biwater Gauff* v. *Tanzania*, paras. 310 et seq.; Zivkovic 2012 with further references.

38 *Salini* v. *Morocco*, para. 52; Grubenmann 2010, 89; Schreuer et al. 2009, Art. 25 N 153; Nadakavukaren Schefer 2016, 87 et seq.; Rubins 2004, 297 et seq.

39 Schreuer et al. 2009, Art. 25 N 153; see also Williams and Foote 2011, 63 et seq.

40 To give just one example, in *Saba Fakes* v. *Turkey*, the Tribunal argued that the objective criteria of a contribution, a certain duration and an element of risk are sufficient to define an investment within the ICSID Convention framework (at paras. 110 and 121). Yannaca-Small calls this the flexible 'objectivist' or pragmatic approach (Yannaca-Small 2010, 258 et seq.).

apparently the tribunals in all cases decided in favour of a 'unity of investment', which means that they considered the combination of different legal rights and obligations that were necessary in order to implement an economic activity as one investment, even if some individual contracts were not typical investments or foresaw a different dispute settlement mechanism.[41] In newer ICSID cases, the decisions on jurisdiction confirm this trend: for example, in *Enron* v. *Argentina*, in which the Tribunal argued that an investment is 'a complex process including various arrangements, such as contracts, licences and other agreements'.[42]

The Legality Requirement BITs often include a definition of investment. Sometimes, those treaties also include the requirement that an investment must be in accordance with the host state's law in order to qualify as an investment.[43] ICSID tribunals consistently interpreted this phrase to mean that an investment has to be legal under the host state's law (legality requirement), and not that the investment has to be defined by reference to the host state's law (as it was sometimes argued by states).[44] Art. 25 of the ICSID Convention itself that regulates jurisdiction does not contain a legality requirement.[45] According to ICSID case law, if the illegality concerns 'the essence of the investment', tribunals regard the legality requirement as an established international legal principle that must be considered even if not mentioned explicitly in a BIT.[46]

[41] Grubenmann 2010, 59 et seq. with reference to ICSID Awards.

[42] *Enron* v. *Argentina*, para. 70; Grubenmann 2010, 63 with further references to ICSID cases.

[43] See, e.g., Schill 2012, 2 et seq.

[44] Grubenmann 2010, 207 et seq.; Knahr 2008, 127; Schreuer et al. 2009, Art. 25 N 199 et seq., all with reference to ICSID Awards in which the tribunals decided about the legality (and illegality) of investments under the host state's law, and in particular to *Salini* v. *Morocco* (para. 46).

[45] *Saba Fakes* v. *Turkey*, para. 112; Moloo and Khachaturian 2011, 1492 et seq.

[46] Fraport v. *Philippines II*, para. 332; *Hamester* v. *Ghana*, para. 124. In *David Minnotte and Robert Lewis* v. *Poland*, the Tribunal stated that – even without an explicit BIT clause that investments must be made in accordance with host state's law – it was generally accepted that an investment based on fraudulent conduct could not benefit from BIT protection (at para. 131). In *Plama* v. *Bulgaria*, the Tribunal found that, even if the applicable Energy Charter Treaty 1994 (ECT) did not contain a provision requiring conformity of the investment with a specific law, the ECT did not mean to protect investments that were contrary to domestic or international law (at para. 138 et seq.). In *Yukos Universal Limited* v. *Russia*, the Tribunal agreed with the proposition of the *Plama* Tribunal (at para. 1352). See also Lamm, Hellbeck and Khan 2015, 566 et seq.; Obersteiner 2014, 267 et seq.

In *Fraport* v. *Philippines*, the Tribunal raised the question of temporality with regard to the legality requirement, arguing that investments must be legal according to the host state's law at the time they are made, and decided on this basis to examine only the so-called 'Initial Investment'.[47] In *Hamester* v. *Ghana*, the Tribunal considered that the applicable Germany-Ghana BIT differentiated between legality of the investment at its initiation and legality during its performance. At the jurisdictional phase, the Tribunal only considered those fraud allegations that related to the initiation of the investment.[48]

Not every kind of violation of host state's law leads to the illegality of an investment;[49] according to the view advanced here, only grave violations can have this consequence. A difference could be made between simple mistakes of form that are minor infringements and a behaviour that typically leads to civil and criminal law sanctions.[50] Furthermore, mistakes in the making of an investment that are made in good faith should not deprive the investor of treaty protection.[51]

Evidence at the Level of Jurisdiction Some ICSID tribunals developed the rule that if the case of the claimant is 'reasonably arguable on its face', jurisdiction is established.[52] However, the question is if there are situations in which a tribunal, at the jurisdictional level, should go beyond this *prima facie* approach and not postpone evidentiary determinations until the merits stage? In *Phoenix* v. *Czech Republic*, the Tribunal stated:

> [A]s a general approach, it is correct that factual matters should provisionally be accepted at face value, since the proper time to prove or disprove such facts is during the merits phase. But when a particular circumstance constitutes a critical element for the establishment of the jurisdiction itself, such fact must be proven, and the Tribunal must take a decision thereon when ruling on its jurisdiction.[53]

47 *Fraport* v. *Philippines II*, paras. 331, 333; see discussion in Chapter 5.

48 *Hamester* v. *Ghana*, para. 129; see discussion in Chapter 5.

49 See Grubenmann 2010, 209 et seq. and Obersteiner 2014, 276 et seq. for ICSID case law.

50 Grubenmann 2010, 211; Knahr 2008, 137 et seq. with reference to the Decision on Jurisdiction in *Tokios Tokelės* v. *Ukraine* (para. 86).

51 Moloo and Khachaturian 2011, 1494 et seq. with reference to *Fraport* v. *Philippines I*, para. 396 (where the good faith of the investor was denied though).

52 Schreuer et al. 2009, Art. 43 N 117 et seq. with references to case law and in particular to *Bayindir* v. *Pakistan*, ICSID Case No. ARB/03/29, Decision on Jurisdiction, 14 November 2005, para. 197.

53 *Phoenix* v. *Czech Republic*, para. 64.

Therefore, according to the *Phoenix* Tribunal, facts that will affect the jurisdiction of a tribunal – e.g. facts related to the legality of an investment – should be proven and a decision thereon taken at the jurisdictional level.[54]

2.1.2.2 The Law Applicable to the Substance of the Dispute

Party Autonomy The ICSID Convention only contains a procedural framework but no substantive rules for the settlement of investment disputes. Some BITs contain a choice of law clause that serves as basis for the choice of law agreement between the disputing parties.[55] In general, Art. 42(1) of the ICSID Convention regulates how the applicable substantive law is determined:

> The Tribunal shall decide a dispute in accordance with such rules of law as may be agreed by the parties. In the absence of such agreement, the Tribunal shall apply the law of the Contracting State party to the dispute (including its rules on the conflict of laws) and such rules of international law as may be applicable.

In principle, the parties to a dispute are free to select the substantive rules they consider the most appropriate; they can choose from any national system of law, international law or a combination of both.[56] International law probably always plays a role in ICSID disputes, even if the parties did not choose it.[57] As Art. 42(1) ICSID Convention refers to 'rules of law' and not to entire systems, the parties can choose the rules they wish to apply from different systems of law.[58] They can also agree to settle a dispute by equitable principles (*ex aequo et bono*).[59] It is rare that parties exclusively refer to the legal system of the host state, or of the investor's home state, or of a third state.[60] Usually, the parties refer to international

54 On burden of proof at the jurisdictional level, see Vasani and Foden 2010.

55 Kreindler 2004, 405 et seq.; Schreuer et al. 2009, Art. 42 N 81 et seq.

56 Schreuer et al. 2009, Art. 42 N 22; Nadakavukaren Schefer 2016, 516. For a detailed analysis of the different options, see Kjos 2013, 157 et seq., 213 et seq., 271 et seq. with further references.

57 Schreuer et al. 2009, Art. 42 N 104 et seq., 115; in detail: Shihata and Parra 1994, 208 et seq.

58 Gaillard and Banifatemi 2003, 410 et seq.; Schreuer et al. 2009, Art. 42 N 39 et seq.

59 Art. 42(3) ICSID 1965.

60 If the host state's law is chosen exclusively, from the investor's perspective it is wise to insert a stabilisation clause to protect from subsequent changes in the law by agreeing that such changes will not be applied *vis-à-vis* the investor (Schreuer et al. 2009, Art. 42 N 116 et seq.).

law or general principles of law in combination with the host state's law.[61] The applicable law may contain conflict of laws rules that direct the parties to another legal system (*renvoi*).[62]

If the parties do not agree on a choice of law, Art. 42(1) in its second sentence provides that the tribunal shall apply the host state's law and international law.[63] An ICSID tribunal should take into account the full range of sources of international law, as provided in Art. 38(1) of the ICJ Statute[64]: treaties (in particular the BITs themselves), customary international law (including the principles on state responsibility),[65] general principles of law (including good faith; the prohibition of corruption;[66] and that the claimant bears the burden of proof), judicial decisions (of international courts and arbitral tribunals), and academic writing. In addition, ICSID tribunals can consider resolutions and guidelines (of the UN General Assembly and of the World Bank, for example).[67]

The relationship between the host state's law and international law is complex.[68] Some ICSID tribunals applied the two systems in parallel, whereas others assigned a supplemental and corrective function to international law. The most pragmatic approach is to apply both systems autonomously:

> [T]ribunals will have to identify the various legal issues before them in their proper legal contexts. Tribunals will then apply international law to some of these issues and domestic law to other issues. Tribunals will not have complete discretion in selecting international and domestic law. They will have to identify the questions to which the respective legal systems apply.[69]

The phrase 'as may be applicable' in Art. 42(1) ICSID Convention should not be understood to mean that only those rules of international law

[61] Schreuer et al. 2009, Art. 42 N 33 et seq.
[62] Schreuer et al. 2009, Art. 42 N 53 et seq., 161 et seq.
[63] Banifatemi 2010, 200 et seq.; Schreuer et al. 2009, Art. 42 N 133 et seq.
[64] Annex to UN 1945.
[65] It has been argued that the prohibition of bribery amounts to a customary rule in public international law (Kreindler 2013a, 245 et seq. and 2010a, 310; Newcombe 2011, 199).
[66] See also Kreindler 2013a, 249 and 2010a, 312.
[67] Schreuer et al. 2009, Art. 42 N 169 et seq.
[68] See Banifatemi 2010, 201 et seq.; Schreuer et al. 2009, Art. 42 N 206 et seq. For a detailed discussion of ICSID case law dealing with the relationship between domestic and international law, see Kulick 2012, 19 et seq.
[69] Schreuer et al. 2009, Art. 42 N 244.

apply that were adopted and incorporated into the host state's domestic law. Rather, it means that the relevant rules of international law apply.[70]

Mandatory Provisions of The Host State's Law A difficult question is whether the parties can opt out of certain mandatory provisions of the host state's law, such as its administrative, labour, monetary, regulatory and criminal law. In those areas, a choice of law other than the law of the host state is probably inconvenient but not impossible (for example, if the investor's state applies higher labour law standards than the host state). Some commentators have argued that the host state should have the power to make such a choice, but that proof of the 'unequivocal intent' of the parties is required.[71] If the parties opt out of the host state's mandatory law, the chosen rules should offer a *higher standard of protection* than the host state's law.

Mandatory Provisions of International Law A decision based on the host state's domestic law may not violate a mandatory rule of international law.[72] It is disputed whether this includes only the rules of *ius cogens*,[73] or international law in general.[74] Arguably, in case a mandatory domestic rule conflicts with the state's international obligation, the latter must prevail.[75]

Transnational Public Policy Public policy is discussed in more detail below in the context of commercial arbitration. To put it short: in ICSID arbitration, transnational public policy can have a decisive impact on the outcome of the proceedings.[76] A well-known example of the important role of transnational public policy in ICSID arbitration is the 2006 *World Duty Free* v. *Kenya* case, in which the tribunal held that bribery was contrary to transnational public policy, and that claims based on bribe contracts or on contracts obtained by bribery cannot be upheld

[70] Schreuer et al. 2009, Art. 42 N 199 et seq.
[71] Schreuer et al. 2009, Art. 42 N 44 et seq. with further references.
[72] Schreuer et al. 2009, Art. 42 N 230.
[73] This is a peremptory norm of international law from which states may not derogate (Art. 53 VCLT), e.g. the prohibitions of use of force, slavery, and genocide (Peters 2016, 85).
[74] For an overview of the different opinions, see Schreuer et al. 2009, Art. 42 N 233 et seq.
[75] Bjorklund 2011, 264.
[76] Crit. Donovan, who argues that the need for the doctrine in international investment arbitration remains to be established (Donovan 2011, 290).

by an ICSID tribunal. Transnational public policy should be distinguished from the question of the applicability of international law (as discussed above).[77]

2.1.2.3 The Applicable Arbitral Procedure

Art. 42 of the ICSID Convention only regulates how the applicable substantive law is determined. Regarding procedure, the Convention contains several provisions. Art. 44 reads:

> Any arbitration proceeding shall be conducted in accordance with the provisions of this Section and, except as the parties otherwise agree, in accordance with the Arbitration Rules in effect on the date on which the parties consented to arbitration. If any question of procedure arises which is not covered by this Section or the Arbitration Rules or any rules agreed by the parties, the Tribunal shall decide the question.

Therefore, if the parties do not agree otherwise, ICSID proceedings are conducted in accordance with the respective provisions of the Convention (in particular Arts. 41–47) and the ICSID Arbitration Rules.[78] The tribunal has the power to fill any gaps by the established methods of treaty interpretation.[79] Art. 43 of the ICSID Convention and Arbitration Rules 34–36 deal with evidence (including witnesses).

The parties are free to exclude or adapt the Arbitration Rules, except when those Rules restate mandatory provisions of the Convention (in particular concerning the tribunal's composition). Under Art. 44 ICSID Convention, national arbitration laws have no role to play, except if the parties agree to apply the provisions of a national legal system. Similarly, domestic public policy has no influence; the parties must, however, observe the international minimum standards of fair procedure.[80] ICSID Awards can neither be appealed in front of the courts of the seat of the arbitration; nor be reviewed by the courts of the state where the enforcement is sought (Arts. 53 and 54 ICSID Convention).[81] The only possibility to set aside an ICSID Award is under Art. 52 of the Convention.[82]

[77] Schreuer et al. 2009, Art. 42 N 52. [78] ICSID 2006.

[79] Schreuer et al. 2009, Art. 44 N 53 et seq.

[80] Schreuer et al. 2009, Art. 44 N 11 et seq., 20 et seq. Unlike other types, ICSID arbitration is completely self-contained and detached from the *lex arbitri* of the tribunal's seat (Schreuer et al. 2009, Art. 62 N 3).

[81] Schreuer et al. 2009, Art. 53 N 20 et seq.; Art. 54 N 81.

[82] Schreuer et al. 2009, Art. 52 N 4.

2.1.2.4 Criminal Law?

The ICSID Convention and Arbitration Rules make no reference to criminal law. In case of alleged criminal conduct in ICSID arbitration – which criminal law provisions apply? From the above discussion, the following principles can be derived:

- If the parties agree that a national legal system should apply (of the host state or of a third state), the tribunal should, in principle, apply the mandatory rules (including criminal law) of that legal system.
- However, by choosing a third state's law, the parties cannot opt out of the mandatory rules of the host state's law, unless they show an unequivocal intent to do so and unless the chosen law offers a higher level of protection than the host state's law.
- If a domestic mandatory rule conflicts with international law, the latter should prevail.
- If the parties agree to apply international law, the tribunal should take into account the full range of sources of international law, including anti-corruption, anti-fraud and anti-money laundering treaties.
- If the parties did not agree on an applicable law, the tribunal will apply the host state's law and international law; if the mandatory rules of the host state's law conflict with international law, the latter should prevail.
- Only if the sources of law mentioned above do not cover the criminal conduct at stake, the tribunal should refer to transnational public policy as a fall-back position, which in all cases sets an absolute limit.

2.1.3 *Other Avenues of Investment Arbitration*

In addition to the ICSID dispute settlement mechanism, other types of investor-state arbitration exist, which can be categorised as:

- non-ICSID institutional investment arbitration (frequently used institutions are the ICC, LCIA, PCA, or Stockholm Chamber of Commerce);[83]
- *ad hoc* investment arbitration based on the UNCITRAL Rules;[84]
- *ad hoc* investment arbitration based on rules as agreed by the parties.[85]

[83] Nadakavukaren Schefer 2016, 443 et seq.

[84] UNCITRAL 2013a; for instance investor-state arbitration under chapter 11 of the NAFTA may be conducted under the UNCITRAL Arbitration Rules (Art. 1120 NAFTA 1992).

[85] Nadakavukaren Schefer 2016, 448.

Thus, non-ICSID institutional investment arbitration relies in principle on the respective institution's own set of rules; and *ad hoc* investment arbitration is based on rules as agreed by the parties.[86]

2.1.4 Summary

Investment (ICSID) arbitration depends on the consent of the parties to this type of dispute settlement mechanism and is characterised by party autonomy, in particular with regard to the applicable substantive law and procedure. Mandatory provisions of law of the host state, public international law and transnational public policy set a limit to party autonomy.

2.2 Commercial Arbitration

Commercial arbitration deals with disputes arising out of commercial relationships. In practice, the term 'commercial' today encompasses all aspects of international business.[87]

2.2.1 The Legal Framework for Commercial Arbitration

2.2.1.1 In General

Commercial arbitration is based on the consent of the parties, which must be expressed in a valid arbitration agreement. This usually takes the form of an arbitration clause in the main contract, or it is expressed in a separate submission agreement drawn up for a particular dispute.[88]

[86] Nadakavukaren Schefer 2016, 451.

[87] Cf. Blackaby et al. 2015, 11 et seq. The UNCITRAL Model Law states that: 'The term "commercial" should be given a wide interpretation so as to cover matters arising from all relationships of a commercial nature, whether contractual or not. Relationships of a commercial nature include, but are not limited to, the following transactions: any trade transaction for the supply or exchange of goods or services; distribution agreement; commercial representation or agency; factoring; leasing; construction of works; consulting; engineering; licensing; investment; financing; banking; insurance; exploitation agreement or concession; joint venture and other forms of industrial or business cooperation; carriage of goods or passengers by air, sea, rail or road.' (UNCITRAL 2006, footnote 2 to Art. 1(1)). Cf. also Swiss law that does not distinguish whether arbitration is concerned with a commercial matter or not: according to Art. 177(1) SPILA, any dispute of financial interest can be settled by arbitration (Berger and Kellerhals 2015, 68 et seq.; Kaufmann-Kohler and Rigozzi 2015, 100 et seq.).

[88] In detail: Blackaby et al. 2015, 12 et seq.; Born 2015b, §1.07.

Parties to arbitration agreements can be individuals, partnerships, corporations, state-owned enterprises or states: in short, any natural or legal person that has the legal capacity to enter into a contract.[89] Commercial arbitration tribunals usually have the competence to decide on their own jurisdiction (in German: *Kompetenz-Kompetenz*).[90]

If the main contract is influenced by criminal conduct in any form, what happens to the arbitration clause? According to the 'separability' (or 'severability' or 'autonomy') principle, the arbitration agreement has its own existence no matter whether it is embedded in the main contract or separate from it. The consent of the parties to arbitrate their disputes must be regarded as separate from their consent regarding the object of the main contract. The separability principle

> recognises the independence of the arbitration clause from the substantive contract in which it is physically embedded, with the consequence that the nullity, non-existence of or other legal defect in the substantive contract will not by itself render invalid an otherwise valid arbitration agreement.[91]

Therefore, criminal conduct influencing the main contract in principle does not invalidate the arbitration agreement, unless the latter is also affected by it. Separability of the arbitral clause is today a standard topic and widely accepted in arbitration rules,[92] in the 2006 UNCITRAL Model Law[93] and in domestic laws on arbitration,[94] in academic writing[95] and in arbitral awards.[96]

Regarding the legal framework for international commercial arbitration, a complex web of rules and laws is applicable to substance and procedure. On the one hand, there are the arbitration rules (of a certain

89 Redfern and Hunter 2004, 145.

90 See, e.g., s. 30 English Arbitration Act 1996; Art. 23(1) LCIA 2014; Art. 186(1) Swiss Private International Law Act (SPILA); Art. 21(1) SRIA; Art. 6(5) ICC 2012; Redfern and Hunter 2004, 252.

91 United Kingdom Department of Trade and Industry Consultation Document on Proposed Clauses and Schedules for an Arbitration Bill (1994), reproduced in 10 *Arbitration International* 189, 226 et seq.

92 Instead of many, see Art. 6(9) ICC 2012; Art. 23(2) LCIA 2014; Art. 23(1) PCA 2012; Art. 21(2) SRIA 2012; Art. 23(1) UNCITRAL 2013a.

93 Art. 16(1) UNCITRAL 2006.

94 E.g. for England: s. 7 English Arbitration Act 1996; for Switzerland: Art. 178(3) SPILA.

95 Instead of many, see Blackaby et al. 2015, 104 et seq.; Born 2015b, §2.04; Redfern and Hunter 2004, 162 et seq. for different theories of separability.

96 See, e.g., *Westinghouse* v. *National Power Corporation*, 19 et seq. and see discussion in Chapter 6.

arbitral institution, or *ad hoc*); on the other hand, domestic (and/or international) laws may apply. There is:

- the domestic arbitration law of the country in whose territory the arbitration has its seat (*lex arbitri*), differing from state to state and governing the conduct of the arbitration, possibly containing mandatory provisions from which the parties cannot derogate;[97]
- the law that governs the arbitral procedure (the parties may choose a different national law to apply other than the *lex arbitri*; however, this is unusual and not practical);[98]
- the law that governs the arbitration agreement and its performance;[99]
- the law applicable to the substance of the dispute;[100]
- possibly, conflict of laws rules (affecting the choice of the law applicable to the arbitration agreement; the law applicable to the substance of the dispute; and the law governing the arbitral procedure)[101] and
- the law governing recognition and enforcement of an award.[102]

The overarching principle regarding the choice of all substantive and procedural rules and laws in international commercial arbitration is party autonomy. The parties – or in the absence of party agreement, the arbitrators – are free to choose the applicable rules and laws. However, mandatory law and/or public policy may set a limit to party autonomy and override a valid choice of law agreement between the parties.[103] This is particularly relevant if alleged criminal behaviour is at stake in arbitration.

2.2.1.2 Mandatory Law

The issue of mandatory rules of law has long been discussed in private international law and also in international (commercial) arbitration.[104] While a uniform definition of the term does not seem to exist, a

[97] For a detailed discussion of the role of the *lex arbitri*, see Born 2014, 1536 et seq.; Cordero-Moss 2013, 9 et seq.; Radicati di Brozolo 2013, 43 et seq.

[98] In detail: Born 2015a, 777 et seq.; Born 2014, 1533 et seq., 1598 et seq.; Cordero-Moss 2013, 14 et seq.; Waincymer 2012, 183 et seq.

[99] In detail: Born 2014, 229 et seq.

[100] In detail: Born 2015a, 961 et seq.; Born 2014, 2616 et seq.

[101] Born 2014, 210 et seq., 472 et seq., 1604 et seq., 2616 et seq.

[102] Blackaby et al. 2015, 157, 605 et seq.; Born 2014, 2897 et seq.

[103] Born 2014, 2690 et seq.

[104] Cf. the academic texts since the mid-1980ies on the subject, including Barraclough and Waincymer 2005; Blessing 1997; Mayer 1986; Voser 1996; see also Shore 2011, 135 et seq.

mandatory rule of law can be described as 'an imperative provision of law which must be applied to an international relationship irrespective of the law that governs that relationship.'[105] Mandatory rules of law therefore override party autonomy.[106] They can be substantive as well as procedural rules.[107] They can be foreign, in the sense that they are not part of the law as chosen by the parties or determined by the arbitrators.[108] The notions of mandatory rules of law and of public policy should not be used interchangeably: mandatory rules are always written down in explicit legal provisions, which can be, but is not necessarily the case with public policy. Mandatory rules also can have a broader content than public policy.[109] Arbitrators confronted with alleged criminal behaviour must decide whether any and which mandatory rules are relevant.

Substantive Criminal Law In international arbitration, provisions of substantive criminal law constitute mandatory rules.[110] If an arbitral tribunal is confronted with alleged criminal conduct, it needs a reference system: it will apply criminal law provisions. However, the difficulty is to identify which provisions apply (mandatorily). Mandatory rules may be found in the law of the seat of the arbitration (*lex arbitri*); in the law applicable to the substance of the dispute; in the law of a third country; or in the law of the place where the award should be enforced.[111]

In the mid-twentieth century it was still common to argue that an arbitral tribunal was obliged to apply the local conflict of laws rules, or the local substantive law, of the arbitral seat. Today however, there is widespread consensus that an arbitral tribunal, unlike a domestic court, does not have a *lex fori*, which means that the law of the state where the arbitration has its seat in principle does not apply on a mandatory basis

105 Mayer 1986, 275.

106 Bermann argues that it is yet unclear whether parties can exclude the application of a mandatory rule by their unequivocal consent (Bermann 2011, 3).

107 Barraclough and Waincymer 2005.

108 Blessing 1997, 23 et seq.; and see right below 'Substantive Criminal Law'. Voser argues that an arbitrator is not a state judge and cannot therefore be the guardian of a specific state's public policy; consequently, all mandatory rules of concerned states are 'foreign' mandatory rules (Voser 1996, 338).

109 Voser 1996, 322; see also Blessing 1997, 24; Kaufmann-Kohler and Rigozzi 2015, 382 et seq. Public policy is discussed in subsection 2.2.1.3.

110 Donovan and Greenawalt 2006, 13; Mourre 2009, 215. See also Sayed 2004, 230 et seq.

111 Cf. Blessing 1997, 26 et seq.

(with the exception of mandatory rules of the *lex arbitri* that will in principle not deal with issues of substantive criminal law).[112] If the parties (or arbitrators) choose the law of a certain country to apply to the substance of the dispute, the arbitral tribunal will also apply the mandatory rules of law of that state,[113] including its criminal law provisions. However, there are limits to this principle:[114]

- If a certain behaviour constitutes a crime under the mandatory rules of the substantive law chosen by the parties, but not under the law of the seat of the arbitration and not under the law of the performance of the contract, the tribunal would – in principle – still apply the mandatory rules of the chosen substantive law.[115]
- If the parties, with the intention to distance their contract from state Z, agree to apply the substantive law of state X (a third state), choose the seat of their arbitration to be state Y, whereas the place of performance of the contract is state Z, the tribunal will – in principle – not be bound by the mandatory laws of state Z (even if the contract is closely connected to the law of state Z).[116]
- However, if a criminal law provision is at stake that is particularly relevant and therefore has a 'very strong title to be applied', the parties' choice of law cannot override the application of this provision.[117] Six criteria can be identified that must be fulfilled for an arbitral tribunal to directly apply a foreign mandatory rule of law – over and above the law as chosen by the parties or determined by the arbitrators:
  - the rule must be of mandatory character;
  - the rule must be such as to impose itself irrespective of the applicable law;
  - the preconditions *ratione personae* and *ratione materiae* must be fulfilled;
  - there must be a close connection between the parties' contract and the state that declared the mandatory rule;

[112] Born 2014, 2629 et seq.; 2637 et seq.; 2709 et seq. On the elements of the *lex arbitri*, see Waincymer 2012, 174 et seq.

[113] Born 2014, 2707 et seq.; Kreindler 2005a.

[114] See the summary in Kreindler 2005a; see also Born 2014, 2696 et seq., 2712 et seq. Shore points out that arbitrators might also be guided by principles of private international law, namely Art. 7(1) of the Rome Convention 1980 that was replaced by Art. 9 of the Regulation (EC) No 593/2008 (Shore 2011, 143 et seq.).

[115] Kreindler 2005b, 432; Mourre 2009, 227.

[116] Kreindler 2005b, 434.

[117] Mourre 2009, 228 et seq.; see also Blackaby et al. 2015, 195 et seq.

- the rule must be 'application-worthy' with regard to the values that it aims to protect and
- there must be an 'appropriate result'.[118]

- In any case, transnational public policy[119] sets an absolute limit. This works in two ways: on the one hand, mandatory rules of law as chosen by the parties that conflict with transnational public policy are precluded from application by the arbitral tribunal.[120] On the other hand, the parties cannot circumvent the law of state Z if such circumvention would be contrary to transnational public policy.[121]

Therefore, party autonomy in international commercial arbitration may be limited by foreign mandatory law if the latter protects relevant interests, and if the effect of the application of the mandatory rule is appropriate.[122]

Civil or Criminal Procedure? If tribunals decide on criminal law issues in arbitral proceedings, the question arises whether certain provisions of civil or criminal procedure – that are fundamental in state court litigation as they protect the parties' right to a fair trial if criminal conduct is alleged – must be taken into account as mandatory rules. This issue will be addressed further below.[123]

2.2.1.3 Public Policy

Since the late 1970s, many commentators addressed the role of public policy in international commercial arbitration.[124] In a nutshell, there exist at least four different notions of public policy:

- public policy;
- international public policy;
- truly international public policy and
- transnational public policy.

[118] Blessing 1997, 32; see also Kaufmann-Kohler and Rigozzi 2015, 384 et seq.; Voser 1996, 345 et seq.

[119] See subsection 2.2.1.3. [120] Born 2014, 2708.

[121] Kreindler 2005a; Kreindler 2005b, 435 et seq.

[122] Blessing 1997, 32 et seq.; see also Barraclough and Waincymer 2005; Mourre 2009, 236; Sayed 2004, 260 et seq.

[123] See Chapter 9.

[124] To name just a few, see the early writings by Böckstiegel 1987; Derains 1987; Lalive 1987; Lew 1978, 531 et seq.; Schwebel and Lahne 1987; as well as Court de Fontmichel 2004, 100 et seq.

The definition and use of those terms is not very clear-cut. In particular, 'truly international' and 'transnational' public policy are sometimes used as synonyms, while other contributors argue that they are not.[125] For the purposes of this text, *public policy* is a term used in the context of domestic law, forming 'a set of rules that parties may not contract out of'.[126] An arbitral award may be set aside by the courts at the tribunal's seat if it violates public policy,[127] or its enforcement may be refused if it would be contrary to the enforcement state's public policy.[128] *International public policy* means 'the concept of public policy as applied in private international law'.[129] *Truly international public policy* means 'the part of public policy which belongs to public international law'.[130]

With regard to allegations of criminal behaviour in international arbitral proceedings, it is especially the notion of *transnational public policy* that is of interest. Transnational public policy functions as follows:

> 'Transnational public policy' can be defined as the set of legal principles, not belonging to the law of a particular State, which may be relied upon by an arbitrator either as a bar to the enforcement of an international commercial contract, or, in a less direct manner, as an obstacle to the application of the State law normally applicable to such contract.[131]

Transnational public policy has a restricted scope, but is universal in its application.[132] While transnational public policy reflects fundamental principles of public international law, it does not form part of public international law:

> Transnational public policy does not form part of the legal orders either of public international law, or any national legal order. The public policy of individual states is divided into domestic public policy and international public policy, with the latter being the (more restricted) public policy of the state as applied to international transactions. By contrast, transnational public policy is the 'common core' of the international public policy of many states, which by its very nature also reflects fundamental principles of public international law.[133]

[125] Mayer 2006, 62; the terms are used as synonyms e.g. in Lalive 1987 and Lalive 2009; see also Blackaby et al. 2015, 600.

[126] Derains 1987, 227. See also Kessedjan 2007, 859.

[127] Art. V 1. (e) New York Convention 1958.

[128] Art. V 2. (b) New York Convention 1958; instead of many, see Barraclough and Waincymer 2005; Voser 1996, 333 et seq.

[129] ILA 2002, at para. 11; Mayer 2006, 61.

[130] Mayer 2006, 61.

[131] Mayer 2006, 62 with reference to Lalive 1987; see also ILA 2000 and Mendes 2009, 834 et seq.

[132] ILA 2000.

[133] Cairns 2009, 2; different: Hunter and Conde e Silva 2003, 378.

Today, the concept of transnational public policy is well established and used in domestic court judgments, international arbitral awards and doctrine.[134] It contains fundamental principles of law, such as the prohibitions of racial or religious discrimination, drug trafficking, terrorism, trade in stolen art objects, traffic in human organs;[135] and the prohibitions of agreements to perform criminal acts, slavery, slave trading, supplying arms to terrorist groups and piracy.[136] Those principles apply mandatorily and override party autonomy in any case.[137]

There is widespread consensus today that the prohibition of foreign public bribery is also part of transnational public policy, as this well-known quote from the *World Duty Free* v. *Kenya* award shows:

> In light of domestic laws and international conventions relating to corruption, and in light of the decisions taken in this matter by courts and arbitral tribunals, this Tribunal is convinced that bribery is contrary to the international public policy of most, if not all, States or, to use another formula, to transnational public policy.[138]

Before the mid-1990s, it was essentially the United States that pushed forward the idea of fighting transnational corruption on the international level, a result of the fear that US businesses would suffer from a competitive disadvantage after the introduction of the Foreign Corrupt Practices Act (FCPA) in 1977.[139] Today however, with the OECD Convention on Bribery of 1997,[140] the UN Convention against Corruption (UNCAC) of 2003,[141] the CoE Criminal Law Convention on Corruption of 1999[142] and other regional treaties,[143] international law provides for binding legal

134 Cf. Lalive 2009, 603 et seq.; Lamm, Pham and Moloo 2010, 707; Hunter and Conde e Silva 2003, 377 et seq.; crit. Reisman, who argues that the content of transnational public policy is imprecise, and its application uncertain (Reisman 2007, 854 et seq.).

135 Mayer 2006, 63.

136 Born 2014, 2716 et seq., who defines transnational public policy as 'certain fundamental principles of law that are considered to be common among developed legal systems'.

137 Born 2014, 2716.

138 *World Duty Free* v. *Kenya*, para. 157; see also *Spentex* v. *Uzbekistan*, paras. 821 et seq.; Born 2014, 2717 et seq.; Cremades and Cairns 2003a, 77 et seq.; Lalive 2009, 605 et seq.; Lalive 1987, 286 et seq.; Lamm, Pham and Moloo 2010, 711 et seq.; Llamzon and Sinclair 2015, 519 et seq. Different: Karrer, who argues that doubts remain whether it is possible to speak of a global consensus against corruption (Karrer 2013b, Art. 187 N 278; see also Wilske and Raible 2009, 264; Court de Fontmichel 2004, 115 et seq.).

139 On the development of the international legal framework against foreign public bribery, see Pieth 2014a, 10 et seq.; Llamzon 2014, 43 et seq.; Sacerdoti 2009; Cremades and Cairns 2003a, 68 et seq.

140 OECD 1997. 141 UNCAC 2003. 142 CoE 1999a.

143 For example, the Inter-American Convention against Corruption (adopted 29 March 1996; entry into force 6 March 1997) and the African Union Convention on Preventing

instruments that are widely signed and ratified by industrialised states as well as a growing number of emerging economies of the South and East. Through their monitoring mechanisms,[144] those treaties not only aim at implementation, but also at enforcement.[145] An important tool in the global fight against foreign public bribery is the confiscation of the bribe as well as of the proceeds of bribery and their return to the state victim of the corruption.[146] Foreign public bribery is also a concern of multilateral development banks (MDBs); and numerous civil society texts and initiatives round off the picture of a global fight against the bribery of foreign public officials.[147]

The difficulty is to identify the content of transnational public policy beyond the above examples. International law in the form of treaties and other international instruments, including soft law, plays an important role here.[148] Further below,[149] the prohibition of private commercial bribery, fraud, and money laundering, and certain fundamental principles of procedure will be discussed.

In a dispute in which criminal behaviour is at stake, is it preferable for arbitrators to apply mandatory rules of law, or to rely on transnational public policy? As discussed above, mandatory rules are always explicit legal provisions (e.g. of criminal law) with a much more precise content than the somewhat vague concept of transnational public policy. For instance, bribery provisions of domestic criminal law specify the objective requirements of the offence in detail. Those requirements prescribe the topic for the evidence.[150] Therefore, if criminal behaviour is at

and Combating Corruption (adopted 11 July 2003; entry into force 5 August 2006). The European Union drafted the Convention on the fight against corruption involving officials of the European Communities or officials of EU Member States (EU 1997a).

[144] Cf. the reports of the OECD Working Group on Bribery (WGB), based on Art. 12 OECD 1997; the UNCAC Conference of States Parties, based on Art. 63 (4)(e) UNCAC 2003; the Group of States against Corruption (GRECO), based on Art. 24 CoE 1999a; and the Mechanism for Follow-Up on the Implementation of the Inter-American Convention against Corruption (MESICIC).

[145] Cf. in particular the OECD WGB's *Tour de Table* mechanism and the Phase 2 and 3 reports; Pieth 2014a, 42 et seq.; Bonucci 2014, 543 et seq., 550 et seq., 568 et seq.

[146] On the history of confiscation as a tool to fight transnational corruption: Mégevand 2013, 43 et seq.; on asset recovery: Pieth (ed.) 2008.

[147] See Pieth 2014a, 29; Vincke 2014; for a detailed account of the existing international treaties, supranational legislative instruments, and soft law norms on corruption: Ivory 2014, 13 et seq.

[148] Lalive 1987, 307; Mourre 2009, 235 et seq. See also Kessedjan 2007, 866 et seq.

[149] See discussion in Chapter 8. [150] See discussion in Chapter 4.

stake, mandatory rules should be identified and applied.[151] Transnational public policy remains important though, as it can lead to the setting aside, or act as a bar to the enforcement, of an arbitral award; preclude the application of mandatory rules chosen by the parties that are contrary to transnational public policy; and prevent the circumvention of certain domestic laws.[152]

2.2.1.4 The Role of International Law

International law plays an important role in international commercial arbitration with regard to the enforceability of arbitration agreements (as well as awards). Starting with the Geneva Protocol of 1923[153] and the Geneva Convention of 1927,[154] international law has evolved in this field and now ensures that arbitration clauses and awards are recognised by all major trading nations. The most relevant international treaty today is still the New York Convention of 1958[155] (that widens the scope of and replaces the earlier Geneva treaties). On the one hand, Art. II(3) of this Convention requires state parties to make sure that their courts, if they are seized with a matter which is subject to a valid arbitration agreement, refer that matter to arbitration. On the other hand, the Convention demands that state parties recognise arbitral awards as binding and enforceable (Art. III), unless one of the grounds for refusal to enforce a foreign arbitral award (listed in Art. V) applies.[156]

International law has furthermore strongly influenced states' domestic arbitration laws. In 1985, the United Nations Commission on International Trade Law (UNCITRAL) developed a 'Model Law on International Commercial Arbitration'[157], that was revised in 2006.[158] It is the 'single most important legislative instrument in the field of international commercial arbitration'.[159] The Model Law contains provisions on all stages of an international commercial arbitration proceeding; it aims at

[151] Cf. Born 2014, 2719; Court de Fontmichel 2004, 115 et seq.; Martin 2003, 9, 11; Mayer 2006, 67 et seq., who points out the difficulties in defining corruption.

[152] In Switzerland, for instance, non-application of a foreign mandatory rule is not a ground for setting aside an award, whereas the failure to apply transnational public policy may result in a setting aside (Kaufmann-Kohler and Rigozzi 2015, 385 with references).

[153] Geneva Protocol 1923.

[154] Geneva Convention 1927.

[155] New York Convention 1958.

[156] In detail: Blackaby et al. 2015, 617 et seq.

[157] UNCITRAL 1985.

[158] UNCITRAL 2006. The Model Law was recommended to the UN member states by General Assembly resolutions A/RES/40/72 of 11 December 1985 and A/RES/61/33 of 18 December 2006.

[159] Born 2014, 134.

harmonising national arbitration laws, and has been highly successful in motivating states to adopt it as their own law of arbitration, or to amend their existing arbitration laws according to the Model Law.[160]

2.2.2 Avenues of Commercial Arbitration

In principle, the above considerations on mandatory rules and public policy apply in all international commercial arbitration proceedings. Four popular avenues are now presented in more detail.

2.2.2.1 The International Chamber of Commerce (ICC)

The International Court of Arbitration of the International Chamber of Commerce, established in 1923 in Paris, offers one possible avenue for international commercial arbitration. ICC arbitrations are governed by the ICC Rules of Arbitration ('ICC Rules').[161]

Jurisdiction The International Court of Arbitration is not a court, but an administrative body. The arbitral tribunals are constituted for each single case.[162] ICC arbitration is characterised by its universality: it covers any kind of disputes, including investment disputes.[163]

The Law Applicable to the Substance of the Dispute Art. 21(1) of the ICC Rules establishes that the parties are free to agree on the law applicable to the merits of their dispute. However, party autonomy is limited by mandatory rules and transnational public policy.[164] In most commercial contracts, the parties will agree to apply a certain domestic legal system to any future dispute. Other possible choices include public international law.[165] If there is no party agreement, the arbitral tribunal applies the rules of substantive law that it determines to be appropriate. The tribunal first examines whether the parties made a(n) (implicit) choice of law. If not, it chooses the applicable law. The arbitral tribunal is not bound to apply the conflict of laws rules of the country where the arbitration has its seat (unless prescribed by a mandatory provision of the *lex arbitri*). Rather, it chooses the applicable law by applying

[160] Blackaby et al. 2015, 62 et seq. [161] ICC 2012. [162] Blackaby et al. 2015, 49.
[163] On the essential features of ICC arbitration: Craig, Park and Paulsson 2000, 1 et seq.
[164] Blackaby et al. 2015, 187 et seq., 195 et seq.; Reiner and Aschauer 2013, 111.
[165] For a more extensive discussion of the possible choices, see Blackaby et al. 2015, 190 et seq., 196 et seq.

appropriate conflict of laws rules; it may also apply different state laws to the various issues of a case.[166]

The Applicable Arbitral Procedure Art. 19 of the ICC Rules states that the proceedings shall be governed by those Rules and, where they are silent, by the rules on which the parties agreed. In the absence of party agreement, the arbitral tribunal is free to choose the applicable procedural law, which may include reference to domestic procedural law. The tribunal is not bound to apply the civil procedure law of the country in which the arbitration is seated – it must, however, respect mandatory provisions on procedure of the *lex arbitri.*[167] In practice, arbitral tribunals often decide procedural issues autonomously, referring to arbitral practice and taking into account domestic rules of procedure only comparatively.[168] Art. 22(4) of the ICC Rules states that the tribunal must treat the parties equally and ensure their right to be heard. In sum, an ICC tribunal must consider three sources to determine the applicable arbitral procedure:

- the ICC Rules;
- the procedural law as agreed by the parties or as determined by the arbitral tribunal;
- mandatory provisions of the *lex arbitri.*

2.2.2.2 Other Institutions for Commercial Arbitration

The LCIA (London Court of International Arbitration) The origins of the LCIA date back to 1892. It has no judicial function, but administers arbitrations that are conducted according to the LCIA Rules.[169] LCIA arbitration can involve all matters of international commerce. The LCIA Secretariat is located in London, but arbitration under the LCIA Rules can be conducted anywhere in the world.[170] In case an LCIA (or any other) arbitration has its seat in England, Wales and Northern Ireland, the English Arbitration Act 1996 (the *lex arbitri*) holds that the parties are free to choose the applicable substantive law. If the parties choose the law of a certain country to apply, the Act states that the

166 Berger and Kellerhals 2015, 483; Blackaby et al. 2015, 218 et seq., 221 et seq., 236; Reiner and Aschauer 2013, 112.

167 In detail: Blackaby et al. 2015, 166 et seq.

168 Reiner and Aschauer 2013, 105 et seq.

169 LCIA 2014.

170 Konrad and Hunter 2013, 416 et seq.

choice is understood to refer to the substantive laws of that country (not to its conflict of laws rules).

In the absence of a party agreement, the arbitral tribunal determines the applicable substantive law according to the conflict of laws rules that it considers applicable (s. 46 of the Arbitration Act 1996 and Art. 22(3) LCIA Rules).[171] In principle, the tribunal decides all matters of procedure and evidence, but the parties have the right to agree on any such matter (s. 34 of the Arbitration Act 1996). The parties and the tribunal are not bound to apply English domestic procedural law.[172] S. 4 of the Arbitration Act 1996 establishes the mandatory and non-mandatory provisions of the Act;[173] the LCIA Rules are designed to address the Act's optional provisions.

The Swiss Chambers' Arbitration Institution In 2004, the Chambers of Commerce and Industry of Basel, Bern, Geneva, Neuchâtel, Ticino, Vaud and Zurich replaced their own arbitration rules with the Swiss Rules of International Arbitration ('Swiss Rules')[174] and founded the Swiss Chambers' Arbitration Institution. The Institution provides, *inter alia*, international arbitration services under any applicable law; it also established the Arbitration Court, which administers arbitrations under the Swiss Rules.[175] Arbitrations governed by the Swiss Rules may have their seat in Switzerland or in any other country.[176] By submitting their dispute to arbitration under the Swiss Rules, the parties confer on the Arbitration Court all powers to supervise the arbitral proceedings (as far as the applicable arbitration law permits it).[177] The Swiss Rules govern the arbitration, unless there is a conflict with mandatory provisions of the *lex arbitri*, in which case the latter prevails.[178]

If the arbitration is seated in Switzerland (under the Swiss Rules or any other), the *lex arbitri* is Arts. 176 et seq. of the Swiss Private International Law Act (SPILA; designed for international arbitration), or Arts. 353 et seq. of the Swiss Civil Procedure Code (SCPC; designed for domestic arbitration). The parties can opt into the other regulation,[179] but it is not

171 Born 2014, 2633 et seq. 172 Konrad and Hunter 2013, 425.
173 See Sheppard 2011, 191 et seq. 174 SRIA 2012.
175 SRIA 2012, Introduction; Wehrli and Stacher 2013, 360 et seq.
176 Art. 1(2) SRIA 2012; Wehrli and Stacher 2013, 346. 177 Art. 1(4) SRIA 2012.
178 Art. 1(5) SRIA 2012.
179 Art. 176(2) SPILA and Art. 353(2) SCPC; Karrer 2013a, 363.

possible to opt out of the SPILA **and** out of the SCPC if the arbitration is seated in Switzerland. For international arbitration, it is not recommended to opt out of the SPILA.[180] Under the Swiss Rules and the SPILA, any dispute of financial nature can be the subject of arbitration.[181] The parties are free to decide on the applicable substantive law. In the absence of party agreement, the arbitral tribunal shall apply the rules of law with which the dispute has the closest connection.[182] The parties can determine the arbitral procedure directly or by reference to arbitration rules. They can also submit the arbitral proceedings to a procedural law of their choice. If the parties do not determine the applicable procedure, the arbitral tribunal will do so directly or by reference to arbitration rules or a statute.[183] In any case, the arbitral tribunal must ensure equal treatment of the parties as well as their right to be heard in adversarial proceedings (Art. 182(3) SPILA).[184]

The arbitral award can be appealed to the Swiss Federal Supreme Court, *inter alia* if the tribunal wrongly determines its jurisdiction or decides about issues that were not raised by the parties; if the parties are not treated equally or their right to be heard is violated; or if the award is contrary to the *ordre public*.[185] Revision of an arbitral award is also possible (although not regulated in the SPILA), *inter alia* if criminal behaviour had an impact on the award.[186]

Other Arbitral Institutions and Claims Tribunals Other institutions for international commercial arbitration include:

- the Singapore International Arbitration Centre (SIAC);
- the Hong Kong International Arbitration Centre (HKIAC);
- the China International Economic and Trade Arbitration Commission (CIETAC);

[180] Karrer 2013a, 367. [181] Art. 177(1) SPILA; Wehrli and Stacher 2013, 351 et seq.

[182] Art. 187(1) SPILA and Art. 33(1) SRIA 2012. On the method how the arbitral tribunal should identify the 'closest connection', see Berger and Kellerhals 2015, 494 et seq.; see also Born 2014, 2632 et seq., 2654 et seq.; Wehrli and Stacher 2013, 372 et seq.

[183] Art. 182(1) and (2) SPILA.

[184] Berger and Kellerhals 2015, 385 et seq. and 392 et seq.; Art. 182(3) SPILA is the only mandatory provision in Swiss arbitration law (Hochstrasser and Fuchs 2013, Einl. 12. Kap. N 238).

[185] Arts. 190 and 191 SPILA.

[186] Kaufmann-Kohler and Rigozzi 2015, 508 et seq.; Wehrli and Stacher 2013, 356 et seq.; BGer 4A_596/2008 of 6 October 2009 (*Thales* v. *Frontier AG*).

- the International Centre for Dispute Resolution (ICDR) of the American Arbitration Association (AAA);
- the International Commercial Arbitration Court (MKAS) at the Chamber of Commerce and Industry of the Russian Federation;
- the German Institution of Arbitration (DIS);
- the Vienna International Arbitral Centre (VIAC);
- the Arbitration Institute of the Finland Chamber of Commerce;
- the Arbitration Institute of the Stockholm Chamber of Commerce;
- the Dubai International Arbitration Centre (DIAC).

Furthermore, there is the Permanent Court of Arbitration (PCA), an inter-governmental organisation established in 1899 and located in The Hague.[187] It provides dispute resolution services for disputes involving various combinations of states, state-controlled entities, inter-governmental organisations and private parties, and has an own set of arbitration rules.[188] The PCA is also involved in commercial and investment disputes (including disputes arising under bi- and multilateral investment treaties).[189]

In terms of specialised arbitration institutions, there exist, *inter alia*, the Geneva-based Arbitration Centre of the World Intellectual Property Organisation (WIPO) for domestic and cross-border intellectual property and technology disputes; and the Court of Arbitration for Sport (TAS/CAS) in Lausanne for sports-related disputes.

International claims tribunals (such as the Iran-US Claims Tribunal or the Claims Resolution Tribunal for Dormant Accounts in Switzerland)

[187] The PCA was set up by the 1899 Convention for the Pacific Settlement of International Disputes (revised in 1907), which was concluded at the first Hague Peace Conference; Blackaby et al. 2015, 55.

[188] PCA 2012.

[189] A very well-known example is the *Yukos* arbitration, for which the PCA served as registry. The Arbitral Tribunal, constituted under the Energy Charter Treaty of 1994 and applying the UNCITRAL Rules, in three Final Awards held unanimously that the Russian Federation had taken measures that had the effect of expropriating the Claimants' investments in Yukos, and had therefore breached its international obligations under the Energy Charter Treaty when it destroyed the Yukos Oil Company. The Tribunal ordered the payment of damages of more than US$50 billion to the Yukos majority shareholders (see *Hulley Enterprises Limited* v. *Russia*; *Veteran Petroleum Limited* v. *Russia*; and *Yukos Universal Limited* v. *Russia*). In April 2016, the Hague District Court set aside the Awards, arguing that the Arbitral Tribunal lacked jurisdiction ('Dutch Court Overturns $50 Billion Ruling Against Russia in Yukos Case', *New York Times*, 20 April 2016 (online edn)). The shareholders are appealing the decision before the Hague Court of Appeal.

and commissions (such as the United Nations Compensation Commission) also apply arbitration mechanisms.[190]

2.2.2.3 The UNCITRAL Rules and *Ad Hoc* Commercial Arbitration

Commercial arbitration can also be conducted *ad hoc*, i.e. without reference to any institutional arbitration rules. In such cases, the parties can refer to the UNCITRAL Rules[191] or draw up their own rules (provided that such rules treat the parties equally and ensure the right to be heard).[192] If the parties agree that their dispute shall be referred to arbitration under the UNCITRAL Rules, they can modify the Rules by agreement.[193] Unless the parties have agreed on the place of the arbitration, the arbitral tribunal will determine it according to the circumstances of the case.[194] If any of the UNCITRAL Rules conflicts with a mandatory provision of the *lex arbitri*, the latter prevails.[195] The Rules leave the arbitral tribunal the freedom to conduct the arbitration proceedings in the manner it considers appropriate; it must, however, ensure equal treatment of the parties as well as their right to be heard.[196]

Party autonomy with regard to the applicable substantive law is foreseen in the UNCITRAL Rules; if the parties fail to designate it, the arbitral tribunal will apply the law it deems appropriate.[197] The parties' choice of a particular national system of law does not include this system's choice of law rules.[198] In the absence of a parties' choice, the tribunal is not required to base its decision on the appropriate applicable law on any choice of law rule.[199] Furthermore, on 1 April 2014, the UNCITRAL Rules on Transparency[200] came into effect. They apply to investor-state arbitration initiated under the UNCITRAL Rules under an investment treaty concluded on or after that date (unless the parties to the treaty agree otherwise). If the investment treaty was concluded before 1 April 2014, the parties can choose to apply the Rules on Transparency.[201] Their purpose is to ensure that treaty-based investor-state arbitration is transparent and accessible to the public.[202]

190 Redfern and Hunter 2004, 60 et seq. 191 UNCITRAL 2013a.
192 Blackaby et al. 2015, 42 et seq. 193 Art. 1(1) UNCITRAL 2013a.
194 Art. 18(1) UNCITRAL 2013a. 195 Art. 1(3) UNCITRAL 2013a.
196 Art. 17(1) UNCITRAL 2013a.
197 Art. 35(1) UNCITRAL 2013a; Born 2014, 2636 et seq.
198 Patocchi and Niedermaier 2013, 1212. 199 Patocchi and Niedermaier 2013, 1215.
200 UNCITRAL 2013b. 201 Art. 1 UNCITRAL 2013b.
202 See www.uncitral.org/uncitral/uncitral_texts/arbitration/2014Transparency.html.

2.2.3 Summary

International commercial (ICC) arbitration is based on the consent of the parties and characterised by party autonomy. Nevertheless, if criminal conduct is alleged in such proceedings, the arbitrators must consider mandatory rules of law when determining the applicable substantive and procedural law. Transnational public policy sets an absolute limit to party autonomy. The arbitration laws of the state where the arbitral tribunal has its seat (*lex arbitri*) and the chosen (*ad hoc* or institutional) arbitral rules are not designed for addressing criminal law issues.

3

Manifestations of Criminal Conduct in International Arbitration

This chapter aims to clarify where criminal conduct may occur in the context of investment or commercial arbitration. The focus is on four criminal offences: the bribery of foreign public officials ('foreign public bribery'), private commercial bribery ('private bribery'), fraud, and money laundering. Obviously, other offences such as embezzlement or document forgery can equally play a role in international arbitration.[1] Those four offences are selected because of their detrimental impact on society and economy, and due to the continuous efforts on the international level to tackle those forms of economic crime. Before discussing criminal conduct, however, it must be explained why this text largely avoids using the term 'illegality'.

3.1 Non-Use of the Term 'Illegality'

In arbitral awards and academic texts, the term 'illegality' (or 'illicitness') is sometimes used. 'Illegality' encompasses more than criminal offences as defined in domestic law, as this would seem too narrow in the context of international arbitration; the term stretches out to all behaviour that is not strictly conforming to the law, without clearly violating it.[2] However, for the purposes of this text, the term 'illegality' appears too vague if it is applied to describe a certain behaviour that allegedly fulfils the objective requirements of a criminal offence. In criminal law, the offences and their requirements must be defined in clear terms – a consequence of the fundamental principle that there is no punishment without a law (*nulla poena sine lege*).[3] If arbitral tribunals decide about alleged criminal conduct, they do refer to applicable criminal laws in order to specify the offence at stake. This text, therefore, rather uses the

[1] See also Kurkela 2008, 285, 287 et seq.
[2] Mistelis 2009, 575 et seq.
[3] In Swiss law: Art. 1 SCrimC.

terms 'criminal behaviour' or 'criminal conduct' instead of 'illegality', or directly names the respective offence.

3.2 Foreign Public Bribery

3.2.1 Definition

Corruption occurs in many different forms.[4] The focus here is on active and passive foreign public bribery (i.e. not on the bribery of domestic officials;[5] not on other forms of corruption such as trading in influence;[6] and not on facilitation payments[7]). Foreign public bribery is the most severe form of transnational corruption and defined differently in each domestic criminal law system and in international treaties. For the purposes of this text, active foreign public bribery is

> the [intentional] promise, offering or giving to a foreign public official or an official of a public international organization, directly or indirectly, of an undue advantage, for the official himself or herself or another person or entity, in order that the official act or refrain from acting in the exercise of his or her official duties, in order to obtain or retain business or other undue advantage in relation to the conduct of international business.[8]

Passive foreign public bribery is

> the [intentional] solicitation or acceptance by a foreign public official or an official of a public international organization, directly or indirectly, of an undue advantage, for the official himself or herself or another person or entity, in order that the official act or refrain from acting in the exercise of his or her official duties.[9]

Foreign public officials include holders of a legislative, executive, administrative or judicial office in a foreign country, and also persons that exercise public functions, e.g. for a public enterprise or agency.[10]

[4] Transparency International (TI) defines corruption as 'the abuse of entrusted power for private gain'; for a brief introduction to the scope of 'corruption', see instead of many Nicholls et al. 2011, N 1.01 et seq.; Ivory 2014, 12 et seq.; Olaya 2009, 34 et seq.

[5] Active and passive bribery of domestic public officials is defined e.g. in Art. 15 UNCAC 2003.

[6] Active and passive trading in influence (influence peddling) is defined e.g. in Art. 18 UNCAC 2003.

[7] For a definition of facilitation payments, see Official Commentary 9 to the OECD Convention on Bribery (OECD 1997) and Zerbes 2014, 171 et seq.

[8] Art. 16(1) UNCAC 2003. [9] Art. 16(2) UNCAC 2003. [10] Art. 2(b) UNCAC 2003.

How does active and passive foreign public bribery allegedly occur in the context of international trade and investment disputes?

3.2.2 *Manifestations of Foreign Public Bribery in International Arbitration*

3.2.2.1 Attempts to Enforce a Bribery Pact

Simply put, this scenario occurs, for instance, if A (a company incorporated in state X) and B (a consultant in state Y) conclude an agreement that A will pay commissions to B in order that B induces C (a public official in state Y) – through the forwarding of a part of the commissions – to a certain behaviour that eventually favours A.[11] The dispute arises if A and B disagree over the payment of the commissions, and B tries to enforce the commission agreement (the bribery pact) by instituting arbitration proceedings.[12]

The legal consequences of such an agreement vary in different legal systems.[13] However, it can be said that the nullity or unenforceability of bribery pacts amounts to a transnational principle of law.[14] In Swiss law, under Art. 20(1) of the Swiss Code of Obligations (SCO), a bribery pact is either illegal (*widerrechtlich*) because its content breaches a Swiss criminal law provision, or it is *contra bonos mores* (*sittenwidrig*) because its content is against Swiss public policy (this is the case if the pact breaches a foreign criminal law provision that protects an interest considered worthy of protection in Swiss law as well). In both instances, the bribery pact is null and void *ex tunc* (from the beginning), and no party can claim its enforcement. Judges must observe the nullity of a bribery pact *ex officio*.[15]

None of the discussed ICSID awards in this text involve an attempt to enforce a bribe contract, which is probably due to the fact that ICSID arbitration deals with investment protection issues. While investments can be influenced by foreign public bribery, the investment itself is not

11 See also Bonell and Meyer 2015, 6; Raeschke-Kessler 2004, 475.

12 For more examples how conflicts between bribe-givers and bribe-takers emerge, and for a detailed corruption scheme, see Khvalei 2014, 16, 19 et seq.

13 For English Law: Yseult 2015.

14 Meyer 2017, 158 et seq., 162; Bonell and Meyer 2015, 10; Meyer 2013, 237 et seq.; see also Raeschke-Kessler 2004, 477 et seq.

15 Berger and Kellerhals 2015, 83; Kissling 2015, 360 et seq.; Huguenin and Meise 2015, Art. 19/20 N 15, 19, 21, 52 et seq.; Kramer 1991, Art. 19–20 N 200; Schmidlin 2013, Art. 28 N 164, 200; Steinbeisser 1977, 27 et seq.; Tercier 1999, 243 et seq.

a bribe contract. Several ICC awards, however, deal with claims that aim at the enforcement of an alleged bribe contract.[16]

3.2.2.2 Allegations That the Main Contract Was Procured by Bribery

A second frequent scenario is that a party to an already existing underlying contract (the 'main contract') alleges that bribery affected the formation of that contract. The main contract contains an arbitration clause. Simplifying again, this occurs, for instance, if company B (incorporated in state Y), which is involved in a bidding process for public works in state X, offers, promises or conveys bribe payments to certain officials of state X who are in charge of awarding the bid, in order that these officials arrange for the conclusion of the main contract between B and state X. The dispute arises if state X finds out about the bribe payments and wants to cancel the main contract.

Again, the legal consequences of such a scenario vary in different jurisdictions.[17] In Swiss law, according to the Swiss Federal Supreme Court, contracts procured by bribery are, as opposed to bribery pacts, neither illegal nor *contra bonos mores*.[18] The main contract is therefore not null and void, but voidable for defect in consent (*Willensmangel*) on the grounds of deliberate deception (*absichtliche Täuschung*, Art. 28 SCO) or fundamental error (*Grundlagenirrtum*, Art. 24(1)(4) SCO).[19] Art. 23 SCO rules that a contract is not binding for the party that is the victim of deception or error when entering the contract. In the above example, state X (but not company B) could unilaterally invoke the defect in consent under Art. 31 SCO.[20] In this case, the contract is in principle invalid *ex tunc* (except when it comes to ongoing obligations that were fully or partly fulfilled).[21] Several ICSID[22]

[16] See below ICC Cases No. 1110 (*Lagergren*), 3916, 4145, 5622 (*Hilmarton* v. *OTV*), 6497, 7047 (*Westacre* v. *Jugoimport*), 8891, 9333, 12472, 13384, 13515, 13914, 14878.

[17] Meyer 2017, 192 et seq.; Bonell and Meyer 2015, 20 et seq.; Raeschke-Kessler 2004, 481 et seq.

[18] BGE 129 III 320, 324 with further references; BGE 119 II 380, 385; Berger and Kellerhals 2015, 83; Kissling 2015, 374; Schmidlin 2013, 202 et seq. For a discussion of agency law: Kissling 2015, 375 et seq.; Tercier 1999, 255 et seq.

[19] Kissling 2015, 381 et seq.; Schmidlin 2013, Art. 28 N 37, 177 et seq., 196 et seq.; Steinbeisser 1977, 58 et seq., 62 et seq.

[20] Kissling 2015, 387 et seq.; Steinbeisser 1977, 69 et seq.

[21] Kissling 2015, 387 et seq. with references to case law and doctrine.

[22] See below *World Duty Free* v. *Kenya*, *Siemens* v. *Argentina*, *African Holding* v. *Democratic Republic of Congo*, *TSA Spectrum* v. *Argentina*, *Sistem* v. *Kyrgyz Republic*, *Niko* v.

and ICC[23] awards deal with such a scenario; it must be kept in mind, however, that in particular in ICSID arbitration, things are much more complex: there is usually not one single main contract at stake, but a web of legal relationships.[24]

3.2.2.3 Bribe Solicitation (or Payments) Related to the Performance of an Investment

In *EDF* v. *Romania*, the Claimant (unsuccessfully) alleged bribe solicitation by a public official in the host state during the performance of the investment, claiming a breach of the obligation to fair and equitable treatment. One could also envisage that bribe offers or payments occur during the performance of an investment, which do not affect its formation in any way. The legal consequences of such conduct would be complex. From the point of view of contract law, the main contract(s) are valid, and there is no defect in consent if at the time the investment was initiated, no bribes were foreseen or offered by any of the parties. The Tribunal in *EDF* v. *Romania* agreed with the Claimant that bribe solicitation would be contrary to the BIT's fair and equitable treatment requirement, as well as to international public policy. The Respondent in such a situation could argue that the investment is not in accordance with host state's law.[25] The bribery pact again would be null and void.

3.3 Private Bribery

3.3.1 *Definition*

In private bribery, no public officials are involved. It is hard therefore to imagine that private bribery could play any role in investment (ICSID) arbitration. The UNCAC defines that private bribery must be committed intentionally and in the course of economic, financial or commercial activities. Active and passive private bribery are:

Bangladesh, *Metal-Tech* v. *Uzbekistan*, *Spentex* v. *Uzbekistan*, and *Fraport* v. *Philippines*. In *RSM* v. *Grenada*, the Claimant unsuccessfully alleged bribe solicitation by a public official in the process of awarding an oil exploration license.

[23] See below ICC Cases No. 6401 (*Westinghouse* v. *National Power Corporation*), 14470.

[24] Raeschke-Kessler 2004, 476 et seq.

[25] See also Llamzon and Sinclair 2015, 463 et seq.; and see discussion in Chapter 5.

> (a) The promise, offering or giving, directly or indirectly, of an undue advantage to any person who directs or works, in any capacity, for a private sector entity, for the person himself or herself or for another person, in order that he or she, in breach of his or her duties, act or refrain from acting;
>
> (b) The solicitation or acceptance, directly or indirectly, of an undue advantage by any person who directs or works, in any capacity, for a private sector entity, for the person himself or herself or for another person, in order that he or she, in breach of his or her duties, act or refrain from acting.[26]

In contrast to public bribery, private bribery provisions do not include separate forms for domestic and foreign bribery. Art. 21 UNCAC therefore covers domestic as well as transnational private bribery. In the absence of published case law, the following scenarios can be envisaged for private bribery, along the lines of foreign public bribery.

3.3.2 *Manifestations of Private Bribery in International Arbitration*

3.3.2.1 Attempts to Enforce a Private Bribery Pact

This occurs, for instance, if company X offers, promises or gives undue commissions to an employee or agent of company Y, in order that the employee or agent favours company X against his duties. By doing this, the employee or agent breaches his relationship of trust towards company Y. A dispute could arise if the employee or agent demands the payment of his commissions.

3.3.2.2 Allegations That the Main Contract Was Procured by Private Bribery

This scenario involves a main contract between company Y and company X. The former learns that the main contract was procured through bribery of one of its employees or agents, and wants to cancel the main contract.[27]

3.3.2.3 Alleged Private Bribery Occurs during the Performance of the Main Contract

If private bribery did not affect the formation of the main contract in any way, the latter is valid and there is no defect in consent between the

[26] Art. 21 UNCAC 2003. [27] Cf. Raeschke-Kessler 2004, 482 et seq.

parties. If private bribery occurs during the performance of the main contract, company Y as the victim of the breach of trust could take action against the 'rogue employee' on the basis of labour or even criminal law, but the main contract would remain valid. The bribery pact would be null and void.

3.4 Fraud

'Fraud' in the context of this text always means fraud as a criminal offence (not civil fraud).

3.4.1 *Definition*

Finding a common denominator for the elements of fraud is difficult, as domestic and international concepts of the offence vary a great deal. Fraud often includes false documentation. As large-scale economic crime, it takes the shape of subsidy, accounting or tax fraud, Ponzi schemes, etc. In Swiss criminal law, the basic fraud provision prescribes *mens rea* (*Vorsatz*) in terms of subjective requirements, as well as the perpetrator's intent to become unjustly enriched (*unrechtmässige Bereicherungsabsicht*). On the objective side, the requirements are:

- error;
- malicious deception;
- a disposal of assets and
- financial damage.[28]

Deception and error as well as error and asset disposal must be related in their motive (*Motivationszusammenhang*). The fraud offence includes that the victim voluntarily causes damage to himself (*Selbstschädigungsdelikt*).[29]

In English criminal law, fraud is not defined in a criminal code, and there exists no basic fraud provision comparable to the one in Swiss law. A number of fraud offences are scattered through statutes and the common law. The English Fraud Act 2006 contains several fraud offences (fraud by false representation, fraud by failing to disclose information, and fraud by abuse of position)[30] that repeal and replace some of the earlier statutory and common law offences and overlap with others. In order to overcome difficulties relating to evidence, the Fraud Act offences

[28] Art. 146(1) SCrimC. [29] In detail: Pieth 2016b, 104 et seq.; Pieth 2014c, 157 et seq.
[30] See s. 1–4 English Fraud Act 2006.

are drafted in inchoate mode: fraudulent conduct is criminalised whether or not someone is deceived successfully, and whether or not any property is obtained.[31]

'Bribery' and 'fraud' are sometimes used interchangeably in arbitral awards and by commentators, in particular by those with a common law (US) background.[32] In Swiss criminal law, the two offences have a different structure and protect different legal interests. However, bribery always includes the deception, and possibly the defrauding, of someone in some form.

3.4.2 *Manifestations of Fraud in International Arbitration*

3.4.2.1 Allegations That the Main Contract Was Procured by Fraud

In two ICSID cases (*Inceysa* v. *El Salvador* and *Hamester* v. *Ghana*) as well as in ICC Case No. 6320, fraud was alleged in relation to the procurement of the underlying main contract. As with bribery, the legal consequences of such a scenario vary in different legal systems; in Swiss law, the main contract would be unilaterally voidable on the grounds of deliberate deception or fundamental error.

3.4.2.2 Alleged Fraud in Relation to the Performance of an Investment

In *Hamester* v. *Ghana*, the Respondent also alleged that fraud occurred during the performance of the investment. The Tribunal eventually did not discuss the legal consequences of such conduct, but those would be complex. From the point of view of contract law, the main contract(s) are valid, and there is no defect in consent if fraud had no impact at all on the establishment of the investment. If the Claimant alleges fraud in the performance of the investment, he might argue that he did not receive fair and equitable treatment; if the Respondent state raises the allegations, it could argue that the investment is not in accordance with host state's law.[33]

3.4.2.3 Other Fraud Scenarios

In *Siag* v. *Egypt*, the Respondent (unsuccessfully) alleged fraud by the Claimant regarding his nationality, arguing that the Claimant did not

[31] Horder 2016, 418. [32] Cf. Llamzon and Sinclair 2015, 469 et seq.
[33] See also Llamzon and Sinclair 2015, 470 et seq.

fulfil the negative nationality requirement of Art. 25(2)(a) ICSID Convention, and that therefore the Tribunal did not have jurisdiction. It is one of many other possible scenarios for fraud allegations in relation to international investment or commercial arbitration.[34]

3.5 Money Laundering

3.5.1 Definition

The definition of money laundering is very similar in the international instruments that cover the offence.[35] In a nutshell, it encompasses:

- the conversion or transfer;
- the concealment;
- the acquisition of property, knowing that it is proceeds of crime (as well as related ancillary offences).[36]

The difficulty with money laundering is that it always involves a predicate offence that will frequently take place in a different jurisdiction than the actual money laundering activity. The range of possible predicate offences varies in different domestic legal systems.

3.5.2 Manifestations of Money Laundering in International Arbitration

3.5.2.1 Money Laundering Allegations by a Party

Money laundering allegations can occur in arbitral proceedings if a party alleges that the other side was involved in a money laundering scheme, and brings this as a defence to the enforcement of the underlying contract: this was the situation in the *X* v. *Y ad hoc* arbitration.[37]

3.5.2.2 An Arbitration Is Conducted in Order to Launder Money

A real issue for arbitrators regarding money laundering is the potential abuse of arbitral proceedings for the laundering of illicit assets. For example, this can happen through the domestic enforcement of an international arbitral award that admits a claim out of a (fake) dispute – e.g. between a European real estate seller and a complicit counterparty

[34] On fraud in relation to document production: Wirth 2009.
[35] See discussion in Chapter 8. [36] Pieth 2014b, 435. [37] See discussion in Chapter 6.

located in a country known for its problems with drug production – over a strongly inflated or non-existent purchase price. In the arbitral proceedings, the respondent will accept the seller's claim, or an award with the agreed wording will be concluded. The award will prevent the seller's bank to question the transfer of a large sum of money from a suspicious source, and the money launderer acquires valuable real estate that can be resold to a third party.[38]

3.5.2.3 The Arbitrator's Legal Obligations in the Face of Money Laundering

Tribunals must be aware of the risk that the arbitration proceedings might be abused for an illegal purpose. However, what are their obligations under domestic criminal and regulatory law in the face of suspected or alleged money laundering?

Are Arbitrators Covered by Criminal Law Money Laundering Provisions? If arbitral proceedings are conducted involving fake claims for the purpose of money laundering, the question is: do arbitrators carry a potential risk of becoming complicit in money laundering? The answer to this question will generally be found in the applicable domestic criminal law of the seat of the arbitration on the basis of the territoriality principle, or possibly, the criminal law of the state of which the arbitrator is a national on the basis of the active nationality principle. Criminal law money laundering provisions apply to arbitrators like they apply to anyone.

For instance, under the Swiss Criminal Code, the money laundering offence requires *mens rea* (*Vorsatz*) by the perpetrator; money laundering through negligence is not possible.[39] *Dolus eventualis* (*Eventualvorsatz*) is sufficient.[40] For an accomplice (*Gehilfe*) to money laundering, *mens rea* is required both with regard to the main offence (in its basic features) as well as to the act of complicity (*doppelter Gehilfenvorsatz*);

[38] Schlabrendorff 2005, 853; Karsten 2003, 18 et seq., both with further examples; cf. also Court de Fontmichel 2004, 346 et seq.; Cremades and Cairns 2003b, 84; Geisinger and Ducret 2011, 115 et seq.; Hiber and Pavić 2008, 463.

[39] Art. 305bis in connection with Art. 12(1) SCrimC.

[40] Pieth 2013, Art. 305bis N 59. Swiss criminal law is narrower than German criminal law in this aspect: according to § 261(5) of the German Criminal Code, money laundering can also be committed by a person that frivolously (*leichtfertig*) does not realise that assets originate from a relevant predicate offence (Stree and Hecker 2014, § 261 N 28; Schlabrendorff 2005, 855).

again, *dolus eventualis*[41] is sufficient.[42] In principle, these subjective requirements will not be fulfilled by arbitrators. However, the possibility of becoming an accomplice with *dolus eventualis* in a money laundering scheme means that arbitrators cannot sit back and relax if they become aware of suspicious circumstances in a case.[43] One option is that they carry out their own investigation and draw the appropriate consequences if they find money laundering to be involved in the case;[44] the second option is to resign.[45] Reporting the suspicious circumstances to the respective arbitral institution is a first step, but possibly not sufficient.[46]

In the United Kingdom, according to s. 328 of the Proceeds of Crime Act 2002 (POCA), arbitrators run the risk of committing a criminal offence if they become involved in an arrangement of which they know, or suspect, that it 'facilitates (by whatever means) the acquisition, retention, use or control of criminal property'. This is the case if an arbitrator – knowing or suspecting that proceeds of crime are being laundered – issues an agreed award following a settlement between the parties.[47]

Are Arbitrators Covered by Regulatory Law? International treaties, the FATF Recommendations 2012, EU law and many domestic legal systems impose certain identification and reporting obligations on banks and other financial intermediaries.[48] Do those regulatory law obligations apply to arbitrators as well? Are they obliged to identify the beneficial owners behind corporate structures, e.g. in a dispute involving shell corporations? If arbitrators suspect money laundering activities, are they obliged to report their suspicions to national anti-money laundering authorities?

In general, arbitrators, in the performance of their duty as arbitrators and the context of arbitral proceedings, do not fall under regulatory law

41 *Dolus eventualis* in this context would mean that an arbitrator thinks it possible that the basic features of a money laundering offence are given in the arbitration, and that he is aiding to this offence; but concedes to both (Art. 12(2) SCrimC).

42 Art. 25 SCrimC; BGE 121 IV 109, 120; Seelmann and Geth 2016, 158.

43 Geisinger and Ducret 2011, 131.

44 As the Tribunal did in the *X* v. *Y ad hoc* arbitration; see discussion in Chapter 6.

45 Geisinger and Ducret 2011, 123 et seq.; cf. also Schlabrendorff 2005, 864 et seq.

46 Cf. Hahn 2010, 388 and see discussion in Chapter 9.

47 CIArb 2010, paras. 3.2.1, 3.2.8, 4.3; Geisinger and Ducret 2011, 130 et seq.

48 For a more detailed discussion of the international instruments against money laundering, see discussion in Chapter 8.

anti-money laundering provisions: they are not obliged to identify the beneficial owners, or to report.[49] If arbitrators got involved in activities resembling those of credit institutions or financial intermediaries (e.g. in the context of the sale of real estate), things would be different – this is, however, hard to imagine in practice, as the function of arbitrators is to settle legal disputes as adjudicators, not to consult or represent clients or to act as notaries.[50] While they are not legally obliged to report, arbitrators can draw lessons from regulatory law anti–money laundering systems, e.g. from the 'risk-based approach' that is applied by banks and other financial intermediaries.[51]

3.6 Other Scenarios

Other scenarios – not discussed here – how criminal behaviour[52] can affect international arbitration include allegations that the formation of the arbitration agreement was influenced by bribery or fraud;[53] that arbitrators, witnesses, neutral experts or other important participants in the proceedings were bribed or defrauded in order to weaken a party's defence;[54] that bribery played a role in the appointment of arbitrators or neutral experts;[55] or that bribery played a role at the enforcement stage of an award.[56]

[49] Cf. Art. 2 of the Swiss Anti-Money Laundering Act (AMLA) that does not include arbitrators in its scope of application; Art. 2 of EU 2015 equally does not extend to arbitrators as it is targeted at financial and legal service providers; the same applies for Art. 22 of the FATF Recommendations 2012. See also Mourre 2009, 231 et seq.; Schlabrendorff 2005, 856 et seq. (for the situation in German law); Blackaby et al. 2015, 332 et seq. Under Singaporean law, however, arbitrators apparently have an obligation to report suspected money laundering (Hwang and Lim 2012, 69 et seq.).

[50] Cf. Schlabrendorff 2005, 858 et seq.

[51] See discussion in Chapter 9.

[52] For an extensive discussion of guerilla tactics in international arbitration: Horvath et al. 2013, 3 et seq.

[53] Cf. Kreindler 2013a, 293.

[54] Cf. Art. 52(1)(c) ICSID 1965; Wilske and Fox 2011, 493 et seq.; in Swiss criminal law, Arts. 322ter, 322^{quater} and 322^{septies} SCrimC cover the active and passive bribery of domestic and foreign arbitrators (Pieth 2013, Art. 322ter N 17); and on fraud in relation to the arbitral proceedings, see, e.g., the decision of the Paris Appeals Court (13/13278) in the *Crédit Lyonnais-Bernard Tapie* dispute.

[55] Cf. Wilske and Fox 2011, 493.

[56] Cf. Wilske and Fox 2011, 494.

4

Evidence

What is evidence? Evidence is required in all legal proceedings. In common law systems, the discipline that deals with evidence is the law of evidence.[1] In continental law systems, evidence is often regulated in civil or criminal procedure law.[2] In general terms, evidence can be defined as 'any material which has the potential to change the state of a fact-finder's belief with respect to any factual proposition which is to be decided and which is in dispute'.[3]

Common law and continental law systems have different conceptions of evidence.[4] In arbitration, in principle no formal rules of evidence apply. This chapter briefly introduces the meaning of evidence both in court litigation (taking the examples of Swiss and English law) as well as in arbitration.

4.1 What Does 'to Prove' Mean in Legal Proceedings?

In all legal proceedings, the parties involved (including state prosecutors) must prove their alleged facts. What does 'to prove' mean under the particular circumstances of court or arbitral proceedings? Two questions guide the process of proving an alleged fact:

- How is the respective past behaviour translated into evidence?
- How is the evidence conveyed to a deciding body and treated by it?[5]

In order to establish the facts of a case, the deciding body must take the evidence and assess it. At the same time, the requirements of an offence

1 E.g. for the United Kingdom: Keane and McKeown 2016, 2.
2 E.g. for Switzerland: Arts. 150 et seq. SCPC and Arts. 139 et seq. SCrimPC.
3 Glover 2015, 2.
4 See, e.g., Engel, who points out that in common law, proof is an objective concept, whereas continental law regards proof as the 'strictly subjective impression in the judge's mind' (Engel 2009, 436); see also Habscheid 1990a (on burden and standard of proof).
5 Pieth 1984, 6.

in criminal law[6] or the substantive provisions of civil law[7] specify what needs to be proven. In criminal law, this results in a circle of alleging a fact – identifying and taking of evidence; assessing the evidence – subsuming under the elements of an offence; and thus drawing up a hypothesis – taking of more evidence to prove or dismiss the hypothesis. This process is called the 'circle of association' (*Assoziationskreisel*).[8] In general, judges as well as arbitrators eventually decide freely, without any formal rules on the evaluation of evidence.[9] However, they have to use their discretion in an objective manner, and make a reasoned decision.[10]

4.2 'Evidence' and 'Truth'

Evidence and truth are not synonyms. In particular, the writings of European criminologists on the notion of 'truth' – strongly influenced by the *Frankfurter Schule* and critical theory about communication and discourse[11] – are very clear in this regard, and in criminology and criminal procedure, two paradigms are now well established:

- First, it is recognised that criminal proceedings, as a particular type of discourse, are not free from power (*kein herrschaftsfreier Diskurs*), but institutionalised and constrained by topic, time, the threat of sanctions and inevitable consequences.[12]
- Second, it is acknowledged that the notion of truth is not absolute. In legal proceedings, it is not possible to establish a past reality: 'A judicial trial is not a search to ascertain the ultimate truth of the past events inquired into, but to establish that a version of what occurred has an acceptable probability of being correct.'[13]

In the context of this text, in particular the second paradigm is interesting as it applies not only to court litigation but also to arbitration. The facts of a case (*Sachverhalt*) should be as close to the truth as possible, but they are always a re-enactment and different from past reality. The crucial element that connects the facts of a case and past reality is the evidence.[14]

[6] For Swiss law: Gless 2014, Art. 139 N 13; for English law: Glover 2015, 21.
[7] For Swiss law: Hasenböhler 2016, Art. 150 N 11; for English law: Glover 2015, 21.
[8] Pieth 1984, 10 et seq. [9] For Swiss law: Art. 157 SCPC and Art. 10(2) SCrimPC.
[10] Pieth 2016a, 185 et seq.; Pieth 1984, 6 et seq.
[11] German-speaking criminologists for instance applied the writings of *Jürgen Habermas* and *Niklas Luhmann* to the criminal law system: cf. Krauss 1980, 65 et seq.
[12] Hassemer 1990, 130 et seq.; see also Lüderssen 1984, 52 et seq. [13] Glover 2015, 3.
[14] Pieth 1984, 5 et seq.

A third paradigm, fundamental in criminal as well as in civil proceedings and possibly also in arbitration, has its roots in human rights law: the search for truth is not without limits, but is constrained by the legality of the proceedings (*Justizförmigkeit des Verfahrens*) – in particular, the rules on the admissibility of evidence must be respected.[15]

4.3 Procedure and Evidence in Common Law and Continental Law

Common law[16] and continental law[17] domestic systems are different in many aspects. This section briefly introduces some of those differences, with a focus on procedure and evidence.

4.3.1 Some Common Law Characteristics (based on the English example)

4.3.1.1 The Doctrine of Judicial Precedent

The term 'common law' has several meanings. Here it refers to the legal tradition that derives from the English legal system and to a form of law-making that is governed by judicial precedent.[18] The English legal doctrine is one of binding precedent: lower courts are bound by decisions of higher courts, and appellate courts in principle are bound by their previous decisions.[19] The basis of English law is case law: the mass of decisions of judges in court cases. Only decisions made by judges, not by juries, constitute case law. The most important source of law in England are statutes, i.e. Acts of Parliament; in principle, they prevail over other sources of law, including case law.[20]

4.3.1.2 Varieties, Admissibility and Weight of Evidence

In English law, courts may receive evidence if it takes the form of oral, documentary or real evidence.[21] Evidence can be direct or circumstantial.[22] In English law, in principle, all evidence that is sufficiently relevant

[15] Gless 2014, Art. 139 N 7; Krauss 1980, 65; Pieth 2016a, 190 et seq.; and see discussion in Chapter 9.

[16] E.g. England and Wales, the United States, Canada and Australia.

[17] E.g. France, Germany and Switzerland.

[18] Wilson et al. 2016, 26.

[19] Martin 2014, 9; Wilson et al. 2016, 149.

[20] Martin 2014, 40; Wilson et al. 2016, 29 et seq.

[21] Glover 2015, 20.

[22] Circumstantial evidence 'requires the tribunal of fact not only to accept the evidence tendered, but also to draw an inference from it' (Glover 2015, 16).

to prove or disprove a fact is admissible, except if it is excluded by the judge because of an exclusionary rule, as a matter of public policy or by the discretion of the judge.[23] In jury trials, the jury determines questions of fact and the judge decides questions of law; admissibility and relevance of evidence are questions of law, whereas the weight of the evidence is a question of fact.[24] The judge has no discretion (in criminal as well as in civil cases) to admit evidence that is legally inadmissible. Whether the judge is allowed to exclude legally admissible evidence is unclear in civil cases. In criminal cases, the judge has the power and the duty to secure a fair trial and must at his discretion exclude or limit evidence which is legally admissible if its 'probative value is outweighed by its potential for unfair prejudice to the accused.'[25] 'Unfair prejudice' means that the evidence could shock or inflame the jury, or predispose it against the accused person.[26]

With regard to illegally or unfairly obtained evidence, the situation in English law is notably different from other legal systems. As a principle of English common law, evidence obtained by means of torture is never admissible in judicial proceedings.[27] In all other cases, evidence is not rendered inadmissible by the manner in which it was obtained (even if it was obtained illegally or unfairly). Consequently, the fruits of illegally obtained evidence are not inadmissible (no *fruit of the poisonous tree* doctrine). Rather, in criminal as well as in civil cases, it is decisive whether the evidence has prejudicial effect, which would result in an unfair trial.[28] At least in criminal cases, the courts have discretion to exclude illegally or unfairly obtained evidence (even if it is legally admissible). In the *Sang*[29] case, the House of Lords established that evidence obtained from the accused after the commission of the offence by a trick or oppression could be excluded by the judge.[30] Furthermore, under s. 78 of the UK Police and Criminal Evidence Act 1984, evidence which is obtained by the use of an *agent provocateur*, or by a subterfuge, ought to be excluded by the court if it would have an adverse effect on the fairness of the proceedings.[31] If the admissibility of the evidence is

23 Keane and McKeown 2016, 30 et seq.
24 Glover 2015, 33 et seq.
25 Glover 2015, 46.
26 Glover 2015, 43 et seq.; cf. also s. 78 of the UK Police and Criminal Evidence Act 1984.
27 Glover 2015, 54 et seq.
28 Glover 2015, 53 et seq., 57 et seq.
29 *R.* v. *Sang* [1980] AC 402.
30 Glover 2015, 62 et seq.; Keane and McKeown 2016, 63 et seq.
31 Glover 2015, 67 et seq. with reference to the *Looseley* case ([2001] UKHL 53); Keane and McKeown 2016, 65 et seq.

clarified, its weight needs to be assessed – this is a question of fact and depends on a multiplicity of factors.[32]

4.3.1.3 Burden and Standard of Proof

Burden of Proof The burden of proof in English law is divided into a legal burden and an evidential burden; however, only the legal burden really is a burden of proof. It can be defined as 'the obligation imposed on a party by a rule of law to prove a fact in issue'.[33] The evidential burden is not a burden of proof and can be defined as 'the obligation on a party to adduce sufficient evidence of a fact to justify a finding on that fact in favour of the party so obliged.'[34] In civil cases under English law, the legal burden of proof as a general rule is on the party that asserts a fact.[35] Substantive law determines the essential elements of claims and defences.[36] In criminal cases, the legal burden of proof for all elements of the charged offence relevant for the prosecution's case, in particular the guilt of the accused person, rests with the prosecution throughout the trial.[37] The evidential burden in both civil and criminal proceedings is generally on the party bearing the legal burden of proof.[38] Regarding civil cases, the evidential burden may shift if the claimant successfully establishes a *prima facie* case:[39] while the legal burden of proof remains with the claimant, the evidential burden shifts to the defendant.[40] Regarding criminal cases, the House of Lords held in the *Lambert*[41] case that the presumption of innocence provided for by Art. 6(2) of the European Convention on Human Rights (ECHR)[42] prohibited the imposition of a legal burden of proof on the defendant; the Lords, however, then 'read down' the legal burden to an evidential burden, which can be imposed on the defendant.[43]

Standard of Proof In English law, the standard of proof designates how cogent or convincing a party's evidence must be for the party to

[32] Glover 2015, 29 et seq.; Keane and McKeown 2016, 33 et seq.
[33] Keane and McKeown 2016, 87; Glover 2015, 76.
[34] Keane and McKeown 2016, 89; Glover 2015, 76 et seq.
[35] Doak, McGourlay and Thomas 2015, 68; Keane and McKeown 2016, 106 et seq.
[36] Glover 2015, 79.
[37] Doak, McGourlay and Thomas 2015, 45; Glover 2015, 85; Keane and McKeown 2016, 91; Powles, Waine and May 2015, 51 et seq.
[38] Keane and McKeown 2016, 109.
[39] *Prima facie* case means that there is enough evidence to entitle a tribunal, in the absence of further evidence, to rule in favour of the claimant (Glover 2015, 77).
[40] Glover 2015, 77 et seq., 84 et seq. [41] [2001] UKHL 37. [42] CoE ECHR 1950.
[43] Glover 2015, 86 et seq., 93 et seq.; Doak, McGourlay and Thomas 2015, 61 et seq.

successfully discharge its burden of proof. Determining the standard of proof is a question of law for the judge, whereas assessing whether the evidence meets the standard is a question of fact and decided by the jury.[44] In civil cases, the standard of proof is the 'balance of probabilities'; this standard also applies if criminal conduct is alleged in civil proceedings.[45] The UK Bribery Act of 2010 does not change the standard of proof in civil cases: the standard of 'balance of probabilities' remains applicable.[46] In criminal cases, the standard of proof traditionally is described as 'beyond reasonable doubt'; a more modern formula is 'proof which makes the jury feel sure'.[47] There is no intermediate standard of proof in English law. However, in cases of serious allegations in civil proceedings, more compelling evidence may be required:

> Although there is a single civil *standard* of proof on the balance of probabilities, it is flexible in its *application*. In particular, the more serious the allegation or the more serious the consequences if the allegation is proved, the stronger must be the evidence before a court will find the allegation proved on the balance of probabilities. Thus the flexibility of the standard lies not in any adjustment to the degree of probability required for an allegation to be proved (such that a more serious allegation has to be proved to a higher degree of probability), but in the strength or quality of the evidence that will in practice be required for an allegation to be proved on the balance of probabilities.[48]

If civil proceedings carry criminal attributes because they affect a person's liberty, the situation is not entirely clear yet in English law, but it appears that the criminal standard of proof would apply.[49]

4.3.1.4 The Privilege against Self-Incrimination

In principle, the privilege against self-incrimination in English law encompasses two aspects: it prohibits any compulsion of witnesses to produce evidence against themselves; and witnesses have the right that

[44] Glover 2015, 107 et seq.; Keane and McKeown 2016, 112 et seq.

[45] Glover 2015, 115 et seq.; Keane and McKeown 2016, 115 et seq.; both with references to English case law, in particular to *Hornal* v. *Neuberger Products Ltd* [1957] 1 QB 247; to *In re Dellow's Will Trusts* [1964] 1WLR 451; and to *In re B (Children)(Fc)* [2008] UKHL 35.

[46] Zadkovich 2011, 108.

[47] Glover 2015, 109 et seq.; Keane and McKeown 2016, 113 et seq.; Powles, Waine and May 2015, 71 et seq.

[48] *R(N)* v. *Mental Health Review Tribunal (Northern Region)* [2006] QB 468, para. 62; Glover 2015, 115 et seq.; see also Smith and Nadeau-Séguin 2015, 137 et seq.

[49] Glover 2015, 119 et seq.

no adverse inference is drawn from their silence.[50] Regarding civil cases, the privilege against self-incrimination is written down in a statute. S. 14 (1) of the English Civil Evidence Act 1968 holds that a witness may refuse to answer any question or to produce documents and things if this would expose him, a spouse, or civil partner to criminal proceedings under UK law. Inferences may not be drawn from the silence or non-production of evidence of the witness.[51]

The picture is more complex in criminal cases, where the privilege against self-incrimination is in fact weaker. While the privilege was long recognised in English common law,[52] it was curtailed by sections 34–37 of the UK Criminal Justice and Public Order Act 1994. In certain situations, those provisions cut into the right to silence by allowing 'proper' inferences to be drawn from an accused person's failure to answer questions.[53] Human rights campaigners severely criticise this as a 'back-door means of coercion' that effectively amounts to 'shifting the burden of proof from the prosecution to the defence'.[54] The legislation has so far not been declared incompatible with Art. 6 of the ECHR.[55] While the right to silence and the right not to incriminate oneself are not explicitly mentioned in Art. 6 ECHR, those are considered 'generally recognised international standards which lie at the heart of the notion of a fair procedure under Article 6'.[56]

4.3.1.5 The English Adversarial Trial

Common law systems in general adopted the *adversarial trial*: the search for truth happens at the trial stage when the parties do the questioning (examination-in-chief, cross-examination and re-examination),[57] and

[50] Doak, McGourlay and Thomas 2015, 165; Glover 2015, 526 et seq.

[51] Doak, McGourlay and Thomas 2015, 184; see also Keane and McKeown 2016, 655 et seq.

[52] See Powles, Waine and May 2015, 324 et seq.

[53] Glover 2015, 523, 583 et seq.; Doak, McGourlay and Thomas 2015, 165, 169 et seq.; Powles, Waine and May 2015, 336 et seq.

[54] Doak, McGourlay and Thomas 2015, 185; see also Sanders and Young 2012, 851.

[55] Doak, McGourlay and Thomas 2015, 185; in *Condron* v. *United Kingdom* (at para. 56), the European Court of Human Rights held that 'it would be incompatible with the right to silence to base a conviction solely or mainly on the accused's silence or on a refusal to answer questions or to give evidence himself.' In *John Murray* v. *United Kingdom* (at para. 47), the Court held that the right to silence did not apply in the absolute. See also Keane and McKeown 2016, 461 et seq.

[56] *Saunders* v. *United Kingdom*, para. 68; see also Doak, McGourlay and Thomas 2015, 185, fn. 124; Gless 2015, 29 et seq.

[57] In the United States: direct-cross-redirect examination.

the judge mainly oversees the fairness of the process. The main features of the adversarial trial include orality (evidence is obtained through live oral witness testimony in court), party control (the parties gather, select and present the evidence before the tribunal of fact whereas the state generally does not intervene) and judicial non-intervention (the judge and jury must rely on the parties for all the material facts and their interferences are minimal).[58]

4.3.2 Some Continental Law Characteristics (based on the Swiss example)

4.3.2.1 A Legal System Based on Codes

In contrast to common law systems, continental law systems are based on codes and use different methods for applying, developing and interpreting the law. In Swiss law, for instance, interpretation has four elements: the linguistic-grammatical, the systematic, the historical, and the teleological.[59]

4.3.2.2 Varieties, Admissibility and Weight of Evidence

In continental law systems, evidence is generally regulated in civil and criminal procedure codes. According to the Swiss Civil Procedure Code (SCPC), the following types of evidence (*Beweismittel*) are admissible: witness statement, documents, inspection, opinion, written advice, questioning of the parties and evidentiary statement (Art. 168 SCPC). In principle, a *numerus clausus* applies and no other types of evidence are allowed than those enumerated.[60] Illegally (*rechtswidrig*) obtained evidence is only considered if there is a predominant interest to find the truth (Art. 152(2) SCPC). 'Illegally' means that the evidence was obtained in breach of a protective rule of substantive law, e.g. Art. 179 SCrimC (opening a letter without authorisation) or Art. 179bis and 179ter SCrimC (recording, as an external person or as a participant, a non-public conversation without the consent of all participants).[61] In order to decide

[58] Doak, McGourlay and Thomas 2015, 20 et seq., 26 et seq.; see also Sanders and Young 2012, 838 et seq.

[59] According to the Swiss Federal Supreme Court, there is no hierarchy of those elements of interpretation; rather, a 'pluralism of methods' (*Methodenpluralismus*) applies (instead of many: BGE 135 III 112, 116).

[60] Sutter-Somm 2017, 213 et seq.; Weibel and Walz 2016, Art. 168 N 1.

[61] In detail: Rüedi 2009, 116 et seq.

whether there is a predominant interest to find the truth, the interests have to be weighed (*Interessenabwägung*). The interest to find the truth must be weighed against the interest to protect the legal object (*Rechtsgut*) that was compromised by the unlawful manner in which the evidence was obtained (e.g. the interest to protect privacy).[62] The violation of procedural rules, e.g. if a witness is not informed about the criminal law consequences of a false testimony (Art. 307 SCrimC), is not covered by Art. 152(2) SCPC. Such mistakes can be repaired by repeating the taking of the evidence after informing about possible criminal law consequences.[63]

The Swiss Criminal Procedure Code (SCrimPC) divides evidence into the categories of 'persons' (*Personalbeweis*)[64] and 'things' (*Sachbeweis*)[65]. There is no *numerus clausus* regarding types of evidence in Swiss criminal procedure. However, evidence must be taken in a way that is in accordance with the law (*justizförmiges Verfahren*),[66] and certain methods of taking evidence are prohibited by Art. 140 SCrimPC.[67] A violation of this provision results in an absolute prohibition to use the evidence in criminal court proceedings; the same applies if the law declares evidence as unusable (Art. 141(1) SCrimPC).[68] In addition, there is a relative prohibition to use evidence in criminal court proceedings if the evidence has been obtained illegally by the authorities, or in violation of a rule on validity (*Gültigkeitsvorschrift*). Rules on validity are, in essence, rules that aim to protect the rights of the accused person.[69] Such evidence is unusable, unless it is necessary to solve a serious crime

[62] Hasenböhler 2016, Art. 152 N 36; Leuenberger and Uffer-Tobler 2016, 241; Rüedi 2009, 148 et seq.; Sutter-Somm 2017, 212 et seq.

[63] Leuenberger and Uffer-Tobler 2016, 241 et seq.

[64] See Art. 142 et seq. SCrimPC on interrogations; this includes witnesses (*Zeugen*), informants (*Auskunftspersonen*), experts (*Sachverständige*) as well as the accused (*Beschuldigte*) and co-accused persons (*Mitbeschuldigte*) (Gless 2014, Art. 139 N 14; Pieth 2016a, 186 et seq.; Schmid 2013, 362 et seq.).

[65] See Art. 192 et seq. SCrimPC; this includes documents (*Urkunden*) and inspections (*Augenschein*) (Gless 2014, Art. 139 N 14; Pieth 2016a, 187; Schmid 2013, 397 et seq.).

[66] Gless 2014, Art. 139 N 14 et seq.; Hauser, Schweri and Hartmann 2005, 275 et seq.; Pieth 2016a, 187 et seq.

[67] This includes evidence taken by the use of coercion, force, threat, promises, deception or by means which influence the cogitation or free will of a person, even if the person has agreed to such methods.

[68] For example, evidence is unusable if the compulsory measures court did not authorise the surveillance of the postal and telecommunication traffic (Art. 277(2) SCrimPC); see Oberholzer 2012, 254; Pieth 2016a, 162 et seq., 191 et seq.

[69] Gless 2014, Art. 141 N 67.

(Art. 141(2) SCrimPC). Evidence which has been obtained in violation of a mere rule on order (*Ordnungsvorschrift*) is always usable (Art. 141(3) SCrimPC).[70] Swiss criminal procedure – to some degree – adopted the *fruit of the poisonous tree* doctrine that applies in US criminal procedure as well. According to that doctrine, secondary evidence obtained on the basis of unusable primary evidence in principle cannot be used. Two situations must be distinguished. In case of an absolute prohibition to use the primary evidence (Art. 141(1) SCrimPC), the secondary evidence is unusable without exception. In case of a relative prohibition (Art. 141(2) SCrimPC), the secondary evidence is unusable if it could not have been obtained without the (illegal) primary evidence (Art. 141(4) SCrimPC).[71]

In principle, Swiss courts evaluate the evidence freely (*freie Beweiswürdigung*), without being bound by rules on the evaluation of evidence, and form their opinion whether there is sufficient evidence on the basis of their so-called inner conviction (*intime conviction*).[72]

4.3.2.3 Burden and Standard of Proof

Burden of Proof In Swiss civil law, the burden of proof (*Beweislast*) is a matter of substantive law: it means that if the party carrying that burden cannot produce evidence of a legally relevant fact, it will lose in the proceedings.[73] Art. 8 of the Swiss Civil Code (SCC) contains the general rule on burden of proof and establishes that:

> E. Rules of evidence
>
> I. Burden of proof
>
> Unless the law provides otherwise, the burden of proving the existence of an alleged fact shall rest on the person who derives rights from that fact.[74]

The burden of proof involves the burden to allege a fact (*Behauptungslast*), the burden to substantiate factual allegations (*Substantiierungspflicht*)

[70] For the difference between rules on validity and rules on order, see Pieth 2016a, 191 et seq.; Wohlers 2014, Art. 141 N 22 et seq.

[71] Pieth 2016a, 198 et seq.; Wohlers 2014, Art. 141 N 15.

[72] Cf. Art. 157 SCPC and Art. 10(2) SCrimPC. The roots of *intime conviction* date back to the French Revolution and in particular to the French *Code d'instruction criminelle* of 1808 (Pieth 2015, 51 et seq.; Pieth 2016a, 30 et seq.).

[73] Berger and Kellerhals 2015, 460; Lardelli 2014, Art. 8 N 38; Leuenberger and Uffer-Tobler 2016, 232; see also Habscheid 1990b, 385 et seq.; Brönnimann 1989, 153 et seq.; Guldener 1955, 16 et seq.

[74] Available at: www.admin.ch (unofficial translation).

and the burden to contest alleged facts (*Bestreitungslast*).[75] If the party alleging a fact does not substantiate the allegation, the court will not take it into consideration when making its decision.[76] Parties should explicitly contest alleged facts of the other side to make sure the court does not consider the facts as granted; they should substantiate the contestation, which may, however, not result in a reversal of the burden of proof.[77] In addition to the general rule, a number of substantive provisions of Swiss civil law specifically distribute the burden of proof (e.g. Art. 97 SCO).[78] Exceptions to the general rule in Art. 8 SCC are mainly found in family law or other situations in which one party is more in need of protection than the other.[79] In Swiss criminal law, the rule on burden of proof derives from what is called the presumption of innocence (*Unschuldsvermutung*): the prosecution must prove the guilt of an accused person, who does not have to prove his or her innocence. If the state is unable to prove guilt, it carries the consequences of the lack of evidence and must acquit the accused. If the court, after assessing the evidence, still has insurmountable doubts that the factual requirements of the accused offence are fulfilled, it is bound to base its decisions on the facts in favour of the accused (*in dubio pro reo*).[80]

Standard of Proof The standard of proof (*Beweismass*) in Swiss civil law determines to which degree of certainty a court, after evaluating the evidence, must be convinced of the existence of an alleged fact to accept it as proven.[81] The standard of proof is (partially) determined by substantive provisions; there is a scale of applicable standards reaching from absolute certainty to credibility (*Glaubhaftmachen*). The generally applicable standard of proof (*Regelbeweismass*) in Swiss civil proceedings is 'fully convinced' (*volle Überzeugung*).[82] This is probably also the applicable standard if criminal conduct is alleged in civil proceedings and

[75] Lardelli 2014, Art. 8 N 29 et seq.; Schmid 2000, 15 et seq.; in detail: Brönnimann 1989, 129 et seq., 165 et seq., 173 et seq. For a comparison of continental European and Anglo-Saxon law with regard to burden and standard of proof, see Habscheid 1990a.

[76] Sutter-Somm 2017, 89.

[77] Lardelli 2014, Art. 8 N 30, 33; Sutter-Somm 2017, 209.

[78] Berger and Kellerhals 2015, 460; Leuenberger and Uffer-Tobler 2016, 234.

[79] Cf. Arts. 446(1) and 314(1) SCC.

[80] Art. 10(1) and (3) SCrimPC; Pieth 2016a, 55, 186; Tophinke 2014, Art. 10 N 19 and 80 et seq.; Verniory 2000, 398 et seq.; Wohlers 2014, Art. 10 N 6 and 11; all with further references.

[81] Leuenberger and Uffer-Tobler 2016, 285 et seq.

[82] Lardelli 2014, Art. 8 N 15 et seq.; Leuenberger and Uffer-Tobler 2016, 286; Sutter-Somm 2017, 238 et seq.; Habscheid 1990b, 380 et seq.; in detail: Berger-Steiner 2008, 41 et seq.

decided as a preliminary matter (*vorfrageweise*). In Swiss criminal law, the inner conviction (*l'intime conviction*)[83] of the judge determines the standard of proof: a conviction 'beyond reasonable doubt' is required in criminal cases.[84]

4.3.2.4 The Privilege against Self-Incrimination

In Swiss civil procedure, the parties have an obligation (*Obliegenheit*) to co-operate in the taking of the evidence (Art. 160 SCPC). Parties have a right to refuse to co-operate *inter alia* if their statement would expose a person close to them (spouses, certain relatives etc.) to the risk of a criminal investigation or civil liability (Art. 163(1)(a) in connection with Art. 165 SCPC). However, the parties cannot refuse to co-operate if they expose *themselves* to the risk of a criminal investigation or civil liability.[85] If a party (or a witness) rightfully refuses to co-operate, the court may not draw any inference from this to the fact that needs to be proven (Art. 162 SCPC). This provision establishes a rule of evidence that is an exception to the principle of free evaluation of the evidence.[86] If a party refuses to co-operate without right, the court will take this into account in the evaluation of the evidence (*Beweiswürdigung*). The court might consider an assertion as true which could not be proven because a party unrightfully refused to co-operate (Art. 164 SCPC); but the court may not automatically draw this conclusion, as in practice this would result in a reversal of the burden of proof.[87] Witnesses – non-parties who directly observed the facts at issue (Art. 169 SCPC) – are summoned by the courts (Art. 170(1) SCPC). They have *inter alia* the right to refuse to give evidence if they would expose themselves or a person close to them to the risk of criminal or civil liability (Art. 166(1)(a) SCPC).[88] If witnesses unlawfully refuse to give evidence, they may *inter alia* be fined or sanctioned according to Art. 292 SCrimC (Art. 167 SCPC; the parties, however, are not fined or sanctioned if they refuse to give evidence).[89]

[83] See subsection 4.3.2.2.

[84] Tophinke 2014, Art. 10 N 82 et seq.; Verniory 2000, 386 et seq.

[85] It is disputed whether this is contrary to the principle of *nemo tenetur se ipsum accusare* enshrined in Art. 32(1) of the Swiss Constitution (SR 101) and Art. 6 ECHR (Leuenberger 2008, 62 et seq.; Leuenberger and Uffer-Tobler 2016, 253; see also BGE 131 IV 36, 40 et seq.).

[86] Hasenböhler 2016, Art. 162 N 5; Higi 2016, Art. 162 N 1.

[87] Hasenböhler 2016, Art. 162 N 4 and Art. 164 N 5 et seq.; Leuenberger and Uffer-Tobler 2016, 254, 283; Sutter-Somm 2017, 216.

[88] Sutter-Somm 2017, 216 et seq.

[89] Sutter-Somm 2017, 235.

Parties as well as witnesses are obliged to speak the truth (Art. 160(1)(a) SCPC).[90] The court must inform parties and witnesses about their obligation to co-operate, their right to refuse to co-operate, and about the consequences, otherwise the evidence that was taken cannot be used unless the respective person agrees, or unless the refusal would not have been rightful (Art. 161 SCPC).[91]

In Swiss criminal procedure, the accused person does not have to incriminate himself and may refuse to give evidence and co-operate in the proceedings (*nemo tenetur se ipsum accusare, Selbstbelastungsfreiheit*, Art. 113(1) SCrimPC). The principle of *nemo tenetur* in criminal proceedings is enshrined in (almost universally recognised) human rights law.[92] According to the European Court of Human Rights, an accused's silence may nevertheless be taken into account when assessing the persuasiveness of the adduced evidence.[93] The prosecuting authorities must inform the accused about the privilege against self-incrimination at the beginning of the first interrogation; if this information is omitted, the evidence is absolutely prohibited to be used in court (Art. 158(1)(b) and (2) SCrimPC).[94] Witnesses – persons not involved in the offence who can make a statement useful for solving it, who are not informers (*Auskunftspersonen*) – are obliged to be present, to give evidence and to speak the truth (Art. 163(2) SCrimPC).[95] A false witness statement is sanctioned according to Art. 307 SCrimC. In certain circumstances, however, witnesses enjoy a right not to testify, which has grown historically. It has its origin in the liberalism of the mid-nineteenth century and the idea that individuals have a private sphere with which the state should in principle not interfere.[96]

Witnesses who are personally related to the accused (spouses, relatives and the like) may refuse to testify (Art. 168(1) SCrimPC). Equally, witnesses who would expose themselves to criminal responsibility may refuse to testify (Art. 169(1)(a) SCrimPC); if they would expose themselves to civil liability, they may refuse to testify if the protected

90 Arts. 306 and 307 SCrimC criminalise a false party or witness statement.

91 Hasenböhler 2016, Art. 161 N 10; cf. also Spühler 2004, 148.

92 Explicitly in Art. 14(3)(g) ICCPR 1966; implicitly in Art. 6 ECHR; see *Saunders* v. *United Kingdom*, para. 68; Gless 2015, 29 et seq.

93 *John Murray* v. *United Kingdom*, para. 47; Safferling 2009, 787 et seq.

94 Pieth 2016a, 192 et seq.

95 The unlawful refusal to testify is fined according to Art. 292 SCrimC and results in criminal proceedings (Art. 176 SCrimPC).

96 Hauser 1974, 13 et seq., 129 et seq.

interest outweighs the interest to prosecute the crime (Art. 169(1)(b) SCrimPC).[97] The prosecuting authorities must inform witnesses about their right to refuse to testify, otherwise the evidence is absolutely prohibited to be used in court (Art. 177(3) SCrimPC).[98] The Swiss Federal Supreme Court left the question open whether the refusal of a witness to testify may be interpreted by a court, in the context of the free evaluation of the evidence, as a fact that creates or corroborates a suspicion.[99]

4.3.2.5 The Inquisitorial Principle in Swiss Criminal Procedure

Some continental law systems (e.g. Switzerland) incorporated the 'inquisitorial' principle for criminal proceedings. In its neutral sense, this means that the state takes over the responsibility to carry out a criminal investigation and to launch court proceedings, and that the presiding judge questions the parties and witnesses at the trial stage. Nowadays, Swiss criminal proceedings are based on a mixture of the adversary[100] and the inquisitorial principle.[101]

4.4 Evidence in International Arbitration

What is the purpose of evidence in international arbitration: ascertaining the truth or resolving the dispute, or something in between?[102] Unlike domestic courts in many states, international arbitral tribunals in principle do not apply strict rules of evidence (they are however free to do so).[103] Nevertheless, evidentiary rules do play a role in international arbitration. The bottom line in all arbitral proceedings are mandatory procedural protections: a party's right to equal treatment and the right to be heard.[104]

97 Pieth 2016a, 202 et seq.; Vest and Horber 2014, Art. 169 N 4.

98 Pieth 2016a, 207.

99 BGE 118 IV 175, 180; several commentators argue that this would be contrary to the object and purpose of the privilege against self-incrimination (Vest and Horber 2014, Vor Art. 168–176 N 7; Donatsch and Schmid 1996 et seq., Vorbem. zu §§ 128 ff., N 36; Hauser 1974, 158 et seq.).

100 See subsection 4.3.1.5.

101 Pieth 2016a, 29, 32; see also Doak, McGourlay and Thomas 2015, 36 et seq.

102 Kreindler 2013a, 314.

103 E.g. Born 2015b, §8.08.

104 See, e.g., Art. 182(3) SPILA (mandatory); Art. 15(1) SRIA 2012; s. 33(1)(a) English Arbitration Act 1996 (mandatory); Art. 14(4)(i) LCIA 2014; Art. 22(4) ICC 2012; Born 2014, 2169 et seq.; O'Malley 2012, 4 et seq.

4.4.1 *In ICSID Arbitration*

In the ICSID system, Art. 43 of the ICSID Convention and Rules 34–36 of the ICSID Arbitration Rules deal with evidence and establish the parties' autonomy to agree on a specific set of evidentiary rules to apply. In practice, tribunals often agree to apply the IBA Rules on the Taking of Evidence in International Arbitration ('IBA Rules of Evidence').[105] Under the ICSID Convention and Arbitration Rules, the tribunal may – unless the parties agree otherwise – at any stage of the proceedings call upon the parties to produce evidence, visit the scene, and conduct enquiries as it deems appropriate. The parties are expected to co-operate with the tribunal in the production of evidence.

4.4.1.1 Admissibility of Evidence

The ICSID Convention is silent about the admissibility of evidence. According to Rule 34(1) of the ICSID Arbitration Rules, the tribunal decides about the admissibility of evidence and its probative value.[106] Similarly, Art. 9(1) of the IBA Rules of Evidence establishes that the tribunal determines the admissibility, relevance, materiality and weight of the evidence. Prohibitions on the use of evidence cannot simply be transferred to ICSID proceedings – each case must be considered individually.[107]

4.4.1.2 Burden and Standard of Proof

The ICSID Convention and Arbitration Rules are silent about burden and standard of proof. Regarding burden of proof, ICSID tribunals developed the following principles:

- normally the burden of proof is with the claimant;
- the burden of proof lies with the party asserting a fact, whether it is the claimant or the respondent;
- if a party adduces evidence that proves *prima facie* the facts alleged, the burden of proof may shift to the other party, who needs to produce evidence to rebut the presumption.[108]

[105] IBA 2010; Schreuer et al. 2009, Art. 43 N 8.

[106] The tribunal has discretion in this regard, but not without limits: Schreuer et al. 2009, Art. 43 N 11 and 15.

[107] Happ 2013, 965 with reference to *EDF* v. *Romania* (see discussion in Chapter 5).

[108] Schreuer et al. 2009, Art. 43 N 116 (references omitted); see also Llamzon and Sinclair 2015, 484 et seq.

In principle, the applicable law as chosen by the parties (or the tribunal) determines burden and standard of proof. However, ICSID current practice shows that in cases of alleged criminal conduct, tribunals usually do not strictly refer to the applicable law.[109]

4.4.1.3 The Privilege against Self-Incrimination?

The ICSID Convention and Arbitration Rules are silent about issues of self-incrimination of parties or witnesses. Rule 35(2) of the ICSID Arbitration Rules only states that witnesses must declare to speak the truth before giving evidence.

4.4.2 In Commercial Arbitration

In commercial arbitration, the *lex arbitri* frequently contains (possibly mandatory) rules of evidence. Equally, the applicable procedural law, as chosen by the parties or by the tribunal, as well as the applicable arbitral rules usually contain evidentiary rules. Within the limits set by mandatory rules of the *lex arbitri*, the parties or, in the absence of party agreement, the tribunal can freely decide whether any and which rules of evidence are to be applied. For instance, if the seat of the arbitration is Switzerland and the Swiss Rules apply, non-mandatory[110] Art. 184 of the SPILA states that in principle, the arbitral tribunal conducts the taking of evidence itself; however, if state legal assistance is required for the taking of evidence, the tribunal or a party with the consent of the tribunal can call on the state judge at the seat of the arbitration, who will apply his own law.[111] Some provisions of the Swiss Rules also address evidence.[112] If the seat of the arbitration is England, Wales or Northern Ireland and the LCIA Rules apply, non-mandatory[113] s. 34 of the English Arbitration Act 1996 establishes that in absence of party agreement, the tribunal decides all matters of procedure and evidence. Some of the provisions of the LCIA Rules also deal with evidence.[114]

[109] See discussion in Chapter 5.
[110] Cf. Hochstrasser and Fuchs 2013, Einl. 12. Kap. N 238.
[111] Wehrli and Stacher 2013, 354 et seq.
[112] E.g. Arts. 24 and 25 (evidence and hearings) SRIA 2012.
[113] Cf. s. 4 and Schedule 1 of the English Arbitration Act 1996.
[114] E.g. Arts. 19 (oral hearings), 20 (witnesses) and 22(1)(vi) (application of rules of evidence) LCIA 2014.

4.4.2.1 Admissibility of Evidence

Admissibility of evidence is a matter of procedure, not substantive law.[115] The general principle in international commercial arbitration is that the arbitral tribunal determines the admissibility, relevance, materiality and weight of the evidence.[116] The Swiss and English *lex arbitri*, for instance, do not contain mandatory provisions on the admissibility of evidence.[117] S. 34(2)(f) of the English Arbitration Act 1996 and Art. 22(1)(vi) LCIA Rules establish that the parties or the tribunal may decide to apply strict rules regarding the admissibility of evidence. The SPILA does not explicitly mention admissibility of evidence. Art. 24(2) of the Swiss Rules states that the arbitral tribunal determines the admissibility, relevance, materiality and weight of the evidence. The admissibility of evidence may, however, be restricted by mandatory provisions of the *lex arbitri* or by transnational public policy.[118]

4.4.2.2 Burden and Standard of Proof

Domestic arbitration laws[119] and arbitration rules[120] are frequently silent about the burden and standard of proof, as are the IBA Rules of Evidence.[121] The UNCITRAL Arbitration Rules[122] and the Swiss Rules,[123] however, state that each party carries the burden of proving the facts on which it relies for its claim or defence. Such provisions on burden of proof in arbitration rules merely state a general principle; they do not override specific rules contained in the applicable law.[124]

Burden of Proof In the absence of mandatory rules of the *lex arbitri*, the burden of proof is determined by the applicable law as chosen by the parties or, in the absence of a parties' choice, by the tribunal.[125] Burden of proof in arbitration is a complex issue in detail; however, the outcome

[115] Waincymer 2012, 792; Berger and Kellerhals 2015, 460; Schneider and Scherer 2013, Art. 184 N 13.
[116] E.g. Art. 9(1) IBA 2010; Art. 27(4) UNCITRAL 2013a.
[117] Cf. Schneider and Scherer 2013, Art. 184 N 13 et seq.
[118] See discussion in Chapter 9.
[119] Cf. e.g. the English Arbitration Act 1996 and ch. 12 of the SPILA.
[120] Cf. e.g. the LCIA Rules 2014.
[121] The IBA Rules contain, however, provisions on adverse inferences; see discussion in Chapter 9.
[122] Art. 27(1) UNCITRAL 2013a. [123] Art. 24(1) SRIA 2012.
[124] Berger and Kellerhals 2015, 460; Haugeneder and Liebscher 2009, 545 with further references.
[125] Cf. Redfern 1994, 321.

of all different approaches under the applicable laws is likely to be the same. The first difficulty is that in some jurisdictions whose law might be chosen to apply, burden of proof is a matter of substantive law, whereas in others it is a matter of procedure.[126] The second issue is that, depending on the legal background of the arbitrator, the term 'burden of proof' may encompass the 'burden of persuasion', the 'burden of production', the 'burden of going forward', the 'burden of allegation' or the 'legal burden'.[127] In a nutshell: in international arbitration, the party that asserts a fact – be it the claimant or the respondent – must prove it (*onus probandi incumbit actori*).[128] However, while the *onus probandi* never shifts between the parties, if the alleging party is able to produce *prima facie* evidence[129] for criminal behaviour, the burden to produce evidence may shift to the alleged party to produce sufficient rebuttal evidence.[130] The *onus probandi* goes further than the burden to produce evidence in that 'a party having the burden of proof must not only bring evidence in support of his allegations, but must also convince the Tribunal of their truth, lest they be disregarded for want, or insufficiency, of proof'.[131]

Standard of Proof It appears that the standard of proof in international commercial arbitration is not regulated in any domestic arbitration laws or arbitration rules. Therefore, the standard of proof is determined by the applicable law as chosen by the parties, or in the absence of a

[126] Generally, in civil law jurisdictions, the burden of proof is an issue of substantive law, whereas in common law jurisdictions it is considered a procedural issue (Carreteiro 2016, 98 et seq.; Lew, Mistelis and Kröll 2003, 560 et seq.; Patocchi and Meakin 1996, 889); cf. also Hanotiau 1994; Reiner 1994, 330 et seq. For Swiss and English law, see discussion earlier in this chapter; and see the *X* v. *Y ad hoc* arbitration, discussed in Chapter 6).

[127] O'Malley 2012, 201 et seq.; see also Mehren 1996, 124 et seq.; Reiner 1994, 328.

[128] Cheng 1987, 327 et seq.; O'Malley 2012, 203; Redfern and Hunter 2004, 297. In ICC Case No. 3344 of 1981, the Tribunal argued that the principle of *onus probandi incumbit actori* (or *actori incumbit probatio*) is part of truly international public policy.

[129] '*Prima facie* evidence' is evidence that does not offer conclusive proof, but serves as a sufficient ground that believing in its truth appears reasonable. It can be rebutted by evidence to the contrary. If such rebuttal evidence could easily be produced, but is not, a tribunal may draw reasonable (possibly adverse) inferences from the non-production (Cheng 1987, 323 et seq.).

[130] O'Malley 2012, 213 et seq.; Sharpe 2006, 552 et seq.; see discussion in Chapter 9 and cf. the *X* v. *Y ad hoc* arbitration, in which the Tribunal argued, with reference to English law, that the legal burden never shifts but the provisional (evidentiary) burden may shift as the case proceeds.

[131] Cheng 1987, 329.

parties' choice, by the tribunal. There is some debate whether to treat the standard of proof as a matter of procedure or of substance; some argue that it should be treated as a matter of substantive law.[132] The above analysis of Swiss and English law demonstrates that the approaches to standard of proof in common and in continental law are quite different.[133] Probably the most generally applied standard of proof in international arbitration is 'preponderance of the evidence'.[134] Should this standard be modified if criminal conduct is alleged?[135]

4.4.2.3 The Privilege against Self-Incrimination?

The Swiss and English *lex arbitri* as well as the Swiss Rules and the LCIA Rules are silent with regard to the privilege against self-incrimination (as probably most domestic arbitration laws and arbitration rules). The applicable procedural law might contain *nemo tenetur* provisions; generally speaking, there is little clarity today whether the privilege against self-incrimination applies in international arbitration.[136]

[132] Smith and Nadeau-Séguin 2015, 145 et seq. and cf. Mehren 1996, 126; Reymond 1994, 326.

[133] See also Smith and Nadeau-Séguin 2015, 137 et seq.; Llamzon 2014, 232 et seq.

[134] Mehren 1996, 127, who explains it in the following terms: '[T]he proponent of a position must do more than create an equilibrium between its position and that of its opponent to prevail. Somehow, the proponent must push its evidence beyond the line of equal weight to a weight greater than that of the other side.'

[135] See discussion in Chapter 9. [136] Waincymer 2012, 814.

PART III

Current Practice Regarding Alleged Criminal Conduct in Arbitration

A growing number of arbitral awards are published that involve allegations of criminal conduct. Due to the significantly different outcomes of those cases, there is little predictability and legal certainty for the parties if such allegations arise in their case. In international arbitration, doctrines of precedent or *stare decisis* do not apply. However, this does not mean that earlier arbitral awards are irrelevant for tribunals. In ICSID arbitration, while there is no *de iure* doctrine of precedent, tribunals closely scrutinise earlier awards and are *de facto* bound by earlier arbitral decisions.[1] In commercial arbitration, of 190 reviewed ICC awards, roughly 15 per cent cited other arbitral decisions (mostly on issues of jurisdiction and procedure and on determining the law governing the merits of the dispute; hardly ever on substantive issues).[2] ICSID tribunals refer to earlier awards in qualitative aspect and much more frequently than ICC tribunals, for two reasons. On the one hand, ICSID awards are consistently published, while commercial arbitral awards are largely confidential. On the other hand, ICC tribunals often apply national laws and rather cite domestic court decisions than other ICC awards.[3] In this part, the aim is to summarise and analyse the existing ICSID and ICC awards regarding certain forms of alleged criminal behaviour.

[1] *Saba Fakes* v. *Turkey* (para. 96) with reference to *Bayindir* v. *Pakistan* (para. 145); Grubenmann 2010, 66 et seq.; Reinisch 2008; Nadakavukaren Schefer 2016, 64 et seq. For an empirical analysis of precedent in investment arbitration, see König 2013, 160 et seq.

[2] Kaufmann-Kohler 2007, 362 et seq. An empirical analysis by König shows that in 23.7 per cent of the reviewed awards, tribunals referred to earlier ICC awards (König 2013, 127 et seq.).

[3] König 2013, 250.

5

Investment Arbitration

Under the heading 'investment arbitration', this chapter discusses ICSID cases that involve allegations of criminal behaviour (foreign public bribery or fraud). The selected cases were considered illustrative to discuss issues of applicable law and evidence when criminal allegations arise; it is not an exhaustive listing.[1] The cases are arranged chronologically in order to show the development in the reasoning of the tribunals.

5.1 ICSID Cases Involving Foreign Public Bribery Allegations

5.1.1 World Duty Free *v.* Kenya (*2006*)

The Claimant in this case was World Duty Free Company Limited ('WDF'), incorporated in the Isle of Man; the Respondent was the Republic of Kenya. In 1989, Kenya concluded an agreement with a company called House of Perfume for the construction, maintenance and operation of duty-free complexes at the international airports of Nairobi and Mombasa. The agreement ran for a period of ten years, renewable for another ten years. Under the terms of the agreement, House of Perfume was to pay to the Kenyan government the sum of US$1 million per year for both complexes. In 1990, the agreement was amended and House of Perfume was substituted by WDF. Both companies were owned by the Al-Ghurair family and managed by Mr Nasir Ibrahim Ali (who signed the 1989 agreement and the 1990 amendment) until 1991, when the Al-Ghurair family sold its shares and Mr Ali became the owner of WDF (directly and through his company Dinky International SA of which he owned 90 per cent and his wife owned the rest).[2]

[1] For a complete list of investment arbitration cases where corruption was alleged by investors or host states, with what result, see Llamzon 2014, 102 et seq., 217, 305 et seq.

[2] *World Duty Free* v. *Kenya*, paras. 62 et seq.

WDF stated that in 1989, to do business in Kenya, Mr Ali was required to make a personal donation to Daniel Arap Moi, the then-President of Kenya, as part of the consideration paid by House of Perfume to obtain the contract. WDF also submitted that in 1992, a massive fraud scheme was drawn up to generate illicit funds for President Moi's re-election campaign, which involved the name of WDF without the company's knowledge or consent. WDF argued that after it had publicly denied any involvement in the fraud, Kenya aimed to take over control of the company. In short, WDF claimed that Kenya had expropriated it and destroyed its rights under the 1989 agreement. WDF demanded compensation in the form of restitution (the return of the two duty free complexes) as well as payment of legal costs and damages.[3] Kenya submitted *inter alia* that the fraud was time-barred and that in any case there was no breach of the 1989 agreement.[4] Furthermore, it alleged that the 1989 agreement was unenforceable and requested that WDF's claims should be dismissed because the agreement was procured by paying a bribe to the then-president.[5] The basis for WDF's claims was an arbitration clause in the 1989 agreement; the ICSID arbitration was therefore contract-based (not treaty-based). The agreement provided that English and Kenyan law should apply.[6]

5.1.1.1 The Existence of a Bribe

The parties did not contest the payment by Mr Ali to the then-president. Rather, they disagreed how this should be qualified: as an illegal bribe or as a legitimate personal donation according to local custom? The Tribunal first asked whether there was a bribe and whether the 1989 agreement had been procured by a bribe. It examined the written witness statement (confirmed in an oral hearing) of Mr Ali, the CEO and shareholder of WDF and former general manager of House of Perfume. It emerged from this statement that Mr Ali had been advised by Mr Sajjad, a Kenyan businessman, that protocol in Kenya required the payment of a personal donation to the president in order to do business with the Kenyan government. The appropriate donation would be US$2 million in cash. Mr Ali arranged for part of this money (US$500,000) through Mr Sajjad, and they took it to a meeting with the president in a briefcase which they

[3] *World Duty Free* v. *Kenya*, paras. 66 et seq.
[4] *World Duty Free* v. *Kenya*, paras. 80 et seq.
[5] *World Duty Free* v. *Kenya*, paras. 105 et seq.
[6] *World Duty Free* v. *Kenya*, paras. 6, 75, 158 et seq.

left by the wall. After the meeting, they fetched the briefcase and saw that the money had been exchanged with fresh corn. Although Mr Ali felt uncomfortable, he was assured that this was lawful and that he had no choice if he wanted the investment contract. Mr Ali fully documented the payment in House of Perfume's records.[7]

Mr Ali added that the president welcomed his proposal for the two duty-free complexes during their meeting, and that Mr Sajjad showed him British newspaper articles relating to 'Harambees' (the Kenyan system of personal donations) officially given to the president. He never thought he was bribing to get the investment agreement. Kenya never denied Mr Ali's payment to the president.[8] In sum, Kenya considered this payment as a bribe in order to procure the investment agreement; WDF thought it was a gift of protocol or a personal donation to the president, to be used later for public purposes, according to the system of 'Harambee', anchored in Kenyan cultural practices.[9]

The Tribunal referred to a Kenyan report, showing that the concept of 'Harambees', originally collective contributions towards individual or communal activities, had changed over the years and had resulted in gross abuses.[10] It stated:

> [T]he Tribunal has no doubt that the concealed payments made by Mr. Ali on behalf of the House of Perfume to President Moi and Mr. Sajjad could not be considered as a personal donation for public purposes. Those payments were made not only in order to obtain an audience with President Moi (as submitted by the Claimant), but above all to obtain during that audience the agreement of the President on the contemplated investment. The Tribunal considers that those payments must be regarded as a bribe made in order to obtain the conclusion of the 1989 Agreement.[11]

5.1.1.2 Transnational Public Policy

Kenya argued that as a matter of international public policy, as well as Kenyan and English law, the 1989 agreement obtained by bribery 'does not have force of law'.[12] The Tribunal first examined the concept of international public policy and noted that this was used with two separate meanings. On the one hand, probably all legal systems know the concept of public policy (*ordre public*). The New York Convention[13] as

[7] *World Duty Free* v. *Kenya*, para. 130.
[8] *World Duty Free* v. *Kenya*, paras. 131 et seq.
[9] *World Duty Free* v. *Kenya*, para. 133.
[10] *World Duty Free* v. *Kenya*, para. 134.
[11] *World Duty Free* v. *Kenya*, para. 136.
[12] *World Duty Free* v. *Kenya*, para. 137.
[13] Art. V 2. New York Convention 1958.

well as the UNCITRAL Model Law[14] state that it is a ground for refusing recognition or enforcement if a foreign judgment or award is contrary to the enforcing state's public policy. Several legislators and courts decided that a narrow concept of public policy should apply to foreign awards in this regard, often referred to as 'international public policy': 'Although this name suggests that it is in some way a supra-national principle, it is in fact no more than domestic public policy applied to foreign awards and its content and application remains subjective to each State.'[15]

On the other hand, the concept is sometimes used with the meaning of an international consensus on universal standards and norms of conduct, which must be applied in all fora. With this meaning, the concept is sometimes referred to as 'transnational public policy' or 'truly international public policy'. The Tribunal stressed that when international arbitral tribunals base their decisions on such transnational public policy, the objective existence of those rules has to be checked carefully by means of international conventions, comparative law and arbitral awards.[16]

In the present case, referring to two Kenyan Acts (1956/2003), the Tribunal held that bribery or influence peddling and active or passive corruption are illegal in most (if not all) countries. It also noted that since the mid-1990ies, the OAS Convention, the OECD Convention on Bribery, the two CoE Conventions, the African Union Convention and the UNCAC had been adopted and had largely entered into force.[17] The Tribunal also referred to domestic court decisions and several ICC awards, which all held that influence peddling or bribery were contrary to international public policy, even if such practices were widespread in a certain country.[18] The Tribunal concluded that,

> In light of domestic laws and international conventions relating to corruption, and in light of the decisions taken in this matter by courts and arbitral tribunals, this Tribunal is convinced that bribery is contrary to the international public policy of most, if not all, States or, to use another formula, to transnational public policy. Thus, claims based on contracts of corruption or on contracts obtained by corruption cannot be upheld by this Arbitral Tribunal.[19]

[14] Art. 36 UNCITRAL 2006. [15] *World Duty Free* v. *Kenya*, para. 138.

[16] *World Duty Free* v. *Kenya*, para. 139.

[17] See OAS 1996; OECD 1997; CoE 1999a and CoE 1999b; AU 2003; UNCAC 2003. Llamzon points out that at the time of the 1989 agreement, none of those conventions was yet in force (Llamzon 2014, 117).

[18] *World Duty Free* v. *Kenya*, paras. 142 et seq. [19] *World Duty Free* v. *Kenya*, para. 157.

5.1.1.3 Bribery under English and Kenyan Law

The Tribunal then turned to English and Kenyan domestic law[20] and stated that the bribe payment was an 'intrinsic part' of the 1989 agreement, without which the latter would not have been concluded. Mr Ali was the *alter ego* of House of Perfume as well as of WDF, and his actions had to be imputed to both companies.[21] The Tribunal argued that the (covert) bribe payment had been made to the Kenyan head of state and could not be imputed to the Respondent: 'Mr. Ali's payment was received corruptly by the Kenyan head of state; it was a covert bribe; and accordingly its receipt is not legally to be imputed to Kenya itself. If it were otherwise, the payment would not be a bribe.'[22] From the outset, the Tribunal had noted that it had no jurisdiction over the Kenyan president, who did not take part in the proceedings.[23]

The Tribunal briefly took note that the local custom of 'Harambee' could not render legal a behaviour that violated transnational public policy or foreign applicable law.[24] The Tribunal concluded that both under English and Kenyan law (which were materially identical), WDF could not maintain its claims due to the principle of *ex turpi causa non oritur actio* (no legal action can be based on an illegal cause).[25]

5.1.1.4 Bribe Solicitation by the Former Kenyan President?

The Tribunal was aware that the unfavourable outcome of the dispute for the Claimant was not uncontroversial:

> It remains nonetheless a highly disturbing feature in this case that the corrupt recipient of the Claimant's bribe was more than an officer of state but its most senior officer, the Kenyan President; and that it is Kenya which is here advancing as a complete defence to the Claimant's claims the illegalities of its own former President. Moreover, on the evidence before this Tribunal, the bribe was apparently solicited by the Kenyan President and not wholly initiated by the Claimant. Although the Kenyan President has now left office and is no longer immune from suit under the Kenyan Constitution, it appears that no attempt has been made by Kenya to prosecute him for corruption or to recover the bribe in civil proceedings. It is not therefore surprising that Mr. Ali feels strongly the unfairness of the legal case now advanced by Kenya.[26]

[20] In particular to a legal opinion by Lord Mustill on general principles of English law regarding avoidance; see *World Duty Free* v. *Kenya*, paras. 164, 183 et seq.

[21] *World Duty Free* v. *Kenya*, paras. 167 et seq., 175.

[22] *World Duty Free* v. *Kenya*, para. 169.

[23] *World Duty Free* v. *Kenya*, paras. 3, 185.

[24] *World Duty Free* v. *Kenya*, para. 172.

[25] *World Duty Free* v. *Kenya*, para. 179.

[26] *World Duty Free* v. *Kenya*, para. 180.

However, neither the former president's apparent bribe solicitation nor Kenya's failure to prosecute him for corruption altered the Tribunal's conclusion. The Tribunal argued that, with regard to public policy, 'the law protects not the litigating parties but the public; or in this case, the mass of tax-payers and other citizens making up one of the poorest countries in the world.'[27] With reference to English case law, the Tribunal stated that Mr Ali's unfairness complaint had been voiced and answered already centuries ago, with the result described above.

In the Award, the Tribunal dismissed all of WDF's claims under the 1989 agreement (as amended in 1990) as a matter of English, Kenyan, and international public policy, and held that Kenya was legally entitled to avoid its obligations under that agreement.[28]

5.1.1.5 Analysis

WDF v. *Kenya* is a remarkable case because WDF itself brought the evidence for the bribe payment – it just did not consider it to be a bribe. Therefore, the Tribunal did not have to worry about evidence or burden and standard of proof issues, but had to clarify the legal situation with regard to the alleged bribery. Concerning applicable law, the Tribunal relied on the existing international anti-bribery conventions (in particular the African Union Convention and UNCAC)[29] as well as earlier commercial arbitration awards to state that bribery was contrary to transnational public policy. It relied on English common law relating to contract (that also applied in Kenya except where modified by Kenyan written law) to establish the general principles regarding avoidance. In order to define the bribery of a public official, the Tribunal explicitly

[27] *World Duty Free* v. *Kenya*, para. 181. It has been criticised that the Award does not protect the public, but rather the opposite as it encourages corruption by public officials if the host state does not have to fear repercussions and receives the investment (Kulick 2012, 320 et seq.; Kulick and Wendler 2010, 68; Litwin 2013; Wilske 2010, 220). It has also been argued, however, that the loss of a neutral forum to arbitrate for corrupt investors may render them more hesitant to invest in states where corruption is endemic; and that the decline in investment may incentivise corrupt governments, that have little reason to change corrupt practices if they continue to receive foreign investment, to take a harder stance on corruption (Menaker 2010, 74 et seq. with further references).

[28] *World Duty Free* v. *Kenya*, para. 188. Donovan points out that English and Kenyan law were sufficient to address the corruption issue, and that transnational public policy was not needed to decide the case (Donovan 2011, 288 et seq.); Bjorklund argues that transnational public policy is a fall-back position: no matter what the Tribunal would have decided applying domestic law, transnational public policy required a dismissal of WDF's claims (Bjorklund 2011, 271 et seq.).

[29] *World Duty Free* v. *Kenya*, paras. 144 et seq.

referred to the relevant sections of the Kenyan Prevention of Corruption Act 1956 (replaced by the Anti-Corruption and Economic Crimes Act 2003).[30]

The Tribunal did not thoroughly discuss either the fact that Kenya did not prosecute its former president for corruption[31] or the conditions under which the corrupt acts of a head of state can be imputed to the state itself.[32] Notably, the dispute was not brought under a BIT, but based on a contract, and the Tribunal did not examine whether the investment was made in accordance with the host state's law at the jurisdictional stage. Affirming its jurisdiction, the Tribunal considered the bribery allegations at the merits stage.

5.1.2 Siemens *v.* Argentina *(2007)*

5.1.2.1 The 2007 Award and the Annulment and Revision Proceedings

In February 2007, an ICSID Tribunal ordered Argentina to pay US$217 million to the German corporation Siemens for breaches of the Germany-Argentina Investment Protection Treaty. In the Award, the Tribunal decided *inter alia* that Argentina had breached the Treaty by expropriating Siemens's investment.[33]

Argentina subsequently sought the annulment of this Award. In July 2008, while the annulment proceedings were in progress before an ICSID *ad hoc* committee, Argentina filed a request with ICSID to revise the Award in light of new evidence that the underlying investment (a contract about national identity cards) had possibly been procured through bribery. Corruption allegations had been surrounding the disputed contract from an early stage but were never proven in a court of law and were contested by Siemens.[34]

30 *World Duty Free* v. *Kenya*, para. 170.

31 Cf. Llamzon 2014, 203 et seq.; crit. of the Tribunal's approach from a development angle: Meshel 2013.

32 Kulick and Wendler argue that the bribe was 'targeted at influencing the President's official decision on a procurement contract', and that under the rules of state responsibility, Moi's acts were attributable to Kenya (Kulick 2012, 319 et seq.; Kulick and Wendler 2010, 66 et seq.); see discussion in Chapter 10.

33 *Siemens* v. *Argentina*, para. 403.

34 'Argentina and Siemens ask annulment panel to suspend proceedings, so original arbitrators can look at bribes evidence', *Investment Arbitration Reporter*, 28 July 2008.

In early 2008, however, a former Siemens executive testified in a German court that the respective contract had been procured through bribery. In the annulment proceedings, Argentina argued that the ICSID Tribunal had rejected essential evidence, namely evidence about the progress of a domestic corruption investigation in Argentina into the Siemens contract. During the proceedings leading up to the 2007 Award, Argentina had sought to examine witnesses in the oral hearings about those corruption allegations. The Tribunal did not admit this evidence, stating that the allegations had been around for a long time and were raised by Argentina only at a late stage in the arbitration. Argentina objected that the new evidence only slowly emerged from the domestic corruption investigations. In fact, Argentina based its July 2008 request for revision of the 2007 Award on the testimony by the Siemens executive, arguing that had this testimony been known at the time of the original proceedings, it might have proven that Siemens's investment was unlawful.[35]

5.1.2.2 Plea Agreements with the US DOJ and Secret Commercial Arbitration

In December 2008, the US Department of Justice (DOJ) and Siemens struck several plea agreements. Siemens AG pled guilty of failure to maintain sufficient internal anti-corruption controls and for violations of the books and records provisions of the US FCPA (not for bribery).[36] Its subsidiary Siemens Argentina SA pled guilty for violations of the FCPA books and records provisions.[37]

In particular, the Statement of Offense agreed upon between the US DOJ and Siemens Argentina revealed that the company had made significant payments to Argentine government officials in exchange for favourable business treatment, characterising those payments in the books as legitimate consulting fees.[38] Through a consulting group, such payments had also been made in relation to the national identity card contract that had been part of the 2007 ICSID proceedings.

[35] 'Argentina and Siemens ask annulment panel to suspend proceedings, so original arbitrators can look at bribes evidence', *Investment Arbitration Reporter*, 28 July 2008.

[36] *US* v. *Siemens AG* Cr. No. 1:08-cr-367-RJL (D. Columbia), Statement of Offense, 15 December 2008, paras. 131 et seq.

[37] *US* v. *Siemens SA (Argentina)*, Cr. No. 1:08-cr-368-RJL (D. Columbia), Statement of Offense, 15 December 2008, paras. 22 et seq.

[38] *US* v. *Siemens SA (Argentina)*, Cr. No. 1:08-cr-368-RJL (D. Columbia), Statement of Offense, 15 December 2008, paras. 30 et seq.

The Statement of Offense revealed that secret commercial arbitration proceedings about the payment of such fees were conducted from 2005–2006 in Zurich between Siemens Argentina and the consulting group. The commercial arbitration was settled with a US$8.8 million payment of Siemens Argentina to the consulting group, and the parties agreed that no information about the claims or the evidence would be released to the public. Notably, during the ICSID proceedings leading up to the 2007 Award, Siemens failed to disclose that secret commercial arbitration proceedings were conducted in parallel. The Statement of Offense points out that 'ICSID does not have jurisdiction to adjudicate claims based on contracts obtained through corruption, and Siemens did not assert or imply during the arbitration that the project was tainted by corruption, despite the confidential record to the contrary in the Argentine Consulting Group arbitration.'[39]

5.1.2.3 Siemens's Waiver of Rights under the 2007 Award

In August–September 2009, Siemens waived its rights under the 2007 Award against Argentina as part of a broader settlement, in which the parties had asked ICSID to discontinue the revision as well as the annulment proceedings. Both also waived their rights to pursue further legal actions in relation to the national identity card contract dispute, and bore their own legal costs and fees.[40]

5.1.2.4 Analysis

The Siemens-Argentina case is one example how ICSID proceedings can be influenced by domestic criminal proceedings. Argentina had sought to examine witnesses on corruption allegations during the proceedings leading up to the 2007 Award. The Tribunal, however, had declined to admit such evidence, and Argentina could not raise the allegations in the oral hearings. In the 2007 Award, nothing indicates that Argentina would have raised a bribery objection to jurisdiction – the Award does not mention corruption, bribery or fraud at all.

[39] *US* v. *Siemens SA (Argentina)*, Cr. No. 1:08-cr-368-RJL (D. Columbia), Statement of Offense, 15 December 2008, paras. 27 and 31 (aa.) et seq.; 'Siemens pleads guilty to breach of Foreign Corrupt Practices Act; evidence of arbitration over illicit payments', *Investment Arbitration Reporter*, 17 December 2008.

[40] 'Siemens waives rights under arbitral award against Argentina, follows company's belated corruption confessions', *Investment Arbitration Reporter*, 2 September 2009.

The testimony of a former Siemens executive in a German court in early 2008 had a decisive impact on Argentina's actions. It pushed Argentina to seek the revision of the 2007 Award. The outcome of the US DOJ investigation, including the guilty pleas by Siemens AG and Siemens Argentina SA and the agreed-upon Statement of Offense between the US DOJ and Siemens Argentina eventually forced Siemens to waive its rights under the 2007 Award.[41]

Two big question marks remain with regard to the secret Zurich commercial arbitration in 2005–2006. On the one hand, if the evidence from those proceedings had been available to the ICSID Tribunal during the proceedings leading up to the 2007 Award, the outcome would quite certainly have been different. On the other hand, it appears that the arbitral tribunal in that commercial arbitration enabled the Claimant, the Argentine Consulting Group, to enforce a bribe contract. The evidence in that arbitration strongly suggested that the Claimant had paid bribes on behalf of Siemens Argentina to Argentine officials. Therefore, the purpose of the consulting agreement was the indirect payment of bribes. When the Argentine government cancelled the national identity card contract, the Argentine Consulting Group sued the Siemens subsidiary for outstanding payments from their bribe contract. The dispute was settled and a Siemens subsidiary paid US$8.8 million to the Claimant.[42] In fact, this payment of US$8.8 million might have been an illegal act in itself (foreign public bribery, money laundering) under the (possibly applicable) laws of Argentina, Switzerland or Germany.

5.1.3 African Holding *v.* Democratic Republic of Congo (*2008*)

Claimants in this case were the African Holding Company of America, Inc. ('African Holding'), established under New Jersey law, and the Congolese company Société africaine de construction au Congo SARL ('SAFRICAS'). The Respondent was the Democratic Republic of Congo ('DRC'). The ICSID arbitration was based on the 1984 BIT between the

[41] See also Yackee 2012, 723 et seq.; on a proposed framework for future FCPA-ICSID interaction: Losco 2014.

[42] 'Siemens pleads guilty to breach of Foreign Corrupt Practices Act; evidence of arbitration over illicit payments', *Investment Arbitration Reporter*, 17 December 2008; see also Olaya 2009, 180 et seq.

United States and the Republic of Zaire.[43] The dispute arose over alleged debts of the DRC towards the Claimants.

5.1.3.1 Contracts Allegedly Tainted by Corrupt Practices

The Respondent alleged that contracts had been awarded by the administration without a public tender, a practice that was allowed under Congolese law only for transactions with a maximum total amount of US$5,000. SAFRICAS, however, was awarded contracts with a total value of US$1,700,555. The DRC argued that this practice was illegal and could only be explained on the basis of corrupt acts and illicit payments.[44]

The Claimants argued that the maximum total amount of US$5,000 only applied in one out of fourteen cases, while for the other contracts, awarding them without public tender was legitimate because SAFRICAS was the only company in place that was capable of executing the works demanded by the government.[45]

5.1.3.2 The Applicable Standard of Proof

The Arbitral Tribunal stated that any corrupt practice would be considered a very serious issue. It demanded irrefutable proof (*preuve irréfutable*) of such a practice, as in criminal proceedings (*'telle que celles qui résulteraient de poursuites criminelles dans les pays où la corruption constitue une infraction pénale'*).[46] The Tribunal concluded that in this case, no such proof was given, but that the DRC's allegations were based on general considerations with regard to the regime of Mobutu and the surrounding political events. It also referred to the *World Duty Free* v. *Kenya* Award (invoked by the Respondent), confirming that jurisdiction may be declined due to corrupt practices, arguing that in that case, such irrefutable proof (in the form of illicit payments admitted by the Claimant itself) had been given.[47]

The Tribunal stressed that in several instances, the Respondent party in investment arbitration had invoked corruption allegations with the aim that the Tribunal would decline jurisdiction, or in order to influence the decision on the merits. Therefore, the Tribunal found that the standard of proof for such allegations must be particularly high (*'la norme*

43 *African Holding* v. *Democratic Republic of Congo*, para. 1.
44 *African Holding* v. *Democratic Republic of Congo*, para. 49.
45 *African Holding* v. *Democratic Republic of Congo*, para. 50.
46 *African Holding* v. *Democratic Republic of Congo*, para. 52.
47 *African Holding* v. *Democratic Republic of Congo*, para. 54.

de preuve doit, à cet égard, être particulièrement élevée').[48] The Tribunal eventually decided that it had no jurisdiction *ratione temporis*.[49]

5.1.3.3 Analysis

The Tribunal dealt with the bribery allegations in this case very briefly. There was clearly a lack of evidence for the allegations that were based on general considerations of the political situation in the DRC. The Tribunal concluded that the standard of proof for corruption allegations would be particularly high, as parties in a number of cases had invoked such allegations. However, the Respondent's allegations probably would have failed already under a lower standard of proof, such as 'more likely than not'. The Respondent's rather blunt and unsubstantiated bribery allegations cannot be taken as basis for a well-founded argument why the standard of proof must be heightened in cases of alleged corruption.[50]

5.1.4 TSA Spectrum *v.* Argentina *(2008)*

The Claimant in this case was the Argentinian company Thales Spectrum de Argentina SA ('TSA Spectrum'), a wholly owned subsidiary of TSI Spectrum International NV, a company registered in the Netherlands. The Respondent was Argentina. The dispute was based on the 1992 Netherlands-Argentina BIT and arose over a concession contract for the administration, management and control of a radio spectrum that had been awarded to TSA Spectrum in 1997. TSA Spectrum filed a request for ICSID arbitration in December 2004.[51]

In July 2001, the Argentinian Anticorruption Office charged – among others – certain persons related to TSA Spectrum with corruption, following an anonymous report on alleged irregularities in the bidding process in which the concession contract had been awarded to the company. In 2008, a federal judge decided to prosecute two persons connected to TSA Spectrum for complicity in fraud. The judge noted that an investigation into alleged bribery was incomplete, and he deferred a decision in this regard.[52]

48 *African Holding* v. *Democratic Republic of Congo*, para. 55.

49 *African Holding* v. *Democratic Republic of Congo*, paras. 108 et seq., 122.

50 According to Llamzon, the President of the Tribunal indicated in an interview that the requirement of a particularly high standard of proof should not be read as a standard of proof higher than 'clear and convincing' evidence (Llamzon 2014, 173).

51 *TSA Spectrum* v. *Argentina*, paras. 1 et seq., 21, 23.

52 *TSA Spectrum* v. *Argentina*, paras. 15 et seq.

5.1.4.1 Argentina's Bribery Objection to Jurisdiction

Argentina raised four jurisdictional issues. As a fourth objection to the Tribunal's jurisdiction, Argentina argued that TSA Spectrum had obtained the concession contract in a manner that was not in accordance with Argentinian law, and the concession was therefore not protected under the BIT.[53] According to Art. 1(a) of the Netherlands-Argentina BIT, an asset had to be invested in accordance with the laws and regulations of the host state in order to qualify as an investment and to be protected under the BIT. Argentina argued that TSA Spectrum was being investigated in Argentina for corruption in relation to the awarding of the concession contract in 1997, and that two persons connected with TSA Spectrum had been charged with criminal offences. Referring to a written witness statement from the domestic criminal proceedings, Argentina argued that there was clear and convincing evidence for bribery.[54]

TSA Spectrum argued that not the Argentine courts, but the ICSID Tribunal had to decide on the issue of alleged bribery. It argued that Argentina had to meet the burden of proving alleged bribery and that the domestic accusations were unfounded: allegations of bribery in arbitration proceedings require 'the most rigorous level of proof', and Argentina had not adduced such proof. The written witness statement was unreliable and would not meet the accepted standard of evidence in arbitration. TSA Spectrum also argued that the question of legality of an investment was a question for the merits stage; and that tribunals that had declined jurisdiction on account of bribery had done so only when there was clear and convincing proof.[55]

5.1.4.2 Parallel Criminal Investigations in Argentina

The Tribunal noted that the bribery investigations in Argentina were still ongoing, despite the indictment of two TSA Spectrum connected persons for complicity in misuse of public office. It held that on the basis of the available materials, it could not conclude that the concession contract was obtained through illicit means. The Tribunal also stated that, if there had been no other obstacle to jurisdiction in this case, it would have joined the fourth jurisdictional objection to the merits of the case.[56]

53 *TSA Spectrum* v. *Argentina*, para. 39.
54 *TSA Spectrum* v. *Argentina*, paras. 163 et seq.
55 *TSA Spectrum* v. *Argentina*, paras. 169 et seq.
56 *TSA Spectrum* v. *Argentina*, paras. 174 et seq.

In the Award, the Tribunal declined jurisdiction, but not because of the bribery allegations. It accepted Argentina's third objection to jurisdiction (that TSA Spectrum was not a national of the Netherlands due to an absence of 'foreign control').[57]

5.1.4.3 Analysis

The Tribunal apparently did not discuss international conventions or domestic laws on public bribery. It also did not discuss earlier arbitral awards dealing with such allegations, or burden and standard of proof. Without further explanation, the Tribunal stated that it would have discussed the bribery objection at the merits stage if it had confirmed jurisdiction in the first place.[58] It seems that the ongoing bribery investigations in Argentina were the reason why the Tribunal was unable to come to a clear conclusion whether the concession was illegally obtained or not.

5.1.5 Sistem *v.* Kyrgyz Republic (*2009*)

The Claimant in this case was the Turkish construction company Sistem Mühendislik İnşaat Sanayi ve Ticaret AŞ ('Sistem'), the Respondent was the Kyrgyz Republic. In 2005, Sistem initiated ICSID arbitration on the basis of the Turkey–Kyrgyz Republic BIT. The dispute arose out of a joint venture formed by Sistem in 1992 with the Kyrgyz company Ak-Keme for the purpose of building and operating the Pinara Hotel in Bishkek, the Kyrgyz capital. In 1995, the relationship between Sistem and Ak-Keme broke down; Ak-Keme took over the operation of the hotel, and Sistem was excluded from participation. In 1998, Ak-Keme was declared bankrupt. In 1999, Sistem bought out its shares and became the sole owner of the hotel. Sistem claimed that in 2005, Ak-Keme ousted Sistem's managers and took physical control of the hotel, and that the Respondent failed to protect Sistem's investment. The Kyrgyz Republic argued that Sistem did not fulfil its obligations regarding the construction of the hotel; that the 1998 bankruptcy procedures and the subsequent purchase of Ak-Keme's shares by Sistem were legally invalid; and that Sistem unlawfully occupied the Pinara Hotel.[59]

[57] *TSA Spectrum* v. *Argentina*, p. 52; 'Divided ICSID Tribunal rules that corporate veil must be pierced so as to determine if a foreigner is in control', *Investment Arbitration Reporter*, 5 January 2009.

[58] See also Llamzon 2014, 178.

[59] *Sistem* v. *Kyrgyz Republic*, paras. 27; 46 et seq.; 53 et seq.; 96 et seq.

5.1.5.1 Attempted Bribery of the Kyrgyz President?

In mid-1995, Sistem refurbished the then–Kyrgyz president's guest residency for distinguished guests. According to Sistem, this happened at the request of the Kyrgyz Republic and as a good-will gesture. The Kyrgyz Republic argued that it was an attempt to bribe the Kyrgyz president.[60] The Tribunal emphasised that it was important to distinguish sponsorship and bribery:

> The refurbishment of a public, State facility is plainly not a direct bribe of any individual; nor, in the view of the Tribunal is the refurbishment in this case something beyond the reasonable scope of sponsorship or good-will gestures of the sort commonly made by companies. While the Tribunal acknowledges that gestures of this kind are made in order to enhance the reputation of the donor company and encourage its favourable reception and treatment, in a world where corporate sponsorship is not merely tolerated but is an accepted part of the system of funding public events and facilities, it is necessary to have a robust distinction between sponsorship and bribery.[61]

5.1.5.2 Applying the OECD Convention: No Causal Link or Improper Advantage

For defining bribery, the Kyrgyz Republic referred to the definition in Article 1 of the OECD Convention on Bribery. Adopting this definition, the Tribunal argued that in the present case, there was no link between the advantage bestowed and any improper advantage obtained. The refurbishment of the guest residency happened in mid-1995. There was no plausible explanation how the 1999 agreement, by which Sistem bought Ak-Keme's shares, could be causally linked to this, and why the refurbishment would constitute an improper advantage to an individual:[62]

> In some circumstances it may happen that regular payments over a period of time effectively 'buy' the long-term goodwill of the recipient, so as to make it difficult to establish a causal link between the bribe and the advantage that it procures. But that is not the case here. This was a

[60] *Sistem* v. *Kyrgyz Republic*, para. 40. [61] *Sistem* v. *Kyrgyz Republic*, para. 41.

[62] *Sistem* v. *Kyrgyz Republic*, para. 43; see also J. Hepburn and L.E. Peterson, 'Arbitral tribunal finds that one-off refurbishment of president's guest residence is corporate sponsorship or goodwill gesture, not a bribe', *Investment Arbitration Reporter*, 19 July 2012.

> one-off transaction, from which no individual derived a personal advantage (the refurbishment being of the President's official accommodation); and it is not suggested that the transaction was made surreptitiously.[63]

In the Award, the Tribunal decided that the Kyrgyz Republic had expropriated Sistem and ordered the payment of US$8.5 million in compensation, plus US$650,000 for legal fees and costs, to Sistem.[64]

5.1.5.3 Analysis

The interesting feature of this case is that the Kyrgyz Republic, in order to define bribery of a foreign public official, invoked Article 1 of the OECD Convention on Bribery (to which Turkey, but not the Kyrgyz Republic, has been a party since 2000 – notably, Turkey was not yet a party during the years when the foreign bribery allegedly took place). The Tribunal found this to be a useful definition and directly applied it with regard to the bribery allegations. No reference was made to transnational public policy or domestic law.

On the basis of the Article 1 definition, the Tribunal concluded that for bribery to be established, an improper advantage must be conferred to an individual. In the present case, according to the Tribunal, the advantage went to the Kyrgyz state (the refurbishment of a state facility). The Tribunal also argued that bribery requires a situation of *quid pro quo* – for the improper advantage conferred to a public official, the official must act or refrain from acting in relation to the performance of his official duties, and an equivalent connection between these events is required: 'From the point of view of the briber, the foreign public official owes him "consideration" for his offer, etc. This consideration should take the form of the direction of his public office to the goal intended by the bribe.'[65] In the case at hand, the Tribunal did not see any link between the mid-1995 refurbishment of the president's guest residency and the 1999 share acquisition by Sistem.

While the first conclusion of the Tribunal seems well founded – the refurbishment of a state facility did not confer an undue advantage to the Kyrgyz president; rather, it was the Kyrgyz state that profited[66] – the second conclusion is more open to critique: the fact that four years lie between the two events does not exclude that they were linked. However, to prove alleged bribery of the Kyrgyz president, (circumstantial)

[63] *Sistem* v. *Kyrgyz Republic*, para. 44. [64] *Sistem* v. *Kyrgyz Republic*, paras. 128, 208.
[65] Zerbes 2014, 168. [66] Cf. Zerbes 2014, 123.

evidence would have been required that the president, directly or indirectly, was offered, promised or given an undue advantage. In sum, the Tribunal's conclusion appears plausible that there was no bribery involved in this case.

5.1.6 EDF *v.* Romania (*2009*)

The Claimant in this case was EDF (Services) Limited ('EDF'), a company incorporated in the Bailiwick of Jersey; the Respondent was Romania. The legal basis for the claims was the Romania-UK BIT (that extends to nationals of the UK's crown dependencies).[67] EDF had participated in two joint ventures with Romanian state-owned enterprises, EDF ASRO SRL ('ASRO') and SKY SERVICES (ROMANIA) SRL ('SKY'). The joint ventures were about building up and operating airport and in-flight sale of goods and duty-free services. The contracts were concluded in 1991 and 1994 for initial periods of ten and fifteen years, respectively, and were both terminated by Romania in 2002.[68] EDF claimed that Romania had violated the BIT by expropriating EDF's investment for arbitrary reasons, after the company had built up almost from scratch the sale of goods and duty-free business in Romanian airports and airplanes.

In particular, EDF alleged that in August 2001, during a meeting of its CEO Mr Weil with Mr Tesu (Chief of Cabinet to then–Romanian Prime Minister Nastase), Mr Tesu requested the payment of a US$2.5 million bribe to the prime minister, which Mr Weil refused to pay. EDF also alleged that in October 2001, Ms Iacob (the State Secretary) repeated the bribe request to Mr Katz (the logistics and operational director of ASRO) in a private conversation at her Bucharest home. After Mr Weil had been informed by Mr Katz and had again refused to pay, Romania allegedly engaged in a concerted attack on EDF's investment.[69] EDF argued that the bribe requests as well as the subsequent actions of the two companies, C.N. Bucarest Aeroport Otopeni ('AIBO') and Compania de Transportationuri Aeriene Romane Tarom SA ('TAROM'), against EDF were attributable to Romania, and violated Romania's obligation under the BIT to provide fair and equitable treatment.[70]

Romania argued that an investigation by the Romanian Anti-Corruption Authority ('DNA') did not find sufficient evidence to substantiate EDF's

[67] *EDF* v. *Romania*, para. 64. [68] *EDF* v. *Romania*, paras. 46 et seq.
[69] *EDF* v. *Romania*, paras. 66, 69 et seq. [70] *EDF* v. *Romania*, paras. 101 et seq.

allegations of corruption; and that the Bucharest Court of Appeal, in a final and irrevocable judgment of September 2007, had rejected EDF's allegations.[71] In addition, Romania argued that the conduct of the companies AIBO and TAROM was not attributable to Romania.[72]

5.1.6.1 Attribution of Companies' Conduct to Romania

The Tribunal first examined whether the acts and conduct of AIBO and TAROM could be attributed to Romania under Article 4, 5 or 8 of the International Law Commission's Draft Articles on State Responsibility.[73] It rejected attribution under Article 4 ('Conduct of organs of a State'),[74] because AIBO and TAROM had separate legal personality under Romanian law and could not be considered state organs.[75] The Tribunal also rejected attribution under Article 5 ('Conduct of persons or entities exercising elements of governmental authority'),[76] because AIBO and TAROM were not agents of Romania and did not exercise governmental functions when performing the acts that EDF alleged to be in breach of the BIT.[77] However, the Tribunal stated that AIBO and TAROM's conduct was attributable to Romania under Article 8 ('Conduct directed or controlled by a State'),[78] because they acted under the direction and control of the state in their performance of the ASRO and SKY contracts. The Tribunal found that AIBO and TAROM's conduct aimed at terminating the contractual arrangements with EDF and ASRO.[79]

[71] *EDF* v. *Romania*, paras. 145 et seq. [72] *EDF* v. *Romania*, paras. 164 et seq.

[73] ILC 2001.

[74] Art. 4 ILC 2001 reads: '(1) The conduct of any State organ shall be considered an act of that State under international law, whether the organ exercises legislative, executive, judicial or any other functions, whatever position it holds in the organization of the State, and whatever its character as an organ of the central Government or of a territorial unit of the State. (2) An organ includes any person or entity which has that status in accordance with the internal law of the State.'

[75] *EDF* v. *Romania*, para. 190.

[76] Art. 5 ILC 2001 reads: 'The conduct of a person or entity which is not an organ of the State under article 4 but which is empowered by the law of that State to exercise elements of the governmental authority shall be considered an act of the State under international law, provided the person or entity is acting in that capacity in the particular instance.'

[77] *EDF* v. *Romania*, para. 198.

[78] Art. 8 ILC 2001 reads: 'The conduct of a person or group of persons shall be considered an act of a State under international law if the person or group of persons is in fact acting on the instructions of, or under the direction or control of, that State in carrying out the conduct.'

[79] *EDF* v. *Romania*, para. 209.

5.1.6.2 Alleged Bribe Solicitation

The Tribunal then turned to the question whether the acts that were attributable to Romania violated the BIT. Regarding the bribery allegations, the Tribunal agreed with EDF that a request for bribery by a state agency would violate the obligation to fair and equitable treatment under the BIT, as well as international public policy. The Tribunal found:

> In any case . . . corruption must be proven and is notoriously difficult to prove since, typically, there is little or no physical evidence. The seriousness of the accusation of corruption in the present case, considering that it involves officials at the highest level of the Romanian Government at the time, demands clear and convincing evidence. There is general consensus among international tribunals and commentators regarding the need for a high standard of proof of corruption. The evidence before the Tribunal in the instant case concerning the alleged solicitation of a bribe is far from being clear and convincing.[80]

The Tribunal examined the available evidence and concluded that the witness statement of Mr Weil was contradicted by Mr Tesu, and that the witness testimonies of Mr Katz were not consistent and of doubtful value, partially based on hearsay evidence. The Respondent indicated that a particular e-mail message sent to Mr Weil, reporting the bribe solicitation by Ms Iacob, might have been manipulated. The Tribunal did not admit an audio tape as new evidence (see next subsection). However, the witness statement of Ms Iacob, denying the bribe request, was also not clear and convincing in the Tribunal's view. The Tribunal mentioned the DNA's bribery investigations and their review by the Romanian courts, which twice resulted in the rejection of EDF's bribery allegations. In sum, the Tribunal concluded that the burden of proving the bribery allegations had been with EDF, and the company had failed to produce clear and convincing evidence; therefore, there was no violation of fair and equitable treatment under the BIT.[81]

5.1.6.3 Admissibility of Certain Evidence

In April 2008, EDF requested the Tribunal to admit an audio tape and a transcript that it had obtained on the same day from a *Financial Times* journalist, as new evidence. The tape recorded the private conversation between Ms Iacob and Mr Katz from October 2001 in her Bucharest

[80] *EDF* v. *Romania*, para. 221.

[81] *EDF* v. *Romania*, paras. 222 et seq., 232, 237, 301; cf. Llamzon 2014, 184 et seq.

home, in the course of which she allegedly had made the bribe request. Romania argued that the new evidence should not be admitted for three reasons: first, the tape was available to EDF from the time when it was recorded (since the male voice on the tape was Mr Katz), and EDF had acted in bad faith when it withheld the tape for seven years; second, the secret tape was obtained illegally as it recorded a private conversation without the consent of the speaker, which constitutes a violation of Romanian constitutional law as well as international human rights law; and third, the tape was not authenticated, incomplete and manipulated.[82] EDF argued that it was unaware how the record was created and that it simply obtained it from the *Financial Times* journalist.[83]

The Tribunal stated that proving corruption was a challenging task, and that the party raising the charge indisputably carried the burden of proof: 'The seriousness of a corruption charge also requires that the utmost care and sense of responsibility be taken to ascertain the truthfulness and genuine character of the evidence that the party intends to offer in support of its claim.'[84] The Tribunal concluded that EDF had failed to meet the burden of proving the authenticity of the audio recording, which had been challenged by Romania. The recording was incomplete and included discontinuities. The Tribunal stated that only the original recording would permit to establish authenticity and the absence of digital edits. In addition, with reference to an earlier arbitral award, the Tribunal held that the recording of the private conversation without Ms Iacob's consent was contrary to the principles of good faith and fair dealing in international arbitration. Referring to Art. 9(2)(g) of the IBA Rules of Evidence, the Tribunal further concluded that by withholding the tape for seven years, EDF had violated its duty of fairness in international arbitration. For all those reasons, the Tribunal rejected the admission of the new evidence.[85]

In the Award, the Tribunal unanimously decided that Romania had not violated the BIT and dismissed all claims by EDF; it also ordered EDF to pay US$6 million to Romania for its legal fees and other costs.[86]

[82] *EDF* v. *Romania*, Procedural Order No. 3, 29 August 2008, paras. 4 et seq.
[83] *EDF* v. *Romania*, Procedural Order No. 3, 29 August 2008, paras. 17 et seq.
[84] *EDF* v. *Romania*, Procedural Order No. 3, 29 August 2008, para. 28.
[85] *EDF* v. *Romania*, Procedural Order No. 3, 29 August 2008, paras. 29 et seq., 36 et seq., 39 et seq.
[86] *EDF* v. *Romania*, para. 330.

5.1.6.4 Analysis

EDF v. *Romania* is a special case in many respects. First of all, the bribery allegation concerns the solicitation of a bribe and not the payment of bribes. Second, the bribery allegation was not raised by the Respondent – it is not the well-known scenario of a bribery objection to jurisdiction due to alleged illegality of the investment. Rather, the Claimant raised the bribery allegations, claiming a breach of the BIT's fair and equitable treatment requirement. Another interesting feature is that the Tribunal invoked the Draft Articles on State Responsibility to decide whether the conduct of the companies AIBO and TAROM was attributable to the Romanian state.[87] Concerning the alleged bribe solicitation, the Tribunal did not rely on international conventions or domestic laws dealing with bribery. Rather, it stated that a bribe request by the Respondent would violate the fair and equitable treatment requirement in the BIT as well as international public policy.

The Tribunal required 'clear and convincing' evidence for corruption, arguing that there was a 'general consensus among international tribunals and commentators regarding the need for a high standard of proof of corruption.'[88] To support this argument, the Tribunal referred to the cases mentioned by the Respondent in its Rejoinder, without specifically listing them. However, case law and doctrine show that opinions are not uniform in this regard.[89] The Tribunal argued that the Claimant had to prove its allegation of bribe solicitation; apparently it did not ask the Respondent to produce any evidence to rebut the allegations. It did, however, examine the Respondent's witnesses.

The Tribunal carefully evaluated the available evidence. It was obviously confronted with the difficulty that the Claimant alleged the solicitation of a bribe, and not that payments had actually been made. All the witnesses (Mr Weil, Mr Katz, Mr Tesu and Ms Iacob) were present at the hearing, but their statements were partly contradicting each other, or inconsistent, or otherwise of doubtful value. Without referring to any provisions of domestic (Romanian) procedural law, but to international law, the Tribunal eventually did not admit the possibly manipulated tape recording of a private conversation, arguing that this would be against the duty of procedural fairness confirmed in Art. 9(2)(g) of the IBA Rules of Evidence.[90]

[87] Cf. Llamzon 2014, 247 et seq.
[88] *EDF* v. *Romania*, para. 221.
[89] See discussion in Chapter 9.
[90] *EDF* v. *Romania*, Procedural Order No. 3, 29 August 2008, para. 47.

Possibly decisive in this case was the fact that a domestic corruption investigation in Romania had not found any evidence of bribery, and that the Bucharest Court of Appeal as the last instance had issued a final judgment in this regard. The ICSID Award was in line with the judgment of the domestic court.

5.1.7 RSM *v.* Grenada *(2009/2010)*

The Claimant in this case was RSM Production Corporation ('RSM'), a US energy company; the Respondent was Grenada, a Caribbean island state with a population of about 100,000 people. In July 1996, RSM concluded an off-shore energy exploration agreement with Grenada according to which Grenada was to issue a licence for oil and natural gas exploration to RSM; RSM had to apply for that licence within 90 days. Instead, RSM invoked a *force majeure* clause of the agreement, which was accepted by Grenada.

In January 2004, RSM revoked the *force majeure* clause and applied for the exploration licence. Grenada refused to issue the licence, arguing that RSM had not filed its application in time, and terminated the exploration agreement in 2005. In August 2004, RSM filed a request for ICSID arbitration based on a clause in the agreement, alleging breach of contract by Grenada.[91]

5.1.7.1 The Proceedings Leading up to the 2009 ICSID Award

During the hearing on the merits, in cross-examination, RSM asked Mr Bowen – the then–Attorney General of Grenada – about a bribe payment that he had allegedly accepted from a company called Global Petroleum Group ('Global Petroleum') in relation to a contract for oil exploration that Global Petroleum had since concluded with Grenada. Mr Bowen denied the alleged bribe payment, confirming, however, that Global Petroleum had provided Grenada with US$2.5 million to fund the arbitration proceedings.[92] RSM did not ask the Tribunal to make a

[91] *RSM* v. *Grenada*, paras. 5 et seq., 42 et seq.; L.E. Peterson, 'Grenada prevails in ICSID contract dispute with US energy company; New York court dismissed separate claims', *Investment Arbitration Reporter*, 17 March 2009; L.E. Peterson, 'Award in RSM v. Grenada arbitration is released; separate contract claim by RSM pending against Central African Republic', *Investment Arbitration Reporter*, 2 April 2009.

[92] *RSM* v. *Grenada*, Annulment Proceeding, para. 5.

finding of fact regarding the alleged bribery, but submitted that the Tribunal should take this evidence into account when deciding about Mr Bowen's credibility.[93] The Tribunal came to the conclusion that:

> On all the evidence adduced in these arbitration proceedings, the Tribunal does not accept any of these personal criticisms of Senator Bowen for the purpose of its decisions in this Award. Moreover, after a firm but fair cross-examination of Senator Bowen during the Main Hearing, RSM's Counsel submitted in his closing oral submissions that RSM was not requesting this Tribunal, in these proceedings, to find Senator Bowen 'corrupt' or 'incompetent' . . . Nor does it.[94]

In March 2009, the ICSID Tribunal rejected all of RSM's claims against Grenada, as well as Grenada's counterclaims, on their merits.[95]

5.1.7.2 The Parallel New York Court Proceedings

In November 2006, while the ICSID arbitration proceedings were ongoing, RSM sued a number of individuals and corporations in front of the District Court for the Southern District of New York, *inter alia* for alleged tortuous interference with RSM's agreement with Grenada. As part of its complaint, RSM alleged bribe solicitation by Mr Bowen, as well as bribe payments to Mr Bowen by RSM's competitors for the oil exploration rights.[96] RSM claimed a violation of the US Foreign Corrupt Practices Act (FCPA) as well as of the OECD Convention on Bribery. However, in February 2009, the Court dismissed all of RSM's claims because the complaint was legally flawed,[97] and there was no factual support for the bribery allegations made in the complaint.[98] The Court noted that if the US DOJ decided to prosecute certain individuals, the alleged bribe payments might constitute a violation of the FCPA. However, the FCPA does not provide for a private right of enforcement.[99]

The ICSID Tribunal in its March 2009 Award was aware of the New York Court proceedings that incurred extensive publicity. Materials from the ICSID proceedings that apparently did not originate from Grenada or Mr Bowen were placed in the public domain; and documents from the New York proceedings were supplied to the ICSID Tribunal.

[93] *RSM* v. *Grenada*, Annulment Proceeding, para. 6.
[94] *RSM* v. *Grenada*, para. 212.
[95] *RSM* v. *Grenada*, paras. 500 et seq.
[96] *RSM et al.* v. *Fridman et al.*, Civ. No. 1:06-cv-11512-EJW (S.D. New York), Judgment, 19 February 2009, 5, 7.
[97] *RSM et al.* v. *Fridman et al.*, 14 et seq.
[98] *RSM et al.* v. *Fridman et al.*, 30 et seq., 42.
[99] *RSM et al.* v. *Fridman et al.*, 40.

The Tribunal took note that Mr Bowen felt unfairly put under pressure by the Court litigation. In the ICSID proceedings, Mr Bowen was neither a party nor separately represented, and protected by Grenada through applications for interim measures. The Tribunal eventually was satisfied that the Court proceedings did not adversely affect Mr Bowen's testimony in the ICSID proceedings, and did not want to comment further on the New York case, as it did not accept any of the personal criticisms of Mr Bowen.[100]

5.1.7.3 The ICSID Annulment Proceedings: Investigating Alleged Bribery?

In June 2009, RSM requested the annulment of the ICSID Award, based on Article 52 of the ICSID Convention. As a preliminary matter, RSM asked the *ad hoc* Annulment Committee to investigate alleged bribery and to inquire whether Grenada's denial of RSM's application for an exploration licence was motivated by a bribe to Mr Bowen. RSM argued that the Annulment Committee possessed an 'inherent jurisdiction to investigate allegations of bribery' that were contrary to international public policy and a universal norm of international law. RSM thus asked the Annulment Committee to do what it specifically had said the ICSID Tribunal need not do, arguing that it was now in a better position to evaluate the evidence, part of which only had emerged at the hearing itself.[101] Grenada replied that RSM had waived its right to argue that Mr Bowen had behaved corruptly because it had assured the ICSID Tribunal that corruption was no part of its case, and because RSM had pursued the corruption allegations in front of the New York District Court (without success).[102]

The Annulment Committee extensively discussed its jurisdiction under Article 52 of the ICSID Convention. RSM asked the Committee to consider and investigate evidence that had already been available before the original Tribunal, as well as additional evidence from the New York court proceedings. Thus, the company's application could not be considered under any of the five grounds for annulment exhaustively listed in Article 52.[103] Regarding RSM's argument that the Committee possessed

[100] *RSM* v. *Grenada*, paras. 30 et seq.

[101] *RSM* v. *Grenada*, Annulment Proceeding, paras. 2, 4 et seq., 8 et seq.; Llamzon 2014, 186 et seq.

[102] *RSM* v. *Grenada*, Annulment Proceeding, paras. 12 et seq.

[103] Cf. Schreuer et al. 2009, Art. 52 N 108.

inherent powers to investigate bribery allegations, the Committee stated that 'such powers cannot be inconsistent with the terms of the relevant constitutive instrument of the international court or tribunal'.[104] The Annulment Committee concluded that the corruption allegations were outside its jurisdictional mandate under the ICSID Convention,[105] and RSM subsequently abandoned the annulment proceedings. RSM could have requested the revision of the 2009 Award on the basis of new evidence, but it chose not to do so.[106]

5.1.7.4 The 2010 ICSID Proceedings Based on a BIT

In January 2010, RSM filed another request for ICSID arbitration, this time alleging a breach of the 1986 US-Grenada BIT. The Claimants in this case were RSM and its three shareholders ('RSM'); the Respondent was Grenada.

RSM alleged five breaches of the BIT, *inter alia* the expropriation of the investment by Grenada.[107] Grenada's main objection was that RSM's claims had already been fully litigated in the 2009 ICSID arbitration proceedings.[108] RSM opposed to this objection *inter alia* that the first ICSID Tribunal had not been asked to examine any corruption allegations, and asserted that it now had proof of corruption that it had uncovered after the commencement of the first ICSID proceeding. Specifically, RSM alleged that it had been denied the exploration licence and was forced out because Global Petroleum had bribed Mr Bowen.[109]

The Tribunal found that due to the doctrine of collateral estoppel, it was bound by the decision of the 2009 Tribunal and unable to re-litigate the first Tribunal's legal and factual findings. Reopening those findings would violate Article 53 of the ICSID Convention, which establishes the finality of ICSID arbitral awards. The Tribunal noted that based on Article 51 of the ICSID Convention (discovery of decisive new facts), RSM could have sought revision of the 2009 Award, but it chose not to do so and initiated annulment proceedings instead.[110] The Tribunal also argued that RSM was aware of almost everything on which it now relied

[104] *RSM* v. *Grenada*, Annulment Proceeding, paras. 15 et seq., 20; Llamzon 2014, 187.
[105] *RSM* v. *Grenada*, Annulment Proceeding, para. 30.
[106] L.E. Peterson, 'ICSID Annulment Committee declines request to investigate alleged bribe', *Investment Arbitration Reporter*, 17 January 2010.
[107] *Grynberg et al.* v. *Grenada*, paras. 3.2.1 et seq.
[108] *Grynberg et al.* v. *Grenada*, paras. 4.1.1 et seq.
[109] *Grynberg et al.* v. *Grenada*, paras. 5.1.3 et seq.
[110] *Grynberg et al.* v. *Grenada*, paras. 7.1.1 et seq., 7.1.9 et seq.

regarding Grenada's alleged corruption already during the first ICSID arbitration, and that an application by RSM to reopen the proceedings (Rule 38(2) of the ICSID Arbitration Rules[111]) had been rejected by the first Tribunal because the fresh evidence adduced by RSM was considered not to be decisive.[112]

The Tribunal concluded that RSM had lost the exploration licence not because of alleged bribery, but because it had failed to apply for the licence in time,[113] and dismissed RSM's claims as manifestly without legal merit based on Article 41(5) of the ICSID Arbitration Rules. In addition, it ordered RSM to pay Grenada's legal and other costs.[114]

5.1.7.5 Analysis

At the core of *RSM* v. *Grenada* are the multiple ICSID and domestic court proceedings. During the proceedings leading up to the 2009 ICSID Award (that were contract-based), RSM already raised allegations of bribery and (unsuccessfully) sought to reopen the proceedings in this regard. In parallel, RSM (unsuccessfully) sued a number of individuals and corporations in a US District Court, *inter alia* for bribe solicitation and bribe payments.

After the dismissal of its claims both in the court proceedings as well as in the 2009 ICSID Award, RSM in a next step (unsuccessfully) applied for the annulment of that Award, raising the bribery allegations with the Annulment Committee, thereby choosing not to ask for the revision of the Award on the basis of new evidence. After the rejection of the annulment application, RSM and its three shareholders eventually filed a request for treaty-based ICSID arbitration and raised detailed bribery allegations. However, in the 2010 Award the Tribunal again dismissed RSM's claims, arguing that there was little new evidence, and that the correct remedy RSM should have chosen was the revision of the 2009 Award.

Both the rejection of RSM's annulment application as well as the dismissal of RSM's claims by the second ICSID Tribunal in 2010 on formal grounds are acceptable. The critical question is, however, whether

[111] ICSID 2006.

[112] *Grynberg et al.* v. *Grenada*, paras. 7.1.18 et seq.; Llamzon 2014, 187 et seq.; see also L.E. Peterson, 'Tribunal nixes Treaty claim against Grenada on expedited basis; arbitrators deem it "impermissible" to pursue claim that re-litigates matters resolved in earlier contract case', *Investment Arbitration Reporter*, 13 December 2010.

[113] *Grynberg et al.* v. *Grenada*, para. 7.2.5.

[114] *Grynberg et al.* v. *Grenada*, para. 9.1.

the first Tribunal should have investigated bribery *ex officio* already in the proceedings leading up to the 2009 ICSID Award (even if RSM said the Tribunal need not do so). The fact that neither the two Tribunals nor the Annulment Committee seriously inquired whether bribery was involved is unsatisfactory and calls into question the integrity of the ICSID dispute settlement mechanism. Revision of an award because new evidence emerges is not always a solution; a party may, for instance, not seek revision for some reason.

The decisions and awards rendered in this case show that the New York District Court and the ICSID Tribunals used documents from each other's proceedings. The outcomes of all decisions and awards are – maybe too much – in line.

5.1.8 Niko v. Bangladesh *(2013, pending)*

The Claimant in this case is Niko Resources (Bangladesh) Ltd. ('Niko'), a company incorporated under the law of Barbados. Its parent company is Niko Resources Ltd., a Canadian company ('Niko Canada'). The Respondents are the Bangladesh Petroleum Exploration & Production Company Limited ('BAPEX') and the Bangladesh Oil Gas and Mineral Corporation ('Petrobangla').[115]

In August 1999, Niko concluded an agreement with BAPEX to develop marginal or abandoned gas fields in Bangladesh. After evaluation, Niko decided to explore two fields, Chattak and Feni. In October 2003, Niko and BAPEX concluded a joint venture agreement ('JVA') in this regard. Gas supplies from the Feni field started in November 2004, and the joint venture partners began to negotiate a gas purchase and sale agreement ('GPSA') with Petrobangla, which was concluded in December 2006. Gas was delivered to Petrobangla already before the conclusion of the GPSA, but Niko claimed that much of it remained unpaid. Development of the Chattak field, however, was less successful, and two blowouts occurred in 2005. In 2008, having estimated the resulting damages, the Bangladesh government and Petrobangla commenced legal action in a domestic district court against Niko, claiming compensation.[116]

[115] *Niko* v. *Bangladesh*, paras. 1 et seq., 13 et seq., 168. The Tribunal noted that the Bangladesh government had never consented to ICSID arbitration, and was therefore no longer a Respondent in the proceedings (*Niko* v. *Bangladesh*, para. 256).

[116] *Niko* v. *Bangladesh*, paras. 1 et seq.

In May 2005, during the negotiations for the GPSA, Niko delivered a CA$190,000 car to the Bangladesh State Minister for Energy and Mineral Resources. In June 2005, Niko Canada invited the minister to Calgary, paying for his travel and accommodation expenses of CA$5,000. When this became public, the minister resigned on 18 June 2005 and returned the car to BAPEX on 20 June 2005. At that time, the draft GPSA had not been approved yet by the government of Bangladesh. After an investigation of those events in Canada, Niko Canada agreed to a Statement of Facts and was convicted in 2011 to a CA$9.5 million fine.[117]

In 2010, according to the respective contract clauses, Niko filed two arbitration requests with ICSID: the first (ARB/10/11) about the Bangladesh government's compensation claim (which Niko argued should be resolved by arbitrators, not domestic courts) and the second (ARB/10/18) about the outstanding payments to Niko under the GPSA. The Respondents objected to the jurisdiction of the Tribunal because of Niko's corrupt behaviour. As a preliminary matter, the Tribunal decided that the two cases should proceed concurrently and that the two Tribunals (referred to as 'the Tribunal') would render their decisions in one single award.[118]

5.1.8.1. The Respondents' Bribery Objection to Jurisdiction

The Respondents argued that the Tribunal should deny jurisdiction because Niko violated the principles of good faith, international public policy and the 'clean hands' doctrine in a manner linked to its investment when it committed the two acts of bribery, and that the Tribunal was responsible to protect the integrity of the ICSID dispute settlement mechanism.[119] According to the Respondents, the good-faith obligation and the requirement that an investment be in accordance with the host state's law applied both to the initiation phase of the investment and to its performance: '[W]hen there is an allegation of fraudulent conduct by the foreign investor, tribunals should examine all the circumstances surrounding the lifespan of the investment, having direct relation to the investment claim.'[120] Elaborating their position, the Respondents argued that in domestic and international law,

[117] *Niko* v. *Bangladesh*, para. 6.

[118] *Niko* v. *Bangladesh*, paras. 6 et seq.; L.E. Peterson, 'In new ruling, investor's corruption conviction is not a bar to jurisdiction over two claims by energy company Niko Resources in Bangladesh arbitrations', *Investment Arbitration Reporter*, 20 August 2013.

[119] *Niko* v. *Bangladesh*, paras. 373 et seq.

[120] *Niko* v. *Bangladesh*, para. 375 with reference to *Phoenix* v. *Czech Republic* and *Hamester* v. *Ghana*.

> an act of bribery is complete when the benefit is provided to the public official, with the intention of influencing that official's performance of his or her functions. Whether or not the bribe in fact causes the official to act as the briber desired is not within the briber's control, and does not affect the gravity of the briber's conduct.[121]

The Respondents explained that a causal link between the bribe and the conclusion of a contract was only relevant if one party argued that the contract was void or voidable. Their point, however, was not that the contract was void or voidable because of corruption. Rather, they were asking: should jurisdiction be denied only to a claimant who succeeds to procure a contract through bribery, or also to the one who attempts it? The Respondents argued that 'The Claimant does not bring this claim in good faith or with clean hands. That is not affected by whether or not, on the facts, the bribery achieved its admitted purpose.'[122]

The Claimants, on the other hand, argued that the Respondents overstated the scope of the good faith and legality requirements when arguing for their application 'throughout the life of the investment'. According to the Claimant, this only applied in the context of particular BITs that required ongoing compliance with domestic law. But the present case was not treaty-based, and the Claimant argued that

> the international law requirements of good faith relate to the creation of the investment, and in some instances the acquisition of an investment for an improper purpose. Obviously, in some instances bad faith performance is relevant, in that rights arising from illegal acts will not be recognized where a BIT requires ongoing compliance with local law. Also, contracts which have corruption as their objective are not enforceable.[123]

Based on this, the Claimant concluded that a nexus was required between alleged corruption and the contract that was to be enforced in a dispute, and that it was the duty of the ICSID Tribunal to examine whether the Claimant's bribery deprived it from having its claims considered by the Tribunal.[124]

5.1.8.2 Bribery Conviction of Niko Canada and Other Indications for Corruption

The Respondents listed the alleged incidents of bribery involving Niko and Niko Canada. Undisputed was the Canadian conviction of 24 June 2011, which held in the Agreed Statement of Facts:

[121] *Niko* v. *Bangladesh*, para. 377.
[122] *Niko* v. *Bangladesh*, para. 377.
[123] *Niko* v. *Bangladesh*, para. 379.
[124] *Niko* v. *Bangladesh*, para. 380.

> The fine reflects that Niko Canada made these payments in order to persuade the Bangladeshi Energy Minister to exercise his influence to ensure that Niko was able to secure a gas purchase and sales agreement acceptable to Niko, as well as to ensure the company was dealt with fairly in relation to claims for compensation for the blowouts, which represented potentially very large amounts of money. The Crown is unable to prove that any influence was obtained as a result of providing the benefits to the Minister.[125]

Niko was having difficulties after it signed the JVA with BAPEX because it had not yet secured the gas sales contract. Niko started to deliver gas when it became available, but it had not yet agreed on a price with Petrobangla. At this point, Niko made the payments in order to persuade the minister.[126] Niko disclosed that the US DOJ had conducted investigations for possible FCPA violations as well but did not think it necessary to prosecute the company in light of the guilty plea in Canada, pointing out, however, that it might decide to restart the inquiry at any time.[127]

The Respondents pointed out a number of other investigations as possible indications for bribery, and requested document disclosure by Niko. *Inter alia*, the Bangladeshi Anticorruption Commission had initiated investigations in 2007 whether public officials accepted bribes in relation to investments in Bangladesh. Niko disclosed documents that showed the charges investigated by the Anticorruption Commission, including a charge against a former prime minister. However, the Bangladeshi investigations and proceedings never led to any trial or conviction.[128]

The Tribunal noted that bribery was difficult to prove and that it had to reach its conclusion with 'very limited means'. However, it also stated that findings of corruption should not be made lightly and had to be based on substantiated facts, not on inferences.[129] In response to far-reaching document disclosure requests by the Respondent, the Tribunal noted that Niko had disclosed the Canadian conviction and Agreed Statement of Facts and provided information about the US investigation. The Tribunal did not request any further disclosure from Niko regarding the proceedings in Canada and in the US; and argued that

[125] *Niko* v. *Bangladesh*, para. 389; a copy of the Agreed Statement of Facts is available at www.osler.com.

[126] *Niko* v. *Bangladesh*, paras. 383 et seq.

[127] *Niko* v. *Bangladesh*, para. 390.

[128] *Niko* v. *Bangladesh*, paras. 393 et seq., 399, 426.

[129] *Niko* v. *Bangladesh*, para. 424 with reference to *Hamester* v. *Ghana*.

regarding the proceedings in Bangladesh, the Respondents were best placed to investigate and collect proof.[130]

The Tribunal concluded that Niko had only committed the acts of bribery that were sanctioned in the Canadian conviction. It took note that the company had never been convicted or sanctioned by a regulatory body for a similar offence before, and that the Supreme Court of Bangladesh had at some point found that no fraudulent means were involved in the making of the JVA. As the Canadian authorities had been unable to prove that Niko obtained any influence out of its payments to the Minister, and because such an allegation had never been made in the arbitration, the Tribunal saw no reason to believe that bribery had influenced the conclusion or content of the JVA or GPSA.[131]

5.1.8.3 No Bribe Contract at Stake in the Present Dispute

The Tribunal stated that the prohibition of bribery is part of international public policy; as such, the 'prohibition of bribery overrides the general principle of party autonomy', and arbitrators cannot give effect to contracts which are contrary to international public policy. The Tribunal referred to numerous domestic court cases and international arbitral awards that declared contracts which had influence peddling or bribery as their object as void or unenforceable.[132]

Specifically, the Tribunal referred to ICC Case No. 1110 (the *Lagergren* case)[133] where the Sole Arbitrator denied jurisdiction as the Claimant sought to enforce a bribe contract. The Tribunal stated that the present case was fundamentally different, because the JVA and GPSA, on which Niko based its claims, had as their legitimate object the development of gas fields and the sale of gas, unlike in the *Lagergren* case, where the contract had bribery as its illicit object. In the present case, the question was: did bribery impact on the validity of the contracts or their arbitration clauses?[134]

5.1.8.4 Contracts Obtained by Corruption

The Tribunal made reference to the *World Duty Free* Award, in which the Arbitral Tribunal stated that 'claims based on contracts of corruption

[130] *Niko* v. *Bangladesh*, paras. 414 et seq., 421 et seq.

[131] *Niko* v. *Bangladesh*, paras. 427 et seq.

[132] *Niko* v. *Bangladesh*, paras. 430 et seq., 434 et seq. with references to court decisions and arbitral awards.

[133] See discussion in Chapter 6.

[134] *Niko* v. *Bangladesh*, paras. 437 et seq.

or on contracts obtained by corruption cannot be upheld by this Arbitral Tribunal'.[135] The Tribunal saw a fundamental difference between the two situations:

> In contracts of corruption, the object of the contract is the corruption of a civil servant and this object is intended by both parties to the contract. In contracts obtained by corruption, one of the parties normally is aware of the corruption and intends to obtain the contract by these means. But this is not necessarily the case for the other side. As explained in the *World Duty Free* award, bribes normally are covert . . . In the case of covert bribes the other side, innocent of the corruption, may have a justified interest in preserving the contract.[136]

The Tribunal referred to Article 50 of the Vienna Convention on the Law of Treaties,[137] Article 34 of UNCAC,[138] and English law[139] to support its argument that 'the innocent victim of an illegality must have the choice whether it accepts the otherwise legal transaction in the terms as concluded or wishes to avoid it'.[140] Before discussing such avoidance, the Tribunal stated that there was a lack of causation in this case: the acts of bribery did not procure the contracts (the JVA and the GPSA) on which Niko's claims were based in the arbitration. The JVA was concluded before the corrupt acts took place, and the GPSA was concluded only eighteen months after the resignation of the minister who had received the benefits. In fact, the Respondents had never alleged such a link – their argument was that 'an attempt to obtain a contract by bribery is sufficient to deny recourse to ICSID arbitration to the party having made such an attempt.'[141]

As different from the Respondent's position in *World Duty Free*, the Respondents in this case did not seek to avoid the agreements

[135] *World Duty Free* v. *Kenya*, para. 157. [136] *Niko* v. *Bangladesh*, paras. 443 et seq.

[137] Art. 50 VCLT 1969 ('Corruption of a representative of a State') reads: 'If the expression of a State's consent to be bound by a treaty has been procured through the corruption of its representative directly or indirectly by another negotiating State, the State may invoke such corruption as invalidating its consent to be bound by the treaty.'

[138] Art. 34 UNCAC 2003 ('Consequences of acts of corruption') reads: 'With due regard to the rights of third parties acquired in good faith, each State Party shall take measures, in accordance with the fundamental principles of its domestic law, to address consequences of corruption. In this context, States Parties may consider corruption a relevant factor in legal proceedings to annul or rescind a contract, withdraw a concession or other similar instrument or take any other remedial action.'

[139] The opinion of Lord Mustill in the *World Duty Free* case (*World Duty Free* v. *Kenya*, para. 164).

[140] *Niko* v. *Bangladesh*, para. 451. [141] *Niko* v. *Bangladesh*, paras. 453 et seq., 455.

(or their arbitration clauses) with Niko (emphasising that they would revisit their position if further disclosure made it appropriate).[142] Rather, the Respondents argued that although the agreements were still in force, Niko could not rely on their ICSID arbitration clauses due to a lack of good faith in the investment because this would jeopardise the integrity of the ICSID dispute settlement mechanism, and due to the doctrine of 'clean hands'.[143]

When new circumstances arose towards the end of the hearing on jurisdiction (the introduction of documents from the proceedings in front of the Bangladeshi Anticorruption Commission in the arbitration), the Respondents stated that those documents suggested that the JVA was obtained by bribery, and if necessary, they would ask for an opportunity to deal with that. However, also at that point, the Respondents did not argue that the JVA or GPSA were void, but – as the Tribunal noted – continued to benefit from those agreements.[144] The Tribunal concluded that under those circumstances, it could not treat the agreements as avoided or invalid.[145]

5.1.8.5 The Decision on Jurisdiction

The Respondents argued that because there was an act of bribery (for which Niko Canada had been convicted) linked to the investment, ICSID jurisdiction should be denied to Niko. The Tribunal stated that '[i]f this position were accepted, Petrobangla and BAPEX could invoke the arbitration clauses but Niko could not'.[146] Examining the Respondents' three lines of arguments, the Tribunal first rejected the one that ICSID arbitration is only available to investments made in good faith. It pointed out that this arbitration was based on two agreements, not on a BIT: 'In a contractual dispute as the present one, alleged or established lack of good faith in the investment does not justify the denial of jurisdiction but must be considered as part of the merits of the dispute.'[147] The Tribunal noted that this was the line taken in the *World Duty Free* v. *Kenya* case (also based on contract): there, Kenya had avoided the agreement. The Tribunal had affirmed jurisdiction and denied the claim on the merits.[148]

On the Respondents' second line of argument – that the integrity of the ICSID dispute settlement mechanism had to be protected – the

[142] *Niko* v. *Bangladesh*, paras. 452, 456. [143] *Niko* v. *Bangladesh*, para. 466.
[144] *Niko* v. *Bangladesh*, paras. 460 et seq. [145] *Niko* v. *Bangladesh*, paras. 463 et seq.
[146] *Niko* v. *Bangladesh*, para. 465. [147] *Niko* v. *Bangladesh*, para. 471.
[148] *Niko* v. *Bangladesh*, para. 472.

Tribunal argued that it actually protected that integrity by resolving the contentions at hand instead of avoiding them:

> In the present case ICSID arbitration is invoked not in pursuit of a claim for corruption nor for claims under an otherwise illegal contract. The Claimant seeks performance of agreements which, despite the Respondents' knowledge about the sanctioned cases of bribery, have not been avoided and from which the Respondents continue to benefit. The Tribunal cannot see why hearing and resolving these claims under the given circumstances would affect the integrity of the ICSID system.[149]

The third line of argument of the Respondent – that Niko did not bring its claim with 'clean hands' – was equally rejected by the Tribunal. The Tribunal examined case law as well as academic writing and noted that the 'clean hands' doctrine is part of equity in common law countries; that it is controversial whether it forms part of international law; and that its content is not very clear.[150] Based on the *Guyana* v. *Suriname* Award[151] of an UNCLOS Arbitral Tribunal, the Tribunal identified the following criteria for applying the doctrine:

> (i) the breach must concern a continuing violation, (ii) the remedy sought must be "*protection against continuance of that violation in the future*", not damages for past violations and (iii) there must be a relationship of reciprocity between the obligations considered.[152]

The Tribunal found that the Respondents' objection did not meet those criteria.[153] The Tribunal also noted that the JVA had already been concluded at the time of Niko Canada's conviction; that the events received much attention in Bangladesh when they became public and led to the resignation of the respective minister; and that Petrobangla and BAPEX were aware of all this when they entered into the GPSA, with the approval of the Bangladeshi government: 'If and to the extent the Claimant or its parent company had unclean hands, the Respondents disregarded this situation. They may not now rely on these events to deny jurisdiction under an arbitration agreement which they then accepted.'[154]

According to the Tribunal, the court proceedings in Canada did not add much to what was already known in Bangladesh at the time the

[149] *Niko* v. *Bangladesh*, para. 475.

[150] *Niko* v. *Bangladesh*, para. 477 et seq.

[151] In particular paras. 420 et seq. of the *Guyana* v. *Suriname* Award (the Arbitral Tribunal was constituted pursuant to Art. 287 and Annex VII of the UN Convention on the Law of the Sea (UNCLOS)).

[152] *Niko* v. *Bangladesh*, para. 481.

[153] *Niko* v. *Bangladesh*, para. 483.

[154] *Niko* v. *Bangladesh*, para. 484.

GPSA was concluded. The Tribunal concluded that the acts of bribery that were established in the Canadian judgment could not justify a refusal to examine the merits of this dispute, in light of the parties' consent to submit it to ICSID arbitration, and it dismissed the Respondents' objection to jurisdiction.[155]

5.1.8.6 Analysis

The Decision on Jurisdiction in *Niko* v. *Bangladesh* does not discuss the applicable law or burden and standard of proof, but rather relies on the outcomes of the domestic proceedings with regard to the bribery allegations in Canada, Bangladesh and the United States, and in particular the company's conviction in Canada. The Tribunal was confronted with an established case of foreign public bribery. The question was how this would impact on the ICSID proceedings.

Niko disclosed a number of documents with regard to the domestic investigations in Canada. The Tribunal found this to be sufficient and rejected the Respondents' request for further document production. Niko was in a difficult position here because it probably would not have wanted to disclose to the Tribunal any incriminating evidence. Such evidence had been collected by the state prosecutors by use of subpoena powers and led to the Canadian bribery conviction. The Respondent obviously wanted to know whether there was any evidence for bribery going beyond that conviction.

Neither the JVA nor the GPSA were void because they were neither bribe contracts nor contracts obtained by bribery, and the Respondents did not seek to avoid them. The Tribunal looked at those contracts (and their respective arbitration clauses) separately and did not consider the investment as one entity. The Respondents argued that the bribery offences committed, even though they had no impact on the conclusion of the JVA and GPSA, were sufficient to deny recourse to ICSID arbitration. Like in *WDF* v. *Kenya*, the arbitration was based on contract, not on an investment agreement, and no 'in accordance with host state's law' clause of a BIT was at stake. Under these circumstances, the Tribunal's conclusion to affirm its jurisdiction appears consistent with the earlier award.

In September 2014, the Tribunal decided on the payment claim, concluding that Petrobangla had withdrawn its request concerning the

[155] *Niko* v. *Bangladesh*, para. 485.

avoidance of the GPSA due to corruption, and ordering Petrobangla to pay approximately US$25 million plus 139 million Bangladeshi Taka to Niko for gas delivered from November 2004 to April 2010.[156] On 25 March 2016, the Respondents filed submissions in which they sought avoidance of the JVA and the GPSA, arguing that the Respondents now had evidence that these agreements were procured through corruption. In May 2016, the Tribunal ordered that Petrobangla immediately had to pay the above amounts to Niko; but it also decided to examine the bribery allegations, referring to its 'responsibility for upholding international public policy'.[157] The case is pending.

5.1.9 Metal-Tech *v.* Uzbekistan *(2013)*

The Claimant in this case was Metal-Tech Ltd. ('Metal-Tech'), a company incorporated in Israel; the Respondent was the Republic of Uzbekistan. In January 2010, Metal-Tech initiated ICSID arbitration, with reference to the Israel-Uzbekistan BIT, claiming *inter alia* the expropriation of its investment by Uzbekistan.[158]

Since December 1998 and throughout 1999, Metal-Tech and the Uzbek government had negotiated about a joint venture to build and operate a molybdenum products plant. The joint venture was eventually formed between Metal-Tech and two state-owned companies, Uzbek Refractory and Resistant Metals Integrated Plant ('UzKTJM') and Almalik Mining Metallurgy Combinate ('AGMK'). By Resolutions No. 15 and 29-F, the joint venture was approved by the Uzbek Cabinet of Ministers in January 2000, under the name of Uzmetal Technology ('Uzmetal'). Metal-Tech should contribute its know-how, technology and international market access; UzKTJM and AGMK should contribute constructions, equipment and raw molybdenum.[159]

From 2000 to 2004, Metal-Tech concluded several consulting agreements with the Swiss company MPC International Investments and Consultants GmbH ('MPC') and its daughter company, MPC-Tashkent. Furthermore, in October 2004, Metal-Tech concluded three individual

[156] *Niko* v. *Bangladesh*, Decision on the Payment Claim, 11 September 2014, paras. 154 et seq., 292.

[157] *Niko* v. *Bangladesh*, Third Decision on the Payment Claim, 26 May 2016, 28 et seq. and Procedural Order No. 13, 26 May 2016; see also Procedural Order No. 15, 7 October 2016.

[158] *Metal-Tech* v. *Uzbekistan*, para. 55.

[159] *Metal-Tech* v. *Uzbekistan*, paras. 6 et seq.

consulting agreements with V. Mikhailov, U. Sultanov (the brother of the then–Uzbek Prime Minister and a former police investigator) and I. Chijenok (a senior government official responsible for human resources functions in the president's office). In February 2005, Metal-Tech concluded a further contract with the three consultants, under which payments were made to Lacey International Corp. ('Lacey'). Uzbekistan argued that those consulting agreements were a sham, used for the purpose of concealing illegal payments to government officials.[160]

Uzmetal's facilities began to operate in October 2002. In June 2006, criminal proceedings were initiated in Uzbekistan that focused on the general director of Uzmetal. In July 2006, Uzbekistan's Cabinet of Ministers abrogated Uzmetal's right to purchase raw materials by resolution. In late December 2006, AGMK initiated domestic court proceedings in order to terminate the contract with Uzmetal for the supply of raw molybdenum; the contract was terminated in May 2007. Also in late December 2006, UzKTJM requested that Uzmetal pay UzKTJM's share of dividends. In July 2007, UzKTJM initiated domestic bankruptcy proceedings for Uzmetal's failure to pay the dividends. In January 2008, the Uzbek Court of Cassation declared Uzmetal bankrupt and initiated liquidation proceedings. In November 2009, liquidation was closed and, according to Metal-Tech, all of Uzmetal's assets were transferred to AGMK and UzKTJM, both of which are controlled by Uzbekistan.[161]

Uzbekistan argued that the Tribunal did not have jurisdiction over the dispute, because Metal-Tech's investment was made and operated in violation of Uzbek law, as the company allegedly engaged in corruption and made fraudulent misrepresentations.[162]

5.1.9.1 Relevance of Previous Awards

As a preliminary matter, the ICSID Tribunal considered how to take into account previous awards handling similar issues. It stated:

> The Tribunal's view is that it is not bound by previous decisions of ICSID or other arbitral tribunals. At the same time, it is of the opinion that it should pay due regard to earlier decisions of international tribunals. The Tribunal is further of the view that, unless there are compelling reasons to the contrary, it has a duty to follow solutions established in a

[160] *Metal-Tech* v. *Uzbekistan*, paras. 28 et seq.
[161] *Metal-Tech* v. *Uzbekistan*, paras. 34 et seq.
[162] *Metal-Tech* v. *Uzbekistan*, para. 110 (i).

> series of consistent cases comparable to the case at hand, but subject, of course, to the specifics of a given treaty and of the circumstances of the actual case.[163]

The Tribunal noted that this was in the interest of a harmonious development of investment law, and also contributed towards certainty of the rule of law on the part of states and investors.

5.1.9.2 Legality Requirement to an Investment in the ICSID Convention?

Regarding Uzbekistan's jurisdictional objection, the Tribunal started by examining its jurisdiction under the ICSID Convention. Article 25(1) states that in order to have jurisdiction, a legal dispute brought before an ICSID Tribunal must arise directly out of an investment. The parties disagreed 'whether such investment must be in conformity with law and, if so, whether it actually was . . . In other words, they diverge on whether the definition of the term "investment" contained in Article 25(1) includes a requirement of legality.'[164] The Tribunal was of the view that the objective definition of the term 'investment' contained in Article 25(1) did not encompass a legality requirement. Such a requirement had to be part of an investment treaty. Consequently, Metal-Tech's 50 per cent participation in Uzmetal met the definition of an 'investment' as contained in Article 25(1) ICSID Convention.[165]

5.1.9.3 The BIT Legality Requirement

The Tribunal then turned to the Israel-Uzbekistan BIT. Article 1(1) of that treaty defined 'investment' as follows: 'The term "investments" shall comprise any kind of assets, implemented in accordance with the laws and regulations of the Contracting Party in whose territory the investment is made.'[166] The parties agreed that Article 1(1) of the BIT contained a legality requirement. Regarding that requirement, the parties disagreed not on its subject matter (that it covered the Uzbek law provisions prohibiting corruption), but on its scope. Uzbekistan argued that the wording of Article 1(1) meant to encompass investments that were made, carried out, or operated in violation of the law of the host state.[167] Metal-Tech argued that Article 1(1) only referred to the

[163] *Metal-Tech* v. *Uzbekistan*, para. 116.
[164] *Metal-Tech* v. *Uzbekistan*, para. 125.
[165] *Metal-Tech* v. *Uzbekistan*, paras. 127 et seq.
[166] *Metal-Tech* v. *Uzbekistan*, para. 130.
[167] *Metal-Tech* v. *Uzbekistan*, paras. 167 et seq.

establishment of an investment, not to its operation.[168] The Tribunal concluded on the basis of its own reading of Article 1(1) that

> the term 'assets implemented' refers to the time when the investment was made. In other words, the Treaty requires that the investment must be legal when it is initially established. Article 1 simply does not address whether or not the investment must be operated lawfully after it is in place.[169]

Consequently, the Tribunal questioned whether Metal-Tech's investment complied with the host state's law at the time when it was established. The Tribunal noted that all the payments to the three consultants had been made between 2001 and 2006 and thus post-dated the establishment of Metal-Tech's investment. However, a witness testimony by one of the Claimant's own witnesses showed that the consultants had been involved much earlier, at least since September 1998, and that they delivered most of their services at the time when Metal-Tech's investment was established. The Tribunal concluded that 'Metal-Tech had promised as early as 1998 to pay the Consultants if and when the Claimant's investment was established.'[170]

5.1.9.4 Burden and Standard of Proof

The parties disagreed with regard to the applicable burden and standard of proof. Uzbekistan argued that the evidence gave rise to a strong presumption of corruption, and that Metal-Tech carried the burden to rebut that presumption. Uzbekistan noted that the Tribunal had issued several Procedural Orders directing Metal-Tech to produce evidence that its consultants had rendered legitimate services, but Metal-Tech had failed to do so without credible explanation. From this, Uzbekistan concluded that Metal-Tech had not been able to meet its burden of proof, and that the Tribunal should draw the inference that kickbacks had been paid to government officials.[171]

Alternatively, Uzbekistan submitted that if facts were inherently difficult to prove, the party alleging those facts should be able to meet its burden of proof through *prima facie* evidence. *Prima facie* evidence should also be sufficient if, as in the present case, the other party has control of the relevant evidence but does not produce it.[172] Further in the

[168] *Metal-Tech* v. *Uzbekistan*, paras. 176 et seq. [169] *Metal-Tech* v. *Uzbekistan*, para. 193.
[170] *Metal-Tech* v. *Uzbekistan*, paras. 267 et seq., 273.
[171] *Metal-Tech* v. *Uzbekistan*, para. 229. [172] *Metal-Tech* v. *Uzbekistan*, para. 230.

alternative, Uzbekistan argued that international tribunals are not bound by strict rules of evidence, with reference to the *Oostergetel* v. *Slovak Republic* case where circumstantial evidence was deemed sufficient to prove corruption, regardless of the standard of proof.[173] On standard of proof, Uzbekistan submitted that 'several ICSID tribunals have noted the uncertainty of the standard of proof for allegations of serious illegality'. Some earlier ICSID awards[174] had required a 'more likely than not to be true' standard. Uzbekistan therefore argued that clear and convincing evidence was not required for alleged corruption. In addition, Uzbekistan submitted that no burden-shifting principles were required in this case, because there was decisive evidence for corrupt practices.[175]

Metal-Tech submitted that Uzbekistan carried the burden to prove the corruption allegations 'by clear and convincing evidence or more'. Metal-Tech argued that for allegations of fraud and corruption, the Respondent bears a particularly heavy burden, referring to the *EDF* v. *Romania* case.[176] Metal-Tech stated that '[a]n over-readiness by international arbitrators to accept illegality defenses may harm an international mechanism which benefits numerous countries that rely on access to international funding, technology and trade.'[177] Metal-Tech argued that there was no precedent in investment arbitration where *prima facie* evidence had been sufficient to shift the burden of proof in cases of alleged bribery or fraud: the cases cited by Uzbekistan were not apposite, as they did not consider burden shifting for alleged bribery or fraud.[178]

The Tribunal resolved to apply international law to decide on burden and standard of proof, noting that it was well established and a general principle of law that each party alleging a fact had to prove it. The Tribunal held that the shifting of the burden of proof in cases of alleged corruption was part of the law applicable to the merits of the arbitration, in the present case the BIT. As the BIT was silent on this, the Tribunal

[173] In the Final Award of that case, the Tribunal stated that 'corruption can also be proven by circumstantial evidence'; however, even circumstantial evidence was entirely lacking in that case, and the corruption allegations rested on mere insinuations (*Oostergetel* v. *Slovak Republic*, para. 303).

[174] Uzbekistan referred to the ICSID cases *Tokios Tokelės* v. *Ukraine* (para. 124) and *Fraport* v. *Philippines I* (para. 399).

[175] *Metal-Tech* v. *Uzbekistan*, paras. 231 et seq. with reference to *WDF* v. *Kenya.*

[176] *EDF* v. *Romania*, para. 221.

[177] *Metal-Tech* v. *Uzbekistan*, para. 234 with reference to *Himpurna California Energy* v. *PT Perusahaan Listruk Negara*, Award, 4 May 1999.

[178] *Metal-Tech* v. *Uzbekistan*, para. 233 et seq.

found that it had relative freedom to decide itself, but that it was not necessary in the dispute at hand to apply the rules on burden of proof or presumptions. The facts that emerged during the hearings had nurtured suspicions of bribery and caused the Tribunal to inquire into the facts by using its *ex officio* powers under Article 43 of the ICSID Convention. When the Tribunal examined the principal witness of Metal-Tech, facts emerged about payments and 'lobbying' activities that Uzbekistan had not alleged. The Tribunal then inquired into the reasons for the payments by use of several Procedural Orders.[179]

With reference to the *World Duty Free* case, the Tribunal noted that the situation was similar: in both cases, the Tribunal had invited the parties to produce additional evidence of the corruption allegations; and in both cases, the decisive evidence came from the Claimant. Both cases eventually did not turn on legal presumptions, rules on burden of proof or on different standards of proof. The Tribunal saw itself in a position to determine whether corruption was established 'with reasonable certainty' on the basis of the evidence it had collected.[180] The Tribunal concluded that 'corruption is by essence difficult to establish and . . . it is thus generally admitted that it can be shown through circumstantial evidence'.[181]

5.1.9.5 A Good-Faith Obligation to Co-Operate

With reference to Rule 34(3) of the ICSID Arbitration Rules[182] and to Article 9(5) of the IBA Rules of Evidence,[183] the Tribunal concluded that parties have a good-faith obligation to co-operate in arbitral proceedings, including the production of evidence, and that the Tribunal may infer that a document is adverse to the interests of a party if the latter does not produce evidence.[184] The Tribunal had asked Metal-Tech to

[179] *Metal-Tech* v. *Uzbekistan*, paras. 237 et seq.

[180] *Metal-Tech* v. *Uzbekistan*, paras. 242 et seq. [181] *Metal-Tech* v. *Uzbekistan*, para. 243.

[182] Rule 34(3) ICSID 2006 ('Evidence: General Principles') reads: 'The parties shall cooperate with the Tribunal in the production of the evidence and in the other measures provided for in paragraph (2). The Tribunal shall take formal note of the failure of a party to comply with its obligations under this paragraph and of any reasons given for such failure.'

[183] Art. 9(5) IBA 2010 ('Admissibility and Assessment of Evidence') reads: 'If a Party fails without satisfactory explanation to produce any Document requested in a Request to Produce to which it has not objected in due time or fails to produce any Document ordered to be produced by the Arbitral Tribunal, the Arbitral Tribunal may infer that such document would be adverse to the interests of that Party.'

[184] *Metal-Tech* v. *Uzbekistan*, paras. 244 et seq.

substantiate what services the consultants had rendered, but Metal-Tech had continuously failed to do so.[185]

5.1.9.6 Violation of Uzbek Criminal Law on Bribery and Its Consequence

Uzbekistan pointed out that its anti-bribery law was consistent with international conventions and the domestic laws of other states (including Israel, the United Kingdom and Switzerland). Uzbekistan alleged a violation of Articles 210–212 of the Uzbek Criminal Code that prohibit 'the giving or taking of bribes, directly or through an intermediary, in exchange for the performance or non-performance of an action'. Uzbekistan argued that Metal-Tech had violated the law when it promised to pay, and later paid, alleged consulting fees in the amount of more than US$4.4 million to a senior government official (Mr Chijenok) and to the prime minister's brother (Mr Sultanov) in return for the Uzbek government's approval of Metal-Tech's investment. Relying on commentaries to the criminal code, Uzbekistan argued that the payment to Mr Chijenok was unlawful, even if he did not have the authority to perform the action for which he was paid, and that the payment to Mr Sultanov for the purpose of influencing the prime minister was unlawful regardless of whether any money had ever been transferred to the prime minister.[186]

The Tribunal cited the relevant provisions of the Uzbek Criminal Code and from the commentaries, also relying on academic writing, and established that under Uzbek law:

> (i) it is unlawful to give or to promise anything of value to a public official or an intermediary of that public official in exchange for the performance or non-performance of certain action that the official must or could have performed; (ii) it is unlawful to enrich a third party, such as a member of an official's family, for the purpose of inducing an official's performance or non-performance of certain action; and (iii) the timing of payment is irrelevant; it can occur before or after the act or omission is sought.[187]

The Tribunal also referred to the international agreements that criminalise corruption, as well as to the *World Duty Free* Award, and cited the following 'red flags' for corruption (based on the list of Lord Woolf, the former Chief Justice of England and Wales):

[185] *Metal-Tech* v. *Uzbekistan*, paras. 246 et seq.
[186] *Metal-Tech* v. *Uzbekistan*, paras. 278 et seq.
[187] *Metal-Tech* v. *Uzbekistan*, para. 289.

> (1) 'an Adviser has a lack of experience in the sector'; (2) 'non-residence of an Adviser in the country where the customer or the project is located'; (3) 'no significant business presence of the Adviser within the country'; (4) 'an Adviser requests "urgent" payments or unusually high commissions'; (5) 'an Adviser requests payments be paid in cash, use of a corporate vehicle such as equity, or be paid in a third country, to a numbered bank account, or to some other person or entity'; (6) 'an Adviser has a close personal/professional relationship to the government or customers that could improperly influence the customer's decision'.[188]

The Tribunal reviewed for a number of persons individually whether they were involved in corrupt activities. It made such findings for two persons: Messrs Chijenok and Sultanov. Both had no relevant experience in the molybdenum industry or other qualifications for the services for which they were allegedly hired; for both, Metal-Tech had been unable to substantiate with documentary evidence what they received their substantial remunerations for; and both were in a position to exercise political and personal influence in order to facilitate Metal-Tech's investment at the time it was being established.[189] In particular, the Tribunal took note that Mr Sultanov was the brother of the then–acting Uzbek prime minister, who was responsible for monitoring the resolution which established Metal-Tech's investment in Uzbekistan.[190]

The Tribunal concluded that corruption and thus a breach of Uzbek law in connection with the establishment of Metal-Tech's investment was sufficiently proven. The investment was not implemented in accordance with the law of the host state and therefore not covered by the definition of an investment according to Article 1(1) BIT. Uzbekistan had consented to ICSID arbitration only for legal disputes that concerned an investment (Article 8(1) BIT). As such, the consent requirement of Article 25(1) ICSID Convention was not fulfilled, and without the consent of the host state under the BIT and the ICSID Convention, the Tribunal did not have jurisdiction.[191]

The Tribunal was perfectly aware of the ongoing debate regarding the corruption defence, its harsh consequences for investor's claims, and exoneration of the host state possibly involved in the corrupt acts:

[188] *Metal-Tech* v. *Uzbekistan*, para. 293; Woolf Committee 2008, 25 et seq.; see also Lamm, Greenwald and Young 2014, 338 et seq.

[189] *Metal-Tech* v. *Uzbekistan*, paras. 295 et seq., 328 et seq.

[190] *Metal-Tech* v. *Uzbekistan*, paras. 337, 347 et seq.

[191] *Metal-Tech* v. *Uzbekistan*, paras. 372 et seq.; see also Schreuer et al. 2009, Art. 25 N 199 et seq.

> It is true that the outcome in cases of corruption often appears unsatisfactory because, at first sight at least, it seems to give an unfair advantage to the defendant party. The idea, however, is not to punish one party at the cost of the other, but rather to ensure the promotion of the rule of law, which entails that a court or tribunal cannot grant assistance to a party that has engaged in a corrupt act.[192]

The Tribunal also noted Metal-Tech's co-operative attitude throughout the proceedings.

5.1.9.7 Impact of the Successful Bribery Defence on Costs

On the one hand, the Tribunal took into account the parties conduct during the proceedings, stating that while Metal-Tech sought to minimise the costs (legal fees of US$1.1 million), Uzbekistan did not (legal fees of US$7.5 million). On the other hand, the Tribunal linked its decision on costs to the ground for denial of jurisdiction:

> The Tribunal found that the rights of the investor against the host State, including the right of access to arbitration, could not be protected because the investment was tainted by illegal activities, specifically corruption. The law is clear – and rightly so – that in such a situation the investor is deprived of protection and, consequently, the host State avoids any potential liability. That does not mean, however, that the State has not participated in creating the situation that leads to the dismissal of the claims. Because of this participation, which is implicit in the very nature of corruption, it appears fair that the Parties share in the costs.[193]

In the Award, the Tribunal decided that it lacked jurisdiction over claims and counterclaims; that the parties should each bear its own legal costs; and equally share the ICSID costs.[194]

5.1.9.8 Analysis

Metal-Tech v. *Uzbekistan* discusses the applicable law and issues of burden and standard of proof in detail. The outcome is similar to *World Duty Free* v. *Kenya*, with the difference that the latter arbitration was based on contract, whereas the present case was based on the Israel-Uzbekistan BIT. While the Tribunal did not feel bound by earlier arbitral awards, it felt a duty to follow a line of consistent case law if there was no compelling reason to decide an issue differently, subject to the specific circumstances of the case.

[192] *Metal-Tech* v. *Uzbekistan*, para. 389.
[193] *Metal-Tech* v. *Uzbekistan*, para. 422.
[194] *Metal-Tech* v. *Uzbekistan*, para. 423.

The Tribunal found a legality requirement in the applicable BIT, encompassing the bribery provisions of the Uzbek Criminal Code (as the applicable law of the host state). Regarding the timing of the legality requirement, the Tribunal decided that the investment had to be legal only when it was initially established (as the BIT was silent whether the investment had to be performed in accordance with host state's law after its setting up). However, the Tribunal found that although the bribe payments had been made only after the establishment of Metal-Tech's investment, the consultants had already been involved before.

Burden and standard of proof were not decisive for the outcome of this case. Rather, the Tribunal investigated the suspicions of bribery *ex officio*, and the evidence for bribery came from the Claimant itself (as in *World Duty Free* v. *Kenya*).[195] Without explicitly referring to the applicable standard of proof, the Tribunal argued that corruption had to be established with 'reasonable certainty'.[196] The Tribunal found that circumstantial evidence was sufficient to prove bribery. From the good-faith obligation to co-operate, the Tribunal inferred that a document was adverse to a party's interests if not produced upon request.

Relying directly on the Uzbek Criminal Code, the Tribunal closely analysed the Uzbek bribery provisions and elements of the offence. The Tribunal also referred to the relevant international conventions and listed the 'red flags' for corruption. The Tribunal concluded that corruption in relation to the establishment of Metal-Tech's investment was sufficiently proven and a breach of the Uzbek Criminal Code established. As such, the investment was not implemented in accordance with the host state's law and did not qualify as an investment under the BIT. The consent of Uzbekistan to ICSID arbitration only covered legal disputes concerned with an investment. As there was no investment, host state's consent to ICSID arbitration was missing and therefore, the Tribunal denied jurisdiction. In the decision on costs, the Tribunal took into account the Respondent's participation in the corruption.

5.1.10 Fraport *v.* Philippines (*2007/2014*)

5.1.10.1 The First ICSID Proceedings

The 2007 Award The Claimant in this case was Fraport AG Frankfurt Airport Services Worldwide ('Fraport'), a company incorporated in Germany; the Respondent was the Republic of the Philippines. Fraport

[195] See also Lamm, Greenwald and Young 2014, 330. [196] Llamzon 2014, 120.

initiated ICSID arbitration in September 2003 on the basis of the Germany-Philippines BIT, claiming breaches by the Philippines of its obligations towards Fraport as an investor.[197]

The dispute, briefly summarised, arose as follows. In 1990, the Philippines initiated the project to build an international passenger terminal at Ninoy Aquino International Airport in Manila ('Terminal 3'). The concession for the Terminal 3 project was eventually awarded to Philippine International Air Terminals Co. ('PIATCO') in 1996–97. PIATCO was controlled by the Cheng family. The concession was renegotiated in 1998 to allow PIATCO to get financing from international lenders, resulting in the Amended and Restated Concession Agreement ('ARCA') with three supplements.[198] According to the Philippines, the Terminal 3 concession was a public utility.[199]

In 1998, Fraport was invited to join PIATCO in the Terminal 3 project as a consultant. Fraport asked a Philippine affiliate of Baker & McKenzie to conduct a legal due diligence review of the investment, and was in the subsequent report informed, *inter alia*, of

> (1) the need to consider carefully any shareholder arrangement other than an equity investment in PIATCO, in view of the Philippine constitutional requirement that foreign nationals can own no more than 40% of the capital of a public utility, and the prohibitions of the [Anti-Dummy Law] that prevent foreign nationals from intervening in the management, operation, administration or control of a company that is a public utility.[200]

In 1999, Fraport began to invest in PIATCO, directly and indirectly through several Philippine companies, and eventually owned 61.44 per cent of PIATCO.[201] Fraport also entered into secret shareholder agreements, which show, according to the Tribunal, that Fraport intended to exercise managerial control over PIATCO and thus 'knowingly orchestrated its investment in flagrant violation of the [Anti-Dummy Law]'.[202] Around that time, Fraport sought to secure long-term financing for PIATCO for completing Terminal 3, and to recoup its bridge loans, by the help of an international lending consortium. The agreement between

[197] *Fraport* v. *Philippines I*, paras. 2 et seq.
[198] *Fraport* v. *Philippines I*, paras. 102 et seq.; *Fraport* v. *Philippines II*, paras. 95 et seq.
[199] *Fraport* v. *Philippines I*, para. 287.
[200] *Fraport* v. *Philippines I*, paras. 120, 308 et seq., 352.
[201] *Fraport* v. *Philippines I*, paras. 79 et seq., 117.
[202] *Fraport* v. *Philippines I*, paras. 124 et seq.

the lending consortium and PIATCO contained seventy-seven conditions that had to be fulfilled before the loans could be drawn down.[203]

After 2001, opposition arose towards the Terminal 3 project from a group of businesses providing services in Terminals 1 and 2, demanding amendments to the allegedly onerous and illegal provisions of the concession agreement.[204] Renegotiations of the terms of the concession agreement between PIATCO and the responsible State Secretary Climaco started in early 2002. However, those were unsuccessful. In 2003, the Philippine Supreme Court declared the 1997 concession agreement null and void due to serious violations of Philippine law and public policy, at a time when the airport terminal was almost completely built.[205] Discussions between Fraport and the Philippine government for compensation were fruitless, and consequently, Fraport filed its request for ICSID arbitration.[206] In 2004, while the ICSID proceedings were ongoing, the Philippines took possession of Terminal 3 and initiated expropriation proceedings.[207]

In its Award of 16 August 2007, the ICSID Tribunal concluded, by majority, that Fraport had knowingly violated the Philippine Anti-Dummy Law ('ADL') when it secretly arranged for the management and control of the Terminal 3 project. As such, Fraport's investment did not qualify as an 'investment' under the German-Philippine BIT, and the Tribunal did not have jurisdiction over the dispute. The Tribunal dismissed Fraport's claims.[208]

In his Dissenting Opinion, Bernardo Cremades argued that the Tribunal did have jurisdiction because the shareholdings of Fraport in Philippine companies did constitute an 'investment' according to Art. 1(1) of the BIT and those shareholdings were an accepted kind of asset under Philippine law, irrespective of any breach of the ADL. The Philippines had failed to demonstrate that PIATCO as the public utility holder had breached the ADL, and therefore Fraport could not be an accomplice. Fraport's shareholding complied with the 'control' test under the ADL. The Terminal 3 concession had been null and void *ab initio* and the Philippines ADL submission violated the good faith

203 *Fraport* v. *Philippines I*, para. 132.
204 *Fraport* v. *Philippines I*, paras. 142 et seq.
205 *Fraport* v. *Philippines I*, paras. 207 et seq., 217, 219.
206 *Fraport* v. *Philippines I*, paras. 219 et seq.
207 *Fraport* v. *Philippines I*, paras. 226 et seq.
208 *Fraport* v. *Philippines I*, paras. 396 et seq.

requirement in international investment arbitration.[209] On illegality and jurisdiction, Cremades stated that,

> The legality of the investment in investment arbitration has its analogy in international commercial arbitration in the validity of the contract. If the applicable law does not insist on the separability of the arbitration agreement from the main contract, then respondents quickly seek to subvert the arbitral process by challenging the validity of the main contract. Similarly, the phrase 'according to the laws and regulations of the Host State' might provide the Achilles Heel of investment arbitration if jurisdiction depends on the Claimant passing a full legal compliance audit.[210]

Cremades concluded that in principle, the legality of the investor's conduct should be decided at the merits stage and that in the jurisdictional phase, the inquiry should be limited to determining whether 'the type of asset is legal in domestic law'.[211]

The 2007 Award was annulled in December 2010. The ICSID *ad hoc* Annulment Committee found that the Tribunal had failed to hear submissions from the parties on crucial evidence, and thus violated the parties' right to be heard.[212] In March 2011, Fraport filed a new ICSID claim against the Philippines.[213]

Parallel ICC Proceedings and Corruption Allegations In parallel to Fraport's claim with ICSID, PIATCO had initiated ICC proceedings against the Philippines in Singapore. In July 2010, the ICC Tribunal affirmed its jurisdiction and dismissed PIATCO's claims due to a violation of the Philippine ADL, arguing in particular that PIATCO had illegally performed the Terminal 3 concession by allowing Fraport to intervene in the management, operation, administration or control of the Terminal. The Tribunal stated that by determining whether there was a violation of the ADL, it did not perform the task of a criminal tribunal,

209 *Fraport* v. *Philippines I*, Dissenting Opinion of Mr Bernardo M. Cremades, para. 35.

210 *Fraport* v. *Philippines I*, Dissenting Opinion of Mr Bernardo M. Cremades, para. 37.

211 *Fraport* v. *Philippines I*, Dissenting Opinion of Mr Bernardo M. Cremades, para. 38; in detail: Llamzon 2014, 164 et seq.; see also Kulick 2012, 324 et seq.; Kulick and Wendler 2010, 71.

212 *Fraport* v. *Philippines I*, Annulment Proceeding, Decision on the Application for Annulment of Fraport AG Frankfurt Airport Services Worldwide, 23 December 2010, paras. 218 et seq.; in detail: Llamzon 2014, 167 et seq.

213 J.E. Hepburn, 'Fraport files new claim at ICSID over expropriation of airport terminal project; annulment committee ruling paved way for new hearing by finding breach of investor's right to be heard', *Investment Arbitration Reporter*, 31 March 2011.

but decided a criminal law issue in a civil proceeding. As such, the Tribunal affirmed arbitrability of this issue. In the ICC proceedings, the Philippines also alleged fraud and corruption by PIATCO in violation of Philippine laws, but the Tribunal did not discuss those allegations, arguing that this was unnecessary due to the conclusion the Tribunal had reached regarding the breach of the ADL.[214] In November 2011, the Singapore High Court dismissed PIATCO's application to set aside the ICC Award.[215]

The parallel ICC proceedings were an issue in the proceedings leading up to the 2007 ICSID Award. The Philippines alleged fraud and corruption by PIATCO shareholders, including Fraport, and contended that relevant evidence could be found in the filings of the ongoing ICC arbitration, as well as in domestic investigations in Germany, the Philippines, the United States and Hong Kong. Fraport subsequently filed a request for document production by the Philippines. The ICSID Tribunal accepted that the issues in the two arbitrations were overlapping, and ordered the Philippines to produce all submissions from the ICC arbitration.[216]

5.1.10.2 The Second ICSID Proceedings

The Parties' Claims In the second ICSID proceedings, Fraport claimed that it was 'subject to an uncompensated and unlawful expropriation' of its investment in PIATCO.[217] The Philippines argued, *inter alia*, that the Tribunal did not have jurisdiction, because Fraport's investment had violated Philippine law, in particular the nationality restrictions of the Anti-Dummy Law, and that Fraport's claims were also inadmissible, because corruption was involved in the obtaining and implementation of the concession.[218]

Proving Corruption The Philippines alleged that Fraport was involved in, or at least aware of, corrupt and fraudulent practices in the implementation of the Terminal 3 project, arguing that there was *prima facie* evidence for corruption and that the Tribunal could rely on recognised 'red flags' and presumption when assessing this evidence; and that

[214] *PIATCO* v. *Republic of the Philippines*; Lamm 2011, 43.

[215] Office of the Solicitor General of the Philippines, Press Release, 'Singapore High Court affirms dismissal of PIATCO claim on ground of illegality', available at www.osg.gov.ph.

[216] *Fraport* v. *Philippines I*, paras. 5, 18; Schreuer et al. 2009, Art. 26 N 122 et seq.

[217] *Fraport* v. *Philippines II*, para. 14.

[218] *Fraport* v. *Philippines II*, para. 15.

Fraport had been unable to produce rebuttal evidence. Fraport argued that corruption allegations require clear and convincing evidence and that the Philippines had failed to meet this high burden of proof.[219]

The Philippines submitted that PIATCO, with the involvement of Fraport, had indirectly – through offshore banking accounts belonging to Mr Liongson, a consultant of PIATCO – paid more than US$10.6 million in bribes to Philippine officials to obtain the necessary government approvals for the Terminal 3 project. Specifically, the Philippines alleged that those payments served to procure discretionary signatures from government officials in order to secure the ARCA and its three supplements. Those were needed to fulfil the seventy-seven conditions by the international lending consortium before their loans could be drawn down, or in other words, to recoup Fraport's short-term bridge loans and to secure the long-term financing of the Terminal 3 project.[220] The Philippines relied on expert reports 'to argue that the nature of these payments, the structure of PIATCO's contract with Liongson, Liongson's lack of qualifications to perform the public relations services for which he was purportedly hired, and an allegedly extraordinarily high level of Project "soft costs" are indicative of bribery.'[221] The Philippines argued that as a consequence, the burden of proof should shift to Fraport to produce evidence that PIATCO did not procure the government approvals through bribery.

Fraport argued that the Philippines had not produced evidence for bribery, relying solely on the inferences of its experts; that the Philippines had not shown the link between alleged payments to corrupt officials and specific government approvals; that no Philippine officials were indicted or convicted for taking bribes in relation to the Terminal 3 concession and that no investigations were ongoing; that the Philippines did not allege corruption with regard to the award of the Terminal 3 concession or to Fraport's making of the investment; and that Liongson did in fact provide public relations services.[222]

The Tribunal's Decision on Jurisdiction The Tribunal first clarified that the ICSID Convention, the Germany-Philippines BIT, international law and provisions of Philippine law (to the extent that they were relevant for determining the Tribunal's jurisdiction) were applicable.

[219] *Fraport* v. *Philippines II*, paras. 226, 477 with reference to *EDF* v. *Romania*.
[220] *Fraport* v. *Philippines II*, paras. 120 et seq.; 228 et seq.
[221] *Fraport* v. *Philippines II*, para. 230. [222] *Fraport* v. *Philippines II*, para. 235.

It also stated that the burden of proof was on the party bringing a claim or defence. If that party had established a *prima facie* case by producing sufficient evidence, the burden would shift to the other party to produce rebuttal evidence, although the ultimate burden to prove the claim or defence was again on the party that raised it.[223]

The Tribunal then examined whether there was an investment under the BIT. To put it short, the Tribunal concluded, on the basis of Article 1 (1) of the BIT that defined the term 'investment', that there was no investment in this case. According to the Tribunal, Article 1(1) only included investments in the scope of the BIT that were lawful according to the host state's law at the time the investment was made.[224] At the jurisdictional level, the Tribunal limited its analysis of Fraport's investments – that span over a period of several years – to the 'Initial Investment' (several equity investments in mid-1999).[225] The Tribunal found that Fraport had violated the Philippine ADL when it made its Initial Investment and that the Initial Investment was therefore illegal. The Tribunal did not have jurisdiction according to Article 25(1) of the ICSID Convention due to the absence of consent.[226]

With regard to the Philippines' objection to ICSID jurisdiction because of Fraport's alleged corruption and fraud, the Tribunal again only looked at Fraport's Initial Investment. The Tribunal argued that most of the Philippines' submissions with regard to corruption and fraud were related to the implementation phase of the Terminal 3 project, after the time of Fraport's Initial Investment. Only the so-called Datacenta Agreement predated the Initial Investment.[227]

The Tribunal was aware of the difficulty of proving bribery by direct evidence and stated that circumstantial evidence was sufficient. This evidence, however, had to be 'clear and convincing' as to 'reasonably make-believe that the facts, as alleged, have occurred'. It concluded that the Philippines had failed to produce clear and convincing evidence for corruption and fraud.[228] With regard to the Datacenta Agreement, the Tribunal found that the events had taken place much before (and after) Fraport's Initial Investment, and that there was 'no basis in conflating PIATCO with Fraport' when Fraport did not know of PIATCO's

223 *Fraport* v. *Philippines II*, paras. 295 et seq.
224 *Fraport* v. *Philippines II*, paras. 331, 333.
225 *Fraport* v. *Philippines II*, paras. 337 et seq.
226 *Fraport* v. *Philippines II*, paras. 467 et seq.
227 *Fraport* v. *Philippines II*, paras. 469 et seq.
228 *Fraport* v. *Philippines II*, para. 479.

allegedly corrupt practices. The Tribunal dismissed the objection to jurisdiction based on corruption.[229]

The Tribunal noted that no government officials had been convicted or indicted for having taken bribes, neither in the Philippines nor in Germany.[230] The Philippines argued in this regard that confidentiality agreements from the first ICSID and the ICC arbitration proceedings hampered it from using the evidence available.[231] In the Award, the Tribunal dismissed Fraport's claims for lack of jurisdiction and ordered it to pay US$5 million towards the Philippines' fees and costs. Each party had to fully bear the remaining fees and costs it incurred, equally sharing the Tribunal's fees and expenses.[232]

5.1.10.3 Analysis

In the 2007 Award, the Tribunal did not (yet) discuss corruption.[233] However, the Award raises two crucial issues that are picked up again in the 2014 Award:

- what does it mean that an investment has to be in accordance with the law of the host state and
- how does a tribunal deal with the situation that illegality occurs not at the initiation of an investment, but only during its performance?

With regard to the second question, the Tribunal in *Fraport* v. *Philippines I* argued that

> the effective operation of the BIT regime would appear to require that jurisdictional compliance be limited to the initiation of the investment. If, at the time of the initiation of the investment, there has been compliance with the law of the host state, allegations by the host state of violations of its law in the course of the investment, as a justification for state action with respect to the investment, might be a defense to claimed *substantive* violations of the BIT, but could not deprive a tribunal acting under the authority of the BIT of its jurisdiction.[234]

In this passage, the Tribunal distinguished two chronological phases of an investment: the time of its initiation and the course of the investment. It argued that those phases must be kept apart with regard to host state

[229] *Fraport* v. *Philippines II*, paras. 480 et seq. [230] *Fraport* v. *Philippines II*, para. 205.
[231] *Fraport* v. *Philippines II*, para. 275. [232] *Fraport* v. *Philippines II*, para. 530.
[233] However, corruption allegations were already raised during the first ICSID proceedings: see Llamzon 2014, 159 et seq.
[234] *Fraport* v. *Philippines I*, para. 345.

law compliance: if non-compliance occurs at the initiation phase, the tribunal will deny jurisdiction. If non-compliance occurs during the course of the investment, the tribunal will assert jurisdiction and discuss illegality at the merits stage.

The consequences of the Tribunal's approach in the 2007 Award clearly show in the 2014 Award, in which the new Tribunal made similar considerations. The Tribunal's conclusion that the Initial Investment did not comply with host state's law (the Philippine ADL), and its denial of jurisdiction can be accepted in the result. However, regarding the allegations of fraud and corruption, it appears incoherent to distinguish the Initial Investment from the course of the investment, and to argue that those allegations mainly related to the latter. Why should the Initial Investment be limited to the equity investments in mid-1999? Can the alleged bribe payments via Mr Liongson, with the purpose of securing government approvals for ARCA to secure long-term financing of the Terminal 3 project, seriously be regarded as separate from the Initial Investment? The consequence of this limitation is that the Tribunal only took a closer look at the Datacenta Agreement, and not at all the other agreements that were surrounded by corruption allegations. Furthermore, one of the general characteristics of criminal law provisions on bribery is that the undue advantage does not have to be conveyed beforehand: corrupt payments etc. that are linked to the initiation of an investment can happen much later.[235]

On applicable law, the 2014 Award shows that the Tribunal invoked the Philippine ADL, but it does not specify whether the Tribunal relied on any other international or domestic legal provisions that deal with bribery or fraud. On standard of proof, the Tribunal argued that circumstantial evidence was sufficient to prove the corruption allegations, but that this evidence had to be clear and convincing.[236] It appears that the parallel criminal proceedings in different jurisdictions, all resulting in no convictions of individuals, also had an impact on the Tribunal's decision regarding corruption. An interesting feature of the parallel ICSID and ICC proceedings in this case is that the ICSID Tribunal denied jurisdiction because of a violation of host state's law (as there was no investment and therefore no consent to ICSID jurisdiction); whereas the ICC

[235] See also discussion in Chapter 10.

[236] The Tribunal did not refer to any other arbitral awards in this regard, while the Claimant had invoked the *EDF* v. *Romania* Award; notably, the *Fraport II* Tribunal was presided by the same arbitrator as the *EDF* Tribunal.

Tribunal affirmed jurisdiction and dismissed the claims on the merits (because of a violation of the applicable Philippine law). This shows that the separability principle that applies in commercial arbitration cannot readily be transferred to treaty-based ICSID arbitration.[237]

5.1.11 Spentex *v.* Uzbekistan *(2016)*

The Claimant in this case was Spentex Netherlands, B.V. ('SNBV'), a company incorporated in the Netherlands. The Respondent was the Republic of Uzbekistan. Spentex initiated ICSID arbitration in September 2013 on the basis of the Netherlands-Uzbekistan BIT, Uzbek investment law, an Investment Agreement between the Uzbek government and Spentex Industries Limited ('SIL') and the ICSID Convention.[238]

SIL was a textile and yarn-spinning company founded under the name CLC Global ('CLC') and renamed SIL after several mergers. SIL was based in New Delhi (India).[239] In February 2004, CLC (later SIL) entered into a services agreement with the company A International ('A', based in New Delhi), according to which A would assist SIL in its global expansion by establishing and operating a spinning mill in Uzbekistan. In May 2004, SIL engaged another consultant, the company B Limited ('B', registered in the United Kingdom), for the same purpose.[240] SIL agreed to pay A 2 per cent of the project cost on a success basis.[241] In October 2004, SIL terminated the services agreement with A due to poor performance.[242]

On 13 April 2006, SIL and the Uzbek state-owned company C concluded an agreement for the establishment of a modern textile manufacturing facility in Uzbekistan.[243] On 21 April 2006, the Uzbek president opened the tender for several textile plants in the country, including the D and E textile plants that were operated by F, LLC ('F'). The initial bid price for F's assets was US$65 million. SIL's bid was set at US$75 million.[244]

On 12 June 2006, SIL engaged G (BVI) Ltd. ('G') to provide 'advice and guidance during the tender process' and 'advice and guidance to ensure good relation[s] with Uzbek authorities'. SIL agreed to

[237] Cremades 2005, 219.
[238] *Spentex* v. *Uzbekistan*, para. 1. At the time of writing, the case was not published yet.
[239] *Spentex* v. *Uzbekistan*, para. 222.
[240] *Spentex* v. *Uzbekistan*, para. 225.
[241] *Spentex* v. *Uzbekistan*, para. 224.
[242] *Spentex* v. *Uzbekistan*, para. 229.
[243] *Spentex* v. *Uzbekistan*, para. 231.
[244] *Spentex* v. *Uzbekistan*, paras. 232 et seq.

remunerate G with 9 per cent of the sales contract. On the same date, SIL engaged B 'to ensure good support' for SIL's bid. B was to receive 2 per cent of the sales contract for its services.[245] On 14 June 2006, SIL submitted a bid to acquire F's assets at a price of US$81 million. SIL explained the increase in the bid price with its commitment to win the bid and on the grounds of 'Hindu luck'.[246] Three companies had qualified to bid for the D and E textile plants: SIL, H International and J. On 20 June 2006, the Uzbek State Commission responsible for overseeing the tender process awarded F's assets to SIL, arguing that the latter had made the 'best proposal in accordance with the requirements of the tender'.[247] In the months following the tender process, B issued invoices to SIL in relation to the F project; no invoices, but only internal vouchers indicating payments were produced regarding G.[248]

In July 2006, SIL established SNBV (the Claimant) as a vehicle for investing in Uzbekistan. The Claimant subsequently incorporated a local subsidiary in Uzbekistan, K LLC ('K'). To put it very short, K defaulted on its cotton payments to Uzbekistan by early 2011 and went bankrupt in 2012.[249] The Claimant alleged violations by Uzbekistan of provisions of the BIT, the Investment Agreement and Uzbek investment law, and demanded compensation and/or damages in the amount of approximately US$130 million.[250] The Respondent objected to the Claimant's claims arguing, *inter alia*, that the Claimant had obtained its investment by paying bribes in the amount of at least US$8.398 million through the companies A, B and G.[251]

5.1.11.1 Corruption as an Issue of Jurisdiction or Admissibility?

In its analysis, the Tribunal first examined the Respondent's bribery allegations, arguing that a positive finding of corruption would potentially dispose of all claims and counterclaims.[252] Before going into evidentiary and factual issues, the Tribunal assessed whether bribery would have an impact on the jurisdiction of the Tribunal, or on the admissibility of the Claimant's claims. The Respondent argued that Article 2 of the Netherlands-Uzbekistan BIT, referring to the host state's admission

245 *Spentex* v. *Uzbekistan*, para. 235. 246 *Spentex* v. *Uzbekistan*, para. 237.
247 *Spentex* v. *Uzbekistan*, para. 238. 248 *Spentex* v. *Uzbekistan*, para. 240.
249 In detail: *Spentex* v. *Uzbekistan*, paras. 241 et seq.
250 *Spentex* v. *Uzbekistan*, para. 328. 251 *Spentex* v. *Uzbekistan*, paras. 332 et seq.
252 *Spentex* v. *Uzbekistan*, para. 814.

of investments within 'the framework of its laws', effectively contained an 'in accordance with host state's law' clause. Alternatively, a legality requirement should be regarded as implicit in all investment treaties. Furthermore, according to the Respondent, claims based on illegal acts such as bribery should be dismissed, as they are contrary to international or transnational public policy. As a general principle of international law and public policy, 'a claimant with unclean hands may not seek relief for claims arising out of its own unlawful conduct'.[253]

The Claimant disputed all those arguments. The Tribunal was aware of the disagreements among the parties as well as among previous tribunals, in particular regarding the question whether illegal acts deprive a tribunal of jurisdiction or render a claim inadmissible. Two Tribunal members found that bribery in the present case should be discussed as a matter of admissibility, whereas one member argued that it was a question of jurisdiction. The Tribunal concluded that in both cases, the claims must be dismissed. Without going any deeper into this issue, it decided that corruption in the making of an investment constituted a core violation of the principle of good faith and a violation of the international *ordre public*, and that a claimant who comes with 'unclean hands' to a tribunal should not be heard.[254] The Tribunal relied on ICC[255] as well as ICSID[256] case law to support its argument that 'an investment procured by corruption will not be protected by an arbitral tribunal set up under the ICSID Convention.'[257]

5.1.11.2 Reference to the OECD Convention on Bribery and UNCAC

In order to define foreign public bribery and to identify which precise acts should be considered contrary to transnational public order, the Tribunal cited Article 1(1) of the OECD Convention on Bribery, as well as Article 16(1) of the UNCAC. The Tribunal found the bottom line to be clear: 'Any promise, offering or giving to a (foreign) public official, directly or indirectly, of an undue financial or other advantage in order that the official act or refrain from acting in the exercise of his or her

[253] *Spentex* v. *Uzbekistan*, para. 818. [254] *Spentex* v. *Uzbekistan*, paras. 819 et seq.

[255] ICC Case No. 1110 (*Lagergren*).

[256] *World Duty Free* v. *Kenya*, *Plama* v. *Bulgaria*, *Phoenix* v. *Czech Republic*, *Hamester* v. *Ghana*, *Metal-Tech* v. *Uzbekistan*, *Fraport* v. *Philippines*, and *Minnotte and Lewis* v. *Poland*.

[257] *Spentex* v. *Uzbekistan*, paras. 824 et seq., 841.

official duties, for the purpose of obtaining business advantages falls under the notion of corruption.'[258] The Tribunal argued that to establish corruption, there had to be evidence that SIL and SNBV through their officers promised, offered or gave financial or other advantages to Uzbek officials, directly or through intermediaries, in order to influence those officials in the exercise of their duties.[259]

5.1.11.3 The Applicable Burden and Standard of Proof

The Respondent argued that 'where a number of "red flags" indicating corrupt practices demonstrably outweigh other evidence that might explain or excuse the seemingly inappropriate conduct', the burden of proof would shift to the Claimant to prove that no corruption had occurred. The Respondent also argued that the Tribunal should apply a 'preponderance of the evidence' standard to the bribery allegations. The Claimant argued that the burden of proof rested with the party objecting to the Tribunal's jurisdiction (or challenging admissibility of the claims), and that a 'clear and convincing' evidence standard applied.[260]

The Tribunal noted that issues of bribery are notoriously difficult to prove in arbitration and that 'there is an inherent danger to dispose of the problem by resorting to strict evidentiary rules that may make proving or disproving corruption practically impossible'. It found that the traditional rule of each party having to prove the facts on which it relied coupled with a heightened standard of proof of 'clear and convincing evidence' made it almost impossible for a party to prove bribery. But it also noted that shifting the burden of proof once a party had produced some corruption indications and then demanding '"clear and convincing evidence" for the absence of corruption from the other party' amounts to a '*probatio diabolica* or *de facto* impossibility to disprove the existence of corruption' for the latter.[261]

The Tribunal decided that it did not matter which standard of proof it applied, because the evidence on the record established corruption. It followed the principle that 'the graver the charge, the more confidence there must be in the evidence relied on'. The Tribunal did not rely on a strict burden of proof, but rather took into account the co-operation of the parties in the fact-finding process. It applied a method of 'connecting the dots', thereby assessing all individual indicia

[258] *Spentex* v. *Uzbekistan*, paras. 842 et seq., 846.
[259] *Spentex* v. *Uzbekistan*, para. 847.
[260] *Spentex* v. *Uzbekistan*, paras. 849 et seq.
[261] *Spentex* v. *Uzbekistan*, para. 856.

in detail and checking the plausibility of a potential picture emerging from putting them together.[262]

5.1.11.4 'Red flags' of Bid Rigging and Bribery

The Respondent alleged that SIL had engaged in bribery to obtain the D and E textile plants. In particular, the Respondent argued that the sudden increase in SIL's bid amount from US$75 million to US$81 million the night before submitting the tender application, and the hiring of consultants remunerated through high success fees, constituted 'red flags' of bid rigging and bribery.[263] The Tribunal analysed each of the red flags raised by the Respondent in great detail. Regarding A, even though e-mails and invoices contained explicit references to 'bribing', the Tribunal noted that legitimate services had been performed and that the payments to A were not clearly disproportionate. The Tribunal also argued that the payments to A made in 2004 were unlikely to have had any influence on the tender process in 2006.[264]

The Tribunal found major red flags established though regarding the payments agreed by SIL to the two consulting firms B and G just days before submitting the tender application:

- The payments agreed, and actually made, in particular to G were suspicious: while it was agreed that B would receive 2 per cent of the purchase price (i.e. US$1.62 million), G was to receive 9 per cent of the purchase price (i.e. US$7.29 million, which was lowered to $6 million, however). The Tribunal found this latter compensation to be 'strikingly high'.[265]
- The Claimant tried to hide the consulting contracts from the Tribunal, and produced only few documents relating to A, B and G in the proceedings.[266]
- The consultants did not have any real qualifications. B was registered in the United Kingdom as a medical office and led by Mr X, described in 2003 as a 'go-between' in the 'kickbacks-for-bosses' business, apparently without any special expertise in the cotton industry. Regarding G, registered in the British Virgin Islands, there was no publicly available information identifying the company's directors, officers or principals.

262 *Spentex* v. *Uzbekistan*, paras. 857 et seq. with further references to case law.

263 *Spentex* v. *Uzbekistan*, paras. 862 et seq.

264 *Spentex* v. *Uzbekistan*, paras. 865 et seq.

265 *Spentex* v. *Uzbekistan*, paras. 877 et seq., 885 et seq.

266 *Spentex* v. *Uzbekistan*, paras. 889 et seq.

In the hearing, it was confirmed that G was headed by the – at the relevant time – twenty-two-year-old Mr Y, whose qualifications remained unclear.[267]

- The descriptions of the services that were to be rendered by the consultants B and G in the respective engagement letters were vague. While B apparently did provide various services to SIL between 2004 and 2006, the Claimant was unable to produce any records demonstrating services rendered by G in exchange for the US$6 million it received.[268]
- The Tribunal found a further red flag established in the fact that the time period between the conclusion of the engagement letter with G (12 June 2006) and the submission of SIL's bid (14 June 2006) was very short: 'It defies imagination to conceive of any valuable reports . . . which could have been produced . . . in a two-day time frame.'[269]
- Even though the Tribunal repeatedly requested the Claimant to produce a formal valuation report allegedly delivered by G shortly before the tender process, the Claimant failed to produce that report, arguing that it was located at K's premises in Uzbekistan to which it no longer had access. The Tribunal found this explanation to be implausible.[270]
- The Claimant failed to produce invoices by G as well as bank records showing where the payments to B and G actually went; apparently, payments went to bank accounts in Luxembourg and the British Virgin Islands.[271]

5.1.11.5 The Role of the Respondent in the Bribery Scheme

The Tribunal noted that 'the only missing link in establishing that the tender process was tainted by corruption is the lack of any direct evidence of payments received by Uzbek officials'.[272] Several Uzbek officials testified in the ICSID proceedings and all denied that there was any corruption. The Tribunal noted that the Respondent's argument contradicted its own witnesses, whilst at the same time implicating them in the corruption. The Tribunal found that the Respondent itself suggested that its officials had taken bribes and its witnesses had falsely testified to the Tribunal. The Tribunal showed concern that Uzbekistan

[267] *Spentex* v. *Uzbekistan*, paras. 892 et seq.
[268] *Spentex* v. *Uzbekistan*, paras. 899 et seq.
[269] *Spentex* v. *Uzbekistan*, para. 908.
[270] *Spentex* v. *Uzbekistan*, paras. 909 et seq.
[271] *Spentex* v. *Uzbekistan*, paras. 916 et seq.
[272] *Spentex* v. *Uzbekistan*, para. 925.

had failed to investigate and prosecute any of its officials for bribery.[273] Nevertheless, the Tribunal concluded that

> 'Connecting the dots' of the individual pieces of evidence described above leads the Tribunal to conclude that the most compelling explanation of the events surrounding the tender process in June 2006 and the making of the investment is clearly that it involved corrupt activities on the part of the investor and of officials of the Respondent.[274]

The Tribunal noted that the Respondent had been far from co-operative in the proceedings, refusing to provide any names of officials who participated in the bribery scheme. The Respondent tried to suggest that one of Spentex's consultants was associated with the daughter of a high Uzbek official and had used this connection to exert corrupt influence; at the same time the Respondent made clear that it was not going to do anything about it. The Tribunal found the Respondent's expert to back this strategy by suggesting the Tribunal should dismiss the Claimant's claims without naming the corrupt officials. The Tribunal argued:

> Such an approach would reinforce perverse incentives for respondent States in the context of corruption. It would ask an investment tribunal to dismiss a claimant's claim, while granting impunity to a respondent State both in respect of the alleged corruption and the claimant's investment claims.[275]

The Tribunal also found that the Respondent's own expert stated that there was no domestic law enforcement in Uzbekistan regarding the corrupt officials. The Tribunal argued that Uzbekistan was unwilling (and not unable) to investigate and prosecute such cases.[276] In conclusion, the Tribunal found that the US$6 million payment to G was made with the purpose to bribe Uzbek officials who had an influence on the tender process. Two Tribunal members found the investor's claims to be inadmissible due to corruption that was against core values of the international *ordre public*; one member denied jurisdiction of the Tribunal.[277]

5.1.11.6 The Impact of Corruption on the Costs Decision

The Tribunal stressed that corruption always takes two: 'those who bribe and those who take bribes'. If a finding of corruption routinely leads to

[273] *Spentex* v. *Uzbekistan*, paras. 926 et seq. [274] *Spentex* v. *Uzbekistan*, para. 934.
[275] *Spentex* v. *Uzbekistan*, para. 940. [276] *Spentex* v. *Uzbekistan*, paras. 942 et seq.
[277] *Spentex* v. *Uzbekistan*, paras. 944 et seq.

the dismissal of the claimant's claims, corrupt investors are punished for their conduct, while corrupt host states are left off the hook.[278] The Tribunal found, however, that for the time being, arbitral tribunals were helpless in trying to 'sanction' corrupt host states. Interestingly, the Tribunal suggested for the future to include certain remedies in BITs:

> On the one hand, the claimant cannot have its claim entertained (due to a lack of either jurisdiction or admissibility). On the other hand, a tribunal should be able to entertain the claim as if no corruption had occurred and, in case it finds the State liable, calculate the damages that a claimant having made an investment without resort to corruption would have been entitled to and then order that such amount be transferred not to the claimant, but to an appropriate body of the UN, the OECD, or any other body fighting against corruption.[279]

In the case at hand, the Tribunal ordered both parties to bear their own costs and fees, and to equally share the costs and fees of the proceedings. In addition, it urged the Respondent to pay US$8 million to the Global Anti-Corruption Initiative administered by the UN Development Programme. By majority, the Tribunal decided that if the Respondent failed to make this payment, it would have to bear all the costs and fees of the proceedings, as well as three-quarters of the Claimant's legal fees.[280]

5.1.11.7 Analysis

Spentex v. *Uzbekistan* sets another milestone. For the first time, an ICSID tribunal decided that bribery was successfully proven on the basis of an accumulation of major 'red flags', even if the final recipients of the bribe payments were not known. The Tribunal found that a claimant who comes with 'unclean hands' should not be heard by an ICSID tribunal. It relied on international anti-corruption conventions (OECD, UNCAC) to formulate its own definition of bribery. The Tribunal did not apply a rigid formula regarding burden and standard of proof, but 'connected the dots'. In sum, the Tribunal must be commended for its modern, well-reflected approach and its courage to ask the right questions and to draw the proper conclusions.

The Tribunal points out the dilemma emerging from the fact that 'it takes two to tango': bribery always involves a bribe giver and a bribe taker. Letting the host state off the hook by dismissing the investor's

[278] *Spentex* v. *Uzbekistan*, paras. 973 et seq.

[279] *Spentex* v. *Uzbekistan*, paras. 978 et seq.

[280] *Spentex* v. *Uzbekistan*, paras. 981 et seq.

claims, even if the host state does not co-operate in the proceedings and does nothing to prosecute its corrupt officials, is unsatisfactory. The Tribunal takes a novel approach to remedy this by urging the Respondent to pay US$8 million to an anti-corruption institution. Two questions are raised by the Tribunal's arguments at this point: (1) What are the rights of parties and witnesses in cases of alleged crime in arbitration proceedings?[281] (2) Should host states be held responsible for the corrupt acts of their officials?[282]

5.1.12 Summary

A string of ICSID Awards dealing with alleged foreign public bribery emerged in the last two decades. Llamzon argues that in only four cases, corruption was outcome-determinative.[283] On the basis of the eleven cases discussed here, the development when it comes to proving bribery can be summarised as follows. In contract-based arbitration, *World Duty Free* v. *Kenya* set a milestone because it showed the impact of a successful corruption defence. The evidence – brought forward by the Claimant – was clear in that case. At the merits stage, the Tribunal found that bribery was contrary to transnational public policy, and dismissed all of the Claimant's claims, allowing the Respondent to avoid the contract.

Siemens v. *Argentina*, *African Holding* v. *Democratic Republic of Congo*, *TSA Spectrum* v. *Argentina* and *Sistem* v. *Kyrgyz Republic* each raised particular issues – the decisive impact that US domestic plea agreements (and a Statement of Offense) can have on ICSID arbitration; the fate of unsubstantiated bribery allegations; the role of ongoing domestic criminal investigations; and the definition of foreign public bribery in international law. However, the next milestone was probably *EDF* v. *Romania*. In this case, the Claimant – and not the Respondent – raised the bribery allegations, claiming solicitation (not the actual payment) of a bribe. EDF did not invoke the host state's anti-bribery laws, but rather claimed a breach of the fair and equitable treatment requirement of the BIT as well as of international public policy. The Tribunal demanded 'clear and convincing evidence' for the alleged bribe solicitation. It was confronted with contradictory and inconsistent witness

[281] See discussion in Chapter 9. [282] See discussion in Chapter 10.

[283] In *World Duty Free* v. *Kenya*; *Metal-Tech* v. *Uzbekistan*; *Siemens* v. *Argentina*; and *Azpetrol* v. *Azerbaijan* (which was settled; see Llamzon 2014, 102 et seq.). *Spentex* v. *Uzbekistan* of 2016 can be added to this list.

statements, and did not admit certain evidence that it considered contrary to the duty of procedural fairness.

RSM v. *Grenada* shows that parties are well advised to raise their corruption allegations as early as possible in ICSID proceedings. If new evidence of bribery is uncovered after an award has been issued, the alleging party should seek revision – and not annulment – of that award. Three more landmark ICSID Awards were issued in the years 2013 and 2014, namely *Niko* v. *Bangladesh* (Decision on Jurisdiction), *Metal-Tech* v. *Uzbekistan* and *Fraport* v. *Philippines*. In all of those cases, the Respondent raised an objection to ICSID jurisdiction on the basis of alleged bribery. While *Niko* was a contract-based arbitration, *Metal-Tech* and *Fraport* were based on BITs. In *Niko*, the Respondent relied on the investor's domestic conviction for foreign public bribery, arguing that ICSID jurisdiction should be denied on the basis of the good faith and legality requirements for investments. The Tribunal, however, rejected the objection to jurisdiction, stating that the established acts of bribery could not justify a refusal to examine the merits of the dispute. The Tribunal also declined the Respondent's requests for far-reaching document production. The case is still pending.

While *Niko* already touched upon it, *Metal-Tech* and *Fraport* bring to light the issue whether the initial phase and the operation of an investment should be distinguished with regard to the legality requirement in BITs. In *Metal-Tech*, the Tribunal closely read the Uzbek Criminal Code (as the applicable law of the host state), concluding that it had been violated and that therefore there was no investment in accordance with host state's law and no consent to ICSID arbitration. The Tribunal found that the legality requirement of Article 1(1) of the BIT only referred to the time of the initial establishment of the investment and did not address the question whether the investment had to be operated lawfully after its initiation. Similarly, in *Fraport*, the Tribunal found in the 2014 Award that the Initial Investment had violated the Philippine Anti-Dummy Law (as the applicable law of the host state), and that therefore there was no investment in accordance with the host state's law as required by Article 1(1) of the applicable BIT, and no consent to ICSID arbitration. For BIT-based ICSID arbitration, the Tribunal argued that illegality at the initial phase of an investment should result in a denial of jurisdiction, whereas violations of host state's law throughout the course of the investment should be discussed at the merits stage. Regarding alleged corruption and fraud, the Tribunal again only looked at Fraport's Initial Investment, arguing that most of the Respondent's respective submissions related to the implementation phase of the investment, and it took into account only a fraction of those allegations.

Metal-Tech is a crucial case when it comes to proving bribery because of the Tribunal's proactive approach. The facts had nurtured bribery suspicions, and the Tribunal consequently used its *ex officio* powers under Article 43 of the ICSID Convention to inquire into the facts. The Tribunal argued that the good-faith obligation of parties to co-operate in arbitral proceedings allows it to infer that a document is adverse to the interests of a party if the latter does not produce such evidence. Eventually, the decisive evidence came from the Claimant. The Tribunal also listed the 'red flags' for corruption; stating that circumstantial evidence was sufficient to prove bribery, the Tribunal concluded that corruption was established 'with reasonable certainty' in this case. Another important feature of *Metal-Tech* is that, in its decision on costs, the Tribunal took into account the harsh consequences of the denial of jurisdiction for the Claimant, as well as the latter's co-operative attitude throughout the proceedings. A pivotal case is *Spentex*, because here the Tribunal accepted that bribery was proven on the basis of accumulated 'red flags', even if the final recipients of the bribe payments were not known. The Tribunal created its own definition of foreign public bribery on the basis of the OECD Convention on Bribery and UNCAC, and found that a Claimant who comes with 'unclean hands' cannot be heard by an ICSID tribunal. The Tribunal criticised the Respondent's lack of co-operation in the proceedings and the latter's unwillingness to investigate its corrupt officials, and ordered it to make a substantial payment to an international anti-corruption institution.

Concerning burden and standard of proof, *Fraport* is important because the Tribunal stated that if a party has established a *prima facie* case, the burden can shift to the other party to produce rebuttal evidence, even if the ultimate burden of proving the claim or defence is again on the party raising it. On standard of proof, the Tribunal argued that 'clear and convincing' evidence was required for alleged corruption and fraud; circumstantial evidence was considered sufficient.

Overall, in ICSID arbitration involving alleged foreign public bribery, the outcome depends on the specific circumstances as well as on the individual arbitrators.[284] On the one hand, in *Spentex*, the Arbitrators

[284] Abdel Raouf distinguishes a passive, 'eyes shut' approach and a proactive, 'zero tolerance' approach by arbitrators in the face of corruption allegations in investment arbitration (Abdel Raouf 2009, 129 et seq.). On techniques how to avoid addressing bribery by tribunals and parties: Rose 2014, 187 et seq.

dismissed all claims and counterclaims, relying on international anti-corruption conventions, 'red flags' and the 'unclean hands' doctrine; and in *Metal-Tech*, the Arbitrators had the courage to conclude that corruption was sufficiently proven and to deny jurisdiction on the basis of a violation of domestic Uzbek law. In *World Duty Free*, the Arbitrators dismissed the claims as a matter of English, Kenyan and transnational public policy. On the other hand, for instance in *Fraport II*, the Tribunal demonstrated a certain awkwardness to accept bribery. It is possible though that the Respondent in that case raised the bribery defence first and foremost in order to strengthen the main argument: lack of jurisdiction due to a violation of the Philippine Anti-Dummy Law.[285]

5.2 ICSID Cases Involving Fraud Allegations

It is beyond the scope of this text to examine all ICSID cases in which fraudulent behaviour played a role.[286] The three cases presented here are illustrative as they discuss issues of applicable law or evidence in relation to alleged fraud.

5.2.1 Inceysa *v.* El Salvador (*2006*)

The Claimant in this case was Inceysa Vallisoletana SL ('Inceysa'), a company incorporated in Spain; the Respondent was the Republic of El Salvador. In June 2000, the Ministry of the Environment and Natural Resources of El Salvador ('MARN') had organised a public bid for contracting vehicle inspection services, including emission control. Inceysa and five other companies participated in the bid. In October 2000, the first place was awarded to Inceysa and the second place to another company named ICASUR. Inceysa and MARN signed a contract in November 2000. In the following months, Inceysa bought land in El Salvador.

In 2002, after problems arose between the parties, Inceysa repeatedly complained to MARN that the Ministry had hired other companies to provide the services which Inceysa had been hired for.[287] In July 2003, Inceysa filed a request for ICSID arbitration on the basis of the Spain-El Salvador BIT, arguing that El Salvador had unilaterally terminated the contract without justification and indirectly expropriated Inceysa of the

[285] Cf. Llamzon and Sinclair 2015, 468 et seq.; Llamzon 2014, 202 et seq.

[286] For a more complete list and discussion of cases: Llamzon and Sinclair 2015, 472 et seq.

[287] *Inceysa* v. *El Salvador*, paras. 22 et seq.

rights granted to it under the contract.[288] El Salvador objected to the jurisdiction of the ICSID Tribunal, arguing that the BIT protects only investments made in accordance with the host state's law, and alleging that Inceysa had committed fraud.[289]

5.2.1.1 The Fraud Allegations

El Salvador alleged that Inceysa had altered its financial statements, used false documents to misrepresent its business experience, and concealed the association between Inceysa and ICASUR. The Tribunal preliminarily discussed those fraud allegations. From the parties' written and oral submissions, the Tribunal gathered that the financial statements submitted by Inceysa with its tender in the bid for the inspection services contract were false and did not display its true financial condition. The statements differed from those that had been filed with the Commercial Registry of Spain: instead of losses, the statements submitted by Inceysa in the bid showed earnings. In addition, it was proven in the ICSID proceedings that the auditor, who had certified the correctness of Inceysa's financial statements, used false credentials: he was not registered as an authorised auditor in Spain. The Tribunal concluded that this behaviour was 'extremely serious', because a company's financial condition is one of the main factors in a bid.[290]

The Tribunal also looked into Inceysa's assertion that its strategic partner for the inspection services project was a public entity named 'Estación ITV de Alcantarilla', which had more than sixteen years of experience in vehicle inspection. In the course of the ICSID proceedings, Inceysa corrected this and affirmed that its strategic partner was a company named 'ITV Alcantarilla SL'. It was demonstrated that this company was incorporated only four months after Inceysa had submitted its tender in the bid and had no experience in vehicle inspection at all. In fact, it turned out that Inceysa itself had no relevant experience, as its main activity before it participated in the bid was selling women's underwear and shoes.[291]

The Tribunal went on to examine the credentials of Mr Martínez, Inceysa's sole administrator. It was proven beyond reasonable doubt in the ICSID proceedings that two letters, which indicated on the one hand

288 *Inceysa* v. *El Salvador*, paras. 37 et seq.
289 *Inceysa* v. *El Salvador*, paras. 45 et seq., 53 et seq.
290 *Inceysa* v. *El Salvador*, paras. 103 et seq., 110.
291 *Inceysa* v. *El Salvador*, paras. 111 et seq.

his membership to an industry association and on the other hand his participation in vehicle inspection projects, were both false. Inceysa thus presented false information about the experience and capacity of its sole administrator.[292]

Furthermore, it was demonstrated in the proceedings that a financial relationship between Inceysa and ICASUR existed, and that Mr Martínez had acted both as an important official of ICASUR and as the general manager of Inceysa. The existence of this connection had not been disclosed to MARN during the bid, which constituted 'a deceit on one of the central aspects of the bid'.[293]

5.2.1.2 The Jurisdiction Objection

Once it had established that Inceysa had committed fraud, the Tribunal discussed the impact of fraud on ICSID jurisdiction. The Tribunal analysed its competence on the basis of the ICSID Convention and the Spain-El Salvador BIT on the one hand and on the basis of the domestic law of El Salvador on the other. El Salvador argued that it did not consent to submit the present dispute to ICSID jurisdiction. The Tribunal found itself competent to decide on its own jurisdiction (*Kompetenz-Kompetenz*[294]), referring to Article 25 of the ICSID Convention that requires consent in writing by the parties to submit their dispute to ICSID. With reference to the BIT, the Tribunal discussed the limitations to consent and questioned whether under that treaty, only investments made in accordance with the laws of the host state were protected. The Tribunal considered the *travaux préparatoires* of the BIT and held that El Salvador had shown its intent to limit the protection of the BIT to investments made in accordance with its domestic laws: 'any investment made against the laws of El Salvador is outside the protection of the [BIT]'.[295]

Consequently, the Tribunal examined whether Inceysa's investment had been made in accordance with El Salvador's laws. Because the BIT, as law of El Salvador, did not contain substantive rules and referred to the generally recognised principles of international law, the Tribunal first examined those principles.[296] It stated that Inceysa's investment violated the principle of good faith from the beginning, notably Inceysa's presentation of false financial information, its false representations

[292] *Inceysa* v. *El Salvador*, paras. 119 et seq. [293] *Inceysa* v. *El Salvador*, paras. 123 et seq.
[294] Art. 41 ICSID 1965. [295] *Inceysa* v. *El Salvador*, para. 203.
[296] For a definition, the Tribunal turned to Art. 38 ICJ Statute 1945.

about experience and capacity and the concealment of the relationship between Inceysa and ICASUR.[297]

Inceysa's investment also violated the general principle *nemo auditur propriam turpitudinem allegans*, or in this case: nobody can benefit from its own fraud. In the view of the Tribunal, there was clear evidence that 'Inceysa acted improperly in order to be awarded the bid that made its investment possible and, therefore, it cannot be given the protection granted by the BIT.'[298] Furthermore, the Tribunal stated that Inceysa's investment had violated international public policy and the principle that prohibits unlawful enrichment.[299] The Tribunal also looked at El Salvador's investment law and decided that Inceysa could not profit from the rights granted to it under that law, because its investment was illegal.[300] In the Award, the Tribunal unanimously decided to accept El Salvador's objection to ICSID jurisdiction. It imposed on Inceysa the entire Tribunal fees and expenses, and ordered that the parties had to pay their own legal costs.[301]

5.2.1.3 Analysis

Inceysa v. *El Salvador* is one example where the Tribunal denied jurisdiction because the investment was illegal according to the host state's law.[302] Notably, when discussing the legality of the investment, the Tribunal looked at it as one unity and did not split it into different chronological stages. The Tribunal examined the fraud allegations as a preliminary issue, relying on international law to determine fraud, and in particular, on general principles of law, namely the principle of good faith and the principle of *nemo auditur propriam turpitudinem allegans.* The Tribunal also considered that in civil law systems, there is a legal principle that prohibits unlawful enrichment. Furthermore, it argued that the inclusion of an 'in accordance with host state's law' clause in a BIT is a manifestation of international public policy,[303] and stated that the fraudulent investment was contrary to international public policy. The Tribunal did not refer to any specific provisions of El Salvadorean law

[297] *Inceysa* v. *El Salvador*, paras. 230 et seq. [298] *Inceysa* v. *El Salvador*, para. 243.
[299] *Inceysa* v. *El Salvador*, paras. 245 et seq., 253 et seq.
[300] *Inceysa* v. *El Salvador*, paras. 258 et seq., 264. [301] *Inceysa* v. *El Salvador*, para. 339.
[302] Grubenmann 2010, 212 et seq.; Kulick criticises the Tribunal's approach to deny jurisdiction because of a violation of host state's law, arguing that this is a merits issue (Kulick 2012, 322 et seq., 340; see also Kulick and Wendler 2010, 69 et seq.).
[303] *Inceysa* v. *El Salvador*, para. 246.

dealing with fraud (e.g. from the Criminal Code).[304] It also did not discuss burden and standard of proof.

5.2.2 Siag *v.* Egypt *(2009)*

The Claimants in this case were Mr Waguih Elie George Siag ('Mr Siag') and Ms Clorinda Vecchi; the Respondent was the Arab Republic of Egypt. The Claimants were Italian citizens and the principal investors in two companies incorporated under the laws of Egypt: Touristic Investments and Hotels Management Company (SIAG) SAE and Siag Taba Company. In 1989, the Claimants bought land in Egypt at the Red Sea in order to develop a tourist resort. The dispute arose over an alleged expropriation by Egypt of the Claimant's investment, through certain acts and omissions commencing in 1995. In May 2005, the Claimants filed a request for ICSID arbitration on the basis of the Italy-Egypt BIT, claiming compensation.[305]

Egypt raised a number of defences, *inter alia* that Mr Siag was at all relevant times an Egyptian national, which would preclude him from bringing a claim against Egypt under the Italy-Egypt BIT. Although the Tribunal had already rejected this contention in its decision on jurisdiction, Egypt pursued it again in the merits proceedings. It argued that Mr Siag had deceived the Tribunal about the fact that he had lost his Egyptian nationality and acquired Lebanese nationality in 1989.[306]

Mr Siag was born in Egypt in 1962 and was an Egyptian national by birth. In December 1989, he received a certificate of Lebanese nationality and applied in Egypt for permission to acquire it. In March 1990, Egypt acknowledged Mr Siag's acquisition of Lebanese nationality, permitted him to retain Egyptian nationality and exempted him from compulsory military service due to his dual nationality. In June 1990, Mr Siag received a Lebanese passport. He subsequently lost Egyptian nationality because he omitted to notify the Egyptian Interior Ministry within one year that he wished to retain it. Later, he married an Italian citizen and acquired Italian nationality in May 1993.[307]

304 Knahr criticises that the Tribunal, when it examined whether the investment was in accordance with host state's law, relied on general principles of law instead of referring to the relevant provisions of El Salvadorean law (Knahr 2008, 132 et seq.). Moloo and Khachaturian, on the other hand, argue that El Salvadorean law referred the Tribunal to such international legal principles (Moloo and Khachaturian 2011, 1479 et seq.).

305 *Siag* v. *Egypt*, paras. 1 et seq., 12 et seq.

306 *Siag* v. *Egypt*, paras. 219 et seq.

307 *Siag* v. *Egypt*, paras. 14 et seq.

5.2.2.1 Egypt's Negative Nationality Defence: Burden of Proof

One of the issues the Tribunal had to deal with was Egypt's allegation that Mr Siag had never lost his Egyptian nationality and thus did not fulfil the negative nationality requirement of Article 25(2)(a) of the ICSID Convention.[308]

According to the Tribunal, the general rule – that the Claimant bears the burden of proof for the facts it alleges, and the Respondent has to prove its defences – meant for the present case: '[W]hile it is clear that the burden of proof in respect of all jurisdictional objections lies with Egypt, at the merits phase Mr Siag must first prove on the balance of probabilities that he acquired Lebanese nationality.'[309] The Tribunal noted that Mr Siag had given extensive *prima facie* evidence of his Lebanese nationality, including Lebanese passports issued in 1990 and 1992. He was able to convince the Tribunal that he had acquired Lebanese nationality, whereby he had satisfied his evidentiary burden.

Accordingly, the Claimants argued that it was on Egypt to prove that Mr Siag had acquired Lebanese nationality on the basis of fraud, forgery or other misconduct, and that it was not on Mr Siag to disprove this. Egypt, however, asserted that it had proven that Mr Siag was not a Lebanese national, and that the burden had shifted. The Tribunal concluded that Egypt had to prove all its jurisdictional objections and substantive defences:

> Because negative evidence is very often more difficult to assert than positive evidence, the reversal of the burden of proof may make it almost impossible for the allegedly fraudulent party to defend itself, thus violating due process standards. It is for this reason that Tribunals have rarely shifted the burden of proof. There are no special circumstances or good reasons for doing so in this case.[310]

The Tribunal found that Egypt had to prove 'fraud, deception, or other dishonest behaviour'. Egypt had stated in its submissions that there had been fraud on the Tribunal. In order to successfully object to the Tribunal's jurisdiction (as against the Tribunal's earlier ruling on jurisdiction), Egypt had to prove that Mr Siag did not lose his Egyptian nationality.[311]

[308] See Schreuer et al. 2009, Art. 25 N 664 et seq. [309] *Siag* v. *Egypt*, para. 316.
[310] *Siag* v. *Egypt*, para. 317. [311] *Siag* v. *Egypt*, paras. 318 et seq.

5.2.2.2 Standard of Proof

The Tribunal then turned to the applicable standard of proof. The Claimants argued that a higher standard of proof applied to the jurisdictional objection because it was based on alleged fraud, and such claims were 'typically held to a heavy standard of proof'. Egypt only submitted that Mr Siag carried the burden of proof, but did not argue that a lower standard of proof than the one suggested by the Claimants should apply. According to the Claimants, a 'clear and convincing evidence' standard should apply that was 'somewhere between the traditional civil standard of "preponderance of the evidence" (otherwise known as the "balance of probabilities"), and the criminal standard of "beyond reasonable doubt"'.[312] The Tribunal agreed with the Claimants' submission, arguing that in most legal systems, fraud allegations were held to a high standard of proof and that the same applied in international proceedings, referring to cases cited by the Claimants including the *Wena* v. *Egypt* Award.[313]

5.2.2.3 Did Mr Siag Obtain Lebanese Nationality by Fraud?

With regard to the alleged fraud, Egypt offered several grounds based on a number of documents. Egypt submitted, *inter alia*, that there was no registration of Mr Siag in Lebanon and that his Lebanese passports were genuine, but based on an invalid document, namely Mr Siag's Individual Record that carried a registry number that had not yet been reached. Egypt produced four letters of Lebanese officials from late 2007 and early 2008 to substantiate its fraud allegations.

Mr Siag argued that his Lebanese nationality was proven by four contemporaneous documents (his Individual Record, nationality certificate and two passports), and that those documents should carry greater weight than Egypt's evidence that had been produced for the purpose of the ongoing legal dispute. Referring to EU, UN and WHO reports, he submitted that the Lebanese civil registry was deficient and incomplete and 'that the absence of a 19-year old record was not proof of anything, let alone fraud'.[314]

312 *Siag* v. *Egypt*, para. 325.

313 That Award, however, only states that the Respondent carried the burden of proof for its affirmative defence (*Wena* v. *Egypt*, paras. 117, 132), and does not discuss standard of proof.

314 *Siag* v. *Egypt*, paras. 334 et seq., 341.

The Tribunal considered the Claimant's evidence for the existing inherent difficulties in the Lebanese registration system as compelling. It gave little weight to the statements of Egypt's witnesses and argued that the reports from respected institutions provided an 'entirely plausible alternative explanation' of why Mr Siag's registration was missing: 'In the face of Claimant's evidence, both as to Mr Siag's Lebanese nationality and as to the state of Lebanon's civil registry, Egypt's evidence falls well short of the required standard.'[315]

The Tribunal also rejected Egypt's other grounds and concluded that there was insufficient evidence to prove fraud, forgery, deception or other misconduct by Mr Siag. Consequently, Egypt's objection to jurisdiction based on the negative nationality requirement of Article 25(2)(a) of the ICSID Convention failed.[316] In the Award, the Tribunal affirmed its jurisdiction because Mr Siag had not been an Egyptian national at all relevant times. It found that Egypt had unlawfully expropriated the Claimants' investment and thus breached the Italy-Egypt BIT. It ordered Egypt to pay US$74.5 million in compensation, as well as US$6 million for legal costs, to the Claimants.[317]

5.2.2.4 The Dissenting Opinion of Professor Vicuña

One member of the Tribunal, Professor Vicuña, disagreed with the others regarding the applicable burden of proof:

> The burden of proof is, in my understanding, still on the Claimant who has to prove that it holds the nationality it claims to have and this it has failed to do in spite of having been directed by the Tribunal to supply the appropriate certification. The Award has taken a different view on this matter in the belief that it is for Egypt to prove fraud, deception or other dishonest behaviour, a proof that would not have been met. While I do not disagree with the need to so prove, I respectfully disagree in respect of the conclusion that this did not happen. I believe that Egypt has so proven by providing ample official documentation on the matter.[318]

Professor Vicuña also dissented on the applicable standard of proof. While the majority of the Tribunal found that a 'clear and convincing evidence' standard should apply, he argued that arbitration tribunals should be

[315] *Siag* v. *Egypt*, para. 346. [316] *Siag* v. *Egypt*, paras. 356 et seq.
[317] *Siag* v. *Egypt*, para. 631.
[318] *Siag* v. *Egypt*, Dissenting Opinion of Professor Francisco Orrego Vicuña, 3 et seq.

> free to choose the most relevant rules in accordance with the circumstances of the case and the nature of the facts involved, as it has been increasingly recognized ... The facts of this case, difficult as they are to establish with absolute certainty, could be best judged under a standard of proof allowing the Tribunal 'discretion in inferring from a collection of concordant circumstantial evidence (*faisceau d'indices*) the facts at which the various indices are directed'.[319]

Professor Vicuña found that the Tribunal should have relied on the information of the Lebanese officials, which should have prevailed over the information of Mr Siag. Otherwise, the assistance of Interpol should have been requested to establish the facts. Professor Vicuña was convinced that 'money changed hands improperly so as to obtain a certificate of a non-existent registration'.[320] He also referred to the *World Duty Free* case and the aim to eradicate domestic and transnational corruption, concluding that the claim should have been dismissed on the merits.[321]

5.2.2.5 Analysis

In *Siag* v. *Egypt*, the Tribunal extensively discussed burden and standard of proof with regard to Egypt's fraud allegations. Regarding burden of proof, the Tribunal argued that it was much more difficult to assert negative evidence than positive evidence, or in other words, it is hard for the allegedly fraudulent party to produce evidence that it actually did not commit the fraud. Therefore, the Tribunal did not accept a reversal of the burden of proof in this case. It did not ask Mr Siag to disprove Egypt's defence that he was at all relevant times an Egyptian national (which would have precluded him from bringing a claim against Egypt because of the negative nationality requirement of Article 25(2)(a) of the ICSID Convention).

Egypt referred to the Egyptian Nationality Law, but not to any criminal code with regard to its fraud allegations. The Tribunal argued that in order to succeed with its defence, Egypt had to prove fraud, deception or other dishonest behaviour. Regarding standard of proof, the Tribunal required clear and convincing evidence. Notably Professor Vicuña dissented with the majority of the Tribunal both on the issue of burden as well as of standard of proof. He argued that Mr Siag carried the burden to prove his nationality and had not discharged of it, and that Egypt on the

[319] *Siag* v. *Egypt*, Dissenting Opinion of Professor Francisco Orrego Vicuña, 4.
[320] *Siag* v. *Egypt*, Dissenting Opinion of Professor Francisco Orrego Vicuña, 4.
[321] *Siag* v. *Egypt*, Dissenting Opinion of Professor Francisco Orrego Vicuña, 4 et seq.

other hand had proven the fraud by submitting official documentation. On standard of proof, he opposed to applying a rigid 'clear and convincing evidence' formula, arguing that the Tribunal should have had discretion in inferring from circumstantial evidence. Furthermore, Professor Vicuña argued that the assistance of Interpol could have been sought to establish the facts.[322]

5.2.3 Hamester *v.* Ghana *(2010)*

The Claimant in this case was Gustav F W Hamester GmbH & Co KG ('Hamester'), a company incorporated in Germany; the Respondent was the Republic of Ghana. In 1992, Hamester (through its predecessor company Schröder) concluded a joint-venture agreement ('JVA') with the Ghana Cocoa Board ('Cocobod'). Through the JVA, Hamester and Cocobod formed West African Mills Company Limited ('Wamco I'), a company under the laws of Ghana. The aim of the JVA was to reactivate an old cocoa-processing factory located in Ghana that was owned by Cocobod. Wamco I was to take over the assets and titles of the old factory; Hamester was to provide the technology, know-how and funding to modernise Wamco I; and Ghana brought in the assets of the old factory and supplied the cocoa beans to be processed at the plant. Wamco I subsequently purchased assets in other old cocoa-processing factories in Ghana from Cocobod, setting up Wamco II and III (collectively referred to as 'Wamco').[323]

In short, the dispute arose over alleged breaches of the JVA and the Germany-Ghana BIT. Hamester claimed damages for such alleged breaches by Ghana (in particular the suspension of delivery of cocoa beans). Ghana objected to ICSID jurisdiction and also rejected Hamester's claims on the merits. The dispute was based on the Germany-Ghana BIT.[324]

5.2.3.1 Ghana's Fraud Objection to Jurisdiction

Ghana objected to the Tribunal's jurisdiction *inter alia* with the argument that the investment was tainted with substantial fraud both at its initiation and throughout its performance over the years, and therefore there was no investment in accordance with Ghanaian law under Article 10 of the Germany-Ghana BIT.[325]

[322] See also Llamzon 2014, 180 et seq.
[323] *Hamester* v. *Ghana*, paras. 3 et seq., 22 et seq.
[324] *Hamester* v. *Ghana*, paras. 1, 68 et seq., 80 et seq.
[325] *Hamester* v. *Ghana*, para. 96.

Ghana alleged that there was fraudulent oppression by the majority shareholder (Hamester) of the minority shareholder (Cocobod). The alleged oppression included the abuse of control by Hamester over Wamco (taking the latter's output at artificially low prices and selling it to own customers with substantial profit); Hamester's charging of sales fees and commissions to Wamco – for the sale of Wamco's output to itself; the sale of property to Wamco (and transfer of the sale price to a director of Wamco) without Board approval; the transfer of 120,000 shares of a Belgian chocolate company by Hamester to Wamco to set off debts and later repurchase at a significant loss for Wamco, again without Board approval; the payment by Wamco of the transfer fee for a Ghanaian football player to his Ghanaian football club and the Ghana Football Association, although the German football club (sponsored by Hamester) that bought the player should have paid the transfer fee; and false invoices.[326]

Hamester agreed that an investment had to be made in 'substantial compliance' with host state law, arguing that its investment had fully complied with Ghanaian law. Hamester in particular argued that the JVA had never foreseen profit sharing with Cocobod; and that Ghana's fraud allegations were not valid defences to BIT claims, but matters of company law that, if established, had to be contested in Ghanaian courts.[327]

5.2.3.2 Timing of Legality of the Investment

The Tribunal found that Article 10 of the Germany-Ghana BIT applicable in this case made a difference between legality of the investment at its initiation and legality during its performance: '[O]n the wording of this BIT, the legality of the creation of the investment is a jurisdictional issue; the legality of the investor's conduct during the life of the investment is a merits issue.'[328] On this basis, the Tribunal considered at the jurisdictional phase only those fraud allegations that related to the initiation of the investment, and not the allegations of fraudulent conduct that arose during the performance of the investment. It examined whether Hamester procured the signing of the JVA on the basis of fraud.[329] In short, Ghana argued that Hamester had presented false invoices for machinery to be delivered to Wamco at the initiation of

[326] *Hamester* v. *Ghana*, paras. 99 et seq. [327] *Hamester* v. *Ghana*, paras. 114 et seq., 119.

[328] *Hamester* v. *Ghana*, para. 127. The Tribunal also cited the *Fraport* v. *Philippines I* Award in this context, stating that this Award had been particularly clear on that issue.

[329] *Hamester* v. *Ghana*, para. 129.

the investment and breached section 131 of the Ghanaian Criminal Code as well as common law rules against fraud.[330]

5.2.3.3 Burden of Proof Regarding the Fraud Objection to Jurisdiction

The Tribunal found that Ghana had not fully met its burden of proof with regard to its fraud allegations. Although there was one invoice to Cocobod that was clearly overstated, and there might have been more, the Tribunal argued that no more evidence had been produced with regard to fraud in the initial investment: 'The Tribunal can only decide on substantiated facts, and cannot base itself on inferences.'[331] The Tribunal also stated that there was no conclusive evidence proving that the alleged fraud was decisive for the securing of the JVA. In conclusion, the Tribunal affirmed its jurisdiction.[332]

5.2.3.4 Fraud Allegations at the Merits Stage?

At the merits stage, the Tribunal did not examine the fraud allegations raised by Ghana that related to the performance of the investment, but dismissed Hamester's claims on other grounds. In the Award, the Tribunal unanimously decided that it had jurisdiction over the dispute, but dismissed all claims because certain acts of Cocobod were not attributable to Ghana; and because the acts of Ghana did not amount to a violation of the BIT.[333]

5.2.3.5 Analysis

Hamester v. *Ghana* of 2010 touches upon an issue that was already raised in the *Fraport* v. *Philippines I* Award of 2007 and comes up again later in *Niko* v. *Bangladesh* (2013), *Metal-Tech* v. *Uzbekistan* (2013) and *Fraport* v. *Philippines II* (2014): does it make a difference whether the illegality occurs at the initiation of an investment, or whether it occurs in the course of its performance? On the basis of Article 10 of the Germany-Ghana BIT, the Tribunal did make such a distinction and argued that illegality at the initial stage of an investment results in a denial of jurisdiction by an ICSID Tribunal; whereas illegality during the performance of an investment is an issue to be discussed at the merits stage.

Ghana alleged that at the initial stage of the investment, Hamester (that was obliged under the JVA to provide technology, know-how and

[330] *Hamester* v. *Ghana*, paras. 130 et seq.
[331] *Hamester* v. *Ghana*, paras. 132 et seq.
[332] *Hamester* v. *Ghana*, paras. 135, 139.
[333] *Hamester* v. *Ghana*, para. 362.

funding) had presented false invoices for machinery that was transferred to Wamco, and had thereby breached the Ghanaian Criminal Code as well as common law. The Tribunal found, however, that Ghana had not fully discharged its burden of proof; in particular, there was no conclusive evidence that the JVA was secured due to the alleged fraud. The Tribunal therefore affirmed jurisdiction; but it did not examine Ghana's fraud allegations relating to the performance of the investment at the merits stage, as it dismissed Hamester's claims on other grounds.

This outcome raises the same questions as discussed earlier in the context of awards dealing with foreign public bribery: when is the initiation phase of an investment finished; and is there no 'unity of investment'? Instead of splitting an investment up into chronological phases, it seems preferable to analyse whether the investment breaches core provisions of the host state's criminal or administrative law, and whether this happens on a large scale or is just a minor infringement.[334]

5.2.4 Summary

In *Inceysa* v. *El Salvador*, the Tribunal looked at the investment as one unity and did not distinguish the initiation and the operation of the investment with regard to the fraud allegations. The Tribunal denied jurisdiction because the investment was not in accordance with the host state's law as required by the BIT, and therefore not protected by the treaty. The Tribunal did not rely on any provisions of El Salvadorean criminal law, but on general principles of law.

Siag v. *Egypt* discusses burden and standard of proof in relation to alleged fraud by the Claimant in detail. The Tribunal found that the Respondent had to prove its objection to jurisdiction. As the Claimants had given *prima facie* evidence and thereby satisfied the evidentiary burden, the Tribunal did not accept any burden shifting, as requested by the Respondent, and did not ask the Claimant to disprove the Respondent's objection, as this would have violated due process standards. The Tribunal also argued that clear and convincing evidence was required with regard to the alleged fraud. One member of the Tribunal disagreed with the majority's findings on burden and standard of proof.

Hamester v. *Ghana* makes the same distinction between the initiation and the operation of an investment when illegality is alleged as the

[334] See discussion in Chapter 10.

Niko v. *Bangladesh*, *Metal-Tech* v. *Uzbekistan* and *Fraport* v. *Philippines* Awards. As *Metal-Tech* and *Fraport*, *Hamester* was a treaty-based arbitration. The Respondent argued that, at the initiation of the investment, the Claimant's behaviour had breached a provision of the Ghanaian Criminal Code as well as common law rules against fraud. The Tribunal found, however, that the Respondent had not fully met its burden of proof in this regard, and affirmed its jurisdiction.

6

Commercial Arbitration

Under the heading 'commercial arbitration', this chapter discusses a selection of ICC cases (and one *ad hoc* arbitration) that involve allegations of criminal behaviour. The vast majority of cases deal with alleged foreign public bribery. Only one fraud and one money-laundering case are discussed.[1] The selected cases are considered illustrative to discuss issues of applicable law and evidence when criminal allegations arise, but the listing is not exhaustive. On the one hand, it is unclear how many commercial arbitration cases involving allegations of criminal behaviour are never published; on the other hand, cases that were arbitrated under others than the ICC Rules are not included. The cases are arranged chronologically, in order to show the emerging patterns of how tribunals handle them.

6.1 ICC Cases Involving Foreign Public Bribery Allegations

6.1.1 The Lagergren *Case (ICC Case No. 1110 of 1963)*

The Claimant in this case (Mr X) was an Argentine engineer and businessman in Buenos Aires. The Respondent (Company A) was a wholly owned UK daughter company of Company B. The shares of Company B were held by Company C.

In 1950, the Argentine authorities planned to increase the production of electrical power in the region of Buenos Aires. The Respondent was interested in supplying the electrical equipment for this project. He asked the Claimant to exercise his influence with the politicians of the Peronista

[1] This is because a string of ICC cases involving alleged foreign public bribery is published, which is not the case with fraud or money laundering. Regarding private bribery, no published cases were found, but the author knows of an arbitration involving such allegations.

government, as well as in commercial and industrial circles, so that orders would be placed with the Respondent. In 1950, the parties concluded an oral agreement (supported by letters)[2] that the Respondent would pay a commission to Mr X for any contract which was awarded to it because of Mr X's efforts. The agreement was reaffirmed in 1953. Two years later, Mr X left Argentina for Germany, apparently for medical reasons. In 1958, after a contract was awarded to the Respondent and another contract to Company C which indirectly held the shares of the Respondent, Mr X claimed his commission. The Respondent refused to pay. The parties then concluded a written agreement to submit their dispute to arbitration subject to the ICC Rules, and chose Paris as the seat of the arbitration.[3]

The Claimant argued that his efforts prior to his departure from Argentina (in June 1955) led to the award of the 1958 contracts. He also argued that the contract awarded to the Respondent himself and the contract awarded to Company C both had to be regarded as awarded to the Respondent, and that he should receive his 10 per cent commission for both contracts. Alternatively, he would reduce his commission claim to the one contract awarded to the Respondent. Of the 10 per cent commission, only 2 per cent were for Mr X himself, the rest would go to his collaborators.[4]

The Respondent, on the other hand, argued that the contracts awarded to him were outside the scope of the commission agreements of 1950 and 1953 with Mr X, and by no means the result of his efforts. He argued that Mr X, if he had remained in Argentina, would not have been *persona grata* with the new military regime that came to power after the overthrow of Perón in September 1955.[5]

The Sole Arbitrator in this case, Judge Lagergren, did not get to the merits stage, but already declined jurisdiction. Although both parties affirmed his 'competence to consider and decide their case',[6] he tested his jurisdiction *proprio motu*. He referred to Article V 2. (b) of the New York Convention 1958, according to which recognition or enforcement of an award on the domestic level may be refused if the

[2] Those letters are quoted in the original award, which is reproduced in Wetter 1994, Annex, 282 et seq.

[3] ICC Case No. 1110, 282 et seq.

[4] ICC Case No. 1110, 285 et seq., 288.

[5] ICC Case No. 1110, 286. For a summary of the facts of the case, see also Lew 1978, 553; Van den Berg 1996.

[6] ICC Case No. 1110, 291.

competent authority finds that this would be contrary to the public policy of the enforcing country.

The parties submitted that Lagergren could not refuse jurisdiction, because the possible offence would only be against Argentine public policy, where the contracts had their *situs*, and not against public policy in France, to which the contracts had no connection, but where the arbitration took place. Lagergren, however, pursued three lines of argument to show that he did not have jurisdiction in this case.

6.1.1.1 Arbitrability According to the French Code of Civil Procedure

Lagergren argued that there were good reasons to treat the agreement to arbitrate as separate from the underlying contract between the parties, and governed by French law.[7] He found that the ICC Arbitration Rules did not contain a provision whether the present case was arbitrable, and since the parties had not chosen any law of procedure, the law of the country where the arbitration was held (i.e. French law) would apply.

The French Code of Civil Procedure foresaw that cases involving French public policy should be treated by ordinary courts. Regarding the breach of foreign laws, Lagergren argued that in cases of infringements of foreign tax law and the like, French public policy was not touched upon; however, cases of 'more serious violations of foreign laws involving grave offences to good morals' would involve French public policy.[8] Lagergren concluded that, due to the gravity of the offences, 'French law cannot admit this case to be settled by arbitration, regardless of whether the adventure was located in France or elsewhere.'[9]

6.1.1.2 Arbitrability According to the Argentine Code of Procedure

Judge Lagergren continued to a second line of argument. According to the 1957 Amsterdam Resolution of the Institut de Droit International on arbitration in private international law, the law applicable to the merits of a case determines whether or not a case is arbitrable. As Argentine law was chosen by the parties to govern the commission agreement between Mr X and the Respondent, it should also apply to the question of arbitrability.[10] The Argentine Code of Procedure said that 'all questions which affect good morals ("la moral y buenas costumbras") are excluded

[7] ICC Case No. 1110, 291. [8] ICC Case No. 1110, 292. [9] ICC Case No. 1110, 292.
[10] ICC Case No. 1110, 292 et seq.

from arbitration'. Judge Lagergren concluded that arbitral jurisdiction was not an option for the dispute at hand. He also referred to Argentine Criminal Law that made bribery a criminal offence.[11]

6.1.1.3 Arbitrability According to General Principles of Law

Lastly, Judge Lagergren referred to the general principle of law that 'contracts which seriously violate *bonos mores* or international public policy are invalid or at least unenforceable and . . . cannot be sanctioned by courts or arbitrators'. Lagergren concluded that this principle was particularly apt in international arbitration that has no *lex fori*.[12]

6.1.1.4 The Impact of Corruption and International Public Policy

Considering the facts of the case, Lagergren decided that it was 'plainly established from the evidence taken by me that the agreement between the parties contemplated the bribing of Argentine officials for the purpose of obtaining the hoped-for business'.[13] While he accepted that during the Perón regime, paying bribes was a common problem for anyone who wanted to do business in Argentina and this practice was at least tolerated at that time, he also stated that the amounts of money involved in this case made it impossible to just overlook the commission payments. He mentioned the 'destructive effect [of amounts of this magnitude] on the business pattern with consequent impairment of industrial progress',[14] and described such corruption as 'contrary . . . to an international public policy common to the community of nations'.[15]

In the Award, Lagergren declined jurisdiction, seeking guidance 'from general principles denying arbitrators to entertain disputes of this nature rather than from any national rules on arbitrability'.[16] Despite his earlier argumentation about the application of French or Argentine law, Judge Lagergren thus based his Award on 'general principles'.

6.1.1.5 Analysis

The Award was subsequently criticised: it was argued that the arbitral clause has to be treated separately from the main contract[17] and that nullity of the main contract does not cause the arbitral clause to

[11] ICC Case No. 1110, 293. [12] ICC Case No. 1110, 293. [13] ICC Case No. 1110, 293.
[14] ICC Case No. 1110, 294. [15] ICC Case No. 1110, 294. [16] ICC Case No. 1110, 294.
[17] For a definition of the separability principle, see discussion in Chapter 2.

be void.[18] It was emphasised that if the arbitral tribunal declines jurisdiction, there is a risk that it will be impossible for the parties to obtain a judgment. This would amount to a denial of justice.[19] The question whether a bribe was paid or not could only be answered if evidence was taken, which could well be done by an arbitral tribunal.[20]

However, it has also been argued that Judge Lagergren's opinion was misrepresented for thirty years and that commentators relied on inaccurate, secondary sources. Lagergren well understood his competence to examine his jurisdiction and the separability of the arbitral clause. As in this case, the arbitration agreement was wholly separate from the main contract, Lagergren had no reason to make explicit reference to the separability principle. What he did, was deny jurisdiction because he considered the case as not arbitrable.[21] Lagergren's point was that such a case was not arbitrable, as it was outside the jurisdiction of any national or international court or tribunal:

> The effect of international public policy was to deny the parties a hearing on their dispute. There was no forum law to uphold nor any foreign law to reject. Rather it was the object of the contract which was considered objectionable with the effect of removing the contract from the realm of legal regulation. This was not to say that the contract was illegal, only that it was outside the jurisdiction of and unenforceable in every national as well as the international legal systems.[22]

Due to the clear facts, Lagergren did not see any problem to skip a few steps: instead of affirming jurisdiction and declaring the main contract invalid at the merits stage, he denied jurisdiction for such a contract from the outset.[23]

Such a decision can only be maintained if on the one hand, the bribery allegations are obvious and not disputed by the parties and the evidence is clear and unambiguous. On the other hand, the dispute between the parties was about the bribe contract between Mr X and the Respondent, Company A, not about the contract between Company A and the Argentine State. While the legal consequences of a bribe contract depend on the applicable law, in many jurisdictions, it is undisputed that such a contract is null and void *ab initio*.

[18] In lieu of many, see BGE 119 II 380, 385 that described the opinion of Judge Lagergren as 'dépassée'; and ICC Case No. 3916, with the relevant passage quoted in El Kosheri and Leboulanger 1984, 14.

[19] ICC Case No. 3916, 934.

[20] BGE 119 II 380, 385.

[21] Wetter 1994, 280.

[22] Lew 1978, 555.

[23] Cf. Pieth 2011, 1378; Cremades and Cairns 2003b, 82.

Nowadays, such a clear situation regarding the evidence will hardly ever be at stake. Parties will be prudent to conceal bribe payments, as foreign bribery laws have become more sophisticated and law enforcement is stepping up. Arbitrators will have to confirm jurisdiction and enter the merits of the case in order to hear the parties' arguments and take the evidence. An exception resulting in a denial of jurisdiction would be a bribery-tainted, and therefore invalid, arbitration agreement. Judge Lagergren's Award is interesting for the purposes of this text, as it presents a viable alternative to deal with bribery if the parties' positions and the evidence are clear.[24] Also, it establishes that bribery is against international public policy and points out that bribery breaching foreign laws can infringe French public policy.

6.1.2 ICC Case No. 3916 (1982)

The Claimant in this case was the director of a department of the Iranian state; the Defendant was a Greek company. According to the contract concluded by the parties in Tehran, the Claimant, acting on behalf of a 'group', was to assist the Defendant through information, advice and actions to obtain orders from various administrative entities of the Iranian state. The Defendant was to remunerate the Claimant with a commission of at least 2 per cent of the value of each contract that was signed. The Defendant obtained several contracts with the Iranian administration, but the 1979 Revolution put an end to the activities of the Greek company in Iran, resulting in a considerable loss for the company. The Defendant only paid part of the promised commissions to the Claimant, corresponding to the payments the company had received from the Iranian state.[25]

6.1.2.1 Evidence for Bribery

The Sole Arbitrator in this case took note that the Claimant had been able to get contracts for the Greek company with astonishing rapidness, and that the Claimant had refused to explain the nature of his intervention or the composition of his 'group'. The Arbitrator also emphasised that during the years when the Greek company was active in Iran, it was almost impossible to obtain contracts for public works without resorting to bribe payments or to trading in influence. The Arbitrator concluded that the activity of the Claimant could only have been to exercise his

[24] Philip 2003, 148. [25] ICC Case No. 3916, 932.

influence over the persons who decided to whom the Iranian state would award contracts for public works.[26]

6.1.2.2 Legal Consequences of a Bribery Pact

The Arbitrator decided that French and Iranian laws were applicable in this case. According to both laws, the bribery pact between the Iranian director and the Greek company was null and void. The Arbitrator noted that a number of anti-corruption laws were in force in Iran. The Arbitrator also referred to ICC Case No. 1110, arguing that bribe agreements were contrary to international public policy and therefore invalid or at least unenforceable. He concluded that even if corrupt practices were generally accepted in a certain country at a certain time, from the point of view of good governance and business ethics, one could not close one's eyes to the destructive effect of such practices. The Arbitrator stated that the rule of *nemo auditur propriam turpitudinem allegans* (no one may base a legal claim on its own unlawful act) applies in two ways: it can paralyse the application of an illegal contract. However, after the execution of such a contract, the rule can also paralyse any claims for restitution.[27]

In the Award, the Arbitrator rejected the Claimant's claim and ordered him to pay the costs of the arbitration (except the Respondent's legal fees, according to an agreement between the parties).

6.1.2.3 Analysis

The Sole Arbitrator did not examine bribery to the last detail in this case. For instance, he apparently did not question whether bribes were actually paid, or who the recipients of the bribe payments were. He concluded, on the basis of circumstantial evidence, that the Claimant had influenced the award of contracts for public works. Therefore, the Arbitrator declared the contract between the Iranian director and the Greek company as null and void.[28]

6.1.3 ICC Case No. 4145 (1983, 1984 and 1986)

The Claimant in this case was an establishment of a Middle Eastern country X. The Defendant was a South Asian construction company trying to enter the construction market in country X. In 1978, a ministry

[26] ICC Case No. 3916, 931 et seq. [27] ICC Case No. 3916, 931 et seq.

[28] See also ICC Case No. 3913 of 1981, where a commission of 8 per cent was at stake. The Tribunal concluded that the purpose of the contract was the payment of 'kickbacks' and that the bribery pact was null and void under French law.

of Middle Eastern country X called for tenders for a construction project, and the Defendant was eager to get the contract. It concluded a consultancy agreement with the Claimant, according to which the Claimant would represent the Defendant in the promotion and contracting of the construction projects. The Claimant should 'provide [the Defendant] with such counsel, guidance liaison assistance, facilities, value engineering, complete tender studies, inspections of site, or any additional service as shall be reasonably necessary and required from a Consultant and shall, in general use its best efforts to promote and further the sale of the [construction project]'.[29]

In early 1979, the Defendant was awarded the construction project with a value of US$374 million, and subsequently paid US$50 million to the Claimant, expressing his sincere thanks for excellent efforts. In the same year, the two parties signed an amendment to the consultancy agreement, as the Defendant negotiated an extension of its original construction contract, which it received in 1980. Additional works with a value of approx. US$54.5 million were awarded to the Defendant.

The Claimant complained that with the US$50 million, it had not received the full amount to which it was entitled, and that it should also receive compensation for the extension of the original contract. The Defendant refused to pay anything more, and in 1981, the Claimant submitted the case to the ICC for arbitration (according to a clause in the consultancy agreement), demanding the payment of US$16.5 million. The place of the arbitration was Vienna.[30] The Arbitral Tribunal rendered two Interim Awards (in 1983 on jurisdiction and in 1984 on validity of the consultancy agreement) and a Final Award (in 1986). The consultancy agreement was governed by Swiss law. Issues of bribery were discussed in the Second Interim Award.

6.1.3.1 Not Even Circumstantial Evidence for Bribery

The Defendant argued that the consultancy agreement was null and void because of bribery and extortion. The Arbitral Tribunal applied the Swiss Code of Obligations (SCO) and stated that, if the real intention of the parties (which is the one that has to be considered, not an incorrect statement[31]) was not a consultancy agreement, but an agreement for bribery, and if both parties agreed on this, the agreement would be null and void.[32] However, the Tribunal found that

[29] ICC Case No. 4145, Yearbook, 97 et seq.

[30] ICC Case No. 4145, Yearbook, 97 et seq.; Crivellaro 2003, 122 et seq.

[31] Art. 18 SCO.

[32] Art. 20 SCO.

> The defendant's accusation is not supported by direct evidence or even circumstantial evidence to be retained as convincing. In this respect, it must be stressed that, following general principles of interpretation . . . a fact can be considered as proven even by the way of circumstantial evidence. However, such circumstantial evidence must lead to a very high probability. This is not the case in the present litigation:
>
> - The Agreement obviously does not mention any bribery;
> - Mr. A – the own defendant's principal witness – who was the man who signed the Agreement on behalf of defendant and with whom it was essentially discussed, categorically denied that any bribery was ever intended (three times: 'No').
>
> His declaration is of the utmost importance if one considers that Mr. A's declarations had been carefully prepared in advance . . . and that it was decisive for the defendant's thesis that the answer to such a question would be: 'Yes'.[33]

The Tribunal also argued that the increase in the final price of the contract was due to additional work performed by the Defendant, and that the ministry considerably cut down the final price. Furthermore, the construction projects were constantly supervised by a World Bank team. They also saw no material evidence that the Defendant would have been a victim of extortion.[34]

6.1.3.2 The True Object of the Agreement

In accordance with Art. 18 SCO, the Arbitral Tribunal then determined the true object of the (consultancy) agreement. One provision of the agreement was that the Claimant was paid on a contingency basis, and his compensation depended on a result, namely the awarding of the construction projects to the Defendant. The Tribunal concluded from this, and other elements, that the agreement was in fact an intermediary or brokerage agreement. Such agreements are valid and regulated under Swiss law.[35]

As the agreement was valid (even though an intermediary and not a consultancy agreement), the Arbitral Tribunal finally ruled in the Award that the Defendant had to pay the Claimant US$1.5 million with interest.[36]

6.1.3.3 Analysis

Swiss law was applicable to the consultancy (or rather intermediary) agreement in this case. The Tribunal referred to the Swiss Code of

[33] ICC Case No. 4145, Yearbook, 102. [34] ICC Case No. 4145, Yearbook, 103.

[35] Arts. 412 et seq. SCO; ICC Case No. 4145, Yearbook, 104 et seq.

[36] ICC Case No. 4145, Yearbook, 99, 107 et seq.

Obligations and the Swiss Civil Code, but not to the Swiss Criminal Code (or the criminal law of country X), with regard to the bribery allegations. It also did not refer to any provisions of Swiss procedural law. The Swiss Criminal Code contained provisions on domestic bribery (Articles 288 and 315 of the former Criminal Code), but not on foreign public bribery at that time. International conventions against corruption did not play any role in this case (they were not yet in force).

The Tribunal did not find any circumstantial evidence for bribery, relying heavily on the statement of the Defendant's principal witness (Mr A), who clearly stated that there was no bribery involved in this case. However, it is not very surprising that Mr A, who signed the intermediary agreement, would deny that any bribery was ever intended as he possibly would have incriminated himself. The Tribunal did not really discuss burden and standard of proof, but stated that circumstantial evidence that resulted in very high probability was sufficient to prove a fact.

From today's point of view, it appears that the very high amount of the intermediary's initial commission (US$50 million when the value of the awarded contracts was US$374 million, i.e. approximately 13.7 per cent) and of the commission claimed additionally (US$16.5 million) are indicators that bribes were paid. Also, it is questionable whether the services rendered by the intermediary were sufficiently documented to explain such a high commission. One would also have to consider whether bribery is endemic or not in Middle Eastern country X.

6.1.4 Hilmarton *v.* OTV *(ICC Case No. 5622 of 1988)*

The Claimant in this case was a broker, the English company Hilmarton. The Respondent was a contractor, the French company Omnium de Traitement et de Valorisation ('OTV'). The place of the arbitration was Geneva.[37]

In response to a tender called by the Algerian authorities, OTV took part in the bidding process and submitted an offer. In order to increase its chances of success, OTV concluded a Protocol of Agreement with Hilmarton. According to its terms, Hilmarton should give OTV legal and fiscal advice and co-ordinate its subcontractors. In return, OTV was to pay Hilmarton 4 per cent of the price of the construction contract

[37] Crivellaro 2003, 124.

that OTV would conclude with the Algerian authorities if the bid was successful. When the contract with the Algerian authorities was subsequently awarded to OTV, it paid 50 per cent of the agreed fee to Hilmarton, but refused to pay the rest. As the Protocol of Agreement contained an ICC arbitration clause, Hilmarton initiated arbitration proceedings.[38]

The Sole Arbitrator in this case modified the order of things. Instead of examining first the impact of a mandatory foreign law (the law of Algeria on intermediary activities) on the Protocol of Agreement that was governed by Swiss law, he decided, as a preliminary issue, 'the nature, contents and validity of the contractual relationship between the parties . . . since it is of primary importance to ascertain at the outset what activity, if any, was developed by claimant in Algeria'.[39]

6.1.4.1 Hilmarton's Activities in Algeria

The Arbitrator examined which activities Hilmarton had performed and concluded that there was no written evidence. Both parties were not able to submit a file of what the company was doing in Algeria. Hilmarton claimed its file had been stolen, and OTV apparently never had received a written report of its broker's activities and did not ask for one over the course of three years.[40]

In terms of witnesses, the key people from OTV had been dismissed in the meantime and had not been called as witnesses by the parties (a fact described as 'strange' by the Arbitrator). The Arbitrator thus relied on Hilmarton's witnesses, whose testimonies revealed that Hilmarton

> developed both activities resembling the provision of more or less confidential commercial information, and activities consisting of using its influence on some Algerian authorities, against payment, in order to have defendant's bid preferred to bids from other companies. According to witness C, 85% of claimant's work consisted of the latter activities.[41]

On this basis, the Arbitrator qualified the Protocol of Agreement as a brokerage contract (*Mäklervertrag*) under the SCO.[42]

[38] *Hilmarton* v. *OTV*, Yearbook, 105 et seq.; Crivellaro 2003, 124.

[39] *Hilmarton* v. *OTV*, Yearbook, 106.

[40] *Hilmarton* v. *OTV*, Yearbook, 107, 109.

[41] *Hilmarton* v. *OTV*, Yearbook, 107.

[42] Art. 412 et seq. SCO.

6.1.4.2 A Simulated Contract or Tacit Approval?

The Arbitrator found that Hilmarton's activities did not correspond to the terms of the Protocol of Agreement, where it was said that the company would give legal and fiscal advice and co-ordinate OTV's subcontractors.[43] As Swiss Law applied to the Protocol, the Arbitrator tested whether it was a simulated contract (*acte simulé*) according to Art. 18(1) SCO. He considered that this was at least partially the case, because OTV never objected to the activities that Hilmarton carried out in Algeria – rather, it paid 50 per cent of the fee agreed in the Protocol. Also, this would have explained why OTV's managers who drafted and signed the Protocol were later dismissed and did not appear as witnesses in the arbitration. However, the Arbitrator concluded that, 'in the absence of tangible and clearly defined factors, the Arbitral Tribunal cannot accept this thesis, since claimant and defendant allege, respectively, that there was performance under the Protocol of Agreement'.[44]

From the absence of documentation for Hilmarton's activities the Arbitrator eventually concluded that Hilmarton understood its task to be 'totally different' from what was written down in the Protocol, and that the company had orally informed OTV of its activities. OTV had not objected, but rather tacitly approved and partially paid for those activities, although they differed from what was agreed in the Protocol. The Arbitrator went on to examine the consequences of such tacit approval.[45]

6.1.4.3 Sufficient Evidence for Bribery?

OTV alleged that Hilmarton 'possibly paid bribes and in any case violated Algerian Law No. 78-02 . . . thereby violating either Swiss or international public policy'. The Arbitrator found that no special law existed in Switzerland that dealt with the traffic in influence (except the Federal Law on Unfair Competition, which he declared inapplicable). He argued that Hilmarton indeed had tried to influence the Algerian authorities, but that according to the Swiss Federal Supreme Court, this activity was not *per se* contrary to the principles of fair trading.[46]

Consequently, the Arbitrator questioned whether actual bribes had been paid by Hilmarton to the Algerian authorities to secure the conclusion of their contract with OTV. On the one hand, he noted that the

[43] *Hilmarton* v. *OTV*, Yearbook, 108. [44] *Hilmarton* v. *OTV*, Yearbook, 108 et seq.
[45] *Hilmarton* v. *OTV*, Yearbook, 109 et seq. [46] *Hilmarton* v. *OTV*, Yearbook, 110 et seq.

statement of one of Hilmarton's witnesses was ambiguous in this regard, and found on the other hand that

> the correspondence between the former General Manager of defendant and claimant ambiguously mentions payments 'which would have been made by defendant directly to local representatives', payments which were to be deducted from claimant's fee. Further, the high commission fee could indicate that there has been bribery.[47]

It appears that OTV made direct payments to Algerian officials, and those payments were deducted from Hilmarton's fee. However, the Arbitrator eventually concluded that there was not sufficient indirect evidence to prove bribery beyond doubt:

> In the present case, bribery has not been proved beyond doubt. It is true that it is possible to prove something through indirect evidence and that Art. 8 of the Swiss [Civil Code] does not exclude indirect evidence. However, it is necessary that a sufficient ensemble of indirect evidence be collected to allow the judge to base his decision on something more than likely facts, i.e., facts which have not been proven . . . Thus, evidence of bribery has not been given and the indirect evidence is not sufficiently relevant.[48]

The Arbitrator subsequently examined whether there was a violation of Algerian law that could have an impact on Swiss public policy.

6.1.4.4 Violation of the Algerian Law on Trading in Influence

The Arbitrator stated that the aim of Algerian Law 78-02 was to prohibit all trading in influence, and that Hilmarton's activities violated this Law.[49] The question was how this would impact Swiss law that was applicable to the merits. Art. 20(1) SCO says that a contract is null and void if its content is illegal or against *bonos mores* – however, illegality in this context refers to a violation of Swiss law. If a provision of foreign law is violated, it has to be 'examined from the point of view of a possible affront to morality'.[50]

The Arbitrator stated that Algerian Law 78-02 aimed at fair competition and the objectivity of the authorities in the allocation of contracts for public works. He noted that trading in influence was not only an Algerian concern, but that most European states had specific laws

[47] *Hilmarton* v. *OTV*, Yearbook, 111 et seq.
[48] *Hilmarton* v. *OTV*, Yearbook, 112.
[49] *Hilmarton* v. *OTV*, Yearbook, 112.
[50] *Hilmarton* v. *OTV*, Yearbook, 113, with reference to BGE 76 II 33 (at 8.).

against corruption. He mentioned the efforts of the ICC in this regard and cited Lalive's text on transnational public policy. He also took note that the Swiss Criminal Code (old Articles 288, 314 and 315) sanctioned active and passive corruption as well as the unfair management of public interests.[51]

The Arbitrator concluded that the Algerian Law did not simply aim at serving Algerian interests, but rather

> aims at guaranteeing healthy and fair commercial practices and at fighting against corruption in general. In fact, the Law of Algeria lays down a general principle which must be respected by all legal systems wishing to fight corruption. This is why the violation of this Law, which concerns international public policy, is contrary to the notion of morality based on Art. 20(1) [Swiss Code of Obligations], which is part of Swiss public policy . . . Hence, the brokerage contract is null and void in its entirety since, according to claimant's collaborator, 85% of claimant's activities aimed at obtaining the contract with the Algerian authorities for defendant, collecting information and legal and fiscal advice being only a marginal activity.[52]

The Arbitrator thus considered that the violation of the Algerian law on trading in influence was against Swiss public policy, and that the Hilmarton-OTV Protocol was null and void according to Article 20 (1) SCO.

6.1.4.5 The First Award

On the merits, the Arbitrator declared the Protocol of Agreement null and void and dismissed Hilmarton's claim for the remaining 50 per cent of the fee as well as OTV's request for compensation for the procedural costs.[53]

6.1.4.6 Annulment of the First Award, Second Award and Enforcement

Annulment by the Court of Justice of the Canton of Geneva Hilmarton challenged the First Award in front of the Court of Justice of the Canton of Geneva, claiming a violation of the law. With judgment of 17 November 1989, the Court annulled the Award, stating that there was no evidence that bribe payments were foreseen or paid by the parties. Although the parties had violated the Algerian Law 78-02, which

[51] *Hilmarton* v. *OTV*, Yearbook, 114. [52] *Hilmarton* v. *OTV*, Yearbook, 115.
[53] *Hilmarton* v. *OTV*, Yearbook, 120 et seq.

prohibited the use of intermediaries, this was not contrary to Swiss public policy, as the use of intermediaries is allowed under Swiss law. As long as the intermediary does not take improper influence on public officials by corrupt means, his activities are perfectly legal. In addition, the Court declared that the award was arbitrary. The parties had concluded the Protocol of Agreement in perfect knowledge that Hilmarton's activities would violate Algerian law, and OTV could not invoke this violation in its favour when it had tacitly been approved to be part of the contract. This amounted to an abuse of right according to Art. 2(2) of the Swiss Civil Code.[54]

Approval of the Annulment by the Swiss Federal Supreme Court OTV appealed the decision of the Geneva Court to the Swiss Federal Supreme Court, which approved the annulment. The Federal Supreme Court stated that the Algerian Law 78-02 was too restrictive and of a protectionist nature when it prohibited the use of all intermediaries. It aimed at ensuring a state monopoly on foreign trade. From the point of view of the Swiss legal order, such a law had an adverse effect on the freedom of contract. The Federal Supreme Court held that no bribes had been paid and there was no evidence which would support that Hilmarton had tried to improperly influence the Algerian authorities.[55]

Second Award and Enforcement in France and in the United Kingdom After the First Award had been annulled by the Swiss courts, Hilmarton resumed ICC arbitration. The Second Award of 1992 was in conformity with the decisions of the Swiss courts, and Hilmarton's claim for payment of the remaining 50 per cent of the fee was approved.[56]

Interestingly, the First Award was enforced in France, even though it had been annulled in Switzerland. The French Supreme Court (*Cour de Cassation*) held that according to Art. VII of the New York Convention 1958, OTV could rely on the French law on international arbitration, which did not list the grounds in Art. V of the 1958 New York Convention (including annulment of an award in the country under the law of which it was made) among the grounds for a refusal of recognition and enforcement. The Supreme Court also stated that 'the award rendered in

[54] See *Rivista dell'arbitrato* (1992), 735 et seq. and *ASA Bulletin* (1993), 250 et seq.; see also Crivellaro 2003, 125.

[55] See *Rivista dell'arbitrato* (1992), 739 et seq. and *ASA Bulletin* (1993), 253 et seq.

[56] Crivellaro 2003, 125.

Switzerland is an international award which is not integrated in the legal system of that State, so that it remains in existence even if set aside and its recognition in France is not contrary to international public policy.'[57] The Second Award, on the other hand, was not enforced in France (the Supreme Court considered the respective claim of Hilmarton as inadmissible because of *res iudicata*).[58]

In the United Kingdom, however, the Second Award was enforced and OTV's objections to its enforcement failed. Referring to the New York Convention 1958, the (unreported) Commercial Court decision set the limits for review on the grounds of public policy as follows:

> Only if enforcement of an award conflicts with overriding public policy concerns such as the need to combat drug trafficking, fraud, corruption and terrorism at an international level, will an English court intervene. Domestic public policy concerns have no role to play at the enforcement stage.[59]

6.1.4.7 Analysis

Hilmarton v. *OTV* is a very complex case that has resulted in two arbitral awards and several domestic court decisions regarding annulment and enforcement in three different countries. For the purposes of this text, the Arbitrator's arguments in the First Award are the most interesting for analysis.[60] The Arbitrator did discuss the bribery allegations not as an issue of jurisdiction, but at the merits stage. Swiss law was applicable to the merits and the Arbitrator in particular relied on the SCO. He also mentioned the Swiss Criminal Code and its provisions on active and passive public bribery; however, he did not apply those provisions. He declared that there was not sufficient indirect evidence to prove bribery beyond doubt; and found a situation of trading in influence to be at stake, not bribery. The Arbitrator noted that Swiss law did not contain provisions on trading in influence, as opposed to Algerian law.

The Arbitrator put the standard of proof high with regard to the bribery allegations. From today's point of view, when the efforts to

[57] See *Yearbook Commercial Arbitration* XX (1995), 663 et seq. See also the decision of the Paris Appeals Court (*Cour d'appel*) of 19 December 1991 (*Rivista dell'arbitrato* (1992), 743 et seq.).

[58] See *Yearbook Commercial Arbitration* XXII (1997), 696 et seq.; for the decision by the Versailles Appeals Court (which was overturned by the Supreme Court decision) see *Yearbook Commercial Arbitration* XXI (1996), 524 et seq.

[59] Brown 2000, 35.

[60] See also Sayed 2004, 234 et seq.

combat foreign public bribery have been stepped up considerably in the meantime, it can be questioned whether the fact that Hilmarton's activities were different from those specified in the Protocol; the complete lack of documentation for Hilmarton's activities; the absence of witnesses from OTV; the rather high amount of the commission; and the fact that OTV apparently made direct payments to Algerian officials that were deducted from Hilmarton's fees, would not establish sufficient *prima facie* evidence for bribery, so that an arbitral tribunal would request the parties to produce more evidence and draw adverse inferences if no such evidence was available.

The Arbitrator's argumentation was progressive insofar as he claimed the existence of a transnational public policy against corruption; and as he eventually declared the Protocol null and void under the SCO because it violated foreign mandatory law (the Algerian law on trading in influence) and was therefore contrary to Swiss public policy. The Swiss Federal Supreme Court's interpretation of the Algerian Law 78-02 as a protectionist instrument differs strongly from the Arbitrator's interpretation. A closer examination of the object and purpose of that Law is however beyond the scope of this text.

6.1.5 Westinghouse *v.* National Power Corporation (*ICC Case No. 6401 of 1991*)

While this arbitration also involved claims by a second company, Burns & Roe, the discussion here is limited to the claims that arose out of the contract between Westinghouse Electric SA (a Swiss company) and National Power Corporation ('NPC') of 9 February 1976 for the construction of a nuclear power plant in the Philippines. The construction contract contained a clause for ICC arbitration in Geneva.[61]

In 1973, President Ferdinand Marcos of the Philippines planned to build a nuclear power plant, having been president for eight years, and ten months after he had put into effect martial law that transferred most state powers to him. NPC was a state-owned entity under the direct

[61] *Westinghouse* v. *National Power Corporation*, 1. Westinghouse Electric SA later assigned the contract to Westinghouse International Projects Company (a Delaware (US) company) that in turn assigned part of the contract to Westinghouse Electric Corporation (a Pennsylvania (US) company). Those three companies appeared together as the Claimant in this case and are collectively referred to as 'Westinghouse'.

supervision of the Office of the President.[62] Westinghouse competed with General Electric Corporation and French, German and Japanese companies for the construction contract. In 1974, NPC awarded the contract to Westinghouse.[63] Construction of the plant apparently was finished in 1985, but after the overthrow of the Marcos regime in 1986 and the Chernobyl disaster, the new Aquino government decided not to operate the plant.[64] Until today, the plant that cost US$2.3 billion has remained mothballed and is now a tourist attraction close to the Pinatubo and other active volcanoes.[65] In 1988, Westinghouse (Claimant) initiated ICC arbitration against both NPC and the Republic of the Philippines (Defendants).

Westinghouse claimed that under the construction contract, tens of millions of dollars were owed to it for unpaid items, price adjustments and cost increases from excusable delay. Defendants argued, *inter alia*, that Westinghouse had committed fraud in procuring the construction contract. Defendants also argued that the Republic of the Philippines was not party to the contract and did not consent to the arbitral clause, and that therefore the Arbitral Tribunal did not have jurisdiction over it.[66] The Tribunal issued a Preliminary Award discussing issues of jurisdiction and contract validity, including the allegations of bribery and fraud.

6.1.5.1 Separability of the Arbitral Clause

The Arbitral Tribunal first examined its jurisdiction. It stated that the doctrine of separability of the arbitral clause from the main contract was by then generally accepted. Still, the parties had different views on its precise application in the context of alleged bribery:

> The Claimants contend that in all events the [separability] doctrine applies; the Defendants argue to the contrary that it would not apply if they establish that the main contracts were obtained by bribery. As a matter of principle, the Tribunal would have been ready to accept that the doctrine of separability is not an absolute to be applied in all cases, as contended by the Claimants. There may be instances where a defect going to the root of an agreement between parties affects both the main contract and the arbitration clause. An obvious example is a contract obtained

[62] *Westinghouse* v. *National Power Corporation*, 9 et seq.
[63] *Westinghouse* v. *National Power Corporation*, 11.
[64] *Westinghouse* v. *National Power Corporation*, 15.
[65] 'A Nuclear Plant, and a Dream, Fizzles', *New York Times*, 13 February 2012 (online edn).
[66] *Westinghouse* v. *National Power Corporation*, 3 et seq.

> by threat. With regard to the impact of bribery, it would remain to be seen whether bribery, if proved, affects both the main contract and the arbitration clause and renders both null and invalid.[67]

The Tribunal argued that the separability doctrine does not apply in the absolute: it is possible that bribery affects both the main contract and the arbitration clause and renders both null and void.[68]

6.1.5.2 Applicable Law and Standard of Proof

The Tribunal then determined the applicable law, as the parties had failed to agree on a law to govern the validity and performance of the construction contract.[69] As the arbitration was situated in Geneva, the Tribunal declared that the Swiss law on international arbitration should apply, next to contractual provisions and the ICC Rules.[70] In short, according to the applicable conflict of laws rule (Art. 187(1) of the Swiss Private International Law Act; SPILA), the closest connection was with the location where Westinghouse had its 'principal place of business'. Thus, the validity of the construction contract was in principle governed by the law of Pennsylvania (US). The Tribunal emphasised that it would also take into account international public policy.[71]

With regard to standard of proof, the Tribunal decided to apply Philippine, Pennsylvania and New Jersey practice, as the contracts were 'negotiated, executed and performed in the Philippines and the United States'.[72] The Tribunal compared the standards applicable in civil cases and found that 'preponderance of evidence' was accepted in all three legal orders:

> [A]lthough the function of fact finding in civil cases is typically performed by a jury in the United States and by the court in the Philippines, the standard of proof applied is essentially the same: The party having the burden of persuasion must establish the facts on which it relies by a 'preponderance of evidence.' In other words, it must have the 'superior weight of evidence' and establish that its version of the facts is 'more likely true than not true.'[73]

67 *Westinghouse* v. *National Power Corporation*, 20.
68 To the same end: Redfern and Hunter 2004, 164; cf. also the Swiss Federal Supreme Court in BGE 119 II 380, 384.
69 *Westinghouse* v. *National Power Corporation*, 24.
70 *Westinghouse* v. *National Power Corporation*, 20 et seq.
71 *Westinghouse* v. *National Power Corporation*, 22, 28 et seq.
72 *Westinghouse* v. *National Power Corporation*, 31.
73 *Westinghouse* v. *National Power Corporation*, 33.

The Tribunal went on to examine which standard had to be applied in civil cases involving allegations of fraud and bribery:

> In the Philippines and in the United States, fraud in civil cases 'must be proved to exist by clear and convincing evidence amounting to more than mere preponderance, and cannot be justified by a mere speculation. This is because fraud is never lightly to be presumed.' ... Bribery is a form of fraud and must be established by 'a clear preponderance of the evidence.' ... Similarly, in Pennsylvania fraud must be proven by 'clear, precise and convincing evidence.' ... Thus, the Tribunal will apply a 'clear and convincing evidence' standard to the Defendants' claims of bribery.[74]

After a close examination of domestic case law, the Tribunal concluded that for the bribery allegations, it would apply the higher standard of 'clear and convincing evidence'. But it also noted that with regard to the facts of this case, the standard of proof was of no relevance – the findings of the Tribunal would have been the same no matter which standard it applied.[75]

6.1.5.3 The Definition of Bribery and Its Impact on Standard of Proof

NPC argued first that the construction contract was invalid and unenforceable because it had been procured by bribery, and second that the arbitration clause in that contract was invalid and unenforceable, because NPC had been forced to accept it by pressure from President Marcos, who was bribed.[76] The Tribunal first clarified how it defined bribery. NPC's position, with reference to Philippine, US and Swiss law, was that

> bribery would be established by showing that Claimants intended to pay money or other consideration of value to Marcos, and that he agreed to accept such payments to have the contracts awarded to them, irrespective of whether or not they could establish that Marcos actually received any payments.[77]

In other words, NPC argued that the actual receipt of any money by Marcos was not a required element to establish bribery; the promise to pay and the acceptance of the promise were sufficient.

[74] *Westinghouse* v. *National Power Corporation*, 34 et seq. with references to Philippine, New Jersey and Pennsylvania case law. The Tribunal took note, however, that the Philippine Civil Code indicated that in a civil action for fraud, even without a conviction, the standard of proof was 'preponderance of evidence'.

[75] *Westinghouse* v. *National Power Corporation*, 35.

[76] *Westinghouse* v. *National Power Corporation*, 36.

[77] *Westinghouse* v. *National Power Corporation*, 37 et seq.

The Tribunal did not make explicit reference to any domestic bribery provisions or international conventions to define bribery, but accepted NPC's position. It understood that NPC could not prove that Marcos actually received a payment, but demanded that NPC would establish by clear and convincing evidence:

> (a) that the alleged briber intended to provide a payment or another thing of value to President Marcos and
>
> (b) that President Marcos agreed to accept this consideration, either directly or through Disini, in exchange for his directing that NPC enter into the challenged contract with the briber.[78]

The Tribunal demanded proof of the existence of a bribery pact: of the intention to pay a bribe and the acceptance of the offer in exchange for the awarding of the construction contract. Regarding the standard of proof, the Tribunal argued that the lack of proof of actual bribe payments would raise the applicable standard to prove the existence of the bribery pact: 'Defendants face a higher burden of proof concerning the existence of an agreement if they are unable to prove actual payments.'[79] To put it short: because NPC was unable to prove actual bribe payments, the Tribunal asked it to prove the existence of the bribe pact by a higher standard of proof.

6.1.5.4 Bribery to Obtain the Construction Contract?

Discussing the facts, the Tribunal closely examined the nomination of Herminio Disini, a close friend of Marcos, as Special Sales Representative (SSR) of Westinghouse in the Philippines. Disini was the CEO of Herdis Management, a holding company for diverse businesses, in which Marcos allegedly had a financial interest.[80] The Tribunal concluded that NPC was able to prove the first element of the bribe pact (above at (a)): Westinghouse possibly knew, or at least 'would not have been surprised or bothered' that Marcos received some of their payments to Disini.[81] NPC failed, however, to prove the second element (above at (b)):

> Most significantly, there is no direct evidence that Marcos supported Westinghouse because he expected to benefit from the SSR payments to Herdis. The circumstantial evidence also fails to prove that Marcos

78 *Westinghouse* v. *National Power Corporation*, 41.
79 *Westinghouse* v. *National Power Corporation*, 42.
80 *Westinghouse* v. *National Power Corporation*, 58 et seq.
81 *Westinghouse* v. *National Power Corporation*, 76.

> promoted Westinghouse because he expected to receive some of the SSR payments to Herdis. There is no evidence either of any agreement between Marcos and Westinghouse, or that Disini acted as agent for Marcos. At most, the evidence indicates that some Westinghouse employees thought that Marcos owned some of Herdis and that Marcos had documents in his possession that outlined the commissions Herdis was supposed to receive for the contracts. However, there is no evidence that Marcos received any share of those commissions. Although Defendants argue that the circumstantial evidence establishes that Marcos must have received a share of the commissions, the Tribunal is not persuaded.[82]

The Tribunal argued that although the Defendants had far-reaching access to information from the Swiss government, the Philippines investigation and US Federal Court proceedings, there was no evidence showing transfers from Disini accounts to Marcos-related accounts; no proof of ownership by Marcos of Herdis, or of other entities to which the commissions were transferred; and no basis for a conclusion that Marcos ever agreed to accept, or received, commissions from Westinghouse. The Defendants thus 'failed to carry their burden of proving Westinghouse's alleged bribery'.[83]

6.1.5.5 Validity of the Arbitration Clause

The Tribunal also inquired into the negotiating history of the arbitration clause in the construction contract. Initially, NPC wanted to limit arbitration to 'technical matters', while Westinghouse wanted arbitration to be mandatory. The Tribunal noted that this was not unusual – the foreign company would routinely insist on international arbitration, the local company (or host state) would demand jurisdiction of its state courts or try to limit the scope of arbitration. The Tribunal did not find any 'fundamental disagreement' between the parties with regard to the arbitration clause, and no evidence for bribe-motivated pressure from Marcos on NPC that the company would agree to the arbitration provision.[84]

6.1.5.6 The Preliminary Award

In sum, the Arbitral Tribunal resolved the preliminary issues of jurisdiction and contract validity with regard to the bribery allegations

[82] *Westinghouse* v. *National Power Corporation*, 77 et seq.
[83] *Westinghouse* v. *National Power Corporation*, 78 et seq.
[84] *Westinghouse* v. *National Power Corporation*, 79 et seq., 85.

surrounding the Westinghouse construction contract as follows: it concluded that it had jurisdiction over the case; that a standard of proof of 'clear and convincing evidence' applied; and while NPC was able to demonstrate that Westinghouse intended to pay a bribe to Marcos through Disini and Herdis, NPC failed to prove that Marcos ever received or agreed to accept a bribe in exchange for directing NPC to conclude the construction contract for the nuclear power plant with Westinghouse. Both the construction contract and the arbitration clause were declared valid; the Republic of the Philippines was, however, not bound by the arbitration clause and no longer a party to the arbitration proceedings.[85]

6.1.5.7 Appeal of the Preliminary Award to the Swiss Federal Supreme Court

NPC appealed the Preliminary Award to the Swiss Federal Supreme Court, claiming that the Westinghouse contract was invalid because it had been procured through bribery of President Marcos; that its arbitral clause was equally invalid and the Arbitral Tribunal thus had no jurisdiction. The Federal Supreme Court dismissed the appeal, stating that NPC challenged the Award by applying its own considerations regarding the evidence (*Beweiswürdigung*) and therefore misinterpreting the scope of the cognition (*Kognition*) of the Federal Supreme Court. The Court only annuls an award if the evaluation of the evidence is obviously arbitrary (*willkürliche Beweiswürdigung*). It does not review the fact-finding of an arbitral tribunal like an appeals court. NPC did *not* challenge the Preliminary Award on the basis that the facts had been established in violation of one of the procedural guarantees of Art. 190 SPILA, or in a manner inconsistent with the *ordre public*.[86]

6.1.5.8 Civil Action in Front of US District Court (New Jersey)

The Republic of the Philippines and NPC also pursued a federal action against Westinghouse in front of the US District Court for the District of New Jersey. Westinghouse argued that the parties were collaterally estopped from court litigation because of the ongoing arbitration. The federal judge noted that the Republic of the Philippines was not a party

[85] *Westinghouse* v. *National Power Corporation*, 123 et seq., 129 et seq.
[86] BGE 119 II 380, 382 et seq.

to the arbitration and not bound by the ICC Preliminary Award. He referred all counts against Westinghouse to arbitration, except two counts related to the bribery of President Marcos. As the issues raised in the court proceedings were factually and legally different from the arbitration, and because the Arbitral Tribunal applied a higher standard of proof than a jury, he denied collateral estoppel for those two counts.[87]

The Federal Judge then reviewed and discussed the Preliminary Award. On standard of proof, he said:

> I have reviewed the Award very carefully and can only conclude that . . . the Tribunal applied a significantly heavier burden of proof than would be applied at trial. My conclusion rests primarily on the manner in which the Tribunal considered the evidence. By compartmentalizing and segregating the categories of evidence, the Tribunal deprived it as a whole of is natural collective force in a way in which the evidence might not be so deprived in this Court.
>
> Had the Tribunal actually applied a 'preponderance of the evidence standard,' it still might have arrived at the same conclusions. However, applying that standard it could not have found that there was no evidence of bribery. That would be inconsistent with my . . . Opinion . . . where I ruled that 'there is ample evidence to permit a reasonable jury to find that the Disini commissions were intended to be paid in whole or in part to President Marcos and were in fact paid in whole or in part to him or upon his direction.'[88]

The Judge listed several examples of evidence that lost its 'collective force' because it was not read in context with the other evidence. Nevertheless, he stated that he had 'no quarrel' with the conclusions of the Arbitral Tribunal because he considered different issues applying a different standard of proof. However, the case was set to go to trial. Eventually, the Philippine government and Westinghouse settled the pending lawsuit. Westinghouse was to pay the Philippines US$100 million, and would then be hired to repair and upgrade the plant to current standards, and to operate and maintain it for up to thirty years.[89]

[87] *The Republic of the Philippines and National Power Corporation* v. *Westinghouse Electric Corporation et al.*, Civ. No. 88-5150, Opinion of 4 February 1992 (D. New Jersey), 1 et seq., 5; see also Crivellaro 2003, 132 et seq.

[88] *The Republic of the Philippines and National Power Corporation* v. *Westinghouse Electric Corporation et al.*, Civ. No. 88-5150, Opinion of 4 February 1992 (D. New Jersey), 25 et seq.

[89] 7(3) *Mealey's International Arbitration Report* (1992), 10 et seq.

6.1.5.9 Analysis

Westinghouse v. *National Power Corporation* is another complex arbitration that resulted in an unsuccessful challenge of the Preliminary Award in front of the Swiss Federal Supreme Court. The Award discusses three topics that are relevant for the purposes of this text: separability of the arbitral clause, standard of proof and the definition of bribery. On separability, the Tribunal found that in principle, the arbitral clause is valid even if the underlying contract is null and void because it has an illegal object (e.g. bribe payments); the exception is that the bribery also affects the arbitral clause.

Regarding the standard of proof, the Tribunal referred to domestic case law and the Philippine Civil Code to determine the standard that was applicable in civil cases involving fraud or bribery. On this basis, it applied a 'clear and convincing' standard, even though the Philippine Civil Code apparently only demanded a 'preponderance of the evidence' standard for such cases. Notably, when the Republic of the Philippines and NPC subsequently pursued a civil action in front of a US District Court, the federal judge stated that the Arbitral Tribunal had applied a considerably higher standard of proof than would be applied at trial, and that the Tribunal would necessarily have found evidence for bribery if it had applied a 'preponderance of the evidence' standard. However, the Tribunal did not consider the standard of proof to be decisive in this case.

In order to define bribery, the Tribunal did not refer to any specific bribery provisions of domestic criminal laws. On the basis of NPC's submission, it argued that two elements had to be proven to establish bribery: first, the intention to confer an advantage to President Marcos; and second, that Marcos agreed to accept the advantage, directly or indirectly, in exchange for his directing NPC to conclude the construction contract with Westinghouse. Such a narrow definition of bribery would not be in line with modern international conventions and national bribery laws anymore: today, it is clear that the offer or promise of a bribe is sufficient to establish the offence of active bribery, if all other requirements are fulfilled. The recipient (the passive side) does not have to accept the advantage.[90] For the same reason, the Tribunal's approach to raise the standard of proof for the existence of the bribe pact because there was no proof of actual bribe payments cannot be maintained from

[90] See, e.g., Art. 1(1) of the OECD Convention on Bribery (OECD 1997) and Zerbes 2014, 137.

today's point of view. The standard of proof must be the same for all elements of a criminal offence that is alleged in arbitration proceedings. Besides, it is more difficult to prove an offer for a bribe payment than an actual bribe payment.

Finally, it can be noted that the Tribunal did not refer to earlier arbitral awards with regard to the bribery allegations (probably because it was not aware of any) or to international anti-corruption conventions (they were not in force yet), and only briefly mentioned international public policy. The Tribunal did not discuss mandatory law.

6.1.6 ICC Case No. 6497 (1994)

The Claimant in this case was a consultant from Liechtenstein; the Respondent was a contractor from Germany. Over a period of ten years, the parties entered into a number of consultancy and product agreements. Under those agreements, the Claimant was to assist the Respondent in obtaining construction contracts in different countries, including Middle Eastern country X. The Respondent obtained several contracts in country X during those ten years. Under the consultancy agreements, the Claimant was paid 1.5 per cent of the amounts received by the Respondent; under the product agreements, it was paid additional remuneration of approximately 5.5 per cent of the amounts received by the Respondent. The dispute arose about the payment of such remunerations for several contracts that had been awarded to the Respondent. The Respondent refused to pay and the Claimant initiated ICC arbitration, according to respective clauses in all those consultancy and product agreements. The Respondent argued that the real purpose of all the agreements was to pay bribes in Middle Eastern country X. The arbitration took place in Geneva and Swiss law applied to the merits.[91]

The Arbitral Tribunal took note that the Respondent had no direct written evidence for the alleged bribery, only circumstantial written evidence and witnesses. The Tribunal pointed out that the agreements would be null and void in Swiss law if bribery could be proven, but not because bribery was prohibited under the criminal law of the country where the bribes were paid: under Swiss law, bribes cannot be the object of a valid contract.[92] The Tribunal was aware that such nullity would not necessarily be equitable:

[91] ICC Case No. 6497, 71 et seq.; Crivellaro 2003, 137.
[92] ICC Case No. 6497, 72 with reference to BGE 95 II 37 et seq.

> The enterprise having benefited from the bribes (i.e., having obtained substantial contracts thanks to the bribes) has not a better moral position than the enterprise having organised the payment of the bribes. The nullity of the agreement is generally only beneficial to the former, and thus possibly inequitable. But this is legally irrelevant.[93]

6.1.6.1 Burden of Proof

On burden of proof, the Tribunal stated that the burden was on the party alleging the bribery, in this case on the Respondent (the contractor):

> The demonstration of the bribery nature of the agreement has to be made by the Party alleging the existence of bribes ... A civil court, and in particular an arbitral tribunal, has not the power to make an official inquiry and has not the duty to search independently the truth. A civil court has to hear the allegations and the proofs offered by the parties.[94]

The Tribunal noted that even if it had some doubts regarding the alleged bribery, it would have to reject the argument of the alleging party if its demonstration was not convincing. However, with reference to the Swiss Civil Code, it also recognised the possibility of modifying the burden of proof in special circumstances and for good reasons:

> The 'alleging Party' may bring some relevant evidence for its allegations, without these elements being really conclusive. In such case, the arbitral tribunal may exceptionally request the other party to bring some counter-evidence, if such task is possible and not too burdensome. If the other party does not bring such counter-evidence, the arbitral tribunal may conclude that the facts alleged are proven (Art. 8 Swiss Civil Code).[95]

6.1.6.2 Proving Bribery

The Respondent admitted that the Claimant had rendered services to it and that for some agreements no bribes were contemplated or paid. However, the critical point was the high amount of Claimant's remuneration in relation to its limited costs. The Claimant alluded to costs for subcontractors without being able to identify them, or produce any such subcontracts in writing; and referred to very high remunerations of its top employees in a vague and contradictory manner. Furthermore, the Respondent argued that the non-transparent corporate structure of the Claimant was a sign that some officials of country X might have a financial interest in some companies of the Claimant's group; and that

[93] ICC Case No. 6497, 72. [94] ICC Case No. 6497, 73. [95] ICC Case No. 6497, 73.

the group did not have many employees, but rather people with personal relations to public officials.[96]

The Tribunal stated that the Claimant's refusal to give more precise information about its group weakened its position, but it was no conclusive evidence what the real object of the agreements between the parties was, and whether bribes were paid. Likewise, the written evidence presented by the Respondent (letters and telexes containing nicknames) was no conclusive evidence that all consultancy and product agreements involved bribery. However, one of the Respondent's witnesses (Mr A, a member of the Respondent's board of directors) testified that the Respondent knew most of the names of the persons who were bribed, and that he knew roughly 70 per cent of those names (about 30 names), but not the amount of bribes paid to them. Mr A did not give any such names, because he had received threats in this respect.[97]

Another possible witness (Mr B, a special representative acting under the authority of Mr A) refused to testify in the arbitral proceedings after the Respondent had decided not to call him, even though he was invited by the Arbitral Tribunal and the Claimant. From all this, the Arbitral Tribunal concluded that

> considering the fact that respondent has decided not to tell the many names of beneficiaries which they allegedly knew, it is not appropriate to shift the burden of the proof on claimant and to request them to demonstrate the justification of their global costs for that period of ten years. One may also mention here that it is respondent who took the decision not to call Mr. B as witness . . . Claimant argues that Mr. B would have testified that the real object of the agreements was *not* of bribery nature. This allegation is impossible to verify, but respondent has to bear the consequences of its decision in this respect.[98]

As the Respondent neither gave the names of the bribe recipients nor called Mr B as a witness, the Tribunal eventually did not shift the burden of proof to the Claimant by asking it to provide details on its costs for the ten-year period of the consultancy and product agreements.

6.1.6.3 Bribery Proven in Product Agreement Q

The Tribunal considered Product Agreement Q as different from all other agreements between the Claimant and the Respondent. It contained an extremely unusual commission of 33.33 per cent, to be paid for

[96] ICC Case No. 6497, 73 et seq.

[97] ICC Case No. 6497, 74.

[98] ICC Case No. 6497, 75.

'extraordinary services', without specifying the nature of those services.[99] The Respondent requested that the Claimant would produce bank documents in relation to this Agreement, in order to see the destination of the payments. The Claimant refused to produce such documents because of business secrets, and alleged a conflict of interest when the Tribunal ordered an independent expertise by an accounting firm. The Tribunal decided that the Claimant should produce all subcontracts concluded in relation with Product Agreement Q; the Claimant refused again on the basis of business secrets, and later refused to co-operate with another independent expert appointed by the Tribunal. The Claimant then, however, produced the bank documents that had originally been requested by the Respondent.[100]

The bank documents showed that the account into which payments concerning Product Agreement Q were made was a mere transit account. The document production therefore did not reveal any business secrets (as it had been argued by the Claimant). In combination with affidavits of Mr D that contained untrue statements about that account regarding the turnover per year (Mr D was an auditor for the Claimant group that described himself as independent; he did not appear as a witness in the arbitration although he was invited to); and the opposition of Mr Z (Claimant's top manager) against a testimony of Mr F, the director of the respective bank, about who had instructed the bank to prepare the documents (Mr F was consequently bound by bank secrecy obligations), this was sufficient evidence for the Arbitral Tribunal:

> Taking into account all circumstances, the arbitral tribunal considers (contrary to its decision on all other Agreements . . .) that there is a high degree of probability that the real object of Product Agreement Q was to channel bribes to officials in country X who had the power to decide that both amounts mentioned in the Agreement were to be paid to respondent. Such probability is high enough for the arbitral tribunal to consider that such allegation presented by respondent is to be admitted.[101]

In the Award, the Tribunal concluded that all consultancy and product agreements were valid, except Product Agreement Q that was null and void because its real object was bribery. Thus, the Claimant's claims for payment of its remuneration were accepted with the one exception of Product Agreement Q.[102]

[99] ICC Case No. 6497, 75 et seq. [100] ICC Case No. 6497, 76 et seq.
[101] ICC Case No. 6497, 79. [102] ICC Case No. 6497, 72, 79.

6.1.6.4 Analysis

With regard to the applicable law, the Tribunal in this case apparently did not rely on any specific criminal law provisions of domestic law to determine bribery. It also did not rely on international anti-corruption conventions (they were not in force yet) and did not invoke transnational public policy. From the published excerpt of this Award, it is unclear how the Tribunal understood and defined bribery. On burden of proof, the Tribunal first argued quite restrictively that an arbitral tribunal does not have to inquire into the facts and does not have to independently search for the truth; rather, an arbitral tribunal can rely on the proof offered by the parties. On the basis of Art. 8 of the Swiss Civil Code, however, the Tribunal concluded that it was possible for the alleging party to bring evidence that was not really conclusive, and exceptionally, an arbitral tribunal could then ask the alleged party to bring counterevidence if that was possible and not too burdensome. If the alleged party then does not produce such counterevidence, the arbitral tribunal may conclude that the alleged facts are proven.

Due to the Respondent's behaviour in the arbitration proceedings, the Tribunal eventually did not shift the burden to produce evidence to the Claimant (with one exception). The Respondent did not give the names of bribe recipients and did not call Mr B as a witness. Possibly, the Respondent and its representatives were aware at this point that they were running the risk of incriminating themselves. For the Tribunal, the Respondent's lack of co-operation had more weight than the bribery indicators, *inter alia* the high amount of the Claimant's remuneration and the lack of documentation for subcontractors. The exception is Product Agreement Q: here, the Tribunal did make its own inquiry and requested the Claimant to produce bank documents. Combined, the extremely unusual amount of commission for unspecified services, the Claimant's uncooperativeness, and the untrue affidavits eventually convinced the Tribunal that Agreement Q involved bribery. The Tribunal argued that the inequality created by the nullity of a bribe contract was legally irrelevant.

6.1.7 Westacre *v.* Jugoimport (*ICC Case No. 7047 of 1994*)

In 1988, Westacre (Claimant), a company incorporated in Panama, and Jugoimport (first Defendant), a state-owned corporation in the former Yugoslavia (now in Serbia), concluded an Agreement according to which Westacre was to assist Jugoimport in the sale of military products and armaments to Kuwait, which was represented by their Ministry of Defence (MoD). Under the terms of the Agreement, any contracts that Jugoimport would conclude with third parties in Kuwait were to be regarded irrefutably as the result of Westacre's efforts. The Agreement ran for three years, and the Claimant was to receive fees for consulting services in different amounts. Second Defendant was a state-owned bank that backed up Jugoimport's contractual obligations.[103] For the purposes of this text, the focus will be on the first Defendant, Jugoimport.

In the following year, Jugoimport and the MoD of Kuwait signed a contract for the delivery of 215 M-84 tanks at a price of roughly US$500 million plus GB£11 million. Prior to concluding this contract, the MoD sent Jugoimport two circulars which requested, first, that arms contracts be made directly with the MoD, without involving agents or intermediaries, and second, that MoD contractors would not pay any agents, and prices would not contain any commissions and the like for agents.[104]

Two weeks before signing the MoD contract, Jugoimport sent a letter to Westacre, enclosing the circulars, stating that at the time of conclusion of their Agreement, it did not know of the circulars and of the legal requirements contained therein (but suggesting that Westacre was acquainted with their content at the time of the Agreement signature). Several months later, Jugoimport informed Westacre by another letter that, since the Agreement was not in accordance with the laws of Kuwait, it was ready to negotiate the terms for terminating the Agreement. Jugoimport considered this letter to be the termination of the Agreement. It repeated its request that Westacre cease its activities in subsequent letters. Westacre on the other hand, had sent several unsigned telefax letters to Jugoimport after the Agreement had been concluded, which related mainly to the M-84 tank contract.[105]

Jugoimport claimed that those letters had not given them any support in the conclusion of the tank contract with the MoD, and that Westacre did not carry out any other activities. Westacre disputed this and demanded the payment of the consultant's fees. According to its arbitration clause, Swiss law governed the Agreement. The arbitration took place in Geneva.[106] The Arbitral Tribunal discussed a number of legal

[103] *Westacre* v. *Jugoimport*, Yearbook, 79 et seq.
[104] *Westacre* v. *Jugoimport*, Bulletin, 302.
[105] *Westacre* v. *Jugoimport*, Bulletin, 302 et seq.; *Westacre* v. *Jugoimport*, Yearbook, 80.
[106] *Westacre* v. *Jugoimport*, Bulletin, 304 et seq., 318 et seq.; *Westacre* v. *Jugoimport*, Yearbook, 80; Crivellaro 2003, 139 et seq.

questions arising out of the parties' claims, of which only those related to alleged bribery are discussed here. The Tribunal held that under Swiss law, the Agreement consisted of brokerage and mandate elements.[107]

6.1.7.1 Mandatory Laws of the Former Yugoslavia

Jugoimport claimed that the mandatory laws of the former Yugoslavia also had to be applied, next to Swiss law as chosen by the parties. The Tribunal was ready to consider this, but Jugoimport failed to inform the Tribunal which mandatory laws it deemed violated. The Tribunal stated:

> It is contrary to all experience that a state-owned institution such as [Jugoimport], whose director is appointed directly by the Head of State, engages in activities contrary to the mandatory laws of that country. The Arbitral Tribunal therefore saw no reason to investigate, without further evidence, whether mandatory rules of the [law of the former Yugoslavia] could be violated. Besides, [Jugoimport] did not even allege that the violation of the mandatory laws of [the former Yugoslavia] would be considered a violation of the international ordre public.[108]

6.1.7.2 Mandatory Laws of Kuwait

Jugoimport also claimed that the Agreement violated mandatory laws of Kuwait, arguing that the MoD circular formulated that mandatory law. The Tribunal stated that it was up to Jugoimport to prove that the MoD circular was part of mandatory Kuwaiti law, and to specify the mandatory provisions of the law of Kuwait on which the circular was based. The Tribunal concluded that Jugoimport had said 'nothing in this respect'.[109]

Jugoimport also claimed a breach of compulsory provisions of Kuwait's nationality laws. The Tribunal argued that, as the parties had chosen Swiss law to apply, it would not take into account those provisions. With reference to Art. 19 of the SPILA, the Tribunal argued that the applicability of this Article was disputed in arbitration if the parties had chosen a specific law to apply. The Tribunal argued that Arts. 19 and 20 of the SCO were mandatory rules of the *lex contractus* in this case, but that the mandatory provisions of Kuwaiti law on details of agency could not come under Arts. 19 and 20 SCO; also, such provisions on

[107] *Westacre* v. *Jugoimport*, Bulletin, 323.
[108] *Westacre* v. *Jugoimport*, Bulletin, 319.
[109] *Westacre* v. *Jugoimport*, Bulletin, 330.

agency were, in the permanent practice of international arbitration, not considered part of the *ordre public international*.[110] The Tribunal concluded that

> The parties are to be enabled to subject their legal relations to the law they choose, and to exclude the national law which would otherwise apply. Therefore, provisions of the law which is excluded can only be recognized within the chosen law to the extent that they are part of the ordre public international . . . Examples of this are provisions to fight corruption and bribery.[111]

Therefore, the Tribunal found that the provisions of Kuwaiti law dealing with corruption and bribery were to be recognised in this arbitration, even though the parties had chosen Swiss law to apply. It seems, however, that the Tribunal did not specify any Kuwaiti anti-bribery provisions.

6.1.7.3 Agreement Not Invalid because of Disproportionately High Fees

The Tribunal decided that despite the disproportionately high fees provided for in the parties' Agreement in relation to the services actually rendered by Westacre, the Agreement was not invalid, arguing that

> The Arbitral Tribunal is unanimous that unusually high fees do not as such invalidate the Agreement. From the beginning, the Agreement was intended to bring about the M-84-contract between [Jugoimport] and the MoD (inter alia), by means of services rendered by [Westacre].
>
> The purpose of the Agreement has been achieved in that [Jugoimport] has concluded the M-84-contract with the MoD. Therefore the validity of the Agreement does not depend on the quantity of services [Westacre] had to perform. It is sufficient that it did render services to [Jugoimport] under the Agreement. Of this the Arbitral Tribunal is satisfied.[112]

The fees that Jugoimport was due to Westacre according to the Agreement amounted to 15 per cent of the payments that Jugoimport received under its contract with the MoD for the M-84 tanks.[113]

6.1.7.4 Agreement Not Invalid because of Lobbying

Jugoimport claimed that the Agreement was invalid because of Westacre's illicit lobbying activities. Westacre did not deny lobbying, stating

[110] *Westacre* v. *Jugoimport*, Bulletin, 331 et seq. with reference to *Northrop Corp* v. *Triad Intern. Marketing SA*.

[111] *Westacre* v. *Jugoimport*, Bulletin, 332.

[112] *Westacre* v. *Jugoimport*, Bulletin, 338.

[113] *Westacre* v. *Jugoimport*, Bulletin, 344 et seq.

that it had lobbied the MoD on Jugoimport's behalf, and had supplied Jugoimport with information on its own as well as its competitors' bids. Westacre explained its understanding of lobbying to be the using of personal contacts in the small community of officials in Kuwait, where everyone knew each other (Westacre's two shareholders in fact were nationals of Kuwait).[114]

The two shareholders of Westacre also explained that they did not perform their work publicly, but openly represented Westacre, and that they had tried to protect their know-how against other agents. The Tribunal held that lobbying as such was not an illegal activity. The majority of the Tribunal concluded that it did not see any malicious intent or illicit activities from Westacre's shareholders, when they tried not to disclose their professional knowledge to third parties.[115]

6.1.7.5 Late Bribery Allegations

From the unusually high level of consultant's fees Jugoimport inferred that Westacre intended, already at the time of conclusion of the Agreement, to use part of those fees to bribe MoD officials, without the knowledge of Jugoimport. However, the majority of the Tribunal was not convinced. On the one hand, this was a new allegation put forward by Jugoimport only in its final brief, after the hearing of evidence, and repeated in its oral final pleadings – at a time when it was too late to bring new facts or allegations. In the hearing of evidence, Jugoimport had not clearly asked the witnesses whether the Agreement involved bribery.[116]

On the other hand, the majority of the Tribunal did not see the unsigned letters to Jugoimport that did not identify Westacre's shareholders, and Jugoimport's suspicion that Westacre was an 'international paper vehicle' because it was domiciled in Panama, as substantive evidence for bribery. It declared Jugoimport's allegations that were submitted late as speculative, stating that,

> In arbitration proceedings . . . bribery is a fact which has to be alleged and for which evidence has to be submitted, and at the same time constitutes a defence, nullifying the claims arising from a contract. The consequences of this are decisive.

[114] *Westacre* v. *Jugoimport*, Bulletin, 331 and 338 et seq.
[115] *Westacre* v. *Jugoimport*, Bulletin, 339 et seq.
[116] *Westacre* v. *Jugoimport*, Bulletin, 341.

> If a claimant asserts claims arising from a contract, and the defendant objects that the claimant's rights arising from the contract are null due to bribery, it is up to the defendant to present the fact of bribery and the pertaining evidence within the time limits allowed to him for presenting facts. The statement of facts and the burden of proof are therefore upon the defendant. The word "bribery" is clear and unmistakeable. If the defendant does not use it in his presentation of facts an Arbitral Tribunal does not have to investigate. It is exclusively the parties' presentation of facts that decides in what direction the arbitral tribunal has to investigate … If the claimant's claim based on the contract is to be voided by the defence of bribery, the arbitral tribunal, as any state court, must be convinced that there is indeed a case of bribery.[117]

Hence, the majority of the Tribunal did not say there was no bribery involved in this case. It rather argued that Jugoimport did not present bribery at the right moment during the arbitral proceedings – it should have done so in its written briefs before the hearing of witnesses.

In the Award, the majority of the Tribunal concluded that the Agreement did not infringe the *ordre public international* and that Westacre's activity did not violate *bonos mores*. Therefore, Westacre was entitled to the fees under the Agreement (or the respective damages) to the extent they were due. In numbers, Westacre was entitled to approximately US $46 million and GB£1 million in fees and damages from Jugoimport for the M-84 tanks that had been delivered and paid so far.[118]

6.1.7.6 Appeal of the Award to the Swiss Federal Supreme Court

Jugoimport appealed to the Swiss Federal Supreme Court, seeking annulment of the Award. It argued, *inter alia*, that the Award was incompatible with substantive public policy (*'l'ordre public matériel'*) because the Agreement violated, or at least circumvented, the mandatory law of Kuwait; and that the Agreement was contrary to *bonos mores* and therefore invalid because it promised the payment of bribes (Art. 190 (2)(e) SPILA).[119]

The Federal Supreme Court stated that the Appellants misconceived the nature of the appeal under Art. 190(2)(e) SPILA, as their critique of the Award was in essence appeals-like (*'rein appellatorische Kritik'*). However, the Swiss legislator deliberately had limited the scope of

117 *Westacre* v. *Jugoimport*, Bulletin, 342 et seq.
118 *Westacre* v. *Jugoimport*, Bulletin, 343, 346 et seq., 356 et seq.
119 *ASA Bulletin* (1995), 217 et seq., 222 et seq.

possible appeals under Art. 190(2)(e) SPILA with the aim of restricting the possibility to obstruct international arbitration and safeguarding the effectiveness of arbitral jurisdiction. This effectiveness would not be granted if the Federal Supreme Court would freely revisit the findings of fact of an arbitral tribunal. For this reason, a general appeal regarding arbitrariness in fact-finding or application of law is not possible. The findings of fact of an arbitral tribunal can be criticised before the Federal Supreme Court only on the basis that they have been established in disregard of procedural guarantees of law, or that they are incompatible with procedural public policy (*'l'ordre public procédural'*).[120]

With regard to procedural public policy, the Appellants failed to specify the essential and unanimously acknowledged procedural principles, a violation of which would affect the sense of justice in Switzerland in an unbearable way. Jugoimport alleged that the Arbitral Tribunal misread its own procedure when it established the facts only in the approximate, without respect to the *ex officio*-principle (*'le principe de l'instruction d'office'*), and when it weighed the evidence erroneously. The Federal Supreme Court argued that Jugoimport claimed a false, possibly arbitrary application of the law, but by no means a transgression of procedural public policy. Therefore, the Court decided to base its decision on the facts as established by the Arbitral Tribunal.[121] The Court also stated that Art. 190(2)(e) SPILA demanded for a notion of universal or transnational public policy.[122]

The Appellants also argued that the Agreement violated mandatory laws of Kuwait prohibiting the intervention of intermediaries and agents in the arms trade; according to Art. 19 SPILA, the Tribunal should have observed those mandatory provisions. The Federal Supreme Court stated that the majority of doctrine was of the view that Art. 19 SPILA did not oblige an arbitral tribunal to apply foreign laws to the *lex contractus* as chosen by the parties; and opinions were apparently unanimous that the non-observation of foreign law as such was not contrary to public policy in the sense of Art. 190(2)(e) SPILA.[123]

Furthermore, the Appellants alleged that according to its true content, the Agreement obliged Jugoimport to pay bribes to Westacre. Therefore, the Agreement was invalid under Arts. 19/20 of the SCO and incompatible with substantive public policy.[124] The Federal Supreme Court stated

[120] *ASA Bulletin* (1995), 223. [121] *ASA Bulletin* (1995), 223 et seq.
[122] *ASA Bulletin* (1995), 224 with reference to BGE 120 II 155, 168.
[123] *ASA Bulletin* (1995), 224 et seq. [124] *ASA Bulletin* (1995), 225.

that a promise to pay bribes was contrary to *bonos mores* and thus null and void, and also against public policy. However, in the case at hand, it was not established that the parties to the Agreement had jointly pursued an illicit purpose (like corruption), and it was neither proven in time nor even alleged that Westacre, at the conclusion of the Agreement, had the intent, without the knowledge of Jugoimport, to destine a part of its fees towards the payment of bribes to Kuwaiti officials. As such, the allegations of Jugoimport were contrary to the facts as established by the Arbitral Tribunal. The Tribunal did not violate substantive public policy when it declared the Agreement valid, and the appeal on the basis of Art. 190(2)(e) SPILA was unfounded. In sum, Jugoimport's appeal was rejected.[125]

6.1.7.7 Enforcement of the Award in Front of the High Court

In 1996, Westacre (Plaintiffs) started proceedings in front of the High Court of Justice of England and Wales, seeking to enforce the ICC Award in England. Jugoimport (Defendants) challenged the enforcement of the Award, arguing that this would be contrary to English public policy.[126] The Court *inter alia* dealt with issues of additional evidence and jurisdiction. The Defendants' case rested primarily on an affidavit sworn by their legal counsel Mr Milosavljevic (M.M.) on 13 December 1995. His detailed investigation into the Agreement and the armament contracts showed that there existed a debt-swapping arrangement between the former Yugoslavia and Kuwait, and that around 1988, high-ranking Kuwaiti officials had made it clear that contracts for military equipment with Yugoslavia would only be entered into if a consultancy agreement was first concluded with a nominated consultant. Westacre was to receive large (15 per cent and 20 per cent) commissions on the value of military equipment contracts over an extended period of time (three years for first supply and twenty years for spare parts); and the scheme included that Yugoslav equipment would be preferred over that of other suppliers.[127] Defendants also alleged that a number of witnesses, who gave evidence during the arbitration proceedings, had perjured themselves.[128]

125 *ASA Bulletin* (1995), 225 et seq.
126 *Westacre Investments Inc* v. *Jugoimport-SPDR Holding Co Ltd and Others* [1998] 4 All ER 570 (QBD), 570.
127 [1998] 4 All ER 570 (QBD), 574 et seq.
128 [1998] 4 All ER 570 (QBD), 577.

Before deciding on the issue of new evidence and perjury, Colman J made the following observation on public policy:

> In my judgment, it is relevant . . . to take into account the fact that there is mounting international concern about the prevalence of corrupt trading practices. This concern relates particularly to armaments contracts and to contracts for public works. Ministers and government officials are in certain parts of the world customarily bribed to procure lucrative contracts for the suppliers of arms and the providers building and construction projects. Indeed in the very week when this judgment is being delivered the government of the United Kingdom together with the governments of many other states is signing the OECD Convention on Combating the Bribery of Foreign Officials in International Transactions. Under that convention the parties are, by art 1, to create a specific criminal offence of bribery of foreign public officials . . . It is therefore important that, although the convention has not yet come into force, the English courts should not be seen to be encouraging the corruption of government officials as an instrument of international trade or merely to be paying lip service to such widespread disapproval.[129]

Against the public policy consideration of fighting transnational corruption, Colman J balanced the importance to sustain the finality of international arbitration awards. He concluded that,

> although commercial corruption is deserving of strong judicial and governmental disapproval, few would consider that it stood in the scale of opprobrium quite at the level of drug-trafficking. On balance, I have come to the conclusion that the public policy of sustaining international arbitration awards on the facts of this case outweighs the public policy in discouraging international commercial corruption.[130]

Colman J eventually decided that the possibilities of a party to bring additional evidence and to allege perjury at the enforcement stage of an arbitration award were very limited and required, *inter alia*, that the evidence was not reasonably obtainable at the arbitration hearing. As the Award was valid under Swiss law, enforcement of it in England would not offend international comity. Therefore, Colman J saw no grounds to decline the enforcement of the award.[131]

6.1.7.8 Judgment of the England and Wales Court of Appeal (Civil Division)

Jugoimport's subsequent appeal to the Appeals Court was dismissed by a 2-to-1 majority, and leave to appeal to the House of Lords refused.

[129] [1998] 4 All ER 570 (QBD), 597. [130] [1998] 4 All ER 570 (QBD), 598.
[131] [1998] 4 All ER 570 (QBD), 571.

The Appellants were not allowed to reopen the facts.[132] The disagreeing judge Waller LJ, with reference to an *obiter dictum* in the *Soleimany* case[133] and to other case law, took a positive stance towards a reopening of the facts as they had been established by the arbitrators, when 'commercial corruption' was at stake:

> [T]here will be circumstances in which, despite the prima facie position of an award preventing a party reopening matters either decided by the arbitrators or which the party had every opportunity of raising before the arbitrators, the English court will allow a re-opening. The court is in this instance performing a balancing exercise between the competing public policies of finality and illegality; between the finality that should prima facie exist particularly for those that agree to have their disputes arbitrated, against the policy of ensuring that the executive power of the English court is not abused. It is for those reasons that the nature of the illegality is a factor, the strength of case that there was illegality also is a factor, and the extent to which it can be seen that the asserted illegality was addressed by the arbitral tribunal is a factor.
>
> The judge performed the balancing exercise and narrowly came down on the side of upholding the finality of the award. It would seem that if the case had concerned a drug trafficking contract he might well have taken a different view but he placed 'commercial corruption' at a different level of opprobrium from drug trafficking.
>
> I have reached a different conclusion to that of the judge. I disagree with him as to the appropriate level of opprobrium at which to place commercial corruption. It seems to me that the principle against enforcing a corrupt bargain of the nature of this agreement, if the facts in MM's affidavit are correct, is within that bracket recognised . . . as being based on public policy of the greatest importance and almost certainly recognised in most jurisdictions throughout the world. I believe it important that the English court is not seen to be turning a blind eye to corruption on this scale. I believe that if unanswered the case at present made on MM's affidavit would be conclusive against Westacre being entitled to enforce the agreement and thus the award as a matter of English public policy. I also believe that the judge did not sufficiently consider the extent to which the case now presented on bribery was examined by the Arbitration Tribunal. When one examines the circumstances of this case one can see that in truth the bribery issue has not been ventilated properly before the Swiss arbitral tribunal . . .

[132] *Westacre Investments Inc* v. *Jugoimport-SPDR Holding Co Ltd and Others* [1999] 3 All ER 864, 865 et seq.

[133] *Abner Soleimany* v. *Sion Soleimany* [1999] 3 All ER 847, 859.

> The fact is that the arbitrators simply did not have an opportunity of considering the case as now made, and whatever their suspicions, the majority did not feel it in their place to make inquiries.[134]

Waller LJ argued that commercial corruption involved illegality of a serious nature. Enforcing a bribe contract was contrary to international public policy, and enforcing a respective award was against English public policy. The public policy that the power of an English court may not be abused should outweigh the public policy of the finality of arbitral awards. According to Waller LJ, the bribery issue had not been dealt with properly by the Arbitral Tribunal.

The other two Lord Justices of Appeal, however, were opposed to a reopening of the facts. Since the bribery claim had been 'made, entertained and rejected' during the arbitral proceedings and there was no fresh evidence, they saw no justification to refuse the enforcement of the ICC Award. They argued that any preliminary inquiry whether there was *prima facie* evidence that the ICC Award was based on an illegal contract would lead to the conclusion that a reopening of the facts should be rebuffed:

> First, there was evidence before the tribunal that this was a straightforward, commercial contract. Secondly, the arbitrators specifically found that the underlying contract was not illegal. Thirdly, there is nothing to suggest incompetence on the part of the arbitrators. Finally, there is no reason to suspect collusion or bad faith in the obtaining of the award. The seriousness of the alleged illegality to which Waller LJ gives weight is not, in my judgment, a factor to be considered at the stage of deciding whether or not to mount a full scale inquiry. It is something to be taken into account as part of the balancing exercise between the competing public policy considerations of finality and illegality which can only be performed in response to the second question, if it arises, namely should the award be enforced.[135]

In short, the majority argued that the Appellants should not be allowed to challenge the arbitrators' fact-finding at the enforcement stage, and this issue was to be treated separately from the question of how serious the alleged illegality was.

6.1.7.9 Analysis

Westacre v. *Jugoimport* is a difficult case resulting in a majority Award that was appealed in Switzerland and also at the enforcement stage in the

[134] *Westacre Investments Inc* v. *Jugoimport-SPDR Holding Co Ltd and Others* [1999] 3 All ER 864, 885 et seq.

[135] [1999] 3 All ER 864, 887 et seq.

United Kingdom. The proceedings raise four issues: mandatory law, the duty of an arbitral tribunal to investigate *ex officio*, the timing of bribery allegations and the rising international concern about corruption.

The Tribunal did not apply the mandatory laws of the former Yugoslavia (the state where Jugoimport was incorporated). Notably, the Tribunal did not argue that those laws were not applicable because the parties had chosen Swiss law to apply. Rather, the Tribunal argued that Jugoimport had not specified the mandatory laws that it thought were violated. The Tribunal's argument that it is against all experience that a state-owned corporation would violate mandatory laws of its country is, from today's point of view, not very convincing, as there are enough examples for such behaviour.[136]

Regarding the mandatory laws of Kuwait (the state where the Agreement was performed), the Tribunal held that they were on the one hand not specified by Jugoimport, and on the other hand not applicable because the parties had chosen Swiss law to apply. The mandatory laws of Kuwait on agency did not form part of international public policy. The Tribunal found that the mandatory laws of Kuwait fighting corruption and bribery would be applicable, but did not specify those provisions.

The Tribunal argued that the unusually high fees that Jugoimport had to pay Westacre did not as such invalidate the Agreement, and that lobbying was not an illegal activity. Regarding the bribery allegations, the Tribunal's main argument was that they were raised too late in the proceedings, after the hearing of evidence. The Tribunal also found that there was no substantive evidence for bribery. As Jugoimport had not invoked bribery in its presentation of facts, the Tribunal argued that it was not obliged to investigate. The Tribunal found that it was exclusively the parties' presentation of facts that directed it in its investigation.

Jugoimport failed with its appeal to the Swiss Federal Supreme Court because its criticism was mainly directed at the fact-finding of the Arbitral Tribunal, arguing that the Tribunal had not investigated bribery *ex officio*. However, the possibilities to appeal the fact-finding of an arbitral tribunal to the Supreme Court are limited to situations where the facts were established in disregard of procedural guarantees of law, or when they are incompatible with procedural public policy. The Supreme Court denied both situations in this case and decided to base its decision on the facts as established by the Tribunal, eventually dismissing Jugoimport's appeal.

[136] E.g. in cases of transnational bribery.

Jugoimport's challenge to the enforcement of the Award in England was based on an affidavit that was sworn after the conclusion of the ICC arbitration proceedings. The High Court Judge took into account the OECD Convention criminalising the bribery of foreign public officials that was being signed by the United Kingdom in those days, arguing that English courts should not encourage a business practice that was widely disapproved. However, the Judge found that the possibilities of the parties to bring additional evidence at the enforcement stage were very limited, and saw no reason to decline the enforcement of the Award that was valid under Swiss law.

Jugoimport appealed the High Court decision, but failed, not being allowed to reopen the facts. The Appeals Court decision was taken by a 2-to-1 majority, and the disagreeing Lord Justice of Appeal put strong emphasis on the fight against (commercial) corruption, arguing that the enforcement of a bribe agreement touched upon a public policy of the greatest importance that was almost universally recognised, and that the bribery allegations had not been discussed properly in front of the Arbitral Tribunal, as the Tribunal majority had decided not to make own inquiries. The majority of the Appeals Court put more emphasis on the finality of arbitral awards and argued that there was no fresh evidence that would have justified a reopening of the facts at the enforcement stage.

If one reads the ICC Award and the domestic court decisions, it appears that the arbitrators and judges at each stage had their suspicions that bribery was involved in this case. The Tribunal's decision not to inquire into Jugoimport's late allegations had far-reaching consequences, because the courts at the appeals and enforcement stage did not want to reopen the Tribunal's fact-finding. Therefore, a real inquiry into the allegations never took place.[137] Under such circumstances, there is a risk that a party that unsuccessfully alleges bribery (in this case Jugoimport) in the result is forced to fulfil a bribery agreement. It is unclear whether other legal remedies were available (e.g. revision).

6.1.8 ICC Case No. 8891 (1998)

The Claimant in this case was a consultant, and the Respondent an exporter to state X. The parties concluded a consultancy contract

[137] Cremades and Cairns reject the Tribunal's approach (Cremades and Cairns 2003b, 78, 82 et seq.).

according to which the Claimant was to assist the Respondent in obtaining a price increase in two contracts that the Respondent had already concluded with state X.[138]

6.1.8.1 The Applicable Law

Citing French and Swiss case law, the Arbitral Tribunal took note that those national laws consider corruption as contrary to domestic law as well as to international public policy.[139] Referring to earlier ICC Awards, the Tribunal stated that the illegality of bribe contracts is well established in international arbitration, and that arbitrators usually do not limit themselves to the application of national laws (although corruption is illegal in most domestic legal systems), but also call upon general principles of law or upon international or transnational public policy.[140] With reference to arbitration doctrine, the Tribunal noted that the recourse to international public policy to declare the illegality of a bribe contract was disputed.[141] The Tribunal stated that the consequence of illegality is nullity of the contract; arbitrators are competent to declare nullity of the main contract because of the principle of separability of the arbitral clause.[142]

6.1.8.2 Proving Bribery

On burden of proof, the Tribunal stated that according to the general rule, the party alleging illegality has to prove it, but that this proof is usually difficult to provide because illegality is hidden behind apparently innocuous contractual terms, and arbitrators often have to rely on indicia. Such indicia must be serious, because corporations frequently hire a local agent to represent their interests in a foreign country, which in itself is perfectly legal.[143] Based on arbitral decisions and doctrine, the Tribunal identified the following indicia for illicit activities:

- incapacity of the agent to provide evidence for his activities, since consultants usually document their services, producing written notes and reports;

[138] Crivellaro 2003, 142.

[139] French law was close to the consultancy contract because of the filiation of the Respondent and because of the nationality and domicile of the Claimant's principal actor; Swiss law was close because the Claimant was incorporated in Switzerland (ICC Case No. 8891, 1079).

[140] ICC Case No. 8891, 1076 et seq.

[141] ICC Case No. 8891, 1078.

[142] ICC Case No. 8891, 1079.

[143] ICC Case No. 8891, 1079.

- the duration of the agent's intervention (a very short engagement that nevertheless brings the expected result is an indicia for corruption);
- in a consultancy contract, remuneration through commission payments which are calculated from the amount received by the corporation out of the contracts that it concludes in a certain country;
- high percentage commission payments in relation to the services actually rendered by the agent (in practice, a commission for a simple agent that amounts to more than 1 or 2 per cent is rare and gives rise to a presumption that the intermediary had to forward certain amounts).[144]

Based on those considerations, the Tribunal examined the evidence from the point of view that a contract inciting or favouring bribery of public officials is contrary to transnational public policy, and if such proves to be the object of a consultancy contract, the Tribunal has no other option than to declare the contract null and void.[145]

The Tribunal found that the consultancy contract was initially concluded for roughly two and a half months, which seemed extremely short bearing in mind the task that had been assigned to the consultant. The Tribunal considered this to be indicia for bribery. Concerning the remuneration of the consultant, it found nothing unusual in the fact that this was paid in the form of a success fee (a percentage of the price increase received from the ministry). However, the high percentage of the commission paid to the consultant (18.5 per cent) was indicia for the Tribunal that the Claimant had to direct a substantial part of the received amounts to third parties.[146]

In addition, the dossier substantiating the activities of the Claimant was meagre. The Claimant explained that its primary task was to create a favourable climate for the negotiations with the ministry; however, this activity was hardly documented, and it was difficult to identify actual services rendered by the Claimant. The Tribunal stated that the essential activity of the Claimant was apparently the payment of remunerations to certain persons in order to unblock the situation inside the ministry to the advantage of the Respondent. Although the actual bribe payments could not be proven with certainty and were contested, witness testimonies and written evidence allowed the Tribunal to reason that the Claimant was first and foremost charged with arranging the necessary payments. Also, the absence of the Claimant's PDG (CEO), although he

[144] ICC Case No. 8891, 1079 et seq. with further references.

[145] ICC Case No. 8891, 1080. [146] ICC Case No. 8891, 1080.

had been invited to testify, made the Tribunal think that he deliberately avoided testimony. It was not discernible that such payments could have been destined to remunerate a legitimate service by the public officials. As such, the Tribunal maintained that the activity performed by the Claimant, as it was documented, was particularly strong indicia that the consultancy contract had an illicit content.[147]

The consistent body of indicia eventually led the Tribunal to the conclusion that the object of the consultancy contract was the obtaining of a price increase from the ministry through bribe payments to influential public officials. The Tribunal did not doubt that this was the intention of the parties already at the time when the contract was concluded.[148]

In the Award, the Tribunal declared the consultancy contract null and void, emphasising that the fact that corruption was common practice to obtain business in certain countries did not modify its conclusion. The Tribunal argued that the fight against corruption was intensifying – referring *inter alia* to the negotiations within the OECD towards an anticorruption convention – and that arbitrators had to be conscious of bribery. While the Tribunal was aware that nullity of the bribe contract in this case meant that the Respondent, who had benefitted from the services of the Claimant, did not have to pay the contracted price, and although it called this consequence unpleasant at the least, it did not find this sufficient to legitimise the contract.[149]

6.1.8.3 Analysis

ICC Case No. 8891 was decided at a time when the efforts on the international level to combat the bribery of foreign public officials were achieving concrete results in the form of a multilateral treaty: the OECD Convention on Bribery that was signed in December 1997 and entered into force in February 1999. The Award shows that the Tribunal was perfectly aware of those developments, and that they had an impact on its considerations.

Regarding the applicable law, it appears that the Tribunal did not rely on any specific provisions of French or Swiss criminal law. Rather, it argued that bribery was contrary to transnational public policy. The Tribunal apparently did not discuss burden and standard of proof in depth, but referred to the general principle that the party alleging

[147] ICC Case No. 8891, 1081 et seq. [148] ICC Case No. 8891, 1082.
[149] ICC Case No. 8891, 1082 et seq.

illegality had to prove it and argued that because such proof was often difficult to establish, the arbitrators frequently relied on indicia.

The Tribunal then listed indicia for bribery and analysed the facts of the case in this light. In particular, it examined whether there was documentation for the services performed by the consultant, the duration of the consultant's engagement, as well as the mode and level of the consultant's remuneration. The Tribunal concluded that there were convergent indicia that the object of the consultancy contract was the bribery of foreign public officials. Therefore, it declared the contract null and void.

6.1.9 ICC Case No. 9333 (1998)

Claimant in this case was a Moroccan individual; Respondent was a French corporation. In 1995, the parties signed an agreement according to which the Claimant had to advise and assist the Respondent with the acquisition and execution of a building contract related to a pipeline project in Morocco, in return for a commission. The commission payment was fixed at 1.9 million French francs, if the value of the building contract acquired by the Respondent was not less than 7 million French francs.

The dispute arose over the commission payment. The Claimant alleged that the Respondent had acquired the building contract, but did not pay the full amount of the agreed commission, indicating that the Respondent ceased its payments after it came under the control of a US corporation. The Respondent claimed nullity of the agreement, alleging that its object were bribe payments contrary to the US law against foreign bribery (the Foreign Corrupt Practices Act; FCPA) as well as to the OECD Convention on Bribery. The Claimant argued that the agreement had no unlawful object and was not contrary to *bonos mores*, and that it rightfully claimed its commission as the building contract had in fact been awarded to the Respondent and had entered into force, proving the effectiveness of Claimant's services.[150]

In fulfilment of the agreement, the Respondent had paid 415,000 French francs in March 1995, responding to an invoice by the company International SA from Lausanne, Switzerland. The payment was

[150] ICC Case No. 9333, Collection, 575; ICC Case No. 9333, ASA Bulletin, 757 et seq.; ICC Case No. 9333, ICC Bulletin, 102; Crivellaro 2003, 142 et seq.

effected to a Swiss bank account of this company. In July 1995, R Inc. (a US corporation) acquired the Respondent. Following the acquisition, the Respondent notified its agents and commercial representatives that the remuneration of their services would be paid exclusively in the country in which they were located and where the services were rendered. The Respondent introduced those directives based on the FCPA, which the US mother company as well as the companies that were part of the R group had to respect. In January 1996, the Respondent paid 310,000 French francs in response to an invoice by International SA into the same Swiss bank account as for the first transfer. In March 1996, International SA sent a third invoice to the Respondent for the amount of 435,000 French francs, which remained unpaid. In the absence of payment, the Claimant contacted Mr A ('A', the Respondent's business development manager), who suggested that Mr B ('B', the Respondent's contract manager) should be contacted.[151]

The Claimant and B met in July 1996. The parties gave divergent descriptions of the content of this meeting. B affirmed that he had explained the Respondent's new company policy prohibiting payments for agents to offshore accounts to the Claimant; for this reason, B had refused to continue Claimant's commission payments to the Swiss bank account. The Claimant then became angry and explained that he had to share its remuneration with certain employees of a Moroccan company, who did not want to receive the payments in Morocco. B considered this statement to be a confession by the Claimant that part of its remuneration was used as bribe payments. Consequently, B suspended all payments to the Claimant. The Claimant initiated arbitration based on a clause in the agreement. Seat of the arbitration was Geneva.[152]

The Claimant requested that the Respondent pay him the sum of 1,175,000 French francs, and that commission payments to him be effected in Switzerland. The Respondent, on the other hand, asked the Sole Arbitrator to declare that the 1995 agreement had an unlawful object, was contrary to *bonos mores*, and thus null and void; to state that the Respondent had paid 310,000 and 415,000 French francs to the Claimant under the agreement; and consequently to reduce the amount of the Claimant's request by 725,000 French francs. The 1995 agreement contained a clause that the SCO should apply. The Arbitrator

[151] ICC Case No. 9333, Collection, 575 et seq.; ICC Case No. 9333, ASA Bulletin, 758 et seq.
[152] ICC Case No. 9333, Collection, 576; ICC Case No. 9333, ASA Bulletin, 759 et seq.

characterised the parties' agreement as a brokerage contract (*Mäklervertrag*) according to Arts. 412 et seq. SCO.[153]

6.1.9.1 Bribe Contracts under Swiss law

The Respondent alleged that the agreement's unlawful object was Claimant's bribe payments to certain persons in charge at the Moroccan company. This allegation was based on B's testimony that the Claimant had confessed that the Respondent's payments were not destined to him alone. The Claimant contested to have made such a declaration. The Arbitrator found that, according to Art. 20 SCO, a contract is unlawful if its conclusion is prohibited; or if the service provided for in the contract is prohibited; or if the aim pursued by the parties is against the law. In the case at hand, the contract could not be unlawful under Art. 20 SCO because, according to the Respondent, the Claimant had acted without its knowledge. Therefore, declaring the agreement null and void according to Art. 20 SCO, as the Respondent had asked, was not adequate. Furthermore, the Arbitrator stated that a bribe contract is not considered unlawful under Swiss law but is contrary to *bonos mores* under Art. 20 SCO; however, in the absence of a common intent to bribe a third person, the agreement is not against *bonos mores*. Under the assumption (which none of the parties developed in this case) that the Respondent knew or should have known the intention of the Claimant to pay bribes, the question would have been whether the Respondent was breaching the principle that no one may base a legal claim on its own unlawful act (*nemo auditur propriam turpitudinem allegans*). The Arbitrator concluded that establishing the consequences of the Claimant's alleged disloyalty was anyway unnecessary if the Respondent could not prove bribery.[154]

6.1.9.2 Proving Bribery

The Arbitrator heard B as well as the Claimant, but their factual descriptions were contradictory. The Arbitrator stated that he had no objective reason to privilege one of the testimonies over the other, and consequently analysed other indicia to establish the alleged facts. He did not examine in depth the terms of the 1995 agreement or the common intention of the parties, as none of them had argued that behind innocuous terms a consensus regarding illicit activities was concealed.

[153] ICC Case No. 9333, Collection, 576 et seq.

[154] ICC Case No. 9333, Collection, 577 et seq. with further references.

Rather, the Arbitrator examined the commission payment that amounted to almost 30 per cent and appeared exorbitant at first sight. However, the Arbitrator stated that the context in which the agreement was concluded had to be considered as well – maybe the intermediary was simply greedy and the principal had badly negotiated the contract terms. In the case at hand, the Arbitrator noted based on the statements of A and of Respondent's PDG (CEO) that the circumstances justified the superior commission payment: the Respondent could not have acquired the building contract without the intervention of the Claimant. The Respondent had to consider the absolute amount of the commission payment (and not its percentage) as a necessary 'investment'.[155]

The Arbitrator then discussed the lack of written evidence to substantiate a corruption case on the Respondent's side – one would have expected the Respondent to keep a dossier with proof to demonstrate its version of the facts in potential subsequent arbitration proceedings. Especially as of the moment when the Respondent decided not to pay any more offshore commissions, this would have been prudent. The FCPA obliges corporations to keep detailed books and records. The Respondent was not able (or ready) to produce certain pieces of evidence in the proceedings; for example the notification of the Claimant of the Respondent's new policy regarding payments to agents. The Respondent also did not explain the payment of January 1996 that was made after the entry into force of the new company policy (which should have suspended all such payments). Furthermore, the Claimant had not vigorously objected when the Respondent had, at some point, reduced the commission payments, as one would have expected if the Claimant had to share the commission with public officials. The Arbitrator concluded that the burden of proving alleged bribery was on the Respondent (Art. 8 Swiss Civil Code), who had failed. There was a lack of circumstantial evidence and of a chain of evidence indicating bribery that would have strengthened the probative force of B's testimony.[156]

6.1.9.3 Role of the FCPA and of the OECD Convention on Bribery

The Arbitrator noted that in principle, a contract that is not contrary to Swiss law, but to a foreign law, is not unlawful according to Art. 20 SCO. Exceptionally, a violation of foreign law can be considered as against

[155] ICC Case No. 9333, Collection, 578 et seq.
[156] ICC Case No. 9333, Collection, 579 et seq.

bonos mores under Art. 20 SCO if the violation is irreconcilable with Swiss public policy. Since the Arbitrator had concluded that bribery was not proven, no fundamental values of Swiss public policy had been affected, and a possible violation of foreign law could not be sanctioned according to Art. 20 SCO.[157]

The Arbitrator carried on and stated that a foreign law having the quality of policing law (*loi de police*) might be applied to a contract otherwise governed by Swiss law by resort to Art. 19 SPILA. Assuming that all requirements for applying Art. 19 SPILA were fulfilled, a violation of such *loi de police* could entail the unlawfulness of a contract. However, the application of Art. 19 SPILA in international arbitration was disputed, and the Swiss Federal Supreme Court had left the question open in a decision of 1994 (on *Westacre* v. *Jugoimport*).[158] Eventually, the Arbitrator left the question open as well, for two reasons: the application of the FCPA as a foreign *loi de police* was not justified, and the conditions for applying the FCPA were not fulfilled. Since the Respondent was a French subsidiary of a US mother corporation (itself not party to the arbitral proceedings) and the Claimant was a Moroccan individual, the only connection to US law was the fact that the mother corporation was American. This was insufficient for applying the FCPA under Art. 19 SPILA. The Arbitrator stated that under the FCPA, the US mother corporation is responsible for the actions of its subsidiaries and concluded that he was incompetent to decide on the application of the FCPA, because the US mother corporation was not party to the proceedings. The Arbitrator also dismissed the application of the OECD Convention on Bribery because it had not been possible to establish a bribery case during the proceedings.[159]

In the Award, the Arbitrator ordered the Respondent to pay 1,175,000 French francs to the Claimant (1,900,000 French francs less the two earlier payments of 310,000 and 415,000 French francs).[160]

6.1.9.4 Analysis

ICC Case No. 9333 was decided in the same year as Case No. 8891, but the outcome is completely different. Despite the exceptionally high amount of the broker's commission (almost 30 per cent), the Arbitrator concluded that there was no bribery involved in this case.

[157] ICC Case No. 9333, Collection, 581.

[158] BGer of 30 December 1994, *ASA Bulletin* (1995), 217.

[159] ICC Case No. 9333, Collection, 581 et seq.

[160] ICC Case No. 9333, Collection, 582.

The factual situation and the available evidence were, however, markedly different in those two cases.

Regarding applicable law, the Arbitrator relied on the SCO, as chosen by the parties, and the Swiss Civil Code. He apparently did not consider the application of the Swiss Criminal Code (the parties' choice of law clause only encompassed the SCO), or of French or Moroccan criminal law provisions (as foreign mandatory laws – although the place of performance of the agreement was Morocco; the Claimant was a Moroccan national; and the Respondent was incorporated in France). Yet the Arbitrator considered the application of the US FCPA under Art. 19 SPILA as a foreign *loi de police* (the Respondent had been acquired by a US corporation in 1995). Eventually he decided that the FCPA was not applicable because the only connection to US law was the Respondent's mother corporation (that was not a party to the proceedings). The Arbitrator considered this insufficient to apply the FCPA under Art. 19 SPILA. He also did not apply the OECD Convention on Bribery (that had been invoked by the Respondent), arguing that it had not been possible to establish a bribery case during the proceedings.

The Arbitrator did not discuss the burden and standard of proof, merely stating the general rule of Art. 8 Swiss Civil Code that the party alleging a fact has to prove it. Concerning evidence, the Respondent's bribery allegations were essentially based on B's testimony that the Claimant had confessed bribe payments; the Claimant, however, contested such a statement. The Arbitrator found that the extraordinarily high commission was explained by the fact that the Respondent only acquired the building contract because of Claimant's intervention. It was uncontested that the Claimant had in fact developed activities to resolve the difficulties the Respondent was facing in the course of the project.[161] The Respondent could not produce a written notification of the Claimant about its new policy on payments to agents. In sum, there was not enough circumstantial evidence that would have supported B's testimony, and the Arbitrator decided that the Respondent had not discharged of its burden to prove bribery.

6.1.10 ICC Case No. 12472 (2004)

Claimant in this case was a European company, acting as Respondent's sole sales agent in Middle Eastern state X. The agency agreement was

[161] ICC Case No. 9333, Collection, Observations, 586.

governed by French law. The dispute arose over claims for the agent's commission payment. The Respondent argued for the application of the law of state X as the place of performance of the agency agreement. The law of state X contained mandatory provisions requiring that agents commissioned by foreign companies must be nationals of and registered in state X. The Respondent argued that the agency agreement was void for that reason on the one hand, and on the other hand, because the Claimant had allegedly bribed government officials in order to obtain the sales contracts. The arbitration took place in Paris.[162]

6.1.10.1 The Applicable Law

The agency agreement being governed by French law, the question arose whether the mandatory provisions of the law of state X, where the agreement was performed, were applicable in this case. The Tribunal decided not to give effect to those mandatory provisions, but applied only French law, as agreed by the parties. The Tribunal argued that in this case, the consequences of not applying the mandatory provisions of the law of state X were neither disproportionate nor severe. However, the Tribunal also pointed out that the mandatory provisions of state X should be consulted if the application of the law of the contract demands for it. In the present case, the Tribunal examined the validity of the agency agreement under French law and according to transnational public policy.[163]

The Respondent alleged that the agency agreement involved trading in influence (*trafic d'influence*) and active bribery of a public official, and was therefore null and void due to its unlawful object and because of the demands of transnational public policy. It argued that national and international criminal law prohibited such practices, with specific reference to Article 433-2 of the French Criminal Code (trading in influence) and to the OECD Convention on Bribery (active bribery of foreign public officials).[164]

6.1.10.2 No Evidence of Corruption

The Tribunal noted that the Respondent carried the burden of proving its allegations of criminal behaviour. The Respondent alleged that the Claimant had understood its mission under the agency agreement

[162] ICC Case No. 12472, 46. [163] ICC Case No. 12472, 49.
[164] ICC Case No. 12472, 50.

differently from what had been agreed between the parties, namely to use its connections within the administration of state X in order to obtain contracts for the Respondent. The Claimant, on the other hand, argued that the object of the contract was a mission to gather information and negotiate in favour of the Respondent.[165]

The Tribunal stated that the accusations of the Respondent were based on simple presumptions not supported by probative elements, and that the facts invoked to support the presumptions could have multiple meanings without necessarily characterising criminal behaviour. The Tribunal argued that the Respondent knew (as shown by the correspondence between the parties) that the Claimant was establishing contacts within the state X administration in order to promote the products of the Respondent. It also argued that the amount of the commission payments could not be a sign for bribery of a public official if the amount was long discussed between the parties and where the Respondent knew that several persons had to intervene to consolidate its position in the market of state X. The Tribunal noted that the Respondent had informed the Claimant that it could legally pay 10 per cent commissions abroad, and argued that it was not proven that the various intervening persons, who had to be paid, had searched to abuse their influence, and that it was also not proven that one of those persons had been a public official. The Tribunal concluded that there was no certainty that a specific person or public body had received, or solicited, or been promised an undue remuneration in order to gain access to a market or other benefit.[166] In the Award, the Tribunal rejected to declare the agency agreement null and void on the basis of influence trading and corruption of public officials.

6.1.10.3 Analysis

In ICC Case No. 12472, the Tribunal refused to apply mandatory provisions on nationality and registration of agents of the state where the agreement was performed, as the consequences of the non-application were not disproportionate. The parties had chosen French law to govern the agreement. Concerning the bribery allegations, the provisions of French criminal law on trading in influence, and the OECD Convention on Bribery were invoked. Transnational public policy was also mentioned.

[165] ICC Case No. 12472, 50. [166] ICC Case No. 12472, 51.

On proof, the Tribunal argued that the Respondent's allegations were only based on presumptions, and there was no conclusive evidence for bribery. The amount of the Claimant's commission had for long been discussed by the parties; the Respondent knew that several persons had to intervene on its behalf; and there was no proof that any of the paid persons had been a public official and had tried to abuse its influence. The Tribunal in this case did not simply refer to transnational public policy, but analysed the objective elements of trading in influence and active bribery of foreign public officials. The Tribunal did not specify which standard of proof it applied.

6.1.11 ICC Case No. 12732 (2007)

The following short summary of the facts is published:

> The claimant accused the respondents of breach of contract for failing to fulfil their obligations under what it considered to be an enforceable and binding agreement between them. The respondents objected to the enforceability of the agreement, which they alleged had been made under a combination of duress and misrepresentation. They also asserted that the agreement was part of a corrupt transaction and entailed conduct that was illegal under applicable law.[167]

The arbitration was seated in London.

6.1.11.1 Burden of Proof

The Arbitral Tribunal noted that there was no direct written or oral evidence for the Respondent's corruption defence: that corrupt payments had been made in connection with the negotiation or signature of the agreement; 'Respondents ask the Tribunal to infer from a constellation of facts that the [Agreement] was part of a single unenforceable corrupt arrangement. Claimant's principal witness . . . strenuously denies that he or Claimant participated in any corruption.'[168] The Tribunal stated that the party asserting a fact bears the burden of proving it, and noted that in this case, the Claimant had to prove the existence of the agreement and its breach by the Respondent, whereas the Respondent had to prove the corruption defence.[169]

[167] ICC Case No. 12732, 76.
[168] ICC Case No. 12732, 76.
[169] ICC Case No. 12732, 77.

6.1.11.2 Standard of Proof

The Tribunal then examined the applicable standard of proof, asking whether the fact that bribery and corruption were alleged did raise, or lower, the standard of proof from the usual civil standard. It noted that direct evidence was rare in cases of alleged bribery because such payments were carefully disguised:

> As a result, reliance can and must be placed by the adjudicator on indirect or circumstantial evidence, on surrounding events, and on inferences. Indeed, it has been suggested that, in such circumstances, the standard of proof may be weakened, being based on presumptions arising from other extrinsic indications. The Tribunal notes that there is also support in international arbitral jurisprudence for the view that a higher standard of proof is required where bribery or corruption is alleged. Similarly, the courts of some nations have taken the view that where particularly serious allegations are involved (such as fraud or corruption) the evidence must be stronger or of greater weight than would otherwise be the case in order to meet the balance-of-probability test.[170]

The Tribunal asked whether those issues were part of substantive or of procedural law, but considered this of little importance in the present case where English law applied to the substance as well as to procedure. In English law, the general standard of proof rule for cases of alleged corruption in commercial disputes is that

> the evidence must be such as to show that the asserted facts are more likely than not to exist, applying the balance-of-probability test. Thus, even though the act of corruption may or may not be a criminal offence, the stricter criminal standard requiring evidence of a fact 'beyond a reasonable doubt' is not applicable.[171]

The Tribunal referred to two seminal decisions of English courts on this issue. The first was a (civil) case of alleged child abuse. The Tribunal quoted the following passage on standard of proof in non-criminal proceedings from the House of Lords decision:

> When assessing the probabilities the court will have in mind as a factor . . . that the more serious the allegation the less likely it is that the event occurred and, hence, the stronger should be the evidence before the court concludes that the allegation is established on the balance of probability. Fraud is usually less likely than negligence. . . .

[170] ICC Case No. 12732, 77. [171] ICC Case No. 12732, 77.

> Although the result is much the same, this does not mean that where a serious allegation is in issue the standard of proof required is higher. It means only that the inherent probability or improbability of an event is itself a matter to be taken into account when weighing the probabilities and deciding whether, on balance, the event occurred. The more improbable the event, the stronger must be the evidence that it did occur before, on the balance of probability, its occurrence will be established.[172]

The second was an inheritance law case raising two main questions: what was needed to remove the presumption that the (older) husband had died first; and whether or not the wife had feloniously killed her husband (both had died from coal gas poisoning). The Tribunal quoted:

> It seems ... that in civil cases it is not so much that a different standard of proof is required in different circumstances varying according to the gravity of the issue, but ... the gravity of the issue becomes part of the circumstances which the court has to take into consideration in deciding whether or not the burden of proof has been discharged. The more serious the allegation the more cogent is the evidence required to overcome the unlikelihood of what is alleged and thus to prove it.[173]

The Tribunal applied those principles to the case at hand, concluding that

> the standard of proof need not be, and should not be, weakened, nor that it need be or should be strengthened. The same standard of proof, namely one based upon the balance of probability, should be applied. That standard does not require 'certainty', or even 'likelihood beyond a reasonable doubt'. Nor does it require conclusive, direct evidence. It requires evidence, to be sure, but such evidence may be indirect or circumstantial, to the extent it is sufficient, in the context of the surrounding circumstances, to tip the balance of probability.[174]

The outcome of the Partial Award seems unpublished. The Tribunal emphasised that it was aiming at establishing enough facts to support the ensuing inferences, and in particular at assessing the credibility of the witnesses.[175]

6.1.11.3 Analysis

Little is known about ICC Case No. 12732, but still the case is interesting because the Tribunal discussed standard of proof when criminal behaviour is alleged in civil cases in great detail. The Tribunal on the one hand

[172] *In re H. and Others (Minors)* [1996] AC 563 (586).
[173] *In re Dellow's Will Trusts* [1964] 1 WLR 451, 454 et seq.
[174] ICC Case No. 12732, 78. [175] ICC Case No. 12732, 78.

argued that in the present case, it was of little practical relevance whether the standard of proof was considered an issue of substantive or procedural law. English law applied to substance as well as procedure. This issue would have been more complicated if different national laws had applied.

On the other hand, the Tribunal examined the standard of proof by recourse to two English court decisions. Both decisions in essence argued that the standard of proof does not change if allegations of criminal behaviour arise in civil proceedings; rather, the evidence has to be stronger and more cogent. The Tribunal concluded that for the case at hand, the standard of 'balance of probability' should be applied, and that indirect or circumstantial evidence is sufficient as long as it tips the balance of probability.[176]

6.1.12 *ICC Case No. 12990 (2005)*

Claimant in this case was an oil company; Respondent was African state X ('X'). There existed an agreement ('Protocole') between the parties that was part of a more complex scheme of agreements between X and three oil companies, governed by French law. The declared aim of those agreements was the acquisition of crude oil by the Claimant on the one side and assistance to the Respondent to realise a programme of structural adjustment on the other. The Claimant pretended to have paid the agreed price, but not to have received the full amount of crude oil in return. With regard to the Respondent, the government that had signed the Protocole was subsequently overthrown in a civil war, and the successor government rejected the claims based on the Protocole, arguing that it had been concluded under abnormal circumstances to enrich corrupt public officials. The Respondent asked the Tribunal to determine the illicit character of the Protocole; to declare it null and void; and to order reciprocal restitution of the services rendered, which would, according to the Respondent, result in a balance in its favour that it wanted to reclaim. The arbitration took place in Paris.[177]

6.1.12.1 The Applicable Law

Referring to the French Civil Code (Articles 1108 and 1133), the Arbitral Tribunal stated that corruption is an unlawful cause for an obligation.

[176] See also Ibrahim 2013.

[177] ICC Case No. 12990, Bulletin, 52; ICC Case No. 12990, Collection, 831; ICC Case No. 12990, Journal, 1406 et seq.

The Tribunal noted that a majority of doctrine as well as numerous arbitral awards consider the immorality of corruption and influence trading to be based on a truly international rule that is part of transnational public policy. The Tribunal took note that France had ratified the OECD Convention on Bribery that demands from state parties to criminalise the active bribery of foreign public officials in its Article 1, and that France had implemented the OECD Convention in September 2000 by adopting law No. 2000-595. The Tribunal concluded that France had confirmed and recognised the illicit character of the bribery of foreign public officials in international business transactions, and if corruption were proven in the present case, the Protocole would be null and void (*ne serait pas valide*) under French law as well as under the rules of transnational public policy.[178]

6.1.12.2 Evidence for Corruption

The Respondent alleged that certain abnormal conditions demonstrated the illicit character of the Protocole, calling the cause of the Protocole, namely the structural adjustment programme and the price of US$3 per barrel crude oil, fictitious and derisory. The Tribunal thus questioned whether the contract terms were concealing the real cause of the contract, that is to say corruption. The Tribunal recalled the general principle that the burden of proof regarding the illicit character of a contract is on the party that raises such an allegation, noting that this proof is often hard to furnish because the parties hide the illicit object of the contract behind innocuous terms. It stated that tribunals can, in principle, use all evidence which is admissible under the law, unless they are bound by the terms of the contract. The Tribunal argued that arbitrators have to rely on extra-contractual indications, and that the requirements regarding proof are reduced and can be limited to a presumption based on indicia.[179]

The Tribunal listed the same four elements as in ICC Case No. 8891 as indicia for illicit activities:

- the inability to produce evidence for any activity by the agent;
- the duration of negotiations for an agreement;
- the mode of remuneration (through a percentage fee) and
- a high level of remuneration.

[178] ICC Case No. 12990, Bulletin, 52 et seq.; ICC Case No. 12990, Journal, 1408 et seq.

[179] ICC Case No. 12990, Bulletin, 53 with reference to ICC Case No. 8891; ICC Case No. 12990, Journal, 1410.

The Tribunal nevertheless added a fifth indicia, derived from the *Lagergren* case: if the respective state is notoriously known for its corruption problems.[180]

In the present case, the Tribunal found no evidence that the Claimant had carried out activities for the Respondent. The Tribunal asked the Claimant to produce evidence for its performed services; the Claimant was unable to do that. The Tribunal concluded that the inability of the Claimant to produce evidence for the slightest tangible activity in relation to its contractual obligations gave rise to a strong suspicion of corruption.[181] Examining other indications for unlawful activity, the Tribunal found that the duration of negotiations until a sales contract was concluded in this case (less than two weeks according to the Respondent, three months according to the Claimant) did not allow the conclusion that the contract had a corrupt cause.[182] With regard to the remuneration of the Claimant, however, the Tribunal noted that it was unusual to pay a consultant in a percentage of the value of the contracts awarded to a company. While the Claimant was rather intermediary than consultant, the excessive amount of its commission (close to 15 per cent), as well as the unusual mode of remuneration, were strong corruption indicators for the Tribunal.[183]

Finally, the Tribunal stated that a pertinent indicator for bribery is the fact that the country at stake is facing real corruption issues. It was well known and undisputed between the parties that corruption was endemic in state X. The Tribunal argued that this objectively corroborated its other findings with regard to unlawful activity.[184] The Tribunal concluded that the Respondent had furnished indicia ('*indices*') corroborating a presumption of unlawfulness of the Protocole between the Claimant and state X, and that the Claimant had been unable to refute this presumption.[185]

6.1.12.3 Attribution of the Acts of Public Officials to the State

The Tribunal stated that under French law, if the parties to a contract were involved in an unlawful activity, no claims for restitution were

[180] ICC Case No. 12990, Bulletin, 53 et seq.; ICC Case No. 12990, Journal, 1410 et seq.
[181] ICC Case No. 12990, Bulletin, 54 et seq., 58. [182] ICC Case No. 12990, Bulletin, 58.
[183] ICC Case No. 12990, Bulletin, 58 et seq. with further references.
[184] ICC Case No. 12990, Bulletin, 60 with further references.
[185] ICC Case No. 12990, Bulletin, 61.

admitted (*in pari causa turpitudinis cessat repetitio*). However, this theory only applies if the unlawful activity has been carried out in full knowledge by all parties. Since bribery is a criminal offence, the knowledge of the representatives or agents of the state cannot simply be imputed to the state, because theories of representation or presumed knowledge ('*connaissance présumée*') are only valid for legal acts and do not apply to situations of fact.[186]

The Tribunal then briefly touched upon the question whether certain state representatives had a say regarding substance and execution of the various agreements, and whether they were themselves implicated in bribery pacts, or omitted to take action. Their presumed knowledge would have resulted in the rejection of the Respondent's counterclaim. However, the Tribunal decided not to address these questions and instead argued with a general principle that grave negligence is treated equally to intention (*magna negligentia culpa est; magna culpa dolus est*). In the current case, the Respondent had convincingly argued that five elements were present proving in an evident manner that the Protocole was not concluded in good faith, but tainted with bribery. State representatives should have noticed this when the Protocole was presented to them, and should have refused to execute it.[187]

The Tribunal concluded that the state had acted imprudently when it ratified and executed the Protocole, accepted the payment of US$15 million, delivered the crude oil, and thus approved the illicit cause. It argued that if the state had been prudent, it would not have accepted such a contract without applying a minimum of due diligence. It also argued that a state cannot itself be corrupted, only its leaders, and that the rule *in pari causa turpitudinis cessat repetitio* should not be applied to a state that is precisely the victim of corruption (as in the present case). Nevertheless, the Tribunal concluded that a state where corruption is endemic cannot protect itself behind its own conduct and engage in activities that are tainted with bribery, in order to claim a reimbursement afterwards.[188]

Based on Article 1131 of the French Civil Code, the Tribunal in the Award declared the Protocole between the Claimant and state X null and void, because the real intention of the parties behind the wording of the

[186] ICC Case No. 12990, Journal, 1411. [187] ICC Case No. 12990, Journal, 1411.
[188] ICC Case No. 12990, Journal, 1411 et seq.

contract (and thus the cause of the contract) was unlawful. Insofar as the state should have been aware of the unlawful cause of the Protocole, its request for restitution was unfounded. Therefore, the Tribunal rejected the Respondent's counterclaim.[189]

6.1.12.4 Analysis

Many issues raised by ICC Case No. 12990 were already discussed in earlier ICC Awards. Regarding the applicable law, the Tribunal relied on the French Civil Code (as chosen by the parties), but apparently did not refer to any specific criminal law provisions when discussing the bribery allegations. It took note that France had ratified and implemented the OECD Convention on Bribery, including Article 1 that criminalises the bribery of foreign public officials, and argued that the fight against bribery was part of transnational public policy.

Regarding burden of proof, the Tribunal asked the Claimant to produce evidence for its performed services. The Tribunal argued that in principle, tribunals can use all evidence admissible under the law, and that the requirements regarding proof can be limited to a presumption based on indicia. The Tribunal relied on the same list of corruption indicators as seven years earlier in ICC Case No. 8891, adding as a fifth indicator the involvement of a state where corruption is endemic. The inability of the Claimant to furnish proof of its activities, the mode of remuneration in a percentage fee, the excessive amount of the remuneration, and the involvement of a state where corruption is endemic in combination satisfied the Tribunal that bribery was involved in this case, and it declared the Protocole null and void.

On attribution to the state of acts of its officials, the Tribunal argued that state representatives had been grossly negligent when they approved the Protocole despite elements being present that clearly indicated bribery. Even though the Respondent was the victim of corruption in this case, the Tribunal found that it could not protect itself behind its own conduct, and rejected the Respondent's counterclaim. One commentator even argued that, from the fact that the Respondent did not react to its endemic corruption problems, the Tribunal should not only have deducted a direct responsibility of the state, but also the state's knowledge of and passive participation in bribery.[190]

[189] ICC Case No. 12990, Bulletin, 62; ICC Case No. 12990, Journal, 1411 et seq.
[190] ICC Case No. 12290, Journal, Notes, 1418.

6.1.13 ICC Case No. 13384 (2005)

Claimant in this case was a consultant company established in the Middle East; Respondent was a European company. The parties concluded a consultancy agreement for the purpose of recovering money that was due to the Respondent for a construction project in West Asian state X. The Claimant was to receive 14 per cent of the recovered amounts for its services. The dispute arose when the Respondent terminated the consultancy agreement ahead of time, arguing that it was void due to corruption of public officials of state X. The arbitration took place in Paris.[191]

6.1.13.1 Applicable Law and Standard of Proof

The consultancy agreement was governed by French law. The Respondent also alleged the violation of statutory regulations against corruption of state X and of transnational public policy. The Sole Arbitrator argued that the governing law was still French law (as chosen by the parties), but that the law of state X and transnational public policy might result in the setting aside of French law in case of any contrariety. The Arbitrator noted that corruption is condemned by various international conventions and domestic laws, and that this condemnation may be seen as a material rule of transnational public policy that must apply, irrespective of the national law chosen to govern the contract.[192]

Specifically, the Arbitrator argued that France had implemented the OECD Convention on Bribery in its domestic criminal law by Article 435-3 of the French Criminal Code. If the consultancy agreement involved the bribery of foreign public officials, it would be null and void under French law, and the signatories and their accomplices would be sanctioned personally. According to the Arbitrator, this provision should be interpreted restrictively on the basis of a very careful examination of the facts, and a high standard of proof should apply to ascertain any alleged infringement: 'No mere presumption would suffice to entail liability of the accused party.'[193]

6.1.13.2 The Terms of the Consultancy Agreement

The Arbitrator examined the subject matter of the consultancy agreement, including the true intention of the parties, in order to find out

[191] ICC Case No. 13384, 62. [192] ICC Case No. 13384, 63.
[193] ICC Case No. 13384, 63 et seq.

whether the agreement involved the direct or indirect procurement of an offer, promise or gift to certain persons and whether those persons were public officials in a position to award some kind of advantage in international trade. The Arbitrator found that the Claimant, whom the Respondent agreed to remunerate for its services, did not have any authority to decide on the payment of the outstanding debts by state X to the Respondent. However, the question remained whether the consultancy agreement involved, through the acts of the Claimant, the indirect procurement of undue advantages to public officials who were in a position to illegally favour the Respondent.[194]

6.1.13.3 Application of State X Law

Referring to a provision of a state X statute, the Respondent argued that the high level of the Claimant's remuneration (14 per cent of the recovered amounts) allowed hidden payments to state X officials who were in charge of the decisions in favour of the Respondent. The Arbitrator noted that the state X law criminalising public bribery was compatible with French law, and used it as a complementary base with regard to the facts that were to take place in state X. State X law prohibited the taking, requesting or accepting of promise of a payment with an improper cause, namely the procuring of an undue advantage to a beneficiary through the actions of public officials. The state X statute required proof of an intention in this regard by the party requesting and/or the party promising payment.[195]

6.1.13.4 Evidence for Corruption?

The Arbitrator argued that the agreement in itself was not forbidden by French or state X law. The Claimant had to advise the Respondent and to provide other counsel and intermediation services. This was supported by written as well as oral evidence. The Respondent was not able to produce the necessary counterevidence: there was no proof of either an intention of the parties to corrupt state X officials, or of any corrupt behaviour by the Claimant. In particular, an affidavit by the Respondent's executive director contained a declaration by the Claimant's assistant general manager that was strongly denied by the latter; the Respondent did not ask the executive director to appear for examination at the hearing; and the rest of the affidavit was in part contrary to clear written

[194] ICC Case No. 13384, 64. [195] ICC Case No. 13384, 64.

evidence. Furthermore, the Respondent raised the argument of nullity of the contract at a late stage, and never filed a criminal complaint in state X with regard to the corruption allegations.[196]

The Arbitrator concluded that the high amount of the remuneration was 'not an unavoidable indication' for bribe payments, as the Claimant had established that it had to pay legal consultants and assistants in state X. Despite a certain shortage of written evidence of the Claimant's performed services, the reality of the Claimant's action was proven to the Arbitrator's satisfaction. The Arbitrator was also satisfied that the Claimant, because of the personality and experience of its manager, was capable of performing the required services for the Respondent.[197] In the Award, the Arbitrator dismissed the Respondent's corruption defence as late, flawed and not raised in good faith.[198]

6.1.13.5 Analysis

In ICC Case No. 13384, the Arbitrator took into account the law of the state where the agreement was performed. Although the parties chose French law to govern the consultancy agreement, the Arbitrator complemented the provisions of the French Criminal Code dealing with the active bribery of foreign public officials with the criminal law provisions of state X. The Arbitrator argued that in case of contrariety between French law and the statutory regulations of state X law dealing with corruption, the latter would prevail (as would transnational public policy). However, French law and state X law were compatible with regard to public bribery.

On standard of proof, the Arbitrator argued that a high standard should apply to ascertain any infringement of the bribery provisions of the French Criminal Code. The Arbitrator examined the objective requirements of foreign bribery in detail. While the Claimant's high level of remuneration (14 per cent of the recovered amounts) would have allowed hidden payments to influential officials, the Respondent failed to produce necessary counterevidence to written and oral proof that the Claimant did provide certain services, and was qualified to do so: there was no proof for any corrupt intention or behaviour by the Claimant. Furthermore, the Respondent had produced contradictory evidence, and never filed a criminal complaint regarding the bribery allegations in state X. In sum, this let the Arbitrator conclude that the Respondent had raised the corruption defence in bad faith.

[196] ICC Case No. 13384, 65.
[197] ICC Case No. 13384, 65 et seq.
[198] ICC Case No. 13384, 66.

6.1.14 ICC Case No. 13515 (2006)

Claimant in this case was a company established in North African state X; Respondent was a European manufacturing company. Under a distribution agreement between the parties, Claimant acted as agent in state X, responsible for promoting sales, installing and servicing Respondent's equipment. Claimant was to receive a 40 per cent commission on the sales price of equipment that the Respondent sold, and a 40 per cent discount on the sales it made itself. The dispute arose over the payment of these commissions. The Respondent argued that the distribution agreement was null and void because it was tainted with corruption. The arbitration took place in Paris.[199]

6.1.14.1 The Applicable Law

The parties had chosen French law to govern the distribution agreement. The Arbitral Tribunal noted that nullity of the contract, as claimed by the Respondent, would be based on French law (in particular, Articles 1131 and 1133 of the French Civil Code) as well as transnational public policy; no foreign mandatory provisions had been invoked by the parties. The Tribunal stated that the chosen law could not impede the application of transnational public policy, and that by choosing French law, the parties had overall ('*globalement*') accepted to submit to it. The Tribunal also noted that France had implemented the OECD Convention on Bribery by law No. 2000-595, criminalising the bribery of foreign public officials in the French Criminal Code.[200]

The Tribunal defined transnational public policy as

> constitué de l'ensemble de principes ou de normes supérieurs et fondamentaux pour le commerce international qui visent en toutes hypothèses à protéger certaines valeurs essentielles ainsi que les intérêts de la société internationale.[201]

In a rough translation this reads:

> constituted out of the totality of principles or norms that are superior and fundamental for international trade, which by all means aim to protect certain essential values as well as the interests of the international community.

[199] ICC Case No. 13515, 66. [200] ICC Case No. 13515, 68 et seq.
[201] ICC Case No. 13515, 69.

According to the Tribunal, an international arbitrator accepts the existence of a principle of transnational public policy as soon as it forms the object of a large convergence between different domestic legal systems, and is retained in international conventions; and if he takes notice that the actors in international trade adhere to the principle. The Tribunal argued that this was the case with regard to anti-corruption, as it was proven by the numerous international conventions[202]; by the codes of conduct of multinational enterprises; by the texts of the ICC; and by the work of NGOs such as Transparency International (TI). The Tribunal concluded that, despite possible divergences in national laws and in the behaviour of states with regard to corruption, there existed a material rule that was immediately applicable and imperative, prescribing the nullity of a contract as soon as its unlawfulness because of corruption was established.[203]

6.1.14.2 Proving Corruption

The Tribunal noted that if an arbitrator is confronted with corruption allegations, he has a duty to carefully examine those beyond the terms of the contract. This is complicated by the fact that he does not have any investigative means at his disposal like the state judiciary. If there is no direct proof for illicit payments, the arbitrator can draw his conclusions with regard to illicit behaviour on the basis of solid and convergent indicia ('*indices*'). Due to the opacity that naturally surrounds corruption and trading in influence, arbitrators can take into account all varieties of evidence ('*une telle preuve peut être rapportée par tous les moyens*'). The Tribunal also noted that contracts are presumed valid until the contrary is proven and that the burden of proving the nullity of the contract is on the party alleging it.[204] It did not accept the Respondent's argument that the unlawfulness of the distribution agreement could be derived from the fact that state X was a state where corruption was widespread. The Tribunal argued that regardless of the reputation of state X, one could assume that licit contracts were concluded there as well.[205]

202 The Tribunal mentioned the OECD, CoE, and OAS Conventions as well as the UNCAC (see OECD 1997; CoE 1999a; OAS 1996; and UNCAC 2003).

203 ICC Case No. 13515, 69 et seq.

204 ICC Case No. 13515, 71 with references to earlier ICC Awards.

205 ICC Case No. 13515, 71.

6.1.14.3 Evidence for Corruption

The Tribunal examined the remuneration of the Claimant, stating that neither remuneration in per cent nor an unusually high remuneration were by themselves suspicious. However, if a commission is particularly high compared to the rates that are practised in the respective sector, and/or if the commission does not correspond to remuneration for real services, this does raise suspicion. In the present case, the Tribunal considered the 40 per cent commission for the Claimant as excessively high compared to what is practised in commercial intermediation, and argued that the Claimant had not been able to produce solid and clear evidence of the reality and content of its services.[206]

The Tribunal also found it unusual that the Claimant had empowered one of its employees to manage a contract of such importance on his own, and that the management of the company had only at a very late stage been bothered by the non-payment of the commissions.[207] Furthermore, the modalities of payment (in particular, the account that should have been credited) were not specified in the Claimant's copy of the contract, without any reaction for more than eight years; and the Respondent seemed not to have worried about the fact that payments were made to the personal account of an employee. Payments also were made to offshore accounts.[208]

In the Award, the Tribunal concluded that illicit payments had been the essential and decisive element for the conclusion of the distribution agreement, and that the contract therefore had an unlawful object and was null and void. Both the Claimant's demand for unpaid commissions and the Respondent's counterclaim for restitution of already paid sums were dismissed.[209]

6.1.14.4. Analysis

In ICC Case No. 13515, with regard to the bribery allegations, the Tribunal confirmed some patterns that had been established in earlier ICC Awards. It applied the French Civil Code (as chosen by the parties), also elaborating on and invoking transnational public policy against corruption. Apparently, it neither relied on the French Criminal Code nor on foreign mandatory law. The Tribunal stated, however, that by

[206] ICC Case No. 13515, 71 et seq. with references to earlier ICC Awards.

[207] ICC Case No. 13515, 73.

[208] ICC Case No. 13515, 74 et seq.

[209] ICC Case No. 13515, 75 et seq.

choosing French law, the parties had agreed to submit to the entire body of that law. The Tribunal also mentioned the OECD Convention on Bribery and the French implementing legislation to it.

The Tribunal argued that no direct proof is required in order to establish bribery. Solid and convergent indicia are sufficient, and arbitrators can utilise all varieties of evidence. The Tribunal noted that the fact that corruption was endemic in North African state X was not sufficient proof for bribery. However, other indicia such as the – in comparison with the usual rates in that sector – excessively high remuneration of the Claimant in combination with an inability of the latter to produce any solid evidence for its services, as well as the modalities of contract management and payment, let the Tribunal conclude that bribery was involved in this case.

6.1.15 ICC Case No. 13914 (2008)

Claimant in this case was a businessman who had worked many years with the government of state X. Respondent was a US company that had concluded consulting and other agreements with the Claimant. The aim of the Respondent was the acquisition of the right to conduct seismic surveys off the coast of African state X, for later oil extraction. The agreements provided for lump sum payments as well as commission payments on data sales from the Respondent's surveys. The dispute arose over the commission payments. The Claimant argued that unlawful deductions had been made, whereas the Respondent alleged that the Claimant had bribed officials in state-owned company A that granted the rights for offshore mining in state X. The Respondent argued that the Claimant was not entitled to any payments, and that such payments would infringe the US Foreign Corrupt Practices Act (FCPA). The arbitration took place in London.[210]

6.1.15.1 The Applicable Law

The consulting agreement was governed by the law of the State of Texas. With regard to the bribery allegations, the Arbitral Tribunal cited Article 1(1) of the OECD Convention on Bribery that defines the offence of bribery of foreign public officials, noting that the US had ratified the OECD Convention in 1998 and subsequently amended its own federal

[210] ICC Case No. 13914, 77.

law on foreign bribery, the FCPA. The Tribunal considered the laws of Texas to include US federal law and therefore the FCPA. The FCPA 'prohibits corrupt payments through intermediaries just like the Anti-bribery Convention itself. Thus, it is unlawful under US federal law to make a payment to a third party, while knowing that all or a portion of the payment will go directly or indirectly to a foreign official.'[211]

6.1.15.2 Red Flags

The Tribunal noted that the US government had developed a list of so-called 'red flags' that indicate possible improper payments, promises, or offers by intermediaries or other third parties, including:

- unusual payment patterns or financial arrangements;
- a history of corruption in the country;
- a refusal by the foreign joint venture partner or representative to provide a certification that it will not take any action in furtherance of an unlawful offer, promise, or payment to a foreign public official and not take any act that would cause the US firm to be in violation of the FCPA;
- unusually high commissions;
- lack of transparency in expenses and accounting records;
- apparent lack of qualifications or resources on the part of the joint venture partner or representative to perform services offered, and
- whether the joint venture partner or representative has been recommended by an official of the potential government customer.[212]

The Tribunal also mentioned that the FCPA includes two affirmative defences: that a payment is lawful under the written laws of the foreign country; and a defence for 'reasonable and *bona fide* business expenditures'.[213]

The Tribunal identified a number of red flags in the evidence record of the case: corruption was endemic in state X according to Transparency International's Corruption Perceptions Index 2007; the Claimant received an unusually high commission in relation to the services it was expected to perform for the Respondent, giving rise to the suspicion that part of the commission was forwarded to officials of state-owned company A; the Claimant did not fully produce the requested documents (in particular, bank records) and unilaterally redacted documents,

[211] ICC Case No. 13914, 78. [212] ICC Case No. 13914, 78.
[213] Cf. FCPA Resource Guide 2012, 23 et seq.

without any credible excuse; the Claimant was insufficiently qualified to perform the services as specified in the consulting agreement; and officials of company A had not only proposed to the Respondent to hire the Claimant but also negotiated the Claimant's commission with the Respondent, and taken a personal interest that the commissions were paid to the Claimant. The Tribunal derived from those red flags that a substantial amount of Respondent's commission payments to the Claimant was eventually forwarded to key officials of company A. The evidence record showed that more than US$6 million had been paid to company A officials by the Claimant during a five-year period, without any credible explanation.[214]

6.1.15.3 Clear and Convincing Evidence for Bribery

The Tribunal concluded that the payments to company A officials through the Claimant as the intermediary had been made with the purpose to secure data processing rights for the Respondent. There was 'clear and convincing evidence' that the commission payments qualified as bribes, as they served to influence officials of state-owned company A in their decision-making.[215]

6.1.15.4 Legal Consequences of Bribery

The Tribunal stated that money laundering, corruption and fraud were crimes in most civilised countries and that '[a]nti-corruption is an integral part of the international public policy' as reflected in international conventions[216] and US federal law (including Texas law).[217] It referred to earlier ICC Awards[218] that had dealt with bribery allegations, as well as to Texas case law, citing an opinion by Justice Speedlin of the Court of Appeals of Texas that had been supported by the US Supreme Court and several other Texas courts: 'A contract to do a thing which cannot be performed without violation of the law violates public policy and is void.'[219] The Tribunal noted that if a contract is void due to illegality, Texas courts do not allow restitution to be awarded.[220]

[214] ICC Case No. 13914, 79. [215] ICC Case No. 13914, 80.

[216] The Tribunal listed the UNCAC and the OECD, CoE and OAS Conventions (see UNCAC 2003; OECD 1997; CoE 1999a; and OAS 1996).

[217] ICC Case No. 13914, 80.

[218] The Tribunal mentioned ICC Cases No. 3913, 3916, 6497, 7047 and 8891.

[219] ICC Case No. 13914, 81. [220] ICC Case No. 13914, 82.

In the Award, the Tribunal concluded, based on 'arbitration precedents' and legal authorities, that the consulting agreement and other agreements were null and void *ab initio* because bribery had been 'part of the intent' of those agreements, as established by the evidence. Therefore, the Claimant's requests for damages due to breach of contract and for punitive damages were fully dismissed.[221]

6.1.15.5 Analysis

In ICC Case No. 13914, the Tribunal relied on Article 1 of the OECD Convention on Bribery and on the US FCPA with regard to the bribery allegations. The parties had chosen Texas law to apply to the consulting agreement, and the Tribunal argued that Texas law includes US federal law and thus the FCPA.

In order to prove any improper payments, promises or offers, the Tribunal invoked a list of 'red flags', such as unusual payment patterns, endemic corruption in the respective country, unusually high commissions, lack of transparency in accounting, and lack of qualifications of the agent or intermediary. Several of those red flags were given in the present case. The evidence record indeed showed that substantial sums of the Claimant's commission payments had been forwarded to officials of state-owned company A, without any credible explanation. The Tribunal concluded that there was 'clear and convincing evidence' that the commission payments were used to influence the decision-making of company A officials, and that therefore the payments qualified as bribes. Consequently, in accordance with earlier ICC Awards as well as with Texas case law, the consulting agreement and other agreements were null and void *ab initio*.

6.1.16 ICC Case No. 14470 (2008)

Claimant in this case was a citizen of the United Arab Emirates; Respondent was African state X. The parties concluded a sales contract according to which the Claimant was to sell to state X a certain number of vehicles and spare parts. The Claimant delivered part of the consignment and state X paid part of the contract price. The dispute arose over the payment of the rest of the contract price. The Respondent challenged the validity of the contract due to corruption. The arbitration took place in Paris.[222]

[221] ICC Case No. 13914, 82. [222] ICC Case No. 14470, 90.

6.1.16.1 Impact of a Criminal Conviction

The Respondent argued that the minister of economy, who had signed the sales contract for state X, had subsequently been convicted for a criminal offence by the state X courts. The Arbitral Tribunal found that a criminal conviction alone was not sufficient evidence that the contract, whose validity was challenged, was tainted by corruption. According to the Tribunal, the Respondent should have brought evidence that was related to the disputed contract.[223]

In the Award, the Tribunal concluded that there was no convergent and solid evidence that made it more than probable or almost certain that corruption was involved in the sales contract. It recognised the difficulty of proving corruption, but argued that the evidence produced by the Respondent was not corroborated by other facts. Therefore, it declared the sales contract valid.[224]

6.1.16.2 Analysis

ICC Case No. 14470 discusses several issues that were already addressed in other cases, and it shows that a criminal conviction in the respective state of the Minister who signed the contract at dispute is not sufficient to prove corruption if there is no other convergent evidence related to the contract.

6.1.17 ICC Case No. 14878 (2008)

Claimant in this case was a consultant for the automobile industry; Respondent was a vehicle manufacturer. The parties concluded a consultancy agreement according to which the Claimant should negotiate a deadline extension with the transport ministry of Asian state X for the supply of the Respondent's vehicles. The consultancy agreement was governed by French law. The dispute arose over the payment of the Claimant's commission, when state X charged penalties for late delivery to the Respondent, and the Respondent withheld commission payments because it was the Claimant's job to avoid such penalties. The Respondent also argued that the Claimant had engaged in corrupt practices in the performance of the agreement. The arbitration took place in Paris.[225]

[223] ICC Case No. 14470, 91.

[224] ICC Case No. 14470, 91 et seq.

[225] ICC Case No. 14878, 92.

6.1.17.1 Proving Corruption

The Respondent alleged a violation of Article 432-11 of the French Criminal Code (corruption and influence trading). In short, the Sole Arbitrator noted that the Respondent's arguments that the Claimant had engaged in corrupt practices in the performance of the consultancy agreement were inconsistent, vague and contradictory, and that the Respondent was unable to produce tangible evidence. The Arbitrator stated that even if it is difficult to prove illicit activities in a foreign country for a party belonging to the private sector, the rules of evidence are not softened only because such practices are alleged. It requires evidence in order to convince the Arbitrator ('*pour emporter l'intime conviction de l'Arbitre*'). Neither the reference to earlier arbitral awards that had condemned corruption in international trade nor the fact that corruption did occur in state X were by themselves sufficient to prove illicit practices by the Claimant and its contacts.[226] In the Award, the Arbitrator concluded that the Respondent failed to prove corruption in this case.

6.1.17.2 Analysis

In ICC Case No. 14878, the Respondent directly invoked the French Criminal Code (the consultancy agreement at stake was governed by French law), but was unable to produce any tangible evidence to support its bribery allegations. Therefore, the Respondent failed to convince the Arbitrator of the alleged illicit practices of the Claimant.

6.1.18 ICC Case No. 16090 (2011)

Claimant in this case was an advisor and consultant, appointed by the Respondent under a brokerage contract for the purpose of marketing and supplying industrial equipment in Central America. The Claimant was to receive commission fees for its services. The dispute arose because the Respondent withheld the commission payments, arguing that the brokerage contract concealed illicit payments and therefore was null and void. The arbitration took place in Geneva, and the applicable substantive law was Swiss law.[227]

6.1.18.1 On Burden and Standard of Proof

The Sole Arbitrator in this case argued that the alleging party bears the burden of proof, and that a tribunal should reject the latter's argument if

[226] ICC Case No. 14878, 93. [227] ICC Case No. 16090, 147.

the demonstration is not convincing, even if some doubts about bribery remain (referring to ICC Case No. 6497). The Arbitrator also found that a high standard of proof applied in cases of alleged bribery.[228]

6.1.18.2 Proving Bribery

The Arbitrator found that the amount of the Claimant's commission (2 per cent) was not unusually high and did not constitute a 'red flag'. Witnesses confirmed that this was an average commission paid by the Respondent. The Respondent argued that the Claimant failed to prove the services provided under the brokerage contract. The Arbitrator, however, stated that it is in the nature of brokerage contracts that the broker's commission depends on the award of the main contract to the principal due to the broker's services. In the present case, the Respondent was granted project contracts, and commissions were paid to the Claimant for almost two years, without any inquiry into the services performed. The Arbitrator concluded from this that the Claimant had actually rendered the expected services.[229]

6.1.18.3 No Disclosure of the Claimant's Beneficial Owner

The Claimant refused to disclose information about its beneficial owner(s) and to produce bank documents for tax reasons and for fear that this information would be illegitimately used or disclosed to third parties. The Arbitrator regretted the lack of co-operation but found those reasons to be justified: '[T]ax reasons are very often relied upon to justify a confidentiality concern . . . an overall tax concern with respect to a Swiss bank account is even more justified today since the Swiss bank secrecy is no more as protected as it used to be.'[230] The Arbitrator concluded that the Claimant's explanations were satisfactory; the non-production of evidence did not lead him to draw an inference that such evidence would have been adverse to the interests of the Claimant. The Arbitrator pointed out that in cases of alleged bribery, tribunals should be 'particularly careful' when drawing adverse inferences.[231]

6.1.18.4 Analysis

The Arbitrator in ICC Case No. 16090 decided that alleged bribery was not proven. Too little is known about the underlying facts to allow an assessment of this outcome. From what is known about the case,

[228] ICC Case No. 16090, 148.
[229] ICC Case No. 16090, 148 et seq.
[230] ICC Case No. 16090, 150.
[231] ICC Case No. 16090, 150.

it is questionable, however, whether the Arbitrator thoroughly inquired into the alleged bribery. Nothing indicates that the Arbitrator referred to provisions of domestic criminal law or transnational public policy. Apparently without reflecting arbitral case law in this regard, the Arbitrator applied a high standard of proof. The Arbitrator also shied away from drawing adverse inferences – not disclosing the actual beneficial owner(s) for tax reasons should not be accepted in circumstances of alleged bribery. Identifying the beneficial owners of companies and accounts is crucial to detect bribery (as well as money laundering and tax avoidance).[232] Arbitrators must be aware of this.

6.1.19 Summary

The eighteen ICC cases discussed above all[233] dealing with allegations of foreign public bribery demonstrate that the ways arbitral tribunals handle such cases have changed over the years.[234] Corruption was outcome-determinative in eight of those cases.[235] The development can be summarised as follows. In ICC Case No. 1110 (*Lagergren*), the Arbitrator denied jurisdiction when the enforcement of a bribe contract was at stake as he considered the case as not arbitrable. A unique feature of this case was that the evidence was clear and the bribery allegations were undisputed. The Award also states that bribery is against international public policy and that bribery in violation of foreign laws can infringe French public policy.

In ICC Case No. 3916, the Sole Arbitrator concluded, on the basis of circumstantial evidence, that the Claimant had exercised his influence over the persons who decided to whom the Iranian state would award contracts for public works. He declared the contract between the Iranian Claimant and the Greek Respondent as null and void under French and Iranian law, and as contrary to international public policy.

In ICC Case No. 4145, bribery was alleged without success. The Tribunal applied Swiss private law (as the law applicable to the intermediary agreement at stake), but apparently did not refer to any criminal

232 Stiglitz and Pieth 2016.

233 The published parts of ICC Case No. 12732 do not entirely clarify the alleged criminal conduct.

234 See also Rose 2014, 207 et seq.

235 In ICC Cases No. 1110; 3916; 5622 (the arbitral award was however annulled by the Swiss Federal Supreme Court); 6497 (only for one of the agreements); 8891; 12990; 13515; and 13914. The outcome in ICC Case No. 12732 is unknown to the author.

laws. The Tribunal accepted that bribery could be proven by circumstantial evidence that leads to a very high probability. It reached its conclusion that no bribery was involved on the basis of the statement of the Defendant's principal witness, who denied that bribery was ever intended (not surprisingly, as he had signed the agreement on behalf of the Defendant and would possibly have incriminated himself). From today's point of view, the intermediary's very high commission (approximately 13.7 per cent and more) would demand closer scrutiny.

In ICC Case No. 5622 (*Hilmarton*), the Arbitrator declared the agreement – that was governed by Swiss law – as null and void at the merits stage. The Arbitrator noted that there was no written evidence for any activities by the Claimant and that its activities as described by witnesses did not correspond to the terms of the agreement. However, he found that there was not sufficient indirect evidence to prove bribery beyond doubt. The Arbitrator mentioned the domestic bribery provisions of the former Swiss Criminal Code and examined the impact of a violation of foreign mandatory law (the Algerian Law on trading in influence) on the validity of the agreement under Swiss private law. He concluded that the violation of the Algerian Law was against Swiss public policy. The Court of Justice of the Canton of Geneva subsequently annulled the (First) Award, arguing that the use of intermediaries was allowed under Swiss law. The annulment was approved by the Swiss Federal Supreme Court which argued that a prohibition of the use of all intermediaries was too restrictive and protectionist. A Second ICC Award that was in conformity with the Swiss courts' decisions was subsequently enforced in the United Kingdom. In France however, the First Award was enforced.

When ICC Case No. 6401 (*Westinghouse*) was decided, separability of the arbitral clause was a generally accepted principle. The Tribunal applied a 'clear and convincing evidence' standard of proof, referring to domestic practice in civil cases involving alleged bribery or fraud. Notably, a US federal judge argued – when discussing the ICC Preliminary Award – that the Arbitral Tribunal had applied a 'significantly heavier burden of proof than would be applied at trial' and that the Tribunal would have found evidence for bribery if it had applied a 'preponderance of the evidence' standard. Without referring to any specific domestic criminal provisions, the Tribunal stated that two elements had to be proven to establish bribery: the intention to confer an advantage, and the agreement to accept the advantage – directly or indirectly – in exchange for a certain act by a public official. Only the first element was proven in the present case. The Tribunal stated that if no actual bribe payments can be proven, a higher standard of proof would apply to the existence of the bribery pact.

In ICC Case No. 6497, the Tribunal stated that the burden of proof was on the party alleging bribery and that an arbitral tribunal did not have to inquire into the facts and search for the truth independently. It added, however, that on the basis of Art. 8 of the (here applicable) Swiss Civil Code, the alleging party could bring non-conclusive evidence and exceptionally, an arbitral tribunal could then ask the alleged party to bring counterevidence if possible and not too burdensome. If the alleged party did not produce such evidence, the tribunal could conclude that the alleged facts were proven. With one exception, the Tribunal eventually did not modify the burden of proof due to the Respondent's lack of co-operation in the proceedings. For one product agreement, the Tribunal did ask the Claimant to produce bank documents. The combination of an extremely unusual amount of commission (33.33 per cent for unspecified services), the Claimant's uncooperativeness and untrue affidavits led the Tribunal to the conclusion that bribery was involved regarding that product agreement.

In ICC Case No. 7047 (*Westacre*), the Tribunal found that mandatory foreign laws would be applicable to the extent that they were part of international public policy. However, neither the Defendant nor the Tribunal specified the respective (anti-bribery) provisions. Regarding the bribery allegations, the Tribunal argued that disproportionately high fees did not invalidate the agreement and that lobbying as such was not an illegal activity. The Tribunal stated that the allegations were raised after the hearing of evidence and therefore too late, and that it had not been obliged to investigate as the Defendant had not invoked bribery in its presentation of facts. The Defendant unsuccessfully appealed to the Swiss Federal Supreme Court, arguing *inter alia* that the Award was incompatible with substantive public policy; in particular, the Court did not reopen the facts. At the enforcement stage, the Defendant appealed twice to English courts on the basis of new evidence but failed, although the courts were aware that the international efforts to combat foreign public bribery were stepping up, and that the allegations had not been discussed properly in front of the Arbitral Tribunal – the courts gave more weight to the finality of arbitral awards.

ICC Case No. 8891 is well known because the Tribunal considered foreign public bribery as proven on the basis of serious indicia. Those indicia were the inability of the hired consultant to provide detailed evidence for his activities and the fact that the available evidence indicated illicit payments; the short engagement of the consultant (roughly two and a half months) for a difficult task; and the percentage of the consultant's commission (18.5 per cent); not an indicia for bribery was the remuneration of the consultant in the form of a success fee. The Tribunal concluded that a contract inciting or favouring bribery of public officials was contrary to transnational public policy and therefore null and void. The Tribunal noted that the fight against bribery was intensifying, referring to the negotiations within the OECD towards an anticorruption convention.

Seven years later, in ICC Case No. 12990 of 2005, the Tribunal relied on the same four indicia to prove bribery. In particular, it reversed the burden of proof, asking the Claimant to produce evidence for its performed services. The Claimant was unable to do that. The duration of negotiations for a sales contract was disputed in this case, and the Tribunal did not take it as indicia for bribery. However, the excessive remuneration of the Claimant (close to 15 per cent) and the unusual payment mode of a percentage fee were both considered strong corruption indicators. The Tribunal nevertheless added a fifth indicia: if the respective state is notoriously known for its corruption problems. The sum of the indicia corroborated a presumption of unlawfulness of the agreement at stake and the Claimant was unable to refute that presumption. The Tribunal relied on the respective provisions of the French Civil Code to declare the agreement null and void; it also mentioned transnational public policy against corruption and the OECD Convention on Bribery as well as the French implementing legislation of the Convention. Notably, the Tribunal rejected the counterclaim of the Respondent (a state), arguing that state representatives had been grossly negligent when they approved the agreement at stake despite strong indicators for bribery.

ICC Case No. 13515 confirmed some of the patterns established in the above two cases. The Tribunal relied on provisions of the French Civil Code and mentioned the French implementing legislation of the OECD Convention on Bribery. It argued that the chosen law could not impede the application of transnational public policy that was defined in detail. The Tribunal relied on solid and convergent indicia to prove bribery, in particular the excessive commission of the Claimant (almost 40 per cent) compared to what was practised in the respective business sector. The Claimant was unable to produce clear evidence of the reality and content of its services, and the modalities of contract management and payment were unusual. The Tribunal did not accept the fact that corruption was endemic in the respective state as sufficient proof for bribery. The sum of the other indicia, however, let it conclude that bribery was involved in this case, and all claims and counterclaims were dismissed.

ICC Case No. 13914 also follows similar patterns as the above three cases. The Tribunal cited Article 1(1) of the OECD Convention on Bribery and referred to the US FCPA (the law of the State of Texas applied to the contracts at stake). It relied on a list of 'red flags' to prove bribery when foreign intermediaries are involved, and identified a number of those in the evidence record of the case: endemic corruption in the country at stake, an unusually high commission, the uncooperativeness of the Claimant, as he did not produce some of the requested (bank) documents and unilaterally redacted others, and the insufficient qualifications by the Claimant to perform the offered services. In addition, officials of the involved state-owned company A had proposed to the Respondent to hire the Claimant, negotiated the commissions, and took a personal interest that those were paid to the Claimant. The evidence record also showed that the Claimant had paid more than US $6 million to company A officials without any credible explanation. The Tribunal found that there was 'clear and convincing evidence' for bribery as the commission payments served to influence company A officials in their decision-making. It relied on international public policy, Texas case law and earlier ICC Awards to conclude that the contracts were null and void *ab initio*.

Compared to the above four cases, the outcome was completely different in ICC Case No. 9333: despite a commission amounting to almost 30 per cent, the Arbitrator concluded that no bribery was involved in this case. He stated that the commission was justified by the circumstances of the case and – in its absolute amount – had to be regarded as a necessary 'investment'. Confronted with contradictory witness statements, the Arbitrator eventually found that the Respondent had not presented conclusive circumstantial evidence for bribery. The Arbitrator left the question open whether a foreign law if having the quality of policing law (*loi de police*) could be applied under Art. 19 of the applicable SPILA.

In ICC Case No. 12472, the Tribunal explicitly referred to the French Criminal Code provision that prohibits trading in influence (French law was applicable) and to the OECD Convention on Bribery. As the effects were neither disproportionate nor severe, it denied the application of mandatory provisions on nationality and registration of agents of the law of the state where the agreement was performed. The Tribunal concluded that the bribery allegations were based on presumptions not supported by probative elements. In particular, the amount of the Claimant's commission had long been discussed by the parties, and the Respondent knew that several persons had to intervene on its behalf. There was no proof that any of the paid persons had searched to abuse his or her influence, and had been a public official.

Not much is public about ICC Case No. 12732, in particular not its outcome. However, it discusses standard of proof in detail. The Tribunal asked whether this issue was part of substantive or of procedural law, but considered the question of little practical relevance as English law applied to substance as well as procedure. Examining English case law – i.e. civil court cases where criminal behaviour was alleged – the Tribunal found that in the case at hand, a 'balance of probability' standard of proof should apply, and that circumstantial evidence was sufficient to prove bribery as long as it tipped the balance of probability.

In ICC Case No. 13384, the Arbitrator stated that the criminal law of state X, where the agreement was performed, and transnational public policy might result in the setting aside of the law governing the contract at stake – in this case French law, as chosen by the parties – in case of any contrariety. There was no contrariety and the Arbitrator complemented French law with state X law. He relied on a provision of the French Criminal Code that implemented the OECD Convention on Bribery, arguing that this provision should be interpreted restrictively and a high standard of proof should apply to ascertain any alleged violation: no mere presumption would suffice. Although the high level of remuneration (14 per cent) would have allowed hidden payments to public officials, there was written and oral evidence that the Claimant performed services for the Respondent and had the necessary qualifications. The Respondent was unable to produce counterevidence of an intention to corrupt state officials, or of any corrupt behaviour by the Claimant. The Respondent's evidence was controversial; the corruption defence was raised at a late stage; and the Arbitrator emphasised that a criminal complaint in state X regarding the bribery allegations had never been filed. In sum, the Arbitrator dismissed the corruption defence.

Finally, ICC Case No. 14470 shows that a criminal conviction of a Minister who signed the contract at stake is not sufficient to prove bribery if there is no convergent evidence related to the contract making it more than probable or almost certain that the latter involved corruption. In ICC Case No. 14878, the Respondent directly invoked the French Criminal Code (French law was applicable to the contract), but was unable to produce tangible evidence for the corruption allegations. The reference to earlier arbitral awards and the endemic corruption in the respective state were not sufficient to convince the Arbitrator. In ICC Case No. 16090, the Arbitrator applied a high standard of proof and did not draw an adverse inference from the Claimant's refusal to disclose the identity of its beneficial owner.

6.2 An ICC Case Involving Fraud Allegations

6.2.1 ICC Case No. 6320 (1992)

Claimant in this case was a utility company; Defendant was a power plant equipment manufacturer. The parties concluded a contract with regard to a power plant to be built in the Claimant's country. According to the terms of the contract, the Defendant should supply equipment and engineering for the power plant, and was responsible for planning, scheduling, co-ordination, technical assistance, personnel training and other services. The Claimant bore *inter alia* the responsibility for the overall co-ordination of the power plant, for its construction, for the supply of qualified personnel and for obtaining all necessary licences and other legal documents. The contract provided for the application of local law and contained an ICC arbitration clause.[236]

The construction of the plant was delayed by defects and problems, and the parties settled in a Power Plant Provisional Acceptance Protocol ('Protocol'). In the Protocol, the Claimant accepted the power plant, and the Defendant agreed to correct deficient items and to pay compensation for uncorrected items. The dispute leading to the arbitration proceedings arose about the scope of the contract and the parties' obligations thereunder. The Claimant argued that the Defendant had agreed to design and supply a power plant ready for safe operation for forty years. The Defendant asserted that it only had agreed to supply the equipment and related services for the power plant; that it was not responsible for the construction; and that it had not given a forty years guarantee. The Defendant also argued that all claims had been settled by the Protocol.[237]

In the arbitration, the Claimant claimed damages for three generators, two steam and one electric. In particular, the Claimant alleged that the steam generators were deficiently designed and manufactured, resulting in corrosion and cracking of the steam generator tubes, so that they had

236 ICC Case No. 6320, 62 et seq. 237 ICC Case No. 6320, 63.

to be replaced after thirteen instead of forty years. The Claimant argued that this claim had not been settled by the Protocol, and that the Defendant had known of the corrosion problems and intentionally concealed the scope of the problem from the Claimant. The Claimant alleged, *inter alia*, fraud by the Defendant.[238]

6.2.1.1 Fraud Allegations

The Claimant argued that the Protocol was not valid (and therefore could not limit the Claimant's claims) because it had been induced by fraud, alleging that the Defendant had not disclosed certain serious defects in the steam generators to the Claimant, and stating that it would not have agreed to the Protocol if it had known of those defects.[239]

6.2.1.2 Proving Fraud

The Tribunal noted – in agreement with the parties – that the burden of proving fraud was 'not easily met':

> A party claiming damages on the ground that it was induced by fraud to enter into a contract must prove the intentional concealment of a fact of which it was unaware and that it would not have entered into such a contract had it known that fact. The fact concealed must be a fact which by law, or custom, or due to the nature of the transaction, should have been disclosed. In this Case, the knowledge at issue cannot be more than the knowledge the parties had at the time the Contract (and the Protocol) was entered into. And the proof must be clear and conclusive, presumptions are not sufficient.[240]

The Claimant argued that it had proven three key facts: that the type of steam generator was defective; that the Defendant knew that it was defective; and that the Defendant lied about the defects and covered up their severity. The Tribunal first examined the Claimant's argument that it was in a weaker position than the Defendant with regard to the necessary information for the power plant contract. The Tribunal noted that, as typical in such situations, the Claimant had employed knowledgeable advisers and could rely on them for the information it needed. The Tribunal found that it could not be considered fraud if the Defendant relied on the expectation that the Claimant make such use of its advisers, which the Defendant knew were available to it.[241]

[238] ICC Case No. 6320, 63 et seq. [239] ICC Case No. 6320, 65 et seq.
[240] ICC Case No. 6320, 66. [241] ICC Case No. 6320, 66 et seq.

6.2.1.3 Evidence of Fraud?

The Tribunal first turned to internal minutes of the Defendant, which showed worries and uncertainty about the corrosion problems. The Tribunal found that there had in fact been such problems; that the Defendant was investigating them; and that it had told the Claimant that it was continuing its investigation. The Tribunal also questioned other internal documents of the Defendant and concluded that:

> The picture that emerges . . . is that there were problems in these defendant steam generators, that their design and materials were at the same time 'state of the art', that information about the problems was available and that in a number of instances defendant itself had provided the relevant information.
>
> Based on its extensive review of the record, the Tribunal finds that these same conclusions must be drawn with respect to the allegation of fraud in the inducement of the Contract generally. This finding follows from an analysis not only of the major instances discussed in detail in this section, but also of the remainder of the relevant evidence, which has led the Tribunal to conclude that claimant has not been able to meet the heavy burden of proof required for a [fraud] claim.[242]

The Tribunal stated that the Defendant had made considerable efforts to handle the existing problems with the steam generators, and that employees had been critical and pessimistic about the solutions in the internal communications, but that such aggressive questioning by scientists and engineers was required to progressively develop a product. The Tribunal held that the steam generators had to be measured to the standards applicable at the time they were designed and delivered, and according to those standards, the generators were 'state of the art'. The Tribunal found that no fraud had been involved in the inducement of the Protocol.[243] In the Award, the Tribunal concluded that neither the contract nor the Protocol had been induced by fraud, and that no fraud was proven in the performance of the contract either.[244]

6.2.1.4 Analysis

ICC Case No. 6320 is one example for alleged fraud in arbitration proceedings. It is an interesting case because the Tribunal examined the applicable standard of proof and concluded that clear and conclusive

[242] ICC Case No. 6320, 71. [243] ICC Case No. 6320, 72 et seq.
[244] ICC Case No. 6320, 86.

evidence is required to prove fraud, and that mere presumptions are insufficient. The Tribunal apparently did not rely on any specific criminal law provisions, international conventions or transnational public policy to discuss the fraud allegations.

6.3 An *Ad Hoc* Arbitration Involving Money Laundering Allegations

6.3.1 X *v.* Y (*2004/2006*)

6.3.1.1 The 2004 Geneva Award

The Claimant in this case was X, a corporation registered in the Bermuda Islands. The Respondent was Y, a corporation registered in the British Virgin Islands with offices in the capital of country A. The arbitration took place in Geneva under the ICC Rules. In April 2001, the parties had concluded a call option agreement ('April agreement'), according to which Y granted to X a call option for up to 77.7 per cent of the shares of C, a corporation registered in the Bahamas. In December 2001, the parties concluded a second call option agreement ('December agreement') for the remaining 22.3 per cent of C. The purpose of those agreements was the indirect sale of D, a corporation of country A holding 25.1 per cent of the shares of E, one of the biggest mobile telephone operators in country A. C dominated D to 99.99 per cent. The April agreement contained a clause for arbitration with seat in Zurich; the December agreement contained a clause for ICC arbitration with seat in Geneva.[245]

In 2003, X initiated ICC arbitration in Geneva, arguing that it had validly executed, and paid for, the December 2001 call option, and claiming that Y was obliged to transfer 22.3 per cent of the C shares to X against the payment of US$16 million. Y argued that the December agreement was illegal and therefore unenforceable.[246]

The Geneva Tribunal decided in August 2004 that X had validly executed the December agreement, and was therefore entitled to 22.3 per cent of the C shares; that C held 99.99 per cent of D's share capital; and that D held 25.1 per cent of E's share capital. The Tribunal ordered Y to transfer the 25.1 per cent share of E to X against the payment of US$16 million. The Tribunal argued that Y had failed to substantiate its allegations that the April and December agreements were part of a

[245] BGer 4P.208/2004, at A; *X* v. *Y* (2004 Geneva Award).

[246] BGer 4P.208/2004, at B.

money laundering system. It concluded that G, a Danish lawyer, was the beneficial owner behind a complex offshore structure of companies, banks and trusts. The Tribunal decided that G's explanations that this structure had grown organically and was retained in this form for tax reasons were plausible. The Tribunal was further confirmed in its conclusion by the fact that several law firms had conducted due diligence checks with regard to X, with satisfactory results.[247]

6.3.1.2 Appeal of the 2004 Geneva Award

Y appealed the 2004 Geneva Award to the Swiss Federal Supreme Court, arguing *inter alia* that the Award was contrary to public policy (Art. 190(2)(e) SPILA), because it resulted in a condemnation of Y to participate in money laundering. The Federal Supreme Court rejected the appeal, arguing that the Award would only be contrary to public policy if money laundering had been proven in the arbitral proceedings.[248]

6.3.1.3 The 2004/2006 Zurich Partial Awards

One month after the Geneva ICC arbitration, X initiated *ad hoc* arbitration in Zurich under the respective clause in the April agreement. X claimed that it had validly executed, and paid for, the April 2001 call option and was therefore entitled to 77.7 per cent of C; which held 99.99 per cent of D; which held 25.1 per cent of E. Y argued that the April agreement was illegal and unenforceable.[249] The Zurich Tribunal issued Partial Awards on 19 October 2004 and 16 May 2006. It held that the findings of the Geneva ICC Tribunal did not have the *res iudicata* effect, as the alleged facts in the Zurich proceedings were substantially different from the Geneva Award.[250] The Tribunal applied English law to the substance of the dispute, in accordance with a clause in the April agreement. However, for the determination of certain preliminary issues, it applied the criminal law of country A and Swiss criminal law.[251]

With regard to procedural law, the Tribunal applied – as agreed by the parties – chapter 12 of the SPILA, and neither English procedural law nor the Code of Civil Procedure of the Canton of Zurich (with the exception of the provision on the privilege against self-incrimination of witnesses of the former Zurich Civil Procedure Code). In accordance with Art. 182

[247] BGer 4P.208/2004, at C. [248] BGer 4P.208/2004, at 6.2.
[249] *X* v. *Y* (2004 Zurich Award), 14 et seq., 32 et seq.
[250] *X* v. *Y* (2004 Zurich Award), 113; *X* v. *Y* (2006 Zurich Award), 118 et seq.
[251] *X* v. *Y* (2006 Zurich Award), 117 et seq.

SPILA, the parties and the Tribunal determined their own procedural rules. Regarding matters not addressed in chapter 12 of SPILA, the Tribunal applied generally accepted arbitration practice.[252] The IBA Rules of Evidence[253] were used as guidelines for taking evidence in the proceedings.[254]

The Partial Award of 19 October 2004 The Partial Award of 19 October 2004 enumerated the various illegality defences (the 'broader illegality defence') that Y brought forward against the validity of the April agreement. Those defences went beyond money laundering and included Y's allegations that assets were involved that had been acquired as a result of bribery of public officials, or fraud, and had been laundered through X or by the structure set up with the April agreement.[255] The Tribunal did not make a final determination on Y's broader illegality defence. It noted that it had received serious but not conclusive materials indicating illegality, and ordered that Y should be allowed to substantiate its allegations and their relevance for the April agreement; X, on the other hand, should further explain how the funds were earned through genuine commercial transactions.[256] Referring to several authors of an ICC Dossier[257] dealing with money laundering, corruption and fraud, the Tribunal held that suspicious circumstances existed in this case, and Y did not raise its defence of alleged illegality without basis and for purely tactical reasons. Therefore, the Tribunal concluded that it had a duty not to ignore the suspicions, but to seek an explanation from the parties. The Tribunal also stated that the beneficial ownership of X was not yet determined.[258]

The Partial Award of 16 May 2006 On 16 May 2006, the Tribunal issued a Second Partial Award, now addressing Y's broader illegality defence. Notably, in 2005, while the arbitration proceedings were ongoing, parallel criminal proceedings took place in country B. The criminal investigation in country B was based on a criminal complaint filed by Respondent Y on charges of breach of trust and money

[252] *X* v. *Y* (2006 Zurich Award), 117 et seq.

[253] Cf. IBA 2010 (in their earlier version of 1999).

[254] *X* v. *Y* (2006 Zurich Award), 31.

[255] *X* v. *Y* (2004 Zurich Award), 101 et seq.

[256] *X* v. *Y* (2004 Zurich Award), 104 et seq., 114 et seq.

[257] Karsten and Berkeley (eds.) 2003.

[258] *X* v. *Y* (2004 Zurich Award), 102 et seq., 115 et seq.

laundering against several witnesses in the Zurich arbitration. Criminal investigations were also ongoing in country A, where Claimant X filed criminal complaints with the General Prosecutor for fraud and breach of trust against a witness in the Zurich arbitration.[259]

a. *The privilege against self-incrimination* Regarding those parallel criminal proceedings, the Tribunal (with reference to § 159(1) of the former Zurich Civil Procedure Code) applied the privilege against self-incrimination of witnesses and acknowledged 'the universal notion that witnesses who are subject to criminal investigations have a right against self-incrimination in giving evidence in civil proceedings'.[260] Those witnesses in the Zurich proceedings who were affected by the investigation in country B had the right not to be questioned or cross-examined on certain issues, and some made use of it.[261]

b. *Beneficial ownership of X* The Tribunal first elaborated that the sole beneficial owner of X in April 2001 was not lawyer G, but F, a high-ranking public official of country A. The Tribunal based this finding on written evidence and stated that the Geneva Tribunal had been misled in this regard, as G had given a clearly wrong account that he was the sole beneficial owner of X.[262] The Tribunal then examined whether the April agreement was valid and enforceable, in light of Y's broader illegality defence – as a preliminary issue to be decided before the Tribunal could examine whether that option had been validly exercised. Two of Y's illegality defences are discussed in subsections f. and g. here.[263]

c. *The applicable law* As English law applied to the substance of the dispute, the Tribunal examined its general principles regarding the alleged illegality of the April agreement. It explained the concepts of void and voidable contracts in English contract law and contrasted those to an unenforceable contract: 'An unenforceable contract is one which is valid in all respects except that a party to it may not sue upon it. An example of an unenforceable contract is one which is illegal.'[264] The Tribunal stated that in English law, the majority view was that a contract concluded for an illegal purpose was not void, but unenforceable. This means that the

259 *X* v. *Y* (2006 Zurich Award), 84 et seq.
260 *X* v. *Y* (2006 Zurich Award), 90.
261 *X* v. *Y* (2006 Zurich Award), 90 et seq.
262 *X* v. *Y* (2006 Zurich Award), 130 et seq., 137 et seq.
263 *X* v. *Y* (2006 Zurich Award), 159 et seq.
264 *X* v. *Y* (2006 Zurich Award), 162.

contract does come into existence, but a court or tribunal will refuse to assist in its enforcement (although there were cases in English law in which judges declared such a contract as void).[265] Regarding illegality, the Tribunal stated:

> Illegality . . . is where a transaction is prohibited by law either because it involves the commission of a legal wrong or involves illegal conduct which is contrary to public policy.
>
> English law distinguishes between illegality as to formation of a contract and illegality as to its performance. In both situations the court will not enforce the contract or provide a party with any remedies arising therefrom.[266]

d. *Burden of proof* The Tribunal then examined the applicable burden and standard of proof and first determined the applicable law in this regard. It pointed out that applying the law of the seat of the arbitration (Swiss law), one was directed to the law applicable to the merits of the arbitration, *in casu* English law. In English law, however, burden and standard of proof are issues of procedure and determined not by the substantive law, but by the procedural law of the *lex fori*, *in casu* Swiss procedural law. As this (circular) argumentation did not provide a solution, the Tribunal relied on international arbitral practice, which showed a tendency to apply the substantive law of a dispute to determine burden and standard of proof, *in casu* English law.[267]

Burden of proof in English law is divided into a legal burden imposed by the law itself and a provisional (evidentiary) burden raised by the state of the evidence. The principle is that 'The legal burden does not shift but the provisional burden may shift as the case proceeds where evidence has been adduced.'[268] With regard to illegal contracts, referring to English case law,[269] the Tribunal noted on burden of proof that 'In the context of allegedly illegal contracts there is a general rebuttable presumption in English law in favour of legality. A party alleging illegality of the contract bears the burden of proving it.'[270] The Tribunal concluded that, 'If . . . the

[265] *X* v. *Y* (2006 Zurich Award), 163.
[266] *X* v. *Y* (2006 Zurich Award), 165; see also *Archbolds (Freightage) Ltd* v. *S Spanglett Ltd* [1961] 1 QBD 374.
[267] *X* v. *Y* (2006 Zurich Award), 167.
[268] *X* v. *Y* (2006 Zurich Award), 168 with reference to *Brown* v. *Rolls Royce Ltd* [1960] 1 WLR 210.
[269] *Hire-Purchase Furnishings Co.* v. *Richens* (1887) 20 QBD 387.
[270] *X* v. *Y* (2006 Zurich Award), 168.

contract on its face evidences an illegal intention, the burden lies upon the party seeking to uphold the contract to adduce evidence showing the legality of intention.'[271]

e. *Standard of proof* Regarding standard of proof in English law, the Tribunal noted that the balance of probabilities applied. With reference to case law,[272] the Tribunal concluded that 'the need for more cogent evidence to prove a serious allegation of facts does not mean that in a civil case the standard of proof is anything higher than the balance of probabilities'.[273] Taking into account the very serious allegations of money laundering and illegality in this case, the Tribunal stated that it would 'require cogent and strong evidence on the facts that a particular event occurred in order to decide whether ... a claim is, on the balance of probabilities, founded or not'.[274]

f. *The 'Dilution Defence'* The Tribunal then examined Y's illegality defences. Under the heading 'Dilution Defence', it questioned F's conduct under the criminal law of country A, as a preliminary issue in a civil law dispute:

> In fact, if an illegality under [the] criminal law [of country A] can be determined, the Arbitral Tribunal must examine whether such illegality results under the applicable English law in the illegality of the April Option Agreement. If on the other hand no illegality under [the] law [of country A] can be found, then the April Option Agreement must be considered valid and enforceable if it is legal under English law.[275]

The Tribunal analysed the elements of three provisions of the Criminal Code of country A in the version valid from 2000 to 2002: Art. 160 (misappropriation or embezzlement), Art. 285 (abuse of official powers) and Art. 289 (unlawful participation in business activity). The Tribunal concluded that, regarding the conduct of F, all elements of Art. 160 of the Criminal Code of country A were proven.[276] While the application of

[271] *X* v. *Y* (2006 Zurich Award), 168.

[272] In particular Lord Nicholls' opinion in *In re H. and Others (Minors)* [1996] AC 563 (583 et seq.), which was a civil case dealing with allegations of criminal conduct (cf. above ICC Case 12732); *Secretary of State for the Home Department* v. *Rehman* [2001] UKHL 47, note 55.

[273] *X* v. *Y* (2006 Zurich Award), 169.

[274] *X* v. *Y* (2006 Zurich Award), 170.

[275] *X* v. *Y* (2006 Zurich Award), 227 et seq.

[276] *X* v. *Y* (2006 Zurich Award), 233 et seq., 242.

Art. 160 overrode the application of Art. 285 of the Criminal Code of country A, the Tribunal considered that the conduct of F also fulfilled all elements of Art. 289 of the Criminal Code of country A.[277]

The Tribunal considered the impact of those criminal offences on the April agreement under the applicable English law. Analysing the relevant case law, it concluded that the agreement was unenforceable under English law because it had an illegal purpose; and that there was cogent and strong evidence for this conclusion,[278] stressing that

> the finding on the applicability of Article 160 ... and Article 289 [of the Criminal Code of country A] ... do not amount to a conviction of [F] to criminal sanctions, but is merely a finding on the preliminary issue whether provisions of [the] criminal law [of country A] have been contravened. Moreover, this finding is made within the framework of a civil law dispute to which [F], despite being the beneficial owner of Claimant, is not a party.[279]

g. *The money laundering defence* The Tribunal also examined Y's money laundering defence and looked in detail at two specific payments to X prior to the signing of the April agreement. It stressed that money laundering was a defence which had to be considered as a matter of international public policy.[280]

The Tribunal analysed the so-called Augmentation Payment. It applied Arts. 285 (abuse of official powers) and 289 (unlawful participation in business activity) of the Criminal Code of country A, again with regard to the conduct of F, concluding that 'money received by Claimant from Augmentation and used for payments under the April Option Agreement ... were obtained through a commission by [F] of criminal offences described in Art. 285 and 289 [of the Criminal Code of country A]'.[281] The Tribunal questioned whether the Augmentation Payment constituted money laundering. The parties agreed that in order to determine this question, Swiss criminal law should be applied. The Tribunal agreed on the basis that the relevant elements of the offence (*Tathandlung*), i.e. the alleged money laundering activity, had taken place in Switzerland. The escrow agent was a law firm based in Zurich, the escrow account was with Swiss banks, and relevant payments had

[277] *X* v. *Y* (2006 Zurich Award), 246 et seq.
[278] *X* v. *Y* (2006 Zurich Award), 255 et seq., 259 et seq.
[279] *X* v. *Y* (2006 Zurich Award), 259 et seq. [280] *X* v. *Y* (2006 Zurich Award), 260.
[281] *X* v. *Y* (2006 Zurich Award), 275 et seq., 282.

been made into and transferred from the Swiss escrow account. The Tribunal went even further and stated, with reference to Art. 7 of the then applicable Swiss Criminal Code (SCrimC), that 'The application of Swiss criminal law depends not on the contractual arrangement of the parties on the contractual place of performance, but merely on the place where the act ("*Tathandlung*") has been carried out or the place where the result has been achieved ("*Erfolgsort*").'[282]

Consequently, the Tribunal analysed the objective and subjective requirements of Art. 305bis (money laundering) of the SCrimC in detail. Regarding the objective requirements, the Tribunal first stated that under the Swiss money laundering provision, the perpetrator can be an individual as well as a company.[283] *In casu*, corporation X had accepted the Augmentation Payment and had used it to indirectly receive the interests in E. G as the alleged beneficial owner of X had instructed X to conclude the April agreement and to finance it through the Augmentation Payment, and was therefore an accomplice (*Mittäter*) or instigator (*Anstifter*) according to the SCrimC. The object of money laundering was *in casu* an option portion from the April agreement that had been paid by transfers of money from bank to bank. The option portion was mainly financed through the Augmentation Payment, which was of criminal origin as it was obtained through the commission of criminal offences (Arts. 285 and 289 of the Criminal Code of country A). The Tribunal did not further inquire whether the tainted funds had been commingled with non-tainted funds, because the Augmentation Payment was clearly the major source for funding the option portion.[284]

With regard to predicate offence, the Tribunal stated that Art. 289 of the Criminal Code of country A could not be a predicate offence within the meaning of Art. 305bis because there was no corresponding provision in Swiss criminal law declaring the activity of unlawful participation in business activity by an official as punishable (principle of dual incrimination). However, the criminal conduct described in Art. 285 of the Criminal Code of country A corresponded to Art. 312 SCrimC (*Amtsmissbrauch*, abuse of office). The Tribunal stated that F had engaged in criminal activity within the meaning of Art. 312 by inaction (arguing that F had a so-called *Garantenpflicht*, in this context meaning

282 *X* v. *Y* (2006 Zurich Award), 283.

283 *X* v. *Y* (2006 Zurich Award), 285 et seq. with reference to Art. 100^{quater}(2) of the former SCrimC.

284 *X* v. *Y* (2006 Zurich Award), 286.

an obligation to represent the interests of country A). As this provision qualifies as a crime, and the predicate offence was not time-barred at the time the alleged money laundering activity occurred, the Tribunal concluded that the requirement of dual incrimination was fulfilled, and affirmed the existence of a predicate offence.[285]

The Tribunal also found that the money laundering activity (*Tathandlung*) was established because the illegal profit that F had achieved through the sale of a company was passed through the Augmentation Payment to X, and then paid to the escrow account and from there onwards through another company to E (which carried a different name at that time), a mobile telephone operator engaging in legitimate business activity. Those transactions impeded the confiscation of assets and the determination of their origin (*Herkunftsermittlung*), and constituted a concealment within the meaning of Art. 305bis SCrimC.[286]

Having concluded that all objective requirements of the Swiss money laundering provision were met, the Tribunal stated that the intention of the perpetrator (the subjective requirement of the offence) was also established. X and G knew, or should have known, about the criminal origin of the assets, and that F was involved in the illicit company sale, while at the same time being the beneficial owner of X. The Tribunal went on to examine the impact of money laundering under English contract law.[287]

h. *Unenforceability of the April agreement* The Tribunal eventually did not refer to English statutory law, but to English public policy. It stated that since money laundering by X and G under Swiss criminal law was established, under the applicable English law, the April agreement was unenforceable.[288] In sum, the Tribunal concluded that the April agreement was unenforceable because of the 'Dilution Defence' and the money laundering defence with regard to the Augmentation Payment.[289]

6.3.1.4 Application for Revision of the 2004 Geneva Award

With submissions of 12 April and 14 August 2006, Y called for revision of the August 2004 Geneva Award. The Swiss Federal Supreme Court noted that the SPILA did not contain any provisions on the revision of arbitral awards, but that Federal Court jurisdiction had filled that gap,

[285] *X* v. *Y* (2006 Zurich Award), 287 et seq., 292.
[286] *X* v. *Y* (2006 Zurich Award), 293 et seq. [287] *X* v. *Y* (2006 Zurich Award), 294 et seq.
[288] *X* v. *Y* (2006 Zurich Award), 299. [289] *X* v. *Y* (2006 Zurich Award), 346.

and federal law provided for the extraordinary legal remedy of revision of an international arbitral award to the Supreme Court.[290] Y applied for revision on the grounds of relevant new evidence, submitting an affidavit of an organ of X dated 16 January 2006 in which it is explained on the basis of three documents that the top executive body of X did not maintain its contention that G was the sole beneficial owner of X.[291]

The Supreme Court took note that Y had met the deadline for filing the application for revision, and affirmed that there was new evidence that partly already existed at the time of the 2004 Geneva proceedings, but of which Y could not have any knowledge at that time. The Court also affirmed that the new evidence was relevant because it proved a fact that the Geneva Arbitral Tribunal itself had considered to be relevant: the identity of the beneficial owner of X in light of the money laundering allegations.[292] In sum, the Court endorsed the application for revision of the Award on the basis of relevant new evidence, remanded the Award, and sent the case back to the Arbitral Tribunal for a new assessment of Y's money laundering allegations on the basis of the new evidence, and for a new decision in this matter.[293]

6.3.1.5 Appeal of the May 2006 Zurich Partial Award

X appealed the May 2006 Partial Award of the *ad hoc* Zurich Tribunal to the Swiss Federal Supreme Court, arguing *inter alia* that the Arbitral Tribunal was not competent to decide on violations of the criminal law of country A by X's beneficial owner, because according to public order, only state authorities can impose penalties. The Federal Supreme Court argued, however, that the aim of the Tribunal had not been to impose penalties, but to arbitrate the parties' claims in a dispute of financial interest. The application of criminal law provisions – in particular of country A – happened in the context of the Tribunal's preliminary examination of the validity of the contract (the April agreement) on which the parties' claims were based. The Court concluded that the Tribunal had been competent for the preliminary (*vorfrageweise*) examination of the criminal law aspects of the case. The Court also stated, with reference to doctrine, that arbitral tribunals must take position if bribery or money laundering allegations are at stake.[294] In sum, the Federal Supreme Court dismissed the appeal.

[290] Cf. BGE 118 II 199; Leuenberger and Uffer-Tobler 2016, 508.
[291] BGer 4P.102/2006, at 2.2.
[292] BGer 4P.102/2006, at 4.
[293] BGer 4P.102/2006, at 5.
[294] BGE 133 III 139, at 5.

6.3.1.6 Analysis

X. v. *Y.* is a very complex case that resulted in at least three (unpublished) arbitral awards and three Federal Supreme Court decisions, as well as in court decisions at the enforcement stage. This analysis is mainly focused on the Second Zurich Partial Award of 16 May 2006, in which the money laundering allegations were discussed in detail. In the 2004 Geneva arbitration proceedings under the ICC Rules, the Tribunal found that the Respondent Y had failed to substantiate its money laundering allegations; Y also failed with its appeal of the Geneva Award to the Swiss Federal Supreme Court.

In the Zurich *ad hoc* arbitration, the Tribunal in a First Partial Award in 2004 decided to give Y the possibility to substantiate its illegality defences, as suspicious circumstances existed in the case. In the Second Partial Award in 2006, the Tribunal carried out a detailed preliminary examination of the money laundering allegations and other alleged illegality. One important feature of that arbitration was the parallel criminal investigations against several witnesses in different jurisdictions. Some witnesses made use of the privilege against self-incrimination in civil proceedings and were not questioned or cross-examined on certain issues.

The parties had chosen English law to apply to the substance of the dispute, and chapter 12 of the SPILA to procedure. However, the Tribunal also relied on other laws:

- a provision of the former Zurich Civil Procedure Code to state that witnesses in civil proceedings who were subject to criminal investigation had a privilege against self-incrimination;
- Swiss criminal law to determine the money laundering allegations (as chosen by the parties; the Tribunal agreed because relevant elements of the offence had taken place in Switzerland; the Tribunal even argued that Swiss criminal law would apply notwithstanding the will of the parties if Switzerland was the place where the criminal act was carried out or the place where the result was achieved) and
- the criminal law of country A with regard to the conduct of F (in particular with regard to the predicate offence for money laundering).

The Tribunal noted that in English law, burden and standard of proof are issues of procedure, whereas in Switzerland, substantive law applies; the Tribunal decided, in accordance with international arbitral practice, to apply substantive law to determine burden and standard of proof, *in casu* English law. It differentiated between the legal burden imposed by the law and the provisional (evidentiary) burden raised by the state of the evidence; only the provisional burden can shift. Regarding contracts, they are presumed to be legal, and a party alleging illegality has to prove it. However, if a contract on its face is illegal, the party that wants to uphold it must prove its legality. On standard of proof, the Tribunal argued that the balance of probabilities applied, as usual in a civil case, but that cogent and strong evidence was required to prove the serious money laundering and illegality allegations in this case.

Having established that the sole beneficial owner of X in 2001 was not lawyer G, but public official F of country A, the Tribunal examined Y's illegality defences in detail. It analysed F's conduct under the criminal law of country A, and found that two provisions were fulfilled. On money laundering, the Tribunal applied the respective provision of the Swiss Criminal Code – stating that the money laundering defence had to be considered as a matter of public policy – and found that the objective and subjective requirements of the offence were given. The Tribunal concluded that the April agreement was unenforceable under English public policy, in particular because money laundering by X and G was established under Swiss criminal law.

Y was subsequently successful with its application for revision of the 2004 Geneva Award on the basis of relevant new evidence in front of the Swiss Federal Supreme Court; whereas X's appeal of the May 2006 Zurich Partial Award to the same Court, based on the argument that the Tribunal had not been competent to decide on violations of the criminal law of country A, was dismissed.

7

Interim Conclusion on Current Practice

In this part, thirty-four international investment and commercial arbitration cases (largely ICSID and ICC) were analysed from the perspective of proving alleged criminal behaviour. It shows that over the past fifty years, arbitral tribunals dealt with such allegations in many different ways, as the legal and factual situation varies from case to case: there is no uniform approach, but rather a patchwork of solutions. However, the newer cases demonstrate that certain patterns have emerged and consolidated when it comes to proving bribery. Those patterns can, in principle, also be applied to other criminal offences. While there is no doctrine of precedent in international arbitration, the case analysis shows that tribunals do refer to earlier arbitral awards in the context of alleged crime. Therefore, identifying and assessing established patterns can help to solve such cases in the future.

For certain issues that can arise in the context of alleged crime, there is no established approach by tribunals yet. Those will be discussed in more detail in the next part. The aim of this text is not to develop a boilerplate solution how cases involving alleged crime should be resolved, but rather to draw up a decision tree for arbitrators what they have to keep in mind, and how they can proceed if criminal allegations arise. A decision tree will be useful not only for arbitrators but also for parties and their legal representatives, and it might increase predictability of the outcome of arbitral proceedings involving alleged criminal conduct, and ultimately serve the interest of increased legal certainty. The following picture of established patterns and disputed or unclarified issues emerges.

In investment as well as in commercial arbitration, tribunals increasingly rely directly on provisions of international or domestic criminal law to determine the objective requirements of bribery, fraud or money laundering. Tribunals also frequently invoke transnational public policy. Regarding evidence, in arbitration practice as well as in doctrine, it is undisputed that the alleging party initially carries the burden of proving alleged criminal behaviour. It is equally uncontroversial to say that circumstantial evidence is sufficient to prove criminal behaviour in arbitration – there is no need for direct evidence.[1] With regard to proving alleged bribery, 'red flag' or indicia lists are well established and used today.[2] Next to those established patterns, the following disputed or unclarified issues exist:

Table 7.1 *Issues of applicable criminal law*

Common to ICSID and ICC arbitration	• From which domestic legal system should tribunals draw the objective requirements of foreign public and of private bribery, fraud and money laundering? • Are international treaties dealing with bribery, fraud and money laundering directly applicable? • Does the party alleging criminal conduct have to prove *mens rea*? • Is there a transnational public policy against private bribery, fraud and money laundering?

Table 7.2 *Issues of evidence*

Common to ICSID and ICC arbitration	• If criminal conduct is alleged, can the burden of proof shift? • May adverse inferences be drawn from the non-production of evidence? • Does the privilege against self-incrimination apply in arbitration? • What evidence issues arise out of parallel domestic criminal proceedings? • Which standard of proof applies? • Is all evidence admissible? • Which 'red flags' are there for private bribery, fraud and money laundering? • Do arbitrators have a duty to report suspected criminal conduct to the authorities? • Do arbitrators have to investigate suspected criminal conduct *ex officio*? Are tribunals obliged to identify and apply (foreign) mandatory provisions? • What if allegations of criminal conduct are raised late in the arbitral proceedings?

[1] Next to the above case analysis, see e.g. Lamm, Greenwald and Young 2014, 338.
[2] Khvalei 2014, 21 et seq.; Cremades and Cairns 2003b, 83 with further references.

Table 7.3 *Legal consequences of criminal conduct*

Specific to ICSID arbitration	• What is the temporal scope of the legality requirement? • Does the 'clean hands' doctrine apply? • Should host states be held responsible for bribe solicitation by their officials?
Specific to ICC arbitration	• What are the legal consequences of bribery pacts? • Are there any options if the existence of a bribery pact cannot be proven, but strong suspicions prevail?

The next part will focus on selected issues of applicable criminal law and evidence. The issues that arise from the case analysis with regard to the legal consequences of criminal conduct in arbitration are briefly touched upon. A detailed analysis is, however, beyond the scope of this text.

PART IV

Critical Assessment

8

Issues of Applicable Criminal Law

8.1 Which Provisions Are Applicable?

The analysis of current practice in Part III demonstrates that if crime is alleged in international arbitration, tribunals increasingly rely on criminal law provisions to determine the requirements of the respective offence. This development merits a closer look: if tribunals draw directly from (domestic or international) criminal law – in addition to, or instead of relying on transnational public policy – the requirements of the criminal offence accurately specify what needs to be proven by the evidence.[1] As a consequence, the arbitrators as well as the parties are in a better position to take and assess the evidence. Furthermore, tribunals can rely on domestic case law and doctrine to apply the criminal law provisions. The application of such provisions increases legal certainty and predictability of the outcome of arbitral proceedings. However, identifying the applicable criminal provisions is not an easy task. The basic legal framework for ICSID and commercial arbitration was presented above. This section now focuses specifically on the applicable criminal law.

8.1.1 In ICSID Arbitration

In the case analysis in Chapter 5, tribunals directly relied on domestic or international criminal law provisions in the following situations.

8.1.1.1 Application of Domestic Criminal Law

On the Basis of a BIT 'in Accordance with Host State's Law' Clause If ICSID arbitration is based on a BIT, the treaty might contain an 'in accordance with host state's law' clause. This requirement arguably

[1] See discussion in Chapter 4 on the 'circle of association'.

applies even if it is not explicitly mentioned in the BIT.[2] Tribunals consider such clauses to encompass the host state's criminal laws.[3] If an investment breaches the host state's criminal law provisions prohibiting bribery or fraud, it does not fulfil the BIT's legality requirement and as a result does not qualify as an investment under Article 25 of the ICSID Convention. In such instances, the tribunal has to closely examine the requirements of the provisions of the host state's criminal law.

On the Basis of a Choice of Law Clause ICSID arbitration is based on party autonomy, and choice of law clauses regarding the applicable substantive law can be found in BITs as well as in contracts. In the (contract-based) *WDF* v. *Kenya* arbitration, the tribunal referred to domestic (Kenyan) criminal law on the basis of a choice of law clause that provided for the application of English and Kenyan law.

8.1.1.2 Application of International Anti-Corruption Treaties

International law includes binding international anti-corruption conventions such as the OECD Convention on Bribery. This treaty is considered not self-executing[4] and therefore needs to be implemented in the state parties' domestic law in order to become applicable by the courts in a legal dispute. However, in *Sistem* v. *Kyrgyz Republic*, the Tribunal relied directly on Article 1 of the OECD Convention on Bribery. Is this approach feasible?

Article 1 defines the elements of the offence of foreign public bribery and appears detailed enough to be applied directly. Indeed, the reason why Article 1 is considered not self-executing is because the OECD Convention is based on the principle of 'functional equivalence':

> The approach assumes that every legal system has its own logic, which is not necessarily determined by legal texts alone. Only the holistic appraisal of the law in operation, including informal rules and practices as well as functions assumed by other legal institutions, will allow us to assess whether the overall legal effects produced by a country's legal system adequately meet the requirements of the Convention.[5]

Therefore, states implementing the OECD Convention cannot simply take over the wording of Article 1. They need to adopt it to the specific

[2] See discussion in Chapter 2.

[3] See *Metal-Tech* v. *Uzbekistan* and *Hamester* v. *Ghana*; in *Fraport* v. *Philippines*, the Tribunal relied on the domestic Anti-Dummy Law.

[4] Bonucci 2014, 546; Harari and Jobin 2014, 509; Pieth 2014a, 36.

[5] Pieth 2014a, 37.

features of their domestic legal system.[6] In ICSID arbitration, however, if tribunals directly apply international law, functional equivalence – that is geared towards a harmonisation of domestic legal systems – has no role to play. If the applicable substantive law is international law, it seems possible to rely directly on Article 1 of the OECD Convention. Article 1 (1) and (4) of the OECD Convention read:

> The Offence of Bribery of Foreign Public Officials
>
> 1. Each Party shall take such measures as may be necessary to establish that it is a criminal offence under its law for any person intentionally to offer, promise or give any undue pecuniary or other advantage, whether directly or through intermediaries, to a foreign public official, for that official or for a third party, in order that the official act or refrain from acting in relation to the performance of official duties, in order to obtain or retain business or other improper advantage in the conduct of international business.
>
> ...
>
> 4. For the purpose of this Convention:
>   a) 'foreign public official' means any person holding a legislative, administrative or judicial office of a foreign country, whether appointed or elected; any person exercising a public function for a foreign country, including for a public agency or public enterprise; and any official or agent of a public international organisation;
>   b) 'foreign country' includes all levels and subdivisions of government, from national to local;
>   c) 'act or refrain from acting in relation to the performance of official duties' includes any use of the public official's position, whether or not within the official's authorised competence.

This provision contains the requirements of foreign public bribery as well as definitions of relevant terms, and it is complemented by Official Commentaries and soft law instruments such as the 2009 Recommendation[7] providing further guidance and help to interpret the Convention.[8] Provisions of other anti-bribery conventions with a global (or regional) reach[9] might be directly applicable in the same manner. Notably, in *Spentex* v. *Uzbekistan*, the Tribunal referred to Article 1(1) of the OECD Convention on Bribery as well as Article 16(1) of the UNCAC to create its own definition of active foreign public bribery.

[6] See also Official Commentary 2 to the OECD Convention on Bribery (OECD 1997) and for Switzerland: Pieth 2012b, 261 et seq.

[7] OECD 2009. [8] For a detailed discussion of Article 1: Zerbes 2014.

[9] See discussion in Chapter 2.

Whether an international anti-bribery, anti-fraud or anti–money laundering treaty is directly applicable depends on the choice of law by the parties or by the tribunal. If international law is chosen to apply, those treaties should apply regardless whether the involved states ratified them or not.[10]

8.1.2 In Commercial Arbitration

The analysis of commercial arbitration cases in Chapter 6 shows that tribunals directly rely on domestic or international criminal law provisions in the following situations.

8.1.2.1 In Case a Particular National Law Is Chosen to Apply

The principle in commercial arbitration with regard to the applicable substantive law is party autonomy. If the parties (or the tribunal) choose a particular national law to apply to the substance of their dispute, the question is whether their choice, which will be geared towards private law, includes the criminal law of the respective domestic legal order. It shows that tribunals in several cases have applied provisions of criminal law from the same domestic legal system as the chosen private law.[11]

8.1.2.2 Application of Foreign Mandatory Law

Party autonomy in commercial arbitration with regard to choice of law can be limited by foreign mandatory law, which includes criminal law. In two cases, tribunals discussed such limitations.

Criminal Law of the Place of Performance of a Contract In ICC Case No. 13384, the Arbitrator applied foreign mandatory law, namely the criminal law of the state where the agreement was performed. He argued that in case of any contrariety between the foreign mandatory law and the law as chosen by the parties (the French Criminal Code in this case), the former would prevail. As there was no contrariety, the Arbitrator applied the foreign mandatory law on a complementary base.

Applying Foreign Mandatory Law According to Criminal Law Principles In *X* v. *Y*, English law applied to the substance of the dispute, as chosen by the parties. With regard to the money laundering allegations, the

[10] See discussion in Chapter 2.

[11] See ICC Cases No. 12472; 13384; 13914; and 14878 (where the Respondent invoked the French Criminal Code).

parties chose Swiss law to apply, and the Tribunal agreed because relevant elements of the offence had taken place in Switzerland. Notably, the Tribunal argued that Swiss law would apply notwithstanding the parties' choice if Switzerland were the place where the criminal behaviour was carried out or the place where the result was achieved. The Tribunal argued in terms of domestic criminal law here, where – generally speaking – jurisdiction and applicable law are determined by the principles of territoriality (for instance, Swiss criminal law applies if either the place of performance or the place of effect of a crime are on Swiss territory)[12] as well as of active and passive personality (either the perpetrator or the victim of a crime are nationals of the respective state). With regard to the predicate offence for money laundering, the Tribunal applied the criminal law of the state where the offence was performed, and of which the perpetrator was a national.

Such an approach ensures that the parties cannot circumvent mandatory rules that would impose themselves if the dispute were handled in front of domestic courts. Criminal law provisions of several jurisdictions may apply, as different states may have jurisdiction according to criminal law principles.

Applying Mandatory Law of the Seat of the Arbitration Imagine the situation that an arbitral tribunal, in a case of alleged foreign public bribery, has its seat e.g. in Switzerland. The parties choose the law of a state that does not criminalise foreign public bribery in its domestic law to apply to their dispute, and the only connection of the dispute with Switzerland is that the arbitration is located there. Does the mandatory Swiss law against foreign public bribery play any role in such a scenario?

The answer is yes, but not during the arbitral proceedings themselves. During the arbitration, only the mandatory rules of the Swiss arbitration law (*lex arbitri*) are relevant. However, it would be possible to appeal the arbitral award in front of the Swiss Federal Supreme Court on the basis of a violation of Swiss (and possibly transnational) public policy (Art. 190 (2)(e) SPILA).[13] The difficulty is that the Federal Supreme Court will in principle not reopen the facts. Therefore, the party alleging bribery should bring evidence for its allegations already during the arbitral proceedings and claim a violation of transnational public policy.

[12] Art. 3 in connection with Art. 8 SCrimC.

[13] See Pfisterer 2013, Art. 190 N 73.

8.1.2.3 Application of International Anti-Corruption Treaties

In ICC Case No. 13914, the Tribunal invoked Article 1(1) of the OECD Convention on Bribery. The parties had chosen the law of the State of Texas to apply to the substance of their dispute. As discussed earlier,[14] if the parties (or the tribunal) choose international law to apply, the direct application of international anti-corruption (or anti-fraud or anti–money laundering) treaties in arbitration seems possible if the respective provisions are precise enough to be applied by tribunals.

8.1.3 Summary

More recent investment (ICSID) and commercial (ICC) arbitral awards show that tribunals increasingly rely directly on provisions of domestic or international criminal law in the context of alleged criminal behaviour. In investment as well as commercial arbitration, international or domestic criminal law may come in through the choice of the applicable substantive law. Furthermore, in investment arbitration, domestic criminal law may apply on the basis of an 'in accordance with host state's law' clause in an investment treaty. In commercial arbitration, domestic criminal law may be applicable in the form of mandatory rules of the place of performance of a contract; of the place where the criminal behaviour was carried out; of the place where the result of the criminal behaviour was achieved; or of the state of which the perpetrator or the victim are nationals. If foreign mandatory rules are contrary to the law applicable to the substance of a dispute as chosen by the parties, the former should prevail if they protect interests of such relevance that they form part of transnational public policy. In addition, the criminal law of the state where the tribunal has its seat may become relevant if a party seeks to set aside an award due to a public policy violation. The criminal law of the state(s) where the award is to be enforced will come into play if a party challenges the enforcement of an award due to a public policy violation (Art. V 2. (b) New York Convention)[15].

8.2 Does *Mens Rea* Have to Be Proven in Arbitration?

In criminal law, in order to establish that a criminal offence was committed, certain subjective requirements of the offence must be proven.

[14] See subsection 8.1.1.2. [15] New York Convention 1958.

Generally speaking, most criminal offences require *mens rea*. Definition and scope of *mens rea* vary in different domestic legal systems. In arbitral proceedings, does the party alleging criminal conduct have to prove *mens rea*? Case law, arbitration rules and academic writing do not provide an answer to this question.[16] According to the view advanced here, parties in arbitration do not have to prove *mens rea* if they allege criminal conduct, for the following reasons:

- In principle, the limits of *mens rea* determine the limits of sanctionable behaviour.[17] If the subjective requirements of a criminal offence are not fulfilled, there is generally no sanction imposed (with the exception of offences than can be committed by negligence). This means that *mens rea* is inextricably linked with the concept of criminal sanctions. Since arbitrators never impose criminal sanctions, it does not seem coherent to ask the parties to prove *mens rea*.
- Arbitration proceedings are not suited to decide about individual (or corporate) criminal liability. To put it simple, in criminal proceedings, prosecutors have certain powers to establish the subjective requirements of a criminal offence (e.g. through interrogation). These powers are balanced with procedural safeguards for the accused persons (e.g. the right to defence). All this does not apply in arbitral proceedings.
- It is already very difficult to establish the objective requirements of a criminal offence in arbitration. If the objective requirements are successfully proven, it appears legitimate to derive – from the knowledge of the facts of the party that engaged in the criminal conduct – the element of will.[18]

Therefore, if arbitral tribunals directly rely on domestic criminal law provisions, evidence for the objective requirements of the offence is sufficient to prove criminal conduct.

[16] In *David Minnotte and Robert Lewis* v. *Poland*, the Tribunal held that the Respondent merely alleged negligence by the Claimants, and that deliberate fraud of the Claimants in the initiation and performance of the investment was not proven (at paras. 134 et seq., 163 et seq.); cf. also Llamzon and Sinclair 2015, 469 et seq. (discussing that investment tribunals usually do not distinguish between fraudulent misrepresentation that requires the intent to deceive, or recklessness; and merely negligent misrepresentation) and Lamm, Hellbeck and Khan 2015, 559.

[17] For Swiss criminal law: Stratenwerth 2011, 182.

[18] In criminal law, such a conclusion may be drawn only in limited cases; for Swiss law, see Niggli and Maeder 2013, Art. 12 N 53 et seq.

8.3 The Role of Transnational Public Policy

8.3.1 The Content of Transnational Public Policy

There is widespread consensus today that the prohibition of foreign public bribery is part of transnational public policy.[19] However, is it the same with private bribery, fraud and money laundering?

8.3.1.1 Efforts to Combat Private Bribery

Treaties such as the Council of Europe Corruption Convention, the African Union Corruption Convention and the UNCAC all contain provisions against private bribery,[20] including monitoring mechanisms.[21] While the CoE and AU Conventions oblige state parties to adopt measures to prevent and combat private bribery, this is optional under the UNCAC. On the EU level, there is a 2003 Council Framework Decision[22] that requires Member States to criminalise active and passive private bribery.[23] Private bribery is also criminalised in many domestic legal systems.[24] The sanctions regimes of several multilateral development banks (MDBs) apply to any corrupt practices that aim at improperly influencing the actions of another party, and do not seem to be limited to public bribery.[25] At the OECD, efforts are made to raise awareness of domestic tax examiners and auditors for corrupt payments, covering both public and private bribery.[26]

[19] See discussion in Chapter 2; the case analysis in Part III also shows that regarding alleged foreign public bribery, tribunals frequently invoke transnational public policy.

[20] Arts. 7 and 8 CoE 1999a; Arts. 4(e), 4(f) and 11 AU 2003; and Art. 21 UNCAC 2003; see Nicholls et al. 2011, N 12.22 et seq., 14.23 et seq., 15.23 et seq.

[21] See the reports of the Group of States against Corruption (GRECO), based on Art. 24 CoE 1999a, and of the UNCAC Conference of States Parties, based on Art. 63 (4)(e) UNCAC 2003.

[22] EU 2003. [23] Nicholls et al. 2011, N 14.103 et seq.

[24] E.g. in the UK Bribery Act 2010 (cf. UK MoJ Guidance 2011, 10; Nicholls et al. 2011, N 4.06 and 4.51); in § 299 of the German Criminal Code; and in Arts. 322^{octies} and 322^{novies} of the Swiss Criminal Code. The Swiss anti-corruption law was revised in 2016 with the aim of strengthening the legal framework against private bribery (Botschaft Korruptionsstrafrecht 2014, BBl 2014 3591 et seq.; Pieth 2016b, 186 et seq.). For an overview of the private bribery laws of 13 countries, see Heine, Huber and Rose (eds.) 2003; see also Hwang and Lim 2012, 5 with further references.

[25] Cf. s. 4.2.(a) AfDB 2014; s. 2.16(iii) EBRD 2014; s. 2.2(a) IADB 2015; the World Bank Sanctions Procedures apparently only apply to the bribery of public officials, including World Bank staff and employees of other organisations charged with procurement decisions (s. 1.02(a) and Appendix 1 A. World Bank 2012, fn. 21; World Bank Sanctions Board Decision No. 76 of 6 March 2015, at para. 51).

[26] See OECD 2013, 7, 9.

However, until now, no arbitral awards seem to be published that involve alleged private bribery; and few academic commentators have specifically addressed the question whether the prohibition of private bribery is part of transnational public policy.[27] One difficulty with private bribery is that national laws – if addressing it at all – treat it very differently,[28] and lawmakers' awareness may be limited.[29] Still, in light of the legislative developments of the last fifteen years that indicate an emerging global consensus to prevent and combat private corruption, it is not devious to say that private bribery should be considered as a violation of transnational public policy.[30]

8.3.1.2 Efforts to Combat Fraud

It is safe to say that the prohibition of fraud is part of transnational public policy. The argument is supported by arbitral case law[31] as well as doctrine,[32] and by national and international legislation. The sanctions regimes of MDBs also condemn fraudulent practices.[33] The difficulty with fraud is that it occurs in many different forms and that there is no uniform understanding of what constitutes fraud. Probably most domestic criminal law systems worldwide contain fraud provisions, but the scope of those provisions is different.[34] The Swiss[35] and the German[36] core fraud provisions, for instance, differ in that fraud in Swiss criminal law requires malice (*Arglist*), which is not the case in German law.

On the international level, there are no treaties and monitoring systems in place with a specific focus on fraud (as they were developed for foreign

[27] Srinivasan et al. 2014, 138 et seq. (leaving the question open); Hwang and Lim include both public and private bribery in their definition of corruption when arguing that corruption violates international and perhaps even transnational public policy (Hwang and Lim 2012, 4 et seq., 101 et seq.).

[28] See Heine 2003, 608 et seq. [29] Hess 2009, 22 et seq.

[30] Cf. Zuberbühler and Schregenberger 2016, 3, who note that this issue is not yet entirely clear.

[31] E.g. in *Inceysa* v. *El Salvador*, the Tribunal argued that the fraudulent investment was contrary to international public policy (paras. 250 et seq.); in *David Minnotte and Robert Lewis* v. *Poland*, the Respondent argued that an investment tainted with fraud was contrary to international public order (para. 128).

[32] Lamm, Pham and Moloo 2010, 719; Cremades and Cairns argue that certainly fraud that conceals bribery and money laundering is against transnational public policy (Cremades and Cairns 2003a, 78 and 2010, 43).

[33] S. 4.2.(b) AfDB 2014; s. 2.16(iv) EBRD 2014; s. 2.2(b) IADB 2015; s. 1.02(a) and Appendix 1 A. World Bank 2012; cf. Nicholls et al. 2011, N 15.179 et seq.

[34] See the discussion of Swiss and English law with regard to fraud in Chapter 3.

[35] Art. 146 SCrimC. [36] § 263 German Criminal Code.

public bribery, private bribery and money laundering). Fraud often occurs along with those offences. Cremades and Cairns for example argue that fraudulent record-keeping will frequently be involved to conceal bribe payments, money laundering and other crime, pointing out that

> Accounting practices are a highly technical field more susceptible to national legislation then international regulation, so it is perhaps not surprising that fraud has not witnessed the same degree of international co-operation and rule-making as corruption and money laundering.[37]

The prohibition of fraud is, in some form, a component of many international instruments with a global or regional reach.[38] The OECD Convention contains an article on accounting that targets fraudulent company records, as those help to conceal bribery.[39] On the EU level, there is *inter alia* the 1995 Convention on the Protection of the EU's financial interests,[40] whose aim is to protect the Union's budget and hence the taxpayers from fraud and other financial misuse; and the 2012 Proposal for a Directive to fight fraud against the EU's financial interests by means of criminal law.[41] In terms of institutions, there is the European Anti-Fraud Office (*Office de Lutte Anti-Fraude*, OLAF).[42] In sum, those texts and initiatives reflect a broad global consensus that fraud affects vital interests of individuals and economies.

8.3.1.3 Efforts to Combat Money Laundering

With regard to money laundering, several criminalisation treaties with a global reach exist, in particular the 1988 Vienna Convention on drug trafficking[43] and the 2000 Palermo Convention on transnational organised crime.[44] The UNCAC requires states parties to prevent and

37 Cremades and Cairns 2003a, 76.

38 This can also happen implicitly: Lamm, Pham and Moloo 2010, 717.

39 Art. 8 OECD 1997; Cremades and Cairns 2003a, 76; Bruch and Adkins 2014, 447 et seq.

40 EU 1995; for a detailed discussion of the need for a European fraud legislation, see Vervaele 1992.

41 EU 2012; see Gless 2015, 164 et seq. The Proposal is based on Art. 325(4) of the Treaty on the Functioning of the European Union, which aims at an 'effective and equivalent protection' in the EU Member States; cf. Kaiafa-Gbandi 2012.

42 See Gless 2015, 165 et seq.

43 Art. 3(1)(b)(i) UN 1988 criminalises the 'conversion or transfer of property' that derives from drug offences; Art. 3(1)(b)(ii) criminalises the 'concealment or disguise' of property that derives from drug offences; see Commentary on the Vienna Convention 1988, 61 et seq.

44 Art. 6(2) UN 2000 establishes 'all serious crime' as possible predicate offences to money laundering, including participation in an organised criminal group (Art. 5) and corruption (Art. 8).

criminalise money laundering.[45] The UNCAC as well as the OECD Convention on Bribery consider foreign public bribery a predicate offence for money laundering.[46]

Regional instruments include the 1990 Strasbourg Convention on anti–money laundering[47] and the 2005 Warsaw Convention on anti–money laundering and terrorist financing.[48] On the EU level, efforts since the first anti–money laundering Directive of 1991[49] include the 1997 Second Protocol to the Convention on the Protection of the EU's financial interests;[50] and the fourth anti–money laundering and terrorist financing Directive of 2015.[51]

Many domestic legal systems criminalise money laundering.[52] The work of the Financial Action Task Force (FATF)[53] over the last twenty-five years must be mentioned here, as it is the cornerstone of a global framework against money laundering. The FATF's core document is the FATF Recommendations,[54] a soft law instrument. Through an implementation peer review mechanism, these Recommendations contribute to the harmonisation of domestic anti–money laundering laws worldwide.[55] Furthermore, multi-stakeholder groups such as the Wolfsberg Group developed their own anti–money laundering standards.[56] In sum, it is safe to say that the prohibition of money laundering is part of transnational public policy; this is also supported by academic writing[57] and arbitral case law.[58]

45 Arts. 14 and 23 UNCAC 2003.

46 Art. 23(2)(b) UNCAC 2003 and Art. 7 OECD 1997; see Pieth 2014b, 437.

47 CoE 1990. 48 CoE 2005. 49 See EU 1991. 50 EU 1997b. 51 EU 2015.

52 E.g. for Switzerland: Art. 305bis SCrimC; for the UK: part 7 of the UK Proceeds of Crime Act (POCA) 2002. For an overview of the anti–money laundering measures in forty-one countries, see Muller, Kälin and Goldsworth (eds.) 2007.

53 The FATF is an inter-governmental body established in 1989 with thirty-six members and eight FATF-Style Regional Bodies (see www.fatf-gafi.org). On the history of FATF, see Pieth 2014b, 430 et seq.

54 FATF Recommendations 2012. 55 See www.fatf-gafi.org/topics/mutualevaluations/.

56 Cf. the Wolfsberg Principles 2012; Pieth 2014b, 434 with further references.

57 Cremades and Cairns 2003a, 68 (for a summary of the international response to money laundering, see 70 et seq.); González García 2013, 527; McDougall 2005, 1046 (who points out that the international consensus does not extend to all predicate offences); Nueber 2015, 12 et seq.; Schlabrendorff 2005, 860.

58 See the *X* v. *Y ad hoc* arbitration. In 2017, the Paris Appeals Court set aside an award in an investment arbitration conducted under the UNCITRAL Rules, arguing that the Latvian investor's acquisition and operation of a Kyrgyz bank aimed at concealing money laundering practices, and that money laundering was contrary to international public policy (decision 15/01650 of 21 February 2017 in the matter *Valeri Belokon* v. *Kyrgyz Republic*).

8.3.2 *Fields of Application*

According to the view advanced here, the better approach in ICSID as well as in ICC arbitration than relying (solely) on transnational public policy is to apply specific provisions of domestic or international criminal law if criminal conduct is at stake.[59] However, if the applicable law does not contain provisions on a certain criminal behaviour (e.g. if it does not regulate foreign public bribery or money laundering), transnational public policy still sets an absolute limit and serves as a fall-back position.[60]

8.4 Interim Conclusion

On applicable criminal law, the case analysis shows that regarding foreign public bribery, fraud and money laundering, tribunals increasingly rely directly on provisions of domestic criminal law (or of international anti-corruption treaties). They apply provisions of the law chosen by the parties, but also of the place of performance of the contract and as determined by criminal law principles. International treaties criminalising foreign public bribery, private bribery, fraud and money laundering are part of public international law and may be directly applicable if parties (or the tribunal) choose international law to apply. According to the view advanced here, if tribunals directly rely on criminal law provisions, *mens rea* does not have to be proven. Evidence for the objective requirements of the offence is sufficient.

Foreign public bribery, private bribery, fraud and money laundering are against transnational public policy. Transnational public policy serves as a fall-back position if the applicable criminal law provisions, as identified by the tribunal, do not cover foreign public bribery, private bribery, fraud, and money laundering. Transnational public policy reflects fundamental principles of public international law, but it does not form part of public international law.[61]

[59] Cf. Newcombe 2011, 200; Martin 2003, 9, 11.

[60] Cf. Llamzon and Sinclair 2015, 522 et seq.

[61] See discussion in Chapter 2.

9

Issues of Evidence

In investment as well as in commercial arbitration, no domestic rules of civil or criminal procedure and evidence apply unless chosen by the parties. However, the case analysis raises some fundamental issues regarding evidence if crime is alleged in international arbitration that should be addressed by all tribunals dealing with such a case.

9.1 Can the Burden of Proof Shift in Cases of Alleged Crime?

In principle, the applicable law as chosen by the parties (or the tribunal) determines the burden of proof in international arbitration.[1] In a number of the ICSID[2] and ICC[3] awards discussed earlier in the book, the question came up whether and how a tribunal can modify the burden of proof in cases of alleged criminal behaviour. In international arbitration literature, the majority of commentators argue that shifting the burden of proof to the defendant (who then must disprove any involvement in alleged criminal behaviour) is contrary to the right to a fair trial.[4]

From the case analysis, it appears that tribunals in principle do not shift the legal burden of proof if criminal conduct is alleged.[5] The legal burden of proving criminal conduct remains with the alleging party

[1] See discussion in Chapter 4; in ICC Case No. 6497, the Tribunal referred to the Swiss Civil Code to determine the burden of proof; in the *X* v. *Y ad hoc* arbitration, the Tribunal referred to English law. In *Metal-Tech* v. *Uzbekistan*, the Tribunal invoked international law and the BIT; in *Fraport* v. *Philippines II* and *Siag* v. *Egypt*, the Tribunals referred to well-established rule.

[2] See *Spentex* v. *Uzbekistan*; *Metal-Tech* v. *Uzbekistan*; *Fraport* v. *Philippines II*; *Siag* v. *Egypt*.

[3] See ICC Cases No. 6497; 12990; as well as the *X* v. *Y ad hoc* arbitration.

[4] Cremades and Cairns 2003a, 83; Hwang and Lim 2012, 28 et seq.; Mourre 2009, 219; Partasides 2010, 53. Different: Mills, who argues that if there is a reasonable indication of corruption, the burden may be shifted to the allegedly corrupt party to prove that the legal and good faith requirements were met (Mills 2002, 130; see also Patocchi and Niedermaier 2013, 1165 et seq. in the context of Art. 27(1) UNCITRAL Rules).

[5] The debate about burden-shifting is unresolved yet, however (Lamm, Greenwald and Young 2014, 334 et seq., 337).

throughout the proceedings (*onus probandi incumbit actori*).[6] What tribunals do, however, is shift the risk of non-production of evidence to the alleged party if the alleging party is able to present *prima facie* evidence for criminal conduct.[7] If the alleged party is unable to produce sufficient rebuttal evidence, the risk materialises and the alleging party prevails.[8] This approach is similar to the one found in English civil procedure, where the evidential burden, that is not a burden of proof, may shift.[9] It is also not completely unlike the approach of Swiss civil procedure, where parties carry a burden to explicitly contest alleged facts, and to substantiate the contestation (which may not result in a reversal of the burden of proof though).[10] In effect, even if technically the legal burden of proof does not shift in arbitral proceedings, the burden of the alleged party to produce rebuttal evidence if there is *prima facie* evidence for criminal conduct will feel as if the burden of proof indeed has shifted.[11]

With regard to alleged bribery, a practice has emerged in recent ICSID and ICC cases that if certain 'red flags' or indicia for bribe payments are present, the tribunal will ask the alleged party to produce rebuttal evidence (in particular, to produce documents substantiating the performed services).[12] This approach appears justified because the alleged party, if contracted for real services for which it is qualified, should typically have no difficulty presenting rebuttal evidence.[13]

9.2 Adverse Inferences from the Non-Production of Evidence

Adverse inferences are somewhat the logical consequence of the above-discussed shifting of the risk of non-production of evidence. An adverse

6 Cf. *Siag* v. *Egypt*, para. 317 with reference to De Boisséson 2009. In *Rompetrol* v. *Romania* (at para. 178), the Tribunal argues that the burden of proof is absolute and does not shift from one party to the other (and perhaps back again to the original party); see also Sharpe 2006, 552.

7 *Fraport* v. *Philippines II*, para. 299 with further references; O'Malley 2012, 212 et seq. Different: Greenberg and Lautenschlager, who argue that in some instances, the burden of proof indeed shifts to the party that refuses to produce the requested documents (Greenberg and Lautenschlager 2011, 182).

8 O'Malley 2012, 213 et seq.; Sharpe 2006, 552 et seq.; Van Houtte 2009, 196 et seq.

9 See discussion in Chapter 4. 10 See discussion in Chapter 4.

11 Cf. Rose 2014, 217 et seq., who discusses these issues under 'shifting the burden of proof'.

12 The clearest examples are *Metal-Tech* v. *Uzbekistan* and ICC Case No. 12290. See also ICC Cases No. 13515 and 13914; Llamzon 2014, 230; Llamzon and Sinclair 2015, 487 et seq.; Khvalei 2014, 24.

13 Cf. Lamm, Pham and Moloo 2010, 701; see also Cheng 1987, 330.

inference is not a sanction,[14] but a type of indirect evidence[15] and can be defined as 'the inference that the evidence that is not produced by a party, despite being in its possession, is adverse to the interests of that party'.[16] Arts. 9(5) and (6) of the IBA Rules of Evidence[17] explicitly recognise the possibility of arbitrators to draw adverse inferences from the non-production of requested documents or other evidence (including witness statements) in the absence of arbitrators' power to compel the production of evidence.[18] While under many domestic arbitration laws, arbitral tribunals can seek the assistance of state courts to take evidence,[19] this may be cumbersome or ineffective because the evidence is located in a different jurisdiction from the seat of the arbitral tribunal.[20] Under Rule 34(3) of the ICSID Arbitration Rules, the parties are obliged to co-operate with the tribunal with regard to evidence production. Uncooperativeness by a party may cause the tribunal to draw an adverse inference – it may, for instance, assume that a withheld document is damaging to the interests of that party.[21] The English Arbitration Act equally foresees that if a party does not comply with a peremptory order, the tribunal may draw an adverse inference from the act of non-compliance.[22] In short, adverse inferences are widely recognised as an effective means in an arbitrator's toolbox to balance the lack of coercive powers.[23]

Nevertheless, an analysis of ICC awards showed a certain reluctance by tribunals to draw adverse inferences, for due process concerns.[24] Indeed, the issue of adverse inferences should not be treated lightly by tribunals. They should only be applied if certain conditions are fulfilled. From an analysis of the case law of the Iran-US Claims Tribunal, Sharpe distilled the following requirements:

[14] To the same end: Greenberg and Lautenschlager 2011, 187 et seq.; possibly different: Van Houtte 2009, 199 et seq.

[15] Greenberg and Lautenschlager 2011, 188, 204; Van Houtte 2009, 195.

[16] Van Houtte 2009, 195. [17] IBA 2010.

[18] Ashford 2013, 166; Greenberg and Lautenschlager 2011, 188 et seq.; Sharpe 2006, 549; Zuberbühler et al. 2012, Art. 9 N 54 et seq.

[19] See, e.g., Art. 184(2) SPILA; Art. 44(2) English Arbitration Act 1996; Poudret and Besson 2007, N 669 et seq.

[20] See, e.g., Shore 2009, who discusses the situation in US and English law.

[21] Happ 2013, 966. [22] Art. 41(7)(b) English Arbitration Act 1996.

[23] Sharpe 2006, 550 et seq.; see also Sandifer 1939, 101.

[24] Greenberg and Lautenschlager 2011, 190, 202 et seq.; and see ICC Case No. 16090.

(1) the party seeking the adverse inference must produce all available evidence corroborating the inference sought;
(2) the requested evidence must be accessible to the inference opponent;
(3) the inference sought must be reasonable, consistent with facts in the record and logically related to the likely nature of the evidence withheld;
(4) the party seeking the adverse inference must produce *prima facie* evidence and
(5) the inference opponent must know, or have reason to know, of its obligation to produce evidence rebutting the adverse inference sought.[25]

In order to guarantee the parties' right to a fair trial, notably the last point is crucial: a tribunal should inform the party requested to produce evidence of the consequences of non-production, including of the possibility of adverse inferences.[26] However, a party cannot defend itself solely by arguing that it was not specifically alerted to the consequences of non-production of requested documents.[27]

The preceding case analysis shows that in particular in ICC Cases No. 12990 and 13515, the Tribunals considered the fact that the Claimant did not produce the requested documents to substantiate the services it performed in return for the commission payments as indicia for bribery. In both cases, the tribunals concluded that bribery was involved on the basis of solid and convergent indicia. Apparently, the Tribunals drew an adverse inference from the non-production of the requested documents, and combined this with other indicia.[28] In ICSID practice, the Tribunal in *Metal-Tech* v. *Uzbekistan* invoked Rule 34(3) of the ICSID Arbitration Rules and asked the Claimant to substantiate the reality and legitimacy of the services it performed for the payments, requesting the production of this evidence by issuing several Procedural Orders.[29] The Tribunal

[25] Sharpe 2006, 551 and 554 et seq.; see also Greenberg and Lautenschlager 2011, 197 et seq.; Zuberbühler et al. 2012, Art. 9 N 58 et seq.

[26] Sharpe 2006, 568 et seq.; Greenberg and Lautenschlager 2011, 201 et seq.

[27] Sharpe 2006, 570 with references to case law.

[28] From the published excerpts of the Awards, it is difficult to conclude whether the Tribunals drew a 'proper' or an 'improper' adverse inference. A 'proper' adverse inference fills a genuine gap in the evidence; an 'improper' adverse inference only influences the weight that is attached to already existing evidence (Greenberg and Lautenschlager 2011, 184 et seq.).

[29] *Metal-Tech* v. *Uzbekistan*, paras. 244 et seq.; see also Llamzon and Sinclair 2015, 489 et seq.

put the Claimant on notice that the production of the evidence would assist it in reaching a conclusion about the Respondent's corruption defence.[30] From the dearth of evidence for the Claimant's performed services, the Tribunal eventually inferred that no (legitimate) services were performed at the time of the Claimant's investment.[31] After an analysis of all the evidence, the Tribunal concluded that corruption was established in this case.[32]

In sum, adverse inferences appear as a legitimate and feasible type of indirect evidence for future cases of alleged bribery. But tribunals are well advised to use them diligently and to adhere to the requirements as identified by Sharpe, in order to avoid a challenge of the award for a violation of due process.[33] In principle, a tribunal should issue a procedural order specifying the requested evidence and warning against possible adverse inferences – there are, however, case examples where tribunals drew adverse inferences in the absence of a document production order.[34]

It needs to be emphasised that even if arbitral tribunals deal with alleged criminal behaviour, the proceedings remain of a civil nature: there is no state prosecutor involved, no penal sanctions are imposed, and the aim is not the proof of guilt of an accused person. Rather, the tribunals decide about the parties' contractual claims and defences. Therefore, principles regarding the burden of proof and the weighing of evidence that apply in criminal procedure in order to counterbalance the power of the state – in particular the presumption of innocence of the accused and *in dubio pro reo* – do not apply in arbitral proceedings:[35] those would prohibit the shifting of the risk of non-production of evidence as well as limit the possibility to draw adverse inferences from such non-production.[36]

In this context, Greenberg and Lautenschlager refer to an ICC arbitration with an interesting outcome: one party successfully requested the

[30] *Metal-Tech* v. *Uzbekistan*, para. 253.
[31] *Metal-Tech* v. *Uzbekistan*, para. 265.
[32] *Metal-Tech* v. *Uzbekistan*, para. 372.
[33] Polkinghorne and Rosenberg 2015, 746.
[34] Sharpe 2006, 570 (fn. 125); see also Rose 2014, 214.
[35] Cf. the argument of the Swiss Federal Supreme Court – regarding an application to set aside an arbitral award – that in the area of civil law, the law of evidence cannot be determined after criminal law concepts such as the presumption of innocence (*Unschuldsvermutung*) or the guarantees which derive from the European Convention on Human Rights (BGer 4A_178/2014, at 5.2.); cf. also BGer 4A_488/2011, at 6.2.
[36] Cf. in Chapter 4 the discussion of English and Swiss criminal procedure and the discussion of the privilege against self-incrimination later in this chapter.

arbitral tribunal to draw an adverse inference against the opponent that had called a witness who relied on the privilege against self-incrimination and refused to answer a question related to ongoing criminal investigations. The tribunal argued that the privilege against self-incrimination under the given circumstances was not applicable in ICC arbitration[37] – this argument calls for a closer look.

9.3 The Privilege against Self-Incrimination

While there are other relevant privileges (e.g. the attorney-client privilege) in international arbitration, the focus here is on the privilege against self-incrimination. The case analysis in Part III has shown that in the *X* v. *Y ad hoc* arbitration, several witnesses relied on the privilege against self-incrimination, referring to the former Zurich Civil Procedure Code. In contrast to the ICC arbitration mentioned earlier, the Zurich *ad hoc* Tribunal acknowledged this to be a universal right. The question is, how tribunals should handle situations in which a witness refuses to give evidence – or a party refuses to produce documents – on the basis of the privilege against self-incrimination. Generally, if a witness refuses to testify in arbitration proceedings, the tribunal has no coercive powers to summon the witness.[38] However, if the *lex arbitri* so allows,[39] the tribunal can seek the assistance of the state court judge at the seat of the arbitration, and the latter may summon the witness (or follow the channels of legal assistance if the witness is located abroad). Instead of using this option, tribunals frequently take into account the non-appearance of witnesses when assessing the evidence.[40] Is this latter course of action appropriate if a witness – or a party – refuses to give evidence in arbitration proceedings referring to the privilege against self-incrimination?

9.3.1 With Regard to Witnesses

According to the view advanced here, the privilege against self-incrimination of witnesses should be respected in arbitral proceedings that involve allegations of criminal conduct. The discussion of Swiss and

[37] Greenberg and Lautenschlager 2011, 192 et seq.
[38] Zuberbühler et al. 2012, Art. 4 N 81.
[39] See, e.g., Art. 184(2) SPILA; Art. 44(2) English Arbitration Act 1996.
[40] Zuberbühler et al. 2012, Art. 4 N 83 et seq.; see also Art. 4(9) IBA 2010.

English civil and criminal procedure shows that the privilege has grown historically and is well recognised today in domestic court proceedings.[41] Due to its wide recognition domestically and internationally, the privilege against self-incrimination of witnesses can nowadays be regarded as part of transnational procedural public policy.[42] It also must be kept in mind that even if (commercial) arbitration proceedings may be purely private, in some jurisdictions, a false witness statement in arbitral (or court) proceedings is a criminal offence.[43] It puts witnesses in a tight spot if they are, by threat of criminal sanctions, obliged to speak the truth and thereby to incriminate themselves. Even if arbitration proceedings are confidential and arbitrators are in principle not obliged to report suspected crime to the authorities,[44] a witness probably feels that his statement might get him into difficulty – in particular if parallel criminal proceedings are taking place.[45]

Does the privilege against self-incrimination encompass the right to silence, or in other words: may arbitral tribunals draw adverse inferences from the refusal of a witness to testify? The exact scope of the privilege against self-incrimination of witnesses varies in different legal systems. In Swiss civil procedure, courts may not draw adverse inferences from the rightful refusal of a witness to testify (Art. 162 SCPC). In criminal procedure, the question is yet unanswered by the Swiss Federal Supreme Court. Witnesses are third persons not directly involved in the dispute at stake. If their testimony would expose themselves or a person close to them to criminal or civil liability, they should have a right to silence in arbitration proceedings. This right would be undermined if adverse inferences from their silence were allowed – at least, arbitral

41 See discussion in Chapter 4.

42 Mosk and Ginsburg 2001, 358 et seq., 380 et seq.; a discussion of the relationship between human rights law (e.g. Art. 6 ECHR) and arbitration is beyond the scope of this text, but see Besson 2006; Hodges 2007; Petrochilos 2004, 109 et seq.

43 E.g. for Switzerland: Art. 307 in combination with Art. 309 SCrimC; Poudret and Besson 2007, N 661; cf. also the *Westacre* v. *Jugoimport* case where the Defendants at the enforcement stage alleged that a number of witnesses who gave evidence during the arbitration proceedings had perjured themselves.

44 See discussion in Section 9.8.

45 An interesting case in this regard is *Getma* v. *Guinea*, where two of the Respondent's witnesses readily testified that they had taken bribes for favouring Getma. The Tribunal found it difficult to understand why the witnesses incriminated themselves without hesitation. It also noted that Guinea did not pursue any domestic criminal proceedings for passive corruption. The Tribunal eventually rejected the corruption allegations by the Respondent (*Getma* v. *Guinea*, paras. 185 et seq., 218).

tribunals should not base a decision solely or mainly on the silence of a witness.

If the *lex arbitri* does not contain mandatory rules in this regard, the privilege against self-incrimination of witnesses and its content can be derived from the applicable procedural law. As will be discussed in detail in Section 9.6, like the domestic provisions on the admissibility of evidence, the provisions on the privilege against self-incrimination should be treated as (foreign) mandatory rules that possibly override the parties' or the tribunal's choice of procedure. In ICSID and ICC arbitration, mandatory provisions of the procedure as chosen by the parties should in principle apply. In ICC arbitration, mandatory provisions of the civil procedure at the seat of the arbitration might also be invoked (due to the risk of a later setting aside of the award). The bottom line in any case is transnational procedural public policy: witnesses may not be forced to expose themselves to criminal investigation or prosecution. In order to ensure that the privilege against self-incrimination is not abused in arbitration, witnesses should be asked to make their risk credible – without taking the step to self-incrimination.[46]

9.3.2 *With Regard to Parties*

Concerning parties, things are slightly different. The position of parties differs from the one of witnesses as they are directly involved in the dispute. Again, it must be considered that in some jurisdictions, a false statement by a party in arbitral (or court) proceedings is a criminal offence.[47] The discussion of Swiss domestic civil procedure shows that parties are, on the one hand, not sanctioned if they refuse to co-operate; on the other hand, they have no right to refuse to co-operate if they expose *themselves* to the risk of a criminal investigation (Art. 163(1)(a) in connection with Art. 165 SCPC). If parties refuse to co-operate without right, the court may take this into account when assessing the evidence (Art. 164 SCPC). In short: parties will rather refuse to co-operate and risk an adverse inference by the court than put themselves into trouble by giving a false or self-incriminating statement.

In arbitral proceedings, a similar approach appears sensible. Giving, for instance, the defendant a strong right to refuse to testify would

[46] Cf. Swiss criminal procedure: Pieth 2016a, 204.

[47] E.g. for Switzerland: Art. 306 in combination with Art. 309 SCrimC.

unduly disadvantage the claimant, as often the required evidence will be within the sphere of influence of the defendant, so that it can solely be adduced by the latter. Therefore, drawing adverse inferences from the defendant's silence and lack of co-operation – including from his refusal to produce documents – is justified in arbitral proceedings. As a word of caution, it must be added that by itself, the silence of a party cannot prove anything. In the context of a free overall evaluation of the evidence (*freie Gesamtwürdigung der Beweise*), however, arbitrators should have the possibility to draw adverse inferences from a party's silence. As different from state organs, arbitral tribunals are in principle not obliged to report suspected crime to the authorities.[48] If a party that really has engaged in criminal conduct neither has to reply to tough questions nor fear any reporting to the authorities, it is let off the hook too easily.

It is possible for a party in international arbitral proceedings to become an accused person in parallel or future domestic criminal proceedings. If this is the case, the evidence from the arbitration, including any adverse inferences (as a type of indirect evidence) drawn by the arbitrators, is in principle not admissible in the criminal proceedings. This evidence must be taken anew, respecting the defence rights of the accused person.[49]

9.4 Evidence Issues in Case of Parallel Domestic Criminal Proceedings

There are several possible scenarios how domestic criminal and international arbitral proceedings may interrelate.[50] They can be distinguished temporally and locally:

- domestic criminal and international arbitral proceedings overlap, i.e. they at least partly take place at the same time;[51]

[48] See discussion in Section 9.8.

[49] For Swiss criminal procedure: Gless 2014, Art. 139 N 47 with reference to Art. 362(4) SCrimPC (statements by the parties for the purpose of accelerated proceedings may not be used in any subsequent ordinary criminal proceedings).

[50] See also Tirado, Page and Meagher 2014, 500 et seq.; on the interaction between FCPA enforcement actions and ICSID arbitration proceedings: Losco 2014; see also Bhojwani 2012.

[51] This was apparently the case in *Siemens* v. *Argentina*; *TSA Spectrum* v. *Argentina*; *EDF* v. *Romania*; *RSM* v. *Grenada*; *Niko* v. *Bangladesh*; *Fraport* v. *Philippines*; and in the *X* v. *Y ad hoc* arbitration.

- international arbitral proceedings are concluded before the initiation of domestic criminal proceedings;
- domestic criminal proceedings are concluded before the initiation of international arbitral proceedings;
- in commercial arbitration, domestic criminal proceedings take place in the state where the tribunal has its seat; of which the parties are nationals or are incorporated; or in a third state;
- in investment arbitration, domestic criminal proceedings take place in the host state, in the investor's home state, or in a third state.

Another option is that no domestic criminal proceedings take place, even though criminal law issues are discussed and decided in international arbitral proceedings.[52] With regard to evidence, the impact of parallel criminal investigations on arbitration proceedings must be kept in mind, particularly regarding witnesses.[53] Arbitrators should be aware of potential pressure that is exerted on witnesses by the investigations[54] and respect the privilege against self-incrimination.

Whether an arbitral tribunal or the parties can gain access to the files of the criminal investigation depends on the applicable domestic criminal procedure.[55] A different question is, whether state authorities can gain

[52] This was apparently the case in *World Duty Free* v. *Kenya*; *African Holding* v. *Democratic Republic of Congo*; *Sistem* v. *Kyrgyz Republic*; *Metal-Tech* v. *Uzbekistan*; *Spentex* v. *Uzbekistan*; *Inceysa* v. *El Salvador*; *Siag* v. *Egypt*; *Hamester* v. *Ghana*; and – interestingly – in all of the discussed ICC Cases (ICC Case No. 13384 merely states that no criminal complaint was ever filed with regard to the corruption allegations; and ICC Case No. 14470 discusses a criminal conviction unrelated to the disputed contract).

[53] Interesting issues arise if host states abuse their sovereign powers to institute criminal proceedings against foreign investors: in *Quiborax* v. *Bolivia*, the Tribunal asked the Respondent, as a provisional measure, to suspend criminal proceedings – that were launched because the Claimant had initiated ICSID arbitration – as they threatened the integrity of the ICSID proceedings, in particular by putting pressure on potential witnesses (paras. 121, 142 et seq., 163 et seq.); in detail: Mirzayev 2012; Mouawad and Silbert 2013, 411 et seq.; see also *Rompetrol* v. *Romania* (para. 279).

[54] Cf. the *RSM* v. *Grenada* case.

[55] E.g. in Switzerland, third persons can inspect case documents of pending criminal proceedings if they have an academic or other legitimate interest, and if this is not contrary to overriding public or private interests (Art. 101(3) SCrimPC); it would depend on the specific circumstances of the case whether arbitrators or parties could gain access to the files of criminal proceedings based on this provision. In *TSA Spectrum* v. *Argentina*, the Tribunal made reference to the evidence of the parallel criminal proceedings (at para. 165); see also Rose 2014, 220 et seq.

access to the files of an investment or commercial arbitration.[56] In principle, party or witness statements from the arbitral proceedings should not be admissible in domestic criminal proceedings; this evidence must be taken anew, respecting the defence rights of the accused person(s). Depending on the circumstances of the case, arbitrators might also consider staying the proceedings in order to await the outcome of the criminal investigation (and avoid the risk of revision of the award).[57] However, this might not be practical, as the criminal proceedings can take a long time. Arbitrators are not bound by the decisions of domestic criminal courts; in particular, arbitrators do not address guilt in the same way as a criminal judge does.[58]

9.5 Which Standard of Proof Applies?

The standard of proof in investment and commercial arbitration in cases of alleged criminal conduct is extensively discussed in academic writing.[59] Nevertheless, in the preceding case analysis, in only one instance the standard of proof might at least have co-determined the outcome: in *Siag* v. *Egypt*, the Tribunal argued that Egypt's evidence did not meet the required standard of 'clear and convincing evidence' and concluded that no fraud was involved.[60] All other cases that discussed the standard of proof in more or less detail (from what is published) probably did not turn on that standard:[61]

[56] In *Fraport* v. *Philippines*, the Respondent argued that it was unable to achieve corruption convictions in particular due to confidentiality agreements from the first ICSID and the ICC proceedings, which hindered the Respondent to use the available evidence (*Fraport* v. *Philippines II*, para. 275). Cf. however, the *Azpetrol* v. *Azerbaijan* case, where the Tribunal referred an incriminating witness statement regarding bribe payments to the national prosecuting authorities (Llamzon 2014, 126).

[57] Cf. the *Siemens* v. *Argentina* case, where decisive evidence came to light after the Award was issued; see also Besson 2015, 103 et seq.

[58] In Swiss civil law, Art. 53 SCO holds that a civil judge is not bound by the earlier decision of a criminal judge with regard to the question of guilt and concerning assessment of damages (see Kessler 2015, Art. 53 N 1 et seq.); see also Kendra and Bonini 2014, 450 and cf. Kreindler 2013b, 113 et seq.

[59] See, e.g., Court de Fontmichel 2004, 330 et seq.; De Boisséson 2009, 72 et seq.; Eveleigh 1994; Haugeneder and Liebscher 2009, 545 et seq.; Mehren 1996, 127 et seq.; Partasides 2010, 56 et seq.; Reiner 1994, 335 et seq.; Rosell and Prager 1999; Waincymer 2012, 766 et seq.

[60] Cf. Llamzon and Sinclair 2015, 493 et seq.

[61] Cf. Rose 2014, 197.

- *African Holding* v. *Democratic Republic of Congo* ('irrefutable proof');
- *EDF* v. *Romania* ('clear and convincing evidence');
- *Metal-Tech* v. *Uzbekistan* ('reasonable certainty');[62]
- *Fraport* v. *Philippines II* ('clear and convincing evidence');
- ICC Case No. 4145 ('very high probability');
- *Hilmarton* v. *OTV* (ICC Case No. 5622, 'proof beyond doubt');
- ICC Case No. 6320 ('clear and conclusive evidence');
- *Westinghouse* v. *National Power Corporation* (ICC Case No. 6401, 'clear and convincing evidence' and possibly an even higher standard for the existence of the bribery pact, whereas the US federal judge would have applied a lower standard altogether);
- ICC Case No. 12732 ('balance of probability');
- ICC Case No. 13384 ('high standard of proof');
- ICC Case No. 13914 ('clear and convincing evidence');
- ICC Case No. 16090 ('high standard of proof') and
- the *X* v. *Y ad hoc* arbitration ('balance of probabilities', but evidence has to be cogent and strong).

Still, it is important for arbitrators to have some guidance for the applicable standard of proof in cases of alleged criminal behaviour. In ICSID as well as in ICC arbitration, the applicable law in principle determines the standard of proof.[63] However, it shows that ICSID tribunals usually do not refer to the applicable law in this regard.[64] One exception is *Metal-Tech* v. *Uzbekistan*, where the Tribunal decided to apply international law to the question of the burden of proof (which, in the Tribunal's terminology, probably included the standard of proof).[65] ICC tribunals take a different approach: they frequently rely on the standard of proof as determined by the applicable law.[66] The preceding analysis of English and Swiss domestic law demonstrates that common and continental law treat the standard of proof quite differently.

62 See Llamzon 2014, 120.

63 See discussion in Chapter 4; Smith and Nadeau-Séguin 2015, 151 et seq.

64 See *African Holding* v. *Democratic Republic of Congo*; *EDF* v. *Romania*; and *Fraport* v. *Philippines II*.

65 *Metal-Tech* v. *Uzbekistan*, at para. 237 et seq.

66 See in particular *Hilmarton* v. *OTV* (ICC Case No. 5622); *Westinghouse* v. *National Power Corporation* (ICC Case No. 6401); ICC Case No. 12732; and the *X* v. *Y ad hoc* arbitration.

Therefore, it is difficult to argue for one single applicable standard of proof in international arbitration if criminal conduct is alleged.[67] The standard of proof is a more complex issue than the burden of proof, where the approaches in common and continental laws are less divergent. Regarding ICSID arbitration, at the current stage, it is also difficult to argue that tribunals should adopt the approach of earlier ICSID awards, as it appears that tribunals did not get to the bottom of the discussion of standard of proof in cases of alleged crime yet. Until now, there is no consensus which standard of proof should apply in such cases.[68]

Current practice shows that in cases involving allegations of foreign public bribery, arbitral tribunals tend to apply a higher standard of proof.[69] In a number of cases involving other types of alleged illegal conduct, however, tribunals did not raise the standard of proof, and found to have wide discretion to determine the applicable standard.[70] In fact, there are good arguments to apply the 'normal' standard for civil cases:

[67] Similar: Llamzon 2014, 236; cf. also the Dissenting Opinion of Professor Francisco Orrego Vicuña in *Siag* v. *Egypt*.

[68] Lamm, Greenwald and Young 2014, 331 et seq., 334; Pieth 2011, 1382; see also Scherer 2002, 30. In *Getma* v. *Guinea*, after a thorough analysis of a wide range of earlier ICSID awards, the Tribunal rejected the Claimant's argument that the standard of proof had to be higher for alleged corruption than for any other facts. The Tribunal decided to apply a 'clear and convincing' standard that would allow it to conclude with reasonable certainty whether corruption was involved in that case (*Getma* v. *Guinea*, paras. 181 et seq., 184).

[69] See also Llamzon 2014, 201 et seq.

[70] See, e.g., *Spentex* v. *Uzbekistan*, para. 860 (where the Tribunal found it not helpful to apply either a 'preponderance of probabilities' or 'clear and convincing proof' standard, but argued that 'the graver the charge, the more confidence there must be in the evidence relied on'); *Tokios Tokelės* v. *Ukraine*, para. 124 (where the Claimant was asked to prove the existence of a so-called 'nayizd' – a concerted unlawful campaign by state bodies against the Claimant's investment – by a 'more likely than not' standard); *Rompetrol* v. *Romania*, para. 183 (where the Tribunal applied the standard of 'balance of probabilities' to the generality of the issues at stake, and where necessary, a more nuanced approach concerning the allegations of seriously wrongful conduct by Romanian authorities with regard to an anti-corruption investigation); *Libananco* v. *Turkey*, para. 125 et seq. (where the Tribunal stated, in the abstract, that fraud allegations do not, without more, require a heightened standard of proof); ICC Case No. 12732 (where the Tribunal applied the standard of 'balance of probability' – it is not entirely clear which offence was at stake); and the *X* v. *Y ad hoc* arbitration (where the Tribunal applied 'balance of probabilities', requiring strong and cogent evidence with regard to the money laundering allegations). See also Llamzon and Sinclair 2015, 494 et seq.

Table 9.1 *Points for and against a higher standard of proof*

• Allegations of criminal conduct in civil proceedings are a serious issue with far-reaching consequences, if proven.[71] • Some domestic legal systems apply a higher standard of proof for alleged crime in civil proceedings.[72] • An abuse of the defence of bribery etc. in arbitration cannot be tolerated; therefore, unsubstantiated allegations of criminal conduct must be recognised by arbitrators when assessing the evidence.	• Current practice with regard to the burden of proof in arbitration shows that the principles of civil proceedings apply even if criminal conduct is alleged. It is not coherent to ask for a higher (approaching the criminal) standard of proof if the burden of proof is determined by civil law principles. Arbitrators do not have any of the powers of state prosecutors to collect evidence by use of compulsory measures (such as searching premises). • The higher standard of proof in criminal proceedings is balanced by the prosecutors' powers and correlates with the presumption of innocence and the principle of *in dubio pro reo*. As arbitral proceedings never aim at establishing the guilt of an accused person, it is not against due process to use the civil standard of proof even if criminal conduct is at issue.[73] • The discussion of English law demonstrates that domestic courts there use the standard of 'balance of probabilities' in cases of alleged criminal behaviour in civil proceedings, and do not apply a higher standard of proof; rather, they ask for strong evidence.

[71] Llamzon and Sinclair 2015, 496 with references to case law.

[72] E.g. in US law, there is an intermediate standard of proof between the civil standard of 'preponderance of the evidence' and the criminal standard of 'beyond reasonable doubt'. In civil cases involving allegations of e.g. fraud, the intermediate standard applies that combines the words 'clear', 'cogent', 'unequivocal', and 'convincing' in some form (*Addington* v. *Texas*, 441 US 418, 423 et seq. (1979); Engel 2009, 435).

[73] Cf. *Fraport* v. *Philippines I*, para. 399; Hwang and Lim 2012, 19.

- Bribery, fraud and money laundering are typically concealed by the perpetrators and difficult to prove in any case. In light of this fact, raising the standard of proof is not appropriate.[74]
- In domestic court proceedings, it is possible that the outcome of parallel civil and criminal proceedings, which are based on the same facts, is different (e.g. that the accused person is not criminally convicted, but held civilly liable) because the standard of proof is not the same.

It is important not to be naive: the bribery (etc.) defence may be abused in investment (ICSID) arbitration, as it can be a powerful defence for the host state.[75] In commercial arbitration, there is the possibility of a deliberate disruption of the proceedings by a criminal complaint.[76] Such abusive conduct certainly must be identified by arbitrators. Nevertheless, according to the view advanced here, tribunals should not apply a higher (or lower) standard of proof to allegations of criminal conduct. Rather, they should use the normal civil standard of 'balance of probabilities' or 'preponderance of the evidence' and demand persuasive (circumstantial) evidence for the criminal allegations.[77]

[74] *Spentex* v. *Uzbekistan*, para. 856; Partasides 2010, 55 et seq.

[75] Cf. *African Holding* v. *Democratic Republic of Congo*.

[76] Cf. Mourre 2009, 234.

[77] *Rompetrol* v. *Romania*, paras. 181 et seq. with reference to *Libananco* v. *Turkey*, para. 125. To the same end: Coşar 2015, 538; Crivellaro 2014, 228, 242 et seq.; Lamm, Hellbeck and Khan 2015, 562 et seq.; Llamzon and Sinclair 2015, 496 et seq.; Llamzon 2014, 234 et seq.; Partasides 2010, 56 et seq.; Raeschke-Kessler 2004, 497 et seq.; Rose 2014, 216 et seq.; Stacher 2011, 1051 et seq.; Zuberbühler and Schregenberger 2016, 31 et seq.

9.6 Is All Evidence Admissible?

In *EDF* v. *Romania*, the Tribunal did not admit certain evidence, with reference to the principles of good faith and fair dealing in arbitration and to Art. 9(2)(g) of the IBA Rules of Evidence. Do arbitral tribunals have discretion to admit or refuse evidence – in particular in cases of alleged criminal conduct?[78] One option is that the *lex arbitri* contains mandatory provisions that restrict the admissibility of evidence. It is also possible to argue that transnational procedural public policy prohibits the use of illegally obtained evidence in international arbitration.[79]

According to the view advanced here, if arbitral tribunals are asked to decide whether criminal conduct is involved in a case or not, one can go a step further: similar to domestic substantive criminal law provisions, provisions of domestic procedure that deal with the admissibility of evidence should be treated as mandatory rules, possibly overriding the parties' or the tribunal's choice of procedural law. The aim of those provisions is to guarantee the legality of the proceedings and to protect the parties in the search for the truth. This is important not only in criminal proceedings but also in civil proceedings involving criminal law issues.[80]

Such an argument is not meant to be against the widespread consensus today that domestic procedure and the law of evidence, including the rules on the admissibility of evidence, are in principle not applicable in arbitration.[81] The point is that if mandatory provisions of criminal law

[78] Cf. Waincymer, who argues that tribunals have discretion to admit or refuse illegally obtained evidence, taking into account the circumstances (Waincymer 2012, 797 with reference to *Methanex* v. *United States*, part II, ch. I, 26, para. 54).

[79] Zuberbühler et al. 2012, Art. 9 N 5; Schneider and Scherer 2013, Art. 184 N 14. On the concept and content of transnational procedural public policy, see Gaillard and Savage (eds.) 1999, N 1257 and 1638 et seq.; Mantilla-Serrano 2004; Kreindler 2013a, 347 et seq.; Waincymer 2012, 200 et seq. In the context of Art. 190(2)(e) SPILA (grounds for setting aside an arbitral award), the Swiss Federal Supreme Court has consistently affirmed the existence of procedural public policy; it holds that the latter is violated if fundamental and generally recognised principles of procedure are breached, resulting in an unbearable contradiction with the sense of justice of a kind that the decision appears incompatible with the values recognised in a state governed by the rule of law (BGE 132 III 389, 392; BGE 126 III 249, 253 with further references). The Court does not refer to Swiss domestic public policy here, but rather to essential and widely recognised values that, according to the conceptions prevailing in Switzerland, should constitute the foundation of all legal orders (BGE 132 III 389, 395; Pfisterer 2013, Art. 190 N 73).

[80] See discussion in Chapter 4.

[81] Born 2014, 2198 et seq.; O'Malley 2012, 6 et seq., 194 et seq.

are at stake, certain mandatory provisions of procedure should also apply[82] – without, however, opening Pandora's box and letting domestic procedure creep into arbitration through the back door. At stake are only few mandatory provisions of procedure – those that are of such importance and universal recognition that they would also form part of transnational procedural public policy[83] – and only situations in which arbitrators decide about alleged criminal conduct. Restrictions on the admissibility of evidence and the privilege against self-incrimination fall into this category.

If one in principle accepts this approach, another question comes up: the mandatory provisions of which domestic (or international) system apply? The situation is different in ICSID and in ICC arbitration. In ICSID arbitration, mandatory provisions on the admissibility of evidence may be found in:

- the law of the host state;
- the law of the investor's home state;
- the procedural law as chosen by the parties or the tribunal;
- the law of the state on whose territory the evidence was gathered and
- the law of the state where the award will be enforced.

[82] Berger and Kellerhals argue that the principle of good faith prevents an arbitral tribunal from admitting illegally obtained evidence, pointing out that this rule does not apply in the absolute: the Swiss Federal Supreme Court as well as the European Court of Human Rights accept a balancing of the interest to protect the right that was infringed by the illegally obtained evidence and the interest to establish the truth (Berger and Kellerhals 2015, 461 with reference to BGE 131 I 272, 276 and 278 ff.). In BGer 4A_362/2013 and BGer 4A_448/2013, the Swiss Federal Supreme Court dismissed applications to set aside awards by the *Tribunal Arbitral du Sport/Court of Arbitration for Sport* (TAS/CAS). The applicants argued on the basis of Art. 190(2)(e) SPILA that the Tribunal violated procedural public policy because it admitted illegally obtained evidence; however, the Federal Supreme Court found that the Tribunal had individually weighed the interests (*Interessenabwägung*), not admitting all evidence; therefore, the Court denied a violation of procedural public policy (see also Segesser, Leimbacher and Bell 2014; crit. Voser and Moss, who point out that the Supreme Court failed to comment on the Tribunal's application of the principles of Swiss domestic procedural law (Voser and Moss 2014)). Cf. also the *Adamu* v. *FIFA Award* (paras. 81 et seq., 101 and 104) of the TAS/CAS, in which the Tribunal argued that Swiss domestic civil and criminal procedure did not apply, and after weighing the interests, decided to admit evidence that had been secretly recorded by *Sunday Times* undercover journalists, denying a violation of Swiss procedural public policy (see Gurovits, Livschitz and Frenkel 2013).

[83] Cf. Lalive, who – while not generally being in favour of emerging transnational public policy principles with regard to proof – argued that certain fundamental principles of arbitral procedure, such as equality of the parties (which excludes the admissibility of 'secret proof'), are part of transnational public policy (Lalive 1987, 300).

If the provisions on the admissibility of evidence from those legal orders are not compatible, in ICSID arbitration, the mandatory provisions of procedure as chosen by the parties should apply; admissibility of evidence is also part of an international standard of fair procedure.[84] In ICC arbitration, it must be considered that admissibility of evidence is handled quite differently in civil and common law systems (and also within those systems).[85] Mandatory provisions on the admissibility of evidence may be found in:

- the procedural law of the seat of the arbitration;
- the applicable procedural law as chosen by the parties or the tribunal;
- the law of the states of which the involved parties are nationals or in which they are incorporated;
- the law of the state on whose territory the evidence was gathered and
- the law of the state where the award will be enforced.

In case of conflicting provisions on the admissibility of evidence, two options appear feasible: to apply mandatory provisions of the procedural law as chosen by the parties or the tribunal; or to apply the provisions of the procedural law of the seat of the arbitration.[86] It must be kept in mind that state courts at the seat of the arbitration frequently have the possibility to set aside arbitral awards that violate (procedural) public policy.[87] While an award also may not be enforceable if it is contrary to an enforcement state's public policy, it is not always easy to identify the enforcement state(s) before the award is issued.[88] Therefore, in case of conflicting provisions, it appears to be the best solution to apply the mandatory provisions on the admissibility of evidence of the procedural law of the seat of the arbitration.

[84] In *EDF* v. *Romania*, the Respondent *inter alia* referred to Article 26(1) of the Constitution of Romania (*EDF* v. *Romania*, Procedural Order No. 3, 29 August 2008, para. 9); the Tribunal emphasised however that admissibility of evidence was governed by international law, not municipal law (at note 47). In *Methanex* v. *United States* (part II, ch. I, 26 et seq., para. 53 et seq., 58), when refusing to admit certain unlawfully obtained evidence, the Tribunal relied on the general legal duty of the parties to conduct the arbitration in good faith and to respect the equality of arms between them, with reference to Art. 15(1) UNCITRAL Arbitration Rules 1976; see also O'Malley 2012, 321 et seq.

[85] See the discussion of Swiss and English law in Chapter 4.

[86] Cf. the approach of the Tribunal with regard to the privilege against self-incrimination in the *X* v. *Y. ad hoc* arbitration (see discussion in Chapter 6).

[87] E.g. for Switzerland: Art. 190(2)(e) SPILA; Pfisterer 2013, Art. 190 N 1 and 72 et seq.

[88] Cf. Schlosser 1989, N 647, 827.

In legal systems that distinguish civil and criminal procedure – such as the Swiss system – the mandatory provisions on the admissibility of evidence of civil procedure should be applied, as arbitral proceedings are civil proceedings, even if they involve allegations of criminal conduct.[89] In any case, the bottom line should be transnational procedural public policy – evidence that has been obtained by the use of coercion, force, threat, promises, deception and means that influence the cogitation or free will of a person are absolutely prohibited, even if the respective person agrees to their application.[90]

9.7 'Red Flags'

Since ICC Case No. 8891 of 1998, several ICC tribunals[91] have relied on 'red flags' or indicia lists to prove foreign public bribery.[92] In *Metal-Tech* v. *Uzbekistan* and *Spentex* v. *Uzbekistan*, the Tribunals equally invoked 'red flags'.[93] What are the indicia for other criminal offences?

9.7.1 For Private Bribery

In order to develop an indicia list for private bribery, one can draw from the list for foreign public bribery:

- in commercial relations, commission payments from a third party (the *extraneus*) to an employee or agent of a private corporation (the *intraneus*) do not appear in the records of the third party and/or the employer (the *principal*); or the true purpose of the payments is concealed;
- a lack of documentation for the performed services of the *intraneus* in return for the commission payments by the *extraneus*;
- excessive commission payments by the *extraneus* to the *intraneus*;

[89] Cf. Rüedi 2009, 87 et seq., who argues that the findings on the admissibility of evidence of criminal procedure cannot be transferred to civil procedure as the proceedings differ in their object and purpose.

[90] See, e.g., Art. 140 SCrimPC; in detail: Gless 2014, Art. 140 N 32 et seq.

[91] See ICC Cases No. 12990; 13515; and 13914.

[92] For a summary of earlier ICC cases where the tribunals relied on similar circumstantial evidence (ICC Cases No. 1110; 3916; and 6497): Lamm, Greenwald and Young 2014, 338 et seq.; for a list of red flags for foreign public bribery, see e.g., Zuberbühler and Schregenberger 2016, 7 et seq.

[93] See also Rose 2014, 214 et seq.

- the commissions by the *extraneus* to the *intraneus* are paid in form of a success fee;
- short engagement of the *intraneus* for a difficult task;
- the *intraneus* is not qualified for the type of services for which he is paid.

9.7.2 For Fraud

It is not easy to draw up an indicia list for fraud as it appears in so many different forms. In general, fraud would involve:

- the deception of A – e.g. through the use of false documentation – by claiming the existence of, or by omitting certain facts that are relevant for A's decision;
- the deception is concealed and cannot easily be identified by A;
- as a result of the deception, A errs about relevant facts;
- as a result of the error, A disposes of assets and
- A (or B) consequently suffers a financial damage.[94]

9.7.3 For Money Laundering

Today, there seems to be little clarity on how arbitrators should proceed if they suspect that money laundering is involved in their case. However, in case of suspected money laundering, arbitrators cannot ignore the suspicions.[95] Warning signs that arbitration proceedings might be sham include a very one-sided dispute; a lack of documentation for the background of the dispute; and a lack of business activity of the involved companies.[96] A possible approach for the entire profession would be to draw from the so-called 'Wolfsberg Process'[97] and from the 'risk-based approach' that is nowadays applied in particular by private banking institutions. In a nutshell, risk-based approach means that banks develop compliance systems based on business- and client-specific risk variables; their regulatory and

[94] For Swiss law: Pieth 2016b, 104 et seq.; Pieth 2014c, 158 et seq.

[95] See discussion in Chapter 3.

[96] See www.lawsociety.org.uk/support-services/advice/articles/spotlight-on-international-arbitration/.

[97] The 'Wolfsberg Process' is a multi-stakeholder initiative that brought together twelve major global private banking institutions with civil society entities (Transparency International and the Basel Institute on Governance) and resulted in particular in the development of anti–money laundering standards and training activities (in detail: Pieth and Aiolfi 2003, 268 et seq.; Pieth 2007, 96 et seq.).

criminal responsibility is attached to a failure of that system.[98] In individual cases, arbitrators could ask the following questions:[99]

- If bank transactions are involved – who owns the accounts?
- Who is the beneficial owner behind accounts or private investment companies, trusts etc. (shell corporations, possibly off-shore)?[100]
- Are persons or funds involved that originate from countries with a well-known risk for crime and corruption?
- Are there any politically exposed persons (PEPs) involved?
- Are there any unusual transactions involved, e.g. large cash payments?
- What is the origin of the funds that are at stake? Is there a plausible explanation how those funds were earned legally?

The most difficult part is to prove the illicit origin of the funds, as the predicate offence will usually have been committed abroad. However, e.g. in Swiss criminal law, it is not necessary to strictly prove the predicate offence, i.e. neither the perpetrator nor the exact circumstances of the predicate offence must be known, and no conviction abroad is required. It is sufficient that there is certainty that the funds originate from crime.[101] Furthermore, arbitrators might draw appropriate adverse inferences, e.g. if a party refuses to disclose the identity of a beneficial owner.

If arbitrators strongly suspect money laundering – confronted with recalcitrant parties unwilling to produce evidence – they should thoroughly investigate their suspicions. The second option is to resign (and report). If the arbitrators report their money laundering suspicions to the authorities, they risk consequences such as claims for civil law damages; this depends, however, on the applicable domestic law (see next section).

9.8 A Duty of Arbitrators to Report and/or Investigate Suspected Crime?

9.8.1 A Duty to Report?

Whether arbitrators are legally obliged to report an offence depends on the domestic law of the seat of the arbitration, or of any other legislation

98 Pieth 2007, 97; see also Wolfsberg Principles 2012.

99 See also Cremades and Cairns 2003b, 84.

100 In the *X* v. *Y ad hoc* arbitration (see Chapter 6), the Tribunal in the first 2004 Geneva proceedings did not know the beneficial owner; the Tribunal in the second 2006 Zurich proceedings, however, knew the identity of the beneficial owner, and this was decisive for the outcome of the case.

101 BGE 120 IV 323, 328; Pieth 2016b, 207 et seq.; Pieth 2013, Art. 305bis N 36.

to which the tribunal members are subject.[102] In Switzerland, for instance, only prosecutors (if they do not investigate themselves) and certain magistrates[103] are in principle obliged, by threat of labour or criminal law, or disciplinary sanctions, to report.[104] On the other hand, as individual persons without a specific duty of official secrecy or professional confidentiality under Swiss criminal law (Arts. 320, 321 and 321[bis] SCrimC), arbitrators have a right to report an offence to state authorities;[105] however, they might be held civilly liable for damages that a party suffers as a result of the contractual confidentiality breach.[106]

While arbitrators are generally not state organs,[107] they cannot be regarded as purely private persons either. Swiss criminal law for instance treats arbitrators as functional officials (i.e. as persons exercising a public function, *funktionale Beamte*).[108] Through their domestic arbitration laws, states delegate public competences to arbitrators. The fact that arbitrators are substitutes for state judges supports the argument that arbitrators should report suspected crime to the authorities.[109] Apparently, however, there is no known precedent that an arbitral tribunal notified the state authorities of any illicit behaviour that was discovered in the arbitral proceedings.[110] Another question is to whom an arbitral tribunal would report its suspicions – to the authorities of the state where the arbitration has its seat, or to the authorities of the state that would have jurisdiction according to criminal law principles?[111]

[102] Cremades and Cairns 2003a, 84 et seq.; Hwang and Lim 2012, 69 et seq.; for a discussion of different national legal systems as well as international conventions: Nasarre 2013, 4 et seq.; Nadeau-Séguin 2013.

[103] Swiss federal and cantonal laws regulate the reporting obligations of their authorities in detail.

[104] Art. 302 SCrimPC; Hagenstein 2014, Art. 302 N 10 et seq., 34; Hahn 2010, 388.

[105] Art. 301 SCrimPC; Riedo and Boner 2014, Art. 301 N 7 et seq.

[106] Berger and Kellerhals 2015, 431.

[107] Geisinger and Ducret 2011, 128 et seq.

[108] See Art. 309 SCrimC (putting a false party or witness statement in arbitration proceedings on a par with a false such statement in state court proceedings) and Arts. 322[ter] et seq. SCrimC (criminalising active and passive bribery of domestic and foreign arbitrators in the same way as such bribery of public officials). Cf. also Makinwa 2009, 275 et seq.

[109] Hiber and Pavić 2008, 477; Nasarre 2013, 31.

[110] Crivellaro 2014, 249; see also Blackaby et al. 2015, 333; Kreindler 2005b, 447 et seq.; Mourre 2009, 230 et seq.; Waincymer 2012, 105.

[111] See also Nasarre 2013, 29 et seq.

9.8.2 *The Duty to Investigate and to Apply Mandatory Rules* Ex Officio

A different question is whether arbitrators have the right, or even carry a duty to investigate *ex officio* if a party raises allegations of criminal behaviour, or if the arbitrators suspect it to be involved in their case due to the facts, even if none of the parties raises the allegation. For arbitrators with a background in common law, who are used to adversarial proceedings and document disclosure (in England) or discovery (in the United States) in domestic civil proceedings, such an approach might be quite unexpected.[112] Arbitrators with a continental law background, familiar with inquisitorial proceedings, will be more used to a tribunal asking questions to the parties, and demanding the production of evidence.[113]

In *Westacre* v. *Jugoimport* of 1994, the Tribunal neither specified the applicable mandatory law provisions, nor did it investigate the bribery allegations *sua sponte*.[114] Today, a majority of commentators affirms that tribunals have a duty to investigate suspicions of criminal conduct *ex officio* not only in cases in which one of the parties alleges it[115] but also *sua sponte* where none of the parties raises any allegations.[116] This includes applying the relevant criminal law provisions, even if the parties do not invoke them: the arbitrators have to know the law (*iura novit curia*).[117] In cases of alleged criminal conduct, if interests of such

[112] Instead of many, see Schlosser 1989, N 638 et seq.

[113] E.g. in Switzerland, while civil proceedings are generally governed by the principles of party disposition (*Dispositionsmaxime*) and negotiation (*Verhandlungsgrundsatz*), the court has a duty to inquire if a party's legal or factual submissions are unclear, contradictory, ambiguous or manifestly incomplete (*gerichtliche Fragepflicht*, Art. 56 SCPC; Leuenberger and Uffer-Tobler 2016, 119 et seq.).

[114] This approach was clearly rejected by Cremades and Cairns 2003a, 79 et seq.; see also ICC Case No. 5943, where the Sole Arbitrator neither referred to criminal law provisions nor to transnational public policy, even though bribe payments were involved.

[115] Blackaby et al. 2015, 121.

[116] Albanesi and Jolivet 2014, 35; Cremades and Cairns 2003a, 79 et seq.; Geisinger and Ducret 2011, 120; Hwang and Lim 2012, 14 et seq.; Khvalei 2014, 18 et seq.; Kreindler 2013a, 376 et seq.; Kreindler 2005c, 60; Llamzon 2014, 226 et seq.; Llamzon and Sinclair 2015, 483; Mistelis 2009, 583 et seq., 594; Mourre 2009, 229; Olaya 2009, 148 et seq.; Philip 2003, 153; Pieth 2011, 1381; Stacher 2011, 1052 et seq. (who points out that as private persons, arbitrators do not have a duty to investigate as magistrates do); Zuberbühler and Schregenberger 2016, 14.

[117] Philip 2003, 153; for a comparison of different domestic arbitration laws: Geisinger and Ducret 2011, 126. In Switzerland, *iura novit curia* (and *arbiter*) is well established in the case law of the Federal Supreme Court (Berger and Kellerhals 2015, 501 et seq. with references; Kaufmann-Kohler and Rigozzi 2015, 376 et seq.). Generally, in continental law systems, *iura novit curia* applies in civil proceedings: it means that the court

relevance are at stake that they form part of transnational public policy, tribunals should identify and use the applicable criminal law provisions *ex officio* (including foreign mandatory rules), even if the parties explicitly exclude their application – in particular if it appears that the parties deliberately intend to circumvent mandatory rules by not invoking them.[118] Arbitrators should, however, notify the parties about the application of other legal provisions than those cited in submissions.[119] Today, it could be envisaged that if arbitrators refused to identify and apply (foreign) mandatory rules, this would cause domestic legislators to declare such disputes as non-arbitrable.[120]

In the context of a tribunal's *ex* officio investigation and application of mandatory rules, the maxim of *ultra petita* is sometimes mentioned: the arbitrators cannot go beyond what the parties claim.[121] According to Art. V 1. (c) of the New York Convention 1958, recognition and enforcement of an arbitral award may be refused if the award decides on matters beyond the scope of what the parties submitted to arbitration.[122]

However, Art. V 2. (b) of the New York Convention says that recognition or enforcement of an award may be refused if this would be contrary to the public policy of the enforcing country.[123] In Switzerland, Art. 190(2)(e) SPILA requires the tribunal to take into account public policy. Arbitrators have to render an enforceable award: in commercial arbitration, an arbitral award that ignores suspicions of criminal behaviour might be set aside, or not be enforced by domestic courts as it is against public policy.[124]

identifies and applies the law *ex officio* (for Swiss domestic civil procedure: Leuenberger and Uffer-Tobler 2016, 135 et seq.).

118 Born 2014, 2720 et seq.; Voser 1996, 356; with regard to anti-corruption laws, cf. Sayed 2004, 276; with regard to anti–money laundering laws, Schlabrendorff 2005, 860. If an arbitral tribunal has its seat in Switzerland, it can take guidance in, but is not obliged to apply Art. 19 SPILA (in detail: Berger and Kellerhals 2015, 498 et seq. with further references; Kaufmann-Kohler and Rigozzi 2015, 384 et seq.; Mächler-Erne and Wolf-Mettier 2013, Art. 19 N 28; see also Blessing 1997, 35 et seq.; Schnyder 1995, 307 et seq.; Voser 1996, 329 et seq.).

119 Geisinger and Ducret 2011, 124 et seq.; Kaufmann-Kohler and Rigozzi 2015, 486 et seq.; Waincymer 2012, 108 et seq.

120 Cf. Mayer 1986, 285 et seq.; Voser 1996, 337, 356.

121 Blackaby et al. 2015, 121.

122 See Hwang and Lim 2012, 14 et seq., who also refer to Art. 34(2)(a)(iii) and Art. 36(1)(a)(iii) UNCITRAL 2006, which provide that an arbitral award may be set aside or refused enforcement if it is *ultra petita*.

123 Hwang and Lim 2012, 15.

124 For Switzerland: Kaufmann-Kohler and Rigozzi 2015, 488 et seq., 502, 529 et seq.

According to the view advanced here, the *ultra petita* rule is not designed for, and does not apply to situations in which arbitrators decide to inquire into alleged criminal conduct on their own motion, without the request of a party, or even against the will of the parties.[125] *Ultra petita* refers to the claims of the parties in a civil law dispute and derives from the principle of party disposition (*Dispositionsmaxime*), meaning that a court (or tribunal) awards something more or different than the party has requested, or less than the opposing party has acknowledged.[126] If a tribunal decides to investigate suspicions of crime, this is an issue of public policy not at the disposal of the parties, and only indirectly connected to the question whether the amounts etc. awarded to the parties correspond with their claims.[127] In general, courts tend to treat as *ultra petita* only awards that go beyond the relief sought by the parties, and not awards that reason beyond the parties' submissions, as long as the result is within or reasonably related to the relief sought by the parties. Some annulment courts are (unduly) restrictive though and consider a reasoning that goes beyond, or is different from the one of the parties as *ultra petita*.[128]

If there is *prima facie* evidence for criminal conduct, arbitrators should raise the issue with the parties, and investigate in all cases.[129] Another option is to resign (and report).[130] While this would be an exceptional and extreme scenario, if an arbitral tribunal neglects clear evidence of criminal conduct and issues an award that forces one party to the proceedings to e.g. continue to make bribe payments, or to perform a contract that includes the acceptance of money originating from crime, the question whether the tribunal was aiding and abetting in crime would have to be asked.[131] It is correct to say that – even if the proceedings are purely private and consensual – the arbitrator's function does have a public aspect in the sense that an award has the same force as a state court decision.[132] It is also important to keep in mind that a successful

[125] Cf. Schlabrendorff 2005, 860 and BGer 4P.260/2000, at 5.b) et seq.

[126] E.g. in Swiss civil procedure, this is regulated in Art. 58(1) SCPC; Sutter-Somm 2017, 83.

[127] See Gaillard and Savage (eds.) 1999, N 1631; Hwang and Lim 2012, 16 et seq.; Kreindler 2003a, 14.

[128] Born 2014, 3289 et seq.; Landolt 2012, 192.

[129] Hwang and Lim 2012, 21 et seq.; Philip 2003, 152 et seq.

[130] See Kreindler 2005c, 94 et seq., who argues that resignation of an arbitrator may be regarded as assisting in illegal conduct as the arbitrator does not make use of the possibility to sanction such conduct.

[131] Cf. Scherer 2002, 36; see also discussion in Chapter 3.

[132] Khvalei 2014, 19.

appeal of an award and its findings on criminal conduct is difficult (e.g. in Switzerland, the Federal Supreme Court does not freely revisit the fact-finding of an arbitral tribunal at the appeals stage);[133] arbitrators must be aware that if they do not properly investigate alleged criminal conduct in the first place, this might never happen.[134] Furthermore, there is the risk of a late revision of an arbitral award.[135]

Case law provides for a good example how an arbitral tribunal can proceed. In *Metal-Tech* v. *Uzbekistan*, the Tribunal decided to investigate *ex officio*, as the facts that emerged during the hearings had nurtured suspicions of bribery. It made use of its powers under Article 43 of the ICSID Convention and in particular requested the production of evidence issuing several Procedural Orders.[136] From the published parts of ICC awards, it is difficult to see how actively the tribunals investigated. However, already back in 1963, Judge *Lagergren* decided to refuse to ignore the bribery issue,[137] and in a recent unpublished ICC Award, the Tribunal stated that it had a duty to *sua sponte* investigate suspected corruption.[138]

Next to ordering the production of documents, tribunals might also call certain witnesses (or experts) on their own initiative.[139] Depending on the circumstances, a no-show of a witness that has been called by the tribunal (or by a party) might result in an adverse inference. However,

[133] See *Westinghouse* v. *National Power Corporation* and *Westacre* v. *Jugoimport*. See also the unsuccessful appeal in the *Thomson CSF* v. *Frontier AG Bern et al.* case (BGer of 28 January 1997; *ASA Bulletin* (1998), 118; as well as Berger and Kellerhals 2015, 83 with further case references.

[134] Kreindler 2003b, 247 et seq.; see also Geisinger and Ducret 2011, 121; Hwang and Lim 2012, 73 et seq.

[135] In the *Thales (formerly Thomson CSF)* v. *Frontier AG Bern et al.* case, the Swiss Federal Supreme Court in 2008 accepted a petition for revision of an ICC Award of 1996, arguing that the arbitrators had been fraudulently misled about the fact that undue commissions had been paid, as was proven in a criminal investigation that took place after the Award had been issued (BGer 4A_596/2008 of 6 October 2009, at 4.).

[136] See also Llamzon and Sinclair 2015, 484; cf. however, the annulment proceedings in *Wena* v. *Egypt*, where the *ad hoc* Annulment Committee argued that the Tribunal did not depart from fundamental rules of procedure when it did not ask for further evidence of alleged bribery (*Wena Hotels Limited* v. *Arab Republic of Egypt*, ICSID Case No. ARB/98/4, Decision on Annulment, 28 January 2002, paras. 71 et seq.; Schreuer et al. 2009, Art. 43 N 20).

[137] Cremades and Cairns 2003a, 80.

[138] Khvalei 2014, 18.

[139] In detail: Levine 2015, 318 et seq.; see also Coşar 2015, 535 et seq. who points out that a tribunal 'could also consider modifying its previous orders, holding hearings and issuing a fresh procedural timetable after fully reviewing the parties' submissions on the applications before it'.

the tribunal must carefully consider whether the absence of the witness is justified (e.g. by illness or fear of self-incrimination),[140] and it should be aware of possible witness intimidation practices.[141] Can tribunals go still a step further and appoint private investigators to inquire into the facts, at the cost of the parties to the dispute? If a tribunal decides to take such a step, an important consideration will be equality of arms: a party with fewer financial means may not be disadvantaged compared to its opponent.[142] Private investigations may become very costly.[143]

9.8.3 *Late Allegations and Late Production of Evidence?*

In *Siemens* v. *Argentina*, in the proceedings leading up to the 2007 Award, the Tribunal apparently did not admit certain oral witness evidence from Argentina, arguing that the latter's corruption allegations were raised at a late stage in the arbitration. Similarly, in *Westacre* v. *Jugoimport*, the Defendant put forward its bribery allegations only in its final brief, after the hearing of evidence; the Tribunal argued that this was at a too late stage. In *Fraport* v. *Philippines I* on the other hand, certain decisive documents were produced only at a late stage in the proceedings, at the insistence of the Tribunal's President.[144]

In general, if there is *prima facie* evidence for criminal conduct, tribunals are well advised to admit such evidence even at a late stage in the proceedings or after the closure of the proceedings.[145] Depending on the circumstances, tribunals might consider reopening a hearing.[146] Otherwise, there is a risk that the award is set aside or not enforceable because it is contrary to public policy (in commercial arbitration);[147] or that a party asks for revision of an award (in commercial or ICSID arbitration).

9.9 Interim Conclusion

The above assessment allows the following conclusions regarding evidence in arbitration if criminal conduct is alleged. The legal burden of proof does not shift; it remains with the party alleging criminal conduct throughout

[140] Levine 2015, 345 et seq.; Born 2014, 2351 et seq. [141] See Wilske 2010, 224 et seq.
[142] Cf. Wälde 2010, 173 et seq. [143] Cf. also Rose 2014, 200.
[144] Schreuer et al. 2009, Art. 43 N 48, 67; however, the Award was subsequently annulled due to a violation of Fraport's right to be heard (Sattar 2011, 219).
[145] For ICSID arbitration: Schreuer et al. 2009, 650 with reference to case law; Levine 2015, 322.
[146] Raeschke-Kessler 2004, 494 et seq. [147] Cf. Kreindler 2005c, 53 et seq., 58 et seq.

the proceedings. What shifts is the risk of non-production of evidence if the alleging party is able to produce *prima facie* evidence for criminal conduct. If certain requirements are fulfilled, tribunals can draw adverse inferences from the non-production of evidence of a party. Regarding witnesses, their privilege against self-incrimination must be respected. Parties should in principle not be protected by the privilege against self-incrimination, i.e. adverse inferences may be drawn from their silence. In case of parallel or future criminal proceedings, the evidence from the arbitral proceedings is not admissible and must be taken anew by the criminal court. Depending on the applicable domestic criminal procedure, arbitrators or parties might gain access to the files of a parallel criminal investigation. They are not bound by the decision of a criminal judge.

The standard of proof rarely decides the outcome of arbitral proceedings that involve alleged criminal conduct. In principle, the applicable law determines the standard of proof; continental and common law treat this issue quite differently. While the approaches of different ICSID and ICC tribunals diverge, there is a tendency to apply a higher standard of proof to allegations of criminal behaviour. There is a risk that criminal allegations are raised in an abusive manner in arbitration. Nevertheless, tribunals should not raise (or lower) the standard of proof, but rather apply the standard of 'balance of probabilities' (or 'preponderance of the evidence') and request persuasive (circumstantial) evidence for the criminal allegations. 'Red flags' for foreign public bribery are well established and used nowadays. Such indicia lists can also be drawn up for other criminal offences, e.g. private bribery, fraud and money laundering.

Regarding admissibility of evidence, in particular in cases of alleged criminal conduct, mandatory rules of procedure should be identified and applied in arbitration. Transnational procedural public policy serves as a fall-back position. Evidence that has been gathered by the use of coercion, force, threat, promises, deception and means that influence the cogitation or free will of a person is absolutely prohibited, even if the concerned person agrees to its application. Arbitrators are usually not obliged to report suspected crime, although this depends on applicable domestic laws. If they do report, they might be held civilly liable for the contractual confidentiality breach. Arbitrators do, however, have a duty to investigate alleged or suspected criminal behaviour, even against the will of the parties. This includes applying the relevant criminal law provisions *ex officio*. Tribunals should notify the parties of the application of other legal provisions than those cited in the parties' submissions. If criminal allegations are raised at a late stage of the proceedings, tribunals should nevertheless take them into account if there is *prima facie* evidence for criminal conduct.

10

Legal Consequences of Criminal Conduct

To round off this text, this chapter briefly looks at legal consequences if criminal conduct is proven in international arbitral proceedings.[1]

10.1 In ICSID Arbitration

10.1.1 The Temporal Scope of a BIT Legality Requirement

In particular, *Fraport* v. *Philippines* raises the question of how a tribunal should deal with the situation that criminal conduct takes place during the performance of an investment, and not at its initiation. The Tribunal in that case argued that non-compliance with host state's law at the initiation of an investment would result in a denial of ICSID jurisdiction, whereas non-compliance throughout the performance of the investment would have to be discussed at the merits stage.[2] However, is it possible to determine when the initiation phase of an investment is finished?[3] And is it not contrary to the principle of 'unity of investment' to split an investment into chronological phases?[4] From a criminal law perspective, with regard to foreign public bribery, it must be pointed out that the offence is already fulfilled with the offer or promise of an undue advantage to an

[1] An in-depth analysis is beyond the scope of this text; for a collection of articles about the impact of corruption on international commercial contracts in different legal systems, see Bonell and Meyer 2015.

[2] *Fraport* v. *Philippines I*, para. 345; *Fraport* v. *Philippines II*, para. 331; cf. *Yukos Universal Limited* v. *Russia*, where the Tribunal argued that the right to invoke the Energy Charter Treaty 1994 (ECT) should not altogether be denied to an investor if the latter had breached the law of the host state in the performance (but not in the making) of the investment (at paras. 1354 et seq.).

[3] Borris and Hennecke 2008, 58 et seq.; Grubenmann 2010, 216.

[4] See discussion in Chapter 2.

official – corrupt payments etc. – that are linked to the initiation of an investment can be effected much later.[5]

An investment usually consists of a complex web of legal relationships.[6] Instead of splitting an investment into different phases on a timeline, according to the view advanced here, tribunals should analyse whether an investment at its initiation and/or throughout its performance violates core provisions of a host state's administrative or criminal law, and whether the violation happened on a large scale or constituted just a minor infringement. Such an analysis should take into account the precise scope of an 'in accordance with host state's law' provision in the applicable BIT, but it should not be limited by it.[7]

BIT provisions that require – at the level of jurisdiction – that the *type of asset is legal* according to the host state's law, thereby postponing all other illegality issues to the merits stage, appear too restrictive.[8] Provisions similar to the one in the underlying BIT in *Metal-Tech* v. *Uzbekistan* that require compliance with all of the host state's laws have a far wider reach. The scope of such a clause in principle should not be considered as temporally limited to the initiation of the investment.[9] The wording of the BIT will eventually determine whether a tribunal, in the face of an investment that breaches the laws of the host state, denies jurisdiction or decides that the claims are not admissible.[10]

[5] See *Metal-Tech* v. *Uzbekistan*, where all payments to the consultants post-dated the establishment of the investment; however, the consultants were promised to be paid before the establishment of the investment.

[6] See also Llamzon and Sinclair 2015, 502 et seq.

[7] See *Fraport* v. *Philippines II*, at para. 332, where the Tribunal argued that there is an established international legal principle that an investment has to be legal under the host state's law, even if a BIT does not explicitly mention this.

[8] Cf. however Art. 1(1) of the Germany-Philippines BIT that was applicable in the *Fraport* v. *Philippines* cases; in *Saba Fakes* v. *Turkey*, the Tribunal argued – with reference to the respective BIT provision – that the legality requirement encompassed only the compliance with the host state's laws regarding the admission of investments; and that in all other cases of a breach of domestic law by the investor, the host state could take appropriate action within the framework of its own law (*Saba Fakes* v. *Turkey*, para. 119).

[9] See also Lamm, Hellbeck and Khan 2015, 559, 570 et seq. (strongly arguing that illegality in the performance or implementation of an investment cannot be ignored); but cf. the Tribunal in *Metal-Tech* v. *Uzbekistan* and Obersteiner 2014, 278 et seq.

[10] See discussion later in this chapter; for states interested in securing their right to a corruption defence, Yackee proposes an investment treaty model clause that explicitly requires compliance with the host state's anti-corruption laws (Yackee 2012, 742 et seq.).

10.1.2 The 'Clean Hands' Doctrine, Jurisdiction, and Admissibility

In *Niko* v. *Bangladesh*, the Respondent argued that the Claimant did not bring its claim with 'clean hands' and that therefore the Claimant should not benefit from the ICSID arbitration clause. The Tribunal discussed the origin and applicability of the doctrine, identifying three criteria: a continuing violation; a protection against future violations; and reciprocity between the obligations considered. The Tribunal eventually denied applicability.[11] Is there room for applying the clean hands doctrine in international investment arbitration?

At the core of the doctrine lies the principle that 'he who comes into equity must come with clean hands'.[12] The origin of the doctrine traces back to Roman law; it was identified by name in eighteenth-century common law. Today, common and civil law systems have incorporated the clean hands doctrine in various forms.[13] The existence of the doctrine in public international law is somewhat controversial.[14] In the past years, several commentators argued that the doctrine exists in international law.[15] Some qualified it as a general principle of law (and therefore as a source of international law according to Art. 38(1)(c) ICJ Statute).[16] As a general principle of law, the clean hands doctrine would be applicable in all arbitral proceedings in which international law is chosen to apply. Furthermore, it was argued that the clean hands doctrine has been applied in several commercial arbitration proceedings.[17]

However, in the *Yukos Universal Limited* v. *Russia* Award of July 2014, the Tribunal argued that the Respondent had not been able to cite a majority decision where an international court or arbitral tribunal had applied the clean hands doctrine as a principle of international law. The Tribunal concluded that the clean hands doctrine does not exist as a

[11] *Niko* v. *Bangladesh*, paras. 476 et seq.; the doctrine is also briefly touched upon in *Fraport* v. *Philippines II* (para. 328); *Metal-Tech* v. *Uzbekistan* (para. 417); and *Hamester* v. *Ghana* (para. 317).

[12] *Precision Instrument Mfg. Co.* v. *Automotive Co.*, 324 US 806, 814 (1945).

[13] For the history of the clean hands doctrine: Llamzon 2015, 316 et seq.; Dumberry and Dumas-Aubin 2013, 1 et seq.; Moloo 2010; Kreindler 2010a, 312 et seq.; Kreindler 2010b, 7 et seq.; Lamm, Pham and Moloo 2010, 723 et seq.

[14] Llamzon and Sinclair 2015, 510 et seq.

[15] E.g. Lamm, Pham and Moloo 2010, 723 with further references; Cremades 2005, 214; in detail: Lim 2013.

[16] E.g. Dumberry and Dumas-Aubin 2013, 3; Moloo and Khachaturian 2011, 1485; Kreindler 2010a, 317; Moloo 2010.

[17] Kreindler 2010a, 319 with reference *inter alia* to ICC Cases No. 1110 and 8891.

general principle of international law that would bar an investor's claim.[18] But a few months later, in the *Al-Warraq* v. *Indonesia* arbitration, the Tribunal concluded that the clean hands doctrine rendered the Claimant's claims inadmissible.[19] In December 2016, the Tribunal found in *Spentex* v. *Uzbekistan* that 'The effect of corruption, if established, on arbitral proceedings has been rather unequivocal. Arbitral tribunals have considered that corruption, as a core violation of the principle of "good faith," implies that a claimant approaches the tribunal with "unclean hands" and should thus not be heard.'[20]

Commentators argue that in a number of cases, the same practical result was achieved even if the clean hands doctrine was not named explicitly (e.g. *World Duty Free* v. *Kenya*, *Inceysa* v. *El Salvador*);[21] that the inclusion of an 'in accordance with host state's law' provision in a BIT is a manifestation of the clean hands doctrine and that several tribunals already applied the doctrine to determine jurisdiction and admissibility;[22] and that the principle of clean hands applies even if the applicable investment treaty does not expressly require compliance with the law.[23] In addition, the clean hands doctrine is described as more nuanced in comparison to the legality doctrine because it allows policy considerations (protection of court integrity, proportional punishment and reciprocity) to be taken into account.[24]

It remains to be seen whether other tribunals will apply the clean hands doctrine in the same way as the *Spentex* Tribunal did. Even if the scope and applicability of the clean hands doctrine in investment arbitration may not be entirely clear yet for some, the difficulties are more related to inconsistent terminology than to practical outcome. Notwithstanding terminology, according to the view advanced here, criminal conduct by investors should have the following legal consequences. If an investor's activity seriously violates core provisions of the host state's administrative or criminal law, or of international law, at any stage of the investment, and the applicable investment treaty contains an 'in accordance with host state's law' clause, the investor's activity does not qualify as an investment under the treaty. Therefore, ICSID jurisdiction should be denied because Art. 25 ICSID Convention (that requires an

[18] *Yukos Universal Limited* v. *Russia*, paras. 1362 et seq.

[19] *Al-Warraq* v. *Indonesia*, para. 646; for a comment on the case: Newcombe and Marcoux 2015; see also Cremades 2005, 214 et seq.

[20] *Spentex* v. *Uzbekistan*, para. 823 with an extensive discussion of case law.

[21] Llamzon 2015, 318 et seq.; Kreindler 2010a, 319 et seq.

[22] Dumberry and Dumas-Aubin 2013, 4 et seq.

[23] Lamm, Pham and Moloo 2010, 726.

[24] Llamzon 2015, 324 et seq.

investment) is not fulfilled.[25] If there is no 'in accordance with host state's law' clause in the applicable investment treaty, or if ICSID jurisdiction is based on a contract or national law, the claims by the investor should be declared inadmissible.[26] The advantage of this more nuanced approach (as compared to denying jurisdiction in all cases of investor's misconduct) is the following: if a tribunal exercises its adjudicative power and decides on the admissibility of a claim, this decision is in general final, whereas a denial of jurisdiction in the absence of an 'in accordance with host state's law' clause might be challenged under Art. 52 ICSID Convention for excess of powers of the tribunal.[27]

In terms of procedure, this means that in some cases arbitrators must take and evaluate the evidence relating to alleged criminal conduct already at the jurisdictional level.[28] The consequence of this approach can be severe: an investor might be deprived of protection even if he did act lawfully at the beginning of his engagement. However, in case of serious breaches of relevant laws, such a result appears acceptable. It might contribute to preventing future investors' misconduct.

A different question is how tribunals should handle situations in which a host state endorses an investment in perfect knowledge of criminal conduct that surrounds it. Could estoppel as a principle of international law be applied?[29] According to this principle, the host state would be

[25] See also discussion in Chapter 2. In *Phoenix* v. *Czech Republic*, the Tribunal argued that compliance with host state's law should be regarded as an additional element of an investment and that manifest non-compliance with host state's law would result in a denial of ICSID jurisdiction (at paras. 104 and 114; in detail: Coşar 2015, 543 et seq.).

[26] Cf. *World Duty Free* v. *Kenya*, para. 188 where the Tribunal held that Kenya was legally entitled to avoid the contract; *Al-Warraq* v. *Indonesia*, para. 647; Newcombe 2011, 196 et seq.; Menaker 2010, 74; Moloo and Khachaturian 2011, 1482 et seq., 1499 et seq.; Lamm, Greenwald and Young 2014, 342 et seq.; Llamzon and Sinclair 2015, 507 et seq., 528 et seq. (who still further differentiate admissibility and merits issues); Dumberry and Dumas-Aubin 2013, 7; Cremades 2005, 216. Yackee argues that investor misconduct should always be treated as a jurisdictional issue, as this precludes any equitable balancing exercise at the merits stage that takes into account the state's own blameworthiness (Yackee 2012, 744 et seq.). Douglas argues that illegality in investment treaty arbitration should always be a question of admissibility (Douglas 2014, 155 et seq.).

[27] Newcombe 2011, 199 with reference to case law; Paulsson 2005, 617; Lamm, Hellbeck and Khan 2015, 569 (who describe jurisdiction as the power of a tribunal to hear a case, and admissibility as whether it is appropriate for a tribunal to hear a case; on the conceptual distinction between jurisdiction and competence/admissibility, see Banifatemi 2015; Heiskanen 2014).

[28] See *Phoenix* v. *Czech Republic* in Chapter 2. Cremades points out that 'for practical reasons, the tribunal might prefer to proceed to the merits and hear all the evidence before ruling on the issues of corruption and jurisdiction' (Cremades 2005, 216).

[29] In detail: Lim 2013.

estopped from raising the illegality defence in front of an arbitral tribunal.[30] However, estoppel would require the host state to issue a clear and unconditional statement that bribe payments were lawful, on which the investor relied to his detriment. This will hardly ever be the case.[31] Does state responsibility offer a solution in such a situation?

10.1.3 State Responsibility for Bribe Solicitation

EDF v. *Romania* (as well as *World Duty Free* v. *Kenya*) raise the question whether, in cases of bribe solicitation by public officials of the host state, the officials' acts are attributable to the host state under the Draft Articles on State Responsibility[32] of the International Law Commission (ILC). Articles 4 ('Conduct of organs of a State'), 5 ('Conduct of persons or entities exercising elements of governmental authority'), 6 ('Conduct of organs placed at the disposal of a State by another State') and 8 ('Conduct directed or controlled by a State') regulate the attribution of conduct to a state, and Article 7 ('Excess of authority or contravention of instructions') contains a rule on excess.[33]

From the point of view of criminal law, it is important to keep in mind that one of the objective requirements of foreign public bribery is that a foreign public official solicits or accepts an undue advantage for himself or for another person.[34] If the advantage goes to the state, it is not a case of foreign bribery:

> Linguistically, it is possible to say that the state itself can be called a third party beneficiary. But on a closer look, this fails to capture what foreign bribery law actually wants to protect, because in such cases, there is no *victim* state, which has been injured by the abuse of office: the state profits from the abuse.[35]

If the advantage goes to a public official or a person close to him, the state is the victim of corruption. Holding the state responsible for the act of the official would be contrary to the logic of international anti-corruption conventions in such a case.[36] However, if the advantage goes to the state itself, the objective requirements of foreign public bribery are not fulfilled.[37]

[30] Moloo and Khachaturian 2011, 1497 et seq. with reference to *Fraport* v. *Philippines I*, para. 346.
[31] Greenwald 2015. [32] ILC 2001.
[33] For a detailed discussion of state responsibility and transnational corruption, see Llamzon 2014, 238 et seq., 275 et seq.; Klaw 2015; Lim 2013; see also Kreindler 2013a, 335 et seq.
[34] See, e.g., Art. 16(2) UNCAC 2003.
[35] Zerbes 2014, 123; see also *Sistem* v. *Kyrgyz Republic*. [36] See also ICC Case No. 12990.
[37] *World Duty Free* v. *Kenya*, para. 169.

If the host state as the recipient of the undue advantage raises the bribery defence, the defence therefore should fail and there appears to be no need to apply the principles of state responsibility as the tribunal will admit the claimant's claims (unless there are other reasons to dismiss them). From this angle, the Tribunal's approach in *EDF* v. *Romania* (where the Claimant raised the issue of bribe solicitation) to affirm attribution under Article 8 of the ILC Draft Articles without discussing domestic and international anti-corruption laws, falls short of the applicable legal framework.

A pragmatic solution to take into account the host state's participation in corruption was applied by the Tribunal in *Metal-Tech* v. *Uzbekistan*: although the Respondent prevailed, the Tribunal ordered the parties to each bear its own legal costs, and equally share the ICSID costs.[38] In *Spentex* v. *Uzbekistan*, the Tribunal dismissed all claims and counter-claims, urged the prevailing Respondent to pay US$8 million to an international anti-corruption institution, and ordered that both parties had to cover their own costs, and equally share the costs of the proceedings. If the Respondent failed to pay the US$8 million, the Tribunal ordered that it would have to pay all costs of the proceedings as well as three-quarters of the Claimant's legal costs.[39]

In the context of the responsibility of states towards the international community as a whole and towards the individuals that make up those states, it has been argued that for a state to be allowed to invoke the bribery defence, it must at least prove that it has engaged in a genuine effort to prosecute and punish its corrupt officials.[40] This is a fair demand, but there are several difficulties to it. First of all, transnational foreign bribery investigations and prosecutions are very complex to conduct. It is a challenge even for states with an independent, impartial and efficient judiciary, and much depends on mutual legal assistance. Many states in which corruption is systemic do not have an independent judiciary, and international co-operation in criminal matters is barred to them. There is no political will to prosecute corrupt officials. Second, a criminal bribery conviction requires proof beyond reasonable doubt, whereas in civil court and arbitration proceedings, a lower standard of

[38] *Metal-Tech* v. *Uzbekistan*, para. 423; similarly, in ICC Case No. 6248 (at 139 et seq.), the Tribunal argued that it would be unfair to award the legal costs to the prevailing defendant who had co-operated in the conclusion of the immoral agreements at stake; the parties therefore each had to bear their own legal costs.

[39] *Spentex* v. *Uzbekistan*, para. 993.

[40] Llamzon 2014, 281; see also Abdel Raouf 2009, 135 and Wilske and Obel 2013, 186 et seq. (both arguing that a 'clean hands' requirement should be mandated from the investor as well as from the host state).

proof applies to alleged bribery. Therefore, it is possible that a civil court or arbitral tribunal decides that bribery is proven even though the criminal court acquits the accused person for lack of evidence.[41]

Frequently, the reality in foreign bribery cases is that the recipients of the bribes are never prosecuted. Tackling the demand side of foreign bribery is important, but measures preventing corruption, for instance through collective action,[42] is the better way forward than condoning investor's corruption by barring the corruption defence to the respondent state, or by awarding a remedy to the corrupt investor under the law of state responsibility. On the other hand, it must be kept in mind that if an investor is able to prove that the host state harmed its investment in retaliation because the investor was unwilling to participate in corruption, the state's behaviour will breach the requirement of fair and equitable treatment of investment treaties.[43]

10.2 In ICC Arbitration

10.2.1 Separability

As discussed in Chapter 2, the principle that the arbitral clause has a separate existence from the underlying contract is well established today. Consequently, in ICC arbitration – in contrast to treaty-based ICSID arbitration with an 'in accordance with host state's law' clause – jurisdiction is in principle not denied if criminal conduct is at stake (unless the arbitral clause itself is affected by it). Even in the *Lagergren* case, the Sole Arbitrator did not question the separability principle, but denied jurisdiction because he considered the matter as non-arbitrable (the case is exceptional because the bribe payments were undisputed between the parties). As a rule, ICC tribunals discuss criminal conduct not as a jurisdictional issue, but on the merits stage.

10.2.2 Legal Consequences of Bribery Pacts and of Bribery-Affected Contracts

In principle, the law applicable to the substance of the dispute determines the legal consequences of bribery pacts and of contracts procured by

[41] Greenwald 2015, who also points out that in *World Duty Free* v. *Kenya* and *Metal-Tech* v. *Uzbekistan*, bribery was proven, even though no public officials were prosecuted for corruption by the respondent states.

[42] See, e.g., Pieth (ed.) 2012a.

[43] Menaker 2010, 74.

bribery. In the above-discussed ICC cases, the nullity of bribery pacts was undisputed. If the existence of a bribery pact is proven, any claims for unpaid remunerations must fail.[44] The inequality created between a respondent who benefitted from a claimant's activities without having to pay the contracted price does not legitimise the bribery pact.[45] Tribunals also consistently concluded that regarding bribery pacts, any claims for restitution of already paid sums equally must fail.[46]

In ICC Case No. 12990 (where the Respondent was a state), the Tribunal argued that if both parties to a contract are involved in an unlawful activity, no claims for restitution are admitted if the unlawful activity has been carried out in full knowledge by all parties (*in pari causa turpitudinis cessat repetitio*). The Tribunal found, however, that the knowledge of the representatives or agents of the state cannot simply be imputed to the state and that a state cannot itself be corrupted, only its leaders. The Tribunal argued that the principle *in pari causa turpitudinis cessat repetitio* should not be applied to a state that is precisely the victim of corruption. Nevertheless, the Tribunal concluded that a state where corruption is endemic cannot protect itself behind its own conduct and engage in activities that are tainted with bribery, in order to claim a reimbursement afterwards. The Tribunal declared the contract at stake as null and void, and insofar as the state should have been aware of the unlawful cause of the contract, its request for restitution was unfounded. Therefore, the Tribunal rejected the Respondent's counterclaim.[47]

10.2.3 Reduction of an Excessive Commission?

There are instances in commercial arbitration where bribery cannot be proven, but strong suspicions prevail that a bribery pact is at stake. In such cases, another – not completely unproblematic – option is to reduce the agent's commission to a certain percentage. The inconsistency lies in the fact that even though bribery is not proven, the commission is

44 See also Kreindler and Gesualdi 2015, 401 et seq.

45 See, e.g., ICC Cases No. 6497; 8891.

46 See, e.g., ICC Cases No. 3916 (with reference to the principle *nemo auditur propriam turpitudinem allegans* (no one may base a legal claim on its own unlawful act)); 13515; Raeschke-Kessler 2004, 480 et seq.; for Swiss law: Kissling 2015, 362 et seq.

47 On the legal consequences of bribery-affected contracts and on contractual and restitutionary remedies under the section 'illegality' of the 2010 UNIDROIT Principles of International Commercial Contracts: Kreindler and Gesualdi 2015, 403 et seq.; cf. also ICC Case No. 11307.

reduced.[48] If a tribunal follows this path, it should make the level of the percentage depend on the total contract value and on the actual work performed by the agent. In principle, the higher the contract value is, the lower the percentage of the agent's commission should be; the fee could be capped. The work provided must be proportionate to the fee paid.

10.3 Interim Conclusion

This brief discussion of the legal consequences if criminal conduct is proven in investment and commercial arbitration allows the following conclusions. In ICSID arbitration, instead of identifying temporal stages of an investment, tribunals should analyse whether the investment at any stage violated core provisions of a host state's laws, and whether the violation happened on a large scale or constituted just a minor infringement. In treaty-based ICSID arbitration, the wording of the applicable treaty will determine whether the tribunal denies jurisdiction (if there is an 'in accordance with host state's law' clause) or whether the claimant's claims are inadmissible (the latter is also the consequence in contract- or national law–based ICSID arbitration).

In cases of bribe solicitation, there is no need to apply the principles of state responsibility, because if the state itself benefits from undue payments, it is not a case of foreign bribery, and therefore the bribery defence must fail. Domestic corruption investigations and prosecutions should not be a prerequisite for a state to invoke the bribery defence.

In ICC arbitration, the arbitral clause is in principle valid even if the main contract is null and void, unenforceable or voidable due to criminal conduct (unless the arbitral clause is also affected). Therefore, ICC tribunals in principle do not deny jurisdiction if criminal conduct is at stake. Bribery pacts are generally treated as null and void by ICC tribunals, and claims for unpaid remunerations or for restitution of already paid sums equally fail. This also applies if one party to the dispute is a state if that state should have been aware of the unlawful cause of the contract. If the existence of a bribery pact cannot be proven, but strong suspicions prevail, one option is to reduce the agent's commission.

[48] See BGer 4A_538/2012; Stacher 2014, 1563 et seq.

PART V

Final Remarks

11

Summary of Results

By using an inductive approach, this text has derived, from an analysis of (mostly) ICSID and ICC case law, pertinent issues (and possible solutions) when it comes to proving alleged criminal conduct in international arbitration. It is now time to return to the starting point of this text: the arbitrator's dilemma in the face of criminal conduct. How should arbitrators proceed in order to successfully prove alleged criminal conduct in international arbitration, and distinguish unsubstantiated allegations from real cases?

Imagine the situation that either a party raises the allegation, or that arbitrators themselves suspect, due to certain 'red flags' (with which they should be familiar and of which they must be aware), that:

- a contract has an illegal purpose (e.g. a bribery pact); or that
- a contract was procured by criminal conduct (e.g. foreign public bribery, private bribery, or fraud); or that
- criminal conduct occurred during the performance of the main contract; or that
- a money laundering scheme is involved in the arbitration; or that
- an arbitration is conducted in order to launder money.

As a first step, arbitrators should *ex officio* identify the applicable domestic or international criminal law provisions. They should notify the parties of the application of different rules than those cited in the submissions. In ICC arbitration, foreign mandatory law might override a choice of law by the parties. In ICSID arbitration, in particular mandatory provisions of the host state's law and international treaties should be applied. In treaty-based ICSID arbitration, the legality requirement should apply even if not explicitly mentioned in a BIT, and the investment should be regarded as one unity.

Arbitrators should make full use of the applicable criminal law with the aim of ascertaining the objective requirements of the offence that must be proven by the evidence. Arbitrators can rely on domestic case law and academic writing to interpret the criminal provisions. In arbitral proceedings, proof of the subjective requirements of an offence (*mens rea*) should not be required; rather, arbitrators should be allowed to derive the element of will from the respective persons' knowledge of the facts. If the applicable laws, including foreign mandatory laws, do not contain provisions that cover the offences at stake (here: foreign public bribery, private bribery, fraud, and money laundering), arbitrators should rely on transnational public policy. Transnational public policy therefore serves as a fall-back position, and it includes the prohibition of the four offences just mentioned.

Once the applicable criminal law framework is identified and the objective requirements of the offence at stake are determined, arbitrators will ask themselves how to prove those requirements. No matter whether a party raises allegations or not, if criminal conduct is suspected, arbitrators should investigate *ex officio*; the *ultra petita* rule is not designed to apply to situations in which an arbitrator inquires into criminal allegations *sua sponte*. If there is *prima facie* evidence, allegations of criminal conduct should be investigated by the arbitrators even if they are raised late in the proceedings. The second option for arbitrators is to resign (and report). In case of strong suspicions of e.g. money laundering, arbitrators should keep in mind that ignoring those might be considered as aiding and abetting in crime, depending on the circumstances.

An important factor arbitrators should keep in mind is possible parallel (or future) criminal proceedings in any jurisdiction, as they might have an impact on the willingness of witnesses to testify and on the parties' readiness to co-operate. Depending on the applicable domestic criminal procedure, tribunals might also be able to gain access to the files of the criminal investigation. Arbitrators are not bound by the decisions of domestic criminal courts; whether they are obliged to report suspected criminal conduct depends on the domestic law of concerned states. In case arbitrators breach their contractual confidentiality duties, they might be held civilly liable for damages.

If a party alleges criminal conduct, it must be able to present *prima facie* evidence for the allegations in the first place. It is important that arbitrators distinguish real cases from unsubstantiated allegations or mere insinuations. To prove criminal conduct, arbitrators may rely on circumstantial evidence; direct evidence is not required. While the legal burden to prove criminal conduct always rests on the party that alleges it, the risk of non-production of evidence may shift to the alleged party. In appropriate circumstances, arbitrators may draw adverse inferences from the non-production of rebuttal evidence by the alleged party. Parties should in principle not be able to invoke the privilege against self-incrimination, and arbitrators may draw adverse inferences from their non-production of evidence. Witnesses can in principle rely on the privilege against self-incrimination. Arbitrators should keep in mind that a false witness or party statement may be a criminal offence in certain jurisdictions. In case of parallel or future criminal proceedings, the evidence from the arbitral proceedings is not admissible and should be taken anew by the criminal court.

More issues might arise with regard to the admissibility of evidence. Evidence collected by the use of coercion, force, threat, promises, deception or by means that influence the cogitation or free will of a person is absolutely prohibited, even if the respective person agrees to the application. In other cases, it may be necessary to weigh the interest to find the truth against the interest to protect the legal object compromised by the unlawful manner in which the evidence was obtained. Arbitrators should rely on mandatory provisions of domestic civil procedure, or on international standards of fair trial, to determine the admissibility of evidence as well as the privilege against self-incrimination. In any case, transnational procedural public policy should be the bottom line.

Regarding the standard of proof, arbitrators should determine it according to the applicable law. The concepts of standard of proof vary a great deal in continental and in common law; however, their relevance should not be overestimated, as the standard of proof is rarely decisive for the outcome of arbitral proceedings if criminal conduct is alleged. There are good reasons to argue that an arbitral tribunal should apply neither a higher nor a lower standard of proof in cases of alleged crime, but refer to the usual civil standard of 'balance of probabilities' or 'preponderance of the evidence'.

12

Conclusion

Foreign public bribery, private bribery, fraud and money laundering are forms of (transnational) economic crime that can have a detrimental impact on fair competition, ethical business conduct and particularly on society at large. Allegations of such criminal conduct nowadays regularly occur in the context of international arbitration proceedings. This comes as no surprise, as international investment and commercial arbitration today is the most popular mechanism for globalised dispute settlement, and so it inevitably inherits disputes involving not only licit but also illicit financial flows. Arbitrators are in a difficult situation in the face of alleged or suspected criminal conduct, but they do have options for how to handle such cases. While arbitrators have no powers of state prosecutors, they in principle have much more flexibility on procedure and evidence issues than do prosecutors and criminal courts. Transnational procedural public policy sets the limit.

Arbitrators decide about disputes that potentially involve huge amounts of money, and in particular in investment disputes, the awards also can have political impact. For the sake of the integrity of the international investment and commercial arbitration system, it is crucial that arbitrators take alleged or suspected criminal conduct seriously. Even if party autonomy is at the heart of international arbitration, issues of criminal law cannot be left at the disposal of the parties. The risk is too high that mandatory laws protecting the public interest are circumvented behind the veil of confidentiality – in particular regarding commercial arbitration. If arbitrators in commercial arbitration shy away from thoroughly investigating alleged or suspected criminal conduct in their own motion by making use of the full range of means at their disposal, they should not deal with such issues at all, or in other words: domestic arbitration laws should declare criminal law issues as non-arbitrable. Alternatively, domestic legislators might consider introducing reporting obligations for arbitrators, e.g. in cases of suspected money laundering. The better solution is, however, that the arbitral community develops an approach how to responsibly and effectively deal with alleged or suspected criminal conduct on its own motion.

Investment (ICSID) arbitration is more transparent than commercial arbitration is, but the demand is the same: arbitrators need to have the courage and the skills to thoroughly inquire into suspected criminal conduct and to draw appropriate legal consequences. Condoning investor's corruption by barring the corruption defence to the host state, or by awarding a remedy to the corrupt investor under the law of state responsibility, is not the proper way forward. According to the logic of international anti-bribery conventions, the state is the victim in cases of transnational corruption. If it is not, the objective requirements of foreign public bribery provisions are not fulfilled, and for that reason the host state's bribery defence should fail. Investor's criminal conduct should result in a denial of jurisdiction or non-admissibility of claims not only if it occurs at the initiation of an investment but also if it occurs during its performance.

Over time, certain positive patterns have emerged in how arbitral tribunals deal with alleged criminal conduct: for instance, tribunals nowadays frequently rely on 'red flags', or draw adverse inferences. For other issues, however, tribunals' approaches still appear rather improvised: for example, they sometimes do not thoroughly investigate alleged or suspected criminal conduct, or the awards fall short of the applicable legal framework of domestic or international criminal law. While this comes as no surprise given that each case has its own specifics, that much depends on the courage and skills of the individual arbitrators, and that there is no doctrine of precedent in international arbitration, it is hard to accept if public interest issues are at stake.

The proposal put forward in the Annex to this text is a decision tree for arbitrators. It does not offer a boilerplate solution for every situation: this is simply not possible. However, it might contribute to ensure that pertinent issues regarding applicable criminal law and evidence that arise from the involvement of criminal conduct are addressed in arbitral proceedings, and that criminal behaviour is identified, investigated and successfully proven. Overall, it is useful to keep in mind what it means to prove in legal proceedings: the aim is not to find an ultimate truth, but rather a version of the past events that is acceptably probable to be correct.[1]

[1] See discussion in Chapter 4.

ANNEX: DECISION TREES

For ICSID arbitration

Question (if yes, proceed to next question)	If no
Do the Respondent or the Claimant allege criminal conduct, or are there any 'red flags' for criminal conduct?	normal course of proceedings
Does the tribunal investigate the allegations or suspicions *ex officio*?	The tribunal does not make full use of its powers under Article 43 ICSID Convention. There is the risk of a revision of the award.
In treaty-based ICSID arbitration: does the tribunal apply the legality requirement in all cases and without distinguishing the initiation phase and the performance of the investment?	The legality requirement applies even if it is not explicitly mentioned in a BIT, and the investment should be regarded as one unity.
Does the tribunal apply criminal provisions of the host state's law based on the legality requirement and provisions of domestic criminal law or international treaties as well as procedural standards based on a choice of law?	The tribunal falls short of the applicable legal framework.
If necessary: does the tribunal make reference to transnational (procedural) public policy as a fall-back position?	A party might apply for the annulment of the award under Article 52 ICSID Convention.
Is there *prima facie* evidence for criminal conduct?	normal course of proceedings
Does the tribunal shift the risk of non-production of evidence to the alleged party?	The tribunal puts the stakes too high.

yes

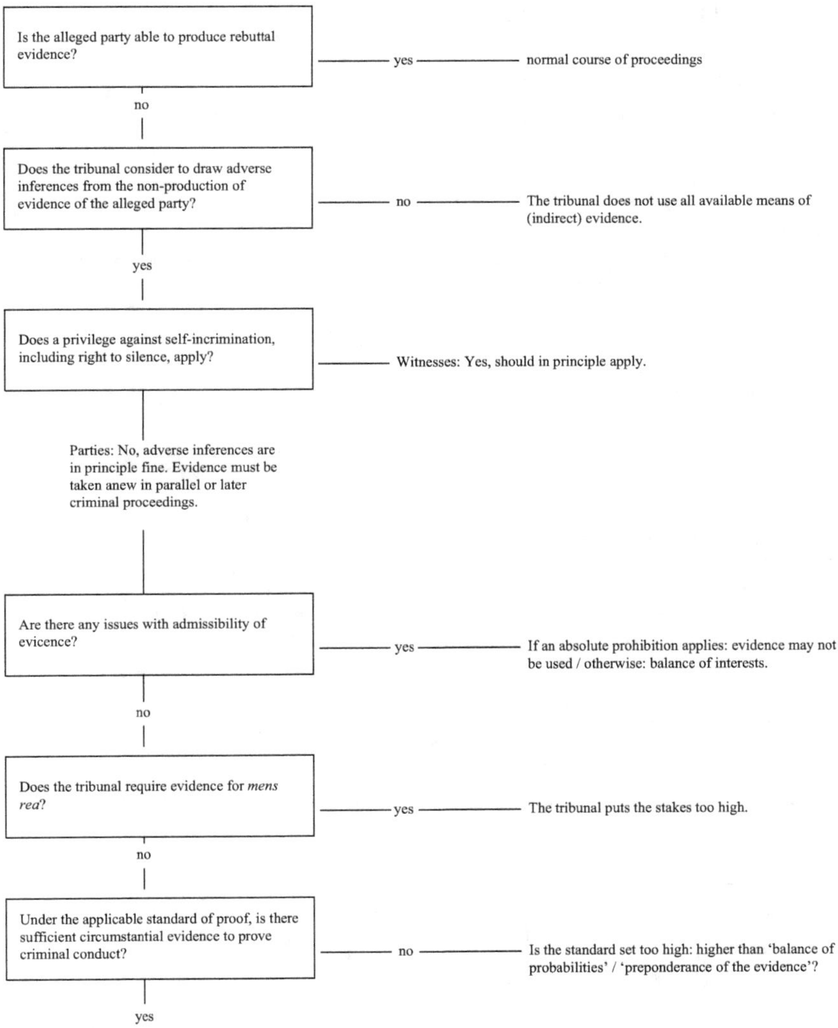
Is the alleged party able to produce rebuttal evidence?
yes
normal course of proceedings
no
Does the tribunal consider to draw adverse inferences from the non-production of evidence of the alleged party?
no
The tribunal does not use all available means of (indirect) evidence.
yes
Does a privilege against self-incrimination, including right to silence, apply?
Witnesses: Yes, should in principle apply.
Parties: No, adverse inferences are in principle fine. Evidence must be taken anew in parallel or later criminal proceedings.
Are there any issues with admissibility of evicence?
yes
If an absolute prohibition applies: evidence may not be used / otherwise: balance of interests.
no
Does the tribunal require evidence for mens rea?
yes
The tribunal puts the stakes too high.
no
Under the applicable standard of proof, is there sufficient circumstantial evidence to prove criminal conduct?
no
Is the standard set too high: higher than 'balance of probabilities' / 'preponderance of the evidence'?
yes

For ICC arbitration

Is crime alleged?
or
Are there any 'red flags' for criminal conduct? — no — normal course of proceedings

yes

Does the tribunal report the suspicions to the authorities? — yes — Risk of civil liability for breach of contractual confidentiality.

no

Does the tribunal investigate the allegations or suspicions *ex officio*? — no — Public policy issues might arise at the seat of the tribunal or in the state where the award is enforced; in case of strong suspicions: risk of aiding and abetting in crime by arbitrators.

yes

Does the tribunal apply (foreign) mandatory rules: domestic criminal law and possibly provisions of domestic civil procedure? — no — The tribunal falls short of the applicable legal framework.

yes

If necessary: does the tribunal make reference to transnational (procedural) public policy as a fall-back position? — no — Public policy issues might arise at the seat of the tribunal or in the state where the award is enforced.

yes

Is there *prima facie* evidence for criminal conduct? — no — normal course of proceedings

yes

Does the tribunal shift the risk of non-production of evidence to the alleged party? — no — The tribunal puts the stakes too high.

yes

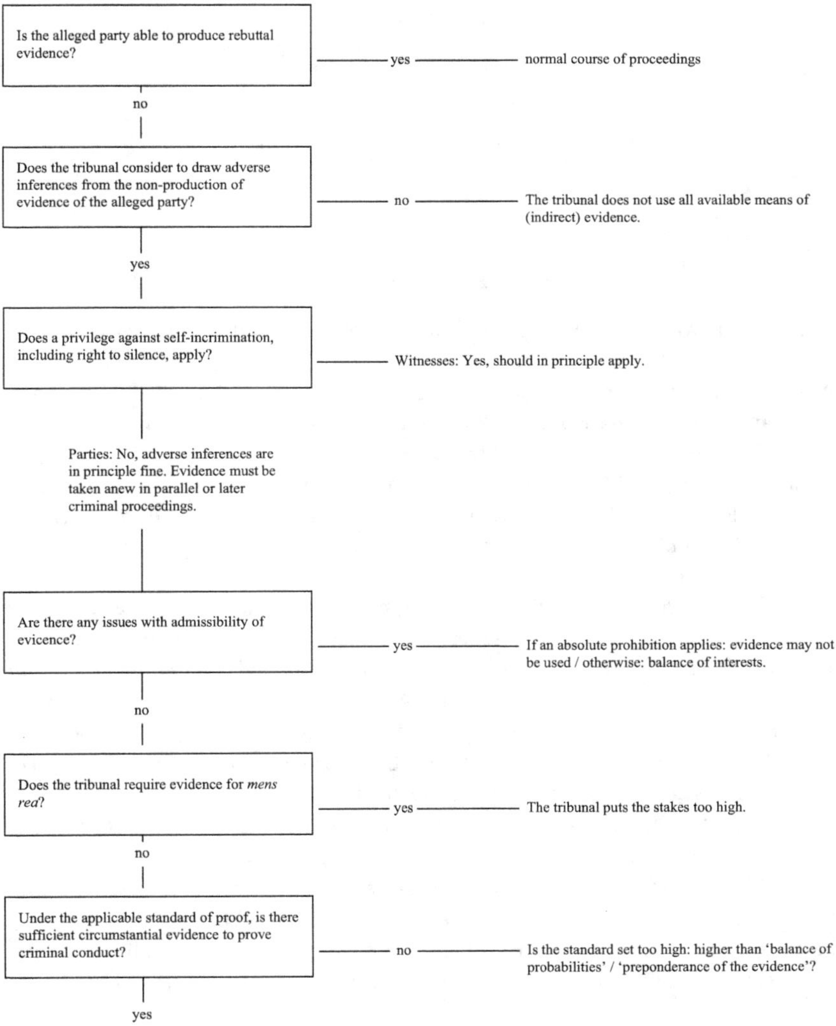
Is the alleged party able to produce rebuttal evidence?
yes
normal course of proceedings
no
Does the tribunal consider to draw adverse inferences from the non-production of evidence of the alleged party?
no
The tribunal does not use all available means of (indirect) evidence.
yes
Does a privilege against self-incrimination, including right to silence, apply?
Witnesses: Yes, should in principle apply.
Parties: No, adverse inferences are in principle fine. Evidence must be taken anew in parallel or later criminal proceedings.
Are there any issues with admissibility of evicence?
yes
If an absolute prohibition applies: evidence may not be used / otherwise: balance of interests.
no
Does the tribunal require evidence for mens rea?
yes
The tribunal puts the stakes too high.
no
Under the applicable standard of proof, is there sufficient circumstantial evidence to prove criminal conduct?
no
Is the standard set too high: higher than 'balance of probabilities' / 'preponderance of the evidence'?
yes

BIBLIOGRAPHY

Books and Articles

Abdel Raouf, M. (2009), 'How Should International Arbitrators Tackle Corruption Issues?', 24 *ICSID Review* 116

Aidt, T.S. (2011), 'Corruption and sustainable development', in: S. Rose-Ackerman and T. Søreide (eds.), *International Handbook on the Economics of Corruption, Volume Two*, Cheltenham, 3

Albanesi, C. and E. Jolivet (2014), 'Dealing with Corruption in Arbitration: A Review of ICC Experience', 24 *ICC International Court of Arbitration Bulletin* (2013), Special Supplement, 'Tackling Corruption in Arbitration', 27

Arfazadeh, H. (2001), 'Considérations pragmatiques sur la compétence respective de l'arbitre et du juge en matière de corruption', 19 *ASA Bulletin* 672

Ashford, P. (2013), *The IBA Rules on the Taking of Evidence in International Arbitration, A Guide*, Cambridge

Banifatemi, Y. (2010), 'The Law Applicable in Investment Treaty Arbitration', in: K. Yannaca-Small (ed.), *Arbitration Under International Investment Agreements, A Guide to the Key Issues*, Oxford, 191

(2015), 'The Impact of Corruption on "Gateway Issues" of Arbitrability, Jurisdiction, Admissibility and Procedural Issues', in: D. Baizeau and R.H. Kreindler (eds.), *Addressing Issues of Corruption in Commercial and Investment Arbitration*, ICC Dossiers, Vol. 13, Paris, 16

Barraclough, A. and J. Waincymer (2005), 'Mandatory Rules of Law in International Commercial Arbitration', 6 *Melbourne Journal of International Law* 205

Berger, B. and F. Kellerhals (2015), *International and Domestic Arbitration in Switzerland*, 3rd edn, Berne

Berger-Steiner, I. (2008), *Das Beweismass im Privatrecht, Eine dogmatische Untersuchung mit Erkenntniswert für die Praxis und die Rechtsfigur der Wahrscheinlichkeitshaftung*, Bern

Bermann, G.A. (2011), 'The Origin and Operation of Mandatory Rules', in: G.A. Bermann and L.A. Mistelis (eds.), *Mandatory Rules in International Arbitration*, Huntington, 1

Besson, S. (2006), 'Arbitration and Human Rights', 24 *ASA Bulletin* 395

(2015), 'Corruption and Arbitration', in: D. Baizeau and R.H. Kreindler (eds.), *Addressing Issues of Corruption in Commercial and Investment Arbitration*, ICC Dossiers, Vol. 13, Paris, 103

Bhojwani, R. (2012), 'Deterring Global Bribery: Where Public and Private Enforcement Collide', 112 *Columbia Law Review* 66

Bjorklund, A.K. (2011), 'Investment Arbitration', in: G.A. Bermann and L.A. Mistelis (eds.), *Mandatory Rules in International Arbitration*, Huntington, 233

Blackaby, N. et al. (2015), *Redfern and Hunter on International Arbitration*, 6th edn, Oxford

Blessing, M. (1997), 'Mandatory Rules of Law *versus* Party Autonomy in International Arbitration', 14 *Journal of International Arbitration* 23

Böckstiegel, K.-H. (1987), 'Public Policy and Arbitrability', in: P. Sanders (ed.), *Comparative Arbitration Practice and Public Policy in Arbitration*, Deventer, 177

Bonell, M.J. and O. Meyer (2015), 'The Impact of Corruption on International Commercial Contracts – General Report', in: M.J. Bonell and O. Meyer (eds.), *The Impact of Corruption on International Commercial Contracts*, Cham et al., 1

Bonucci, N. (2014), 'Article 12 – Monitoring and Follow-up', in: M. Pieth, L.A. Low and N. Bonucci (eds.), *The OECD Convention on Bribery, A Commentary*, 2nd edn, Cambridge, 534

Born, G.B. (2014), *International Commercial Arbitration*, 2nd edn, Alphen aan den Rijn

Born, G. (2015a), *International Arbitration, Cases and Materials*, 2nd edn, New York

Born, G.B. (2015b), *International Arbitration: Law and Practice*, 2nd edn, Alphen aan den Rijn

Borris, C. and R. Hennecke (2008), 'Das Kriterium der Einhaltung von Vorschriften nationalen Rechts in ICSID-Schiedsverfahren – Anmerkungen zum Schiedsspruch in der Sache Fraport v. Philippines', *Zeitschrift für Schiedsverfahren (SchiedsVZ)*, 49

Brönnimann, C.J. (1989), *Die Behauptungs- und Substanzierungslast im schweizerischen Zivilprozessrecht*, Bern

Brown, E. (2000), 'Illegality and Public Policy – Enforcement of Arbitral Awards in England: Hilmarton Limited v. Omnium de Traitement et de Valorisation S.A.', 3 *International Arbitration Law Review* 31

Bruch, G.S. and A.N. Adkins (2014), 'Article 8 – Accounting', in: M. Pieth, L.A. Low and N. Bonucci (eds.), *The OECD Convention on Bribery, A Commentary*, 2nd edn, Cambridge, 447

Cairns, D.J.A. (2009), 'Transnational Public Policy and the Internal Law of State Parties, 6(1) *Transnational Dispute Management*

Carreteiro, M.A. (2016), 'Burden and Standard of Proof In International Arbitration: Proposed Guidelines For Promoting Predictability', 13 *Revista Brasileira de Arbitragem* 82

Cheng, B. (1987), *General Principles of Law as Applied by International Courts and Tribunals*, Cambridge

Cockcroft, L. (2014), *Global Corruption, Money, Power and Ethics in the Modern World*, London and New York

Cordero-Moss, G. (2013), 'International arbitration is not only international', in: G. Cordero-Moss (ed.), *International Commercial Arbitration, Different Forms and Their Features*, Cambridge, 7

Coşar, U. (2015), 'Claims of Corruption in Investment Treaty Arbitration: Proof, Legal Consequences and Sanctions', in: A.J. van den Berg (ed.), *Legitimacy: Myths, Realities, Challenges*, Alphen aan den Rijn, 531

Court de Fontmichel, A. (2004), *L'arbitre, le juge et les pratiques illicites du commerce international*, Paris

Craig, W.L., W.W. Park and J. Paulsson (2000), *International Chamber of Commerce Arbitration*, 3rd edn, New York

Cremades, B.M. (2005), 'Corruption and Investment Arbitration', in: G. Aksen et al. (eds.), *Global Reflections on International Law, Commerce and Dispute Resolution, Liber Amicorum in honour of Robert Briner*, Paris

Cremades, B.M. and D.J.A. Cairns (2003a), 'Transnational public policy in international arbitral decision-making: The cases of bribery, money laundering and fraud', in: K. Karsten and A. Berkeley (eds.), *Arbitration: Money Laundering, Corruption and Fraud*, ICC Dossiers, Paris, 65

(2003b), 'Corruption, International Public Policy and the Duties of Arbitrators', 58(4) *Dispute Resolution Journal* 76

Crivellaro, A. (2003), 'Arbitration case law on bribery: Issues of arbitrability, contract validity, merits and evidence', in: K. Karsten and A. Berkeley (eds.), *Arbitration: Money Laundering, Corruption and Fraud*, ICC Dossiers, Paris, 109

(2014), 'The courses of action available to international arbitrators to address issues of bribery and corruption', in: F. Bonelli and M. Mantovani (eds.), *Corruzione nazionale e internazionale*, Milan, 225

De Boisséson, M. (2009), 'Adducing evidence – anything goes?', Transcript, 12th IBA International Arbitration Day, *Due Process in International Arbitration*, 16 February 2009

Derains, Y. (1987), 'Public Policy and the Law Applicable to the Dispute in International Arbitration', in: P. Sanders (ed.), *Comparative Arbitration Practice and Public Policy in Arbitration*, Deventer, 227

Doak, J., C. McGourlay and M. Thomas (2015), *Evidence in Context*, 4th edn, London and New York

Donatsch, A. and N. Schmid (1996 et seq.), *Kommentar zur Strafprozessordnung des Kantons Zürich*, Zurich

Donovan, D.F. (2011), 'Investment Treaty Arbitration', in: G.A. Bermann and L.A. Mistelis (eds.), *Mandatory Rules in International Arbitration*, Huntington, 275

Donovan, D.F. and A.K.A. Greenawalt (2006), '*Mitsubishi* After Twenty Years: Mandatory Rules Before Courts and International Arbitrators', in: L.A. Mistelis and J.D.M. Lew (eds.), *Pervasive Problems in International Arbitration*, Alphen aan den Rijn, 11

Douglas, Z. (2014), 'The Plea of Illegality in Investment Treaty Arbitration', 29 *ICSID Review* 155

Dumberry, P. and G. Dumas-Aubin (2013), 'The Doctrine of 'Clean Hands' and the Inadmissibility of Claims by Investors Breaching International Human Rights Law', 10(1) *Transnational Dispute Management Special Issue: Aligning Human Rights and Investment Protection*, January 2013

El Kosheri, A.S. and P. Leboulanger (1984), 'L'arbitrage face a la corruption et aux trafics d'influence', 3 *Revue de l'arbitrage* 3

Engel, C. (2009), 'Preponderance of the Evidence versus *Intime Conviction*, A Behavioral Perspective on a Conflict between American and Continental European Law', 33 *Vermont Law Review* 435

Eveleigh, E. (1994), 'General Standards of Proof in Litigation and Arbitration Generally', 10 *Arbitration International* 354

Gaillard, E. and Y. Banifatemi (2003), 'The Meaning of "and" in Article 42(1), Second Sentence, of the Washington Convention: The Role of International Law in the ICSID Choice of Law Process', 18 *ICSID Review* 375

Gaillard, E. and J. Savage (eds.) (1999), *Fouchard, Gaillard, Goldman on International Commercial Arbitration*, The Hague

Gazzini, T. (2012), 'Bilateral Investment Treaties', in: T. Gazzini and E. De Brabandere (eds.), *International Investment Law, The Sources of Rights and Obligations*, Leiden, 99

Geisinger, E. and P. Ducret (2011), 'The Uncomfortable Truth: Once Discovered, What to Do with It?', in: M. Wirth, C. Rouvinez and J. Knoll (eds.), *The Search for 'Truth' in Arbitration, Is Finding the Truth What Dispute Resolution Is About?*, Huntington NY, 113

Gless, S. (2014), Commentary on Arts. 139, 140 and 141, in: M.A. Niggli, M. Heer and H. Wiprächtiger (eds.), *Basler Kommentar, Schweizerische Strafprozessordnung, Jugendstrafprozessordnung, Art. 1–195 StPO*, 2nd edn, Basel

(2015), *Internationales Strafrecht*, 2nd edn, Basel

Glover, R. (2015), *Murphy on Evidence*, 14th edn, Oxford

González García, L.A. (2013), 'Corruption, Money Laundering and International Arbitration', 1 *Latin American Journal of International Trade Law* 509

Greenberg, S. and F. Lautenschlager (2011), 'Adverse Inferences in International Arbitral Practice', in: S. Kröll et al. (eds.), *Liber Amicorum Eric Bergsten, International Arbitration and International Commercial Law: Synergy, Convergence and Evolution*, Alphen aan den Rijn, 179

Greenwald, B. (2015), 'The Viability of Corruption Defenses in Investment Arbitration When the State Does Not Prosecute', *Blog of the European Journal of International Law*, 15 April 2015

Grubenmann, B. (2010), *Der Begriff der Investition in Schiedsgerichtsverfahren in der ICSID-Schiedsgerichtsbarkeit*, Basel

Guldener, M. (1955), *Beweiswürdigung und Beweislast nach schweizerischem Zivilprozessrecht*, Zurich

Gurovits, A., T. Livschitz and D. Frenkel (2013), 'Admissibility of Illegally Procured Evidence in CAS Proceedings – Some Comments to the Adamu Decision', www.sportslawcircle.com, 14 January 2013

Habscheid, W.J. (1990a), 'Beweislast und Beweismass, Ein kontinentaleuropäisch-angelsächsischer Rechtsvergleich', in: H. Prütting (ed.), *Festschrift für Gottfried Baumgärtel zum 70. Geburtstag*, Köln et al.

(1990b), *Schweizerisches Zivilprozess- und Gerichtsorganisationsrecht*, 2nd edn, Basel

Hagenstein, N. (2014), Commentary on Art. 302, in: M.A. Niggli, M. Heer and H. Wiprächtiger (eds.), *Basler Kommentar, Schweizerische Strafprozessordnung, Jugendstrafprozessordnung, Art. 196–457 StPO, Art. 1–54 JStPO*, 2nd edn, Basel

Hahn, A.-C. (2010), 'Schweizer Schiedsgerichte und der internationale Kampf gegen Korruption', *Schweizerische Zeitschrift für Wirtschafts- und Finanzmarktrecht*, 382

Hanotiau, B. (1994), 'Satisfying the Burden of Proof: The Viewpoint of a "Civil Law" Lawyer', 10 *Arbitration International* 341

Happ, R. (2013), 'Chapter XIV – ICSID Rules', in: Schütze, R.A. (ed.), *Institutional Arbitration, Article-by-Article Commentary*, Munich, 923

Harari, M. and D. Jobin (2014), 'Articles 9–11 – International Co-operation', in: M. Pieth, L.A. Low and N. Bonucci (eds.), *The OECD Convention on Bribery, A Commentary*, 2nd edn, Cambridge, 486

Hasenböhler, F. (2016), Commentary on Arts. 150, 152, 161, 162 and 164, in: T. Sutter-Somm, F. Hasenböhler and C. Leuenberger (eds.), *Kommentar zur Schweizerischen Zivilprozessordnung (ZPO)*, 3rd edn, Zurich

Hassemer, W. (1990), *Einführung in die Grundlagen des Strafrechts*, 2nd edn, Munich

Haugeneder, F. and C. Liebscher (2009), 'Corruption and Investment Arbitration: Substantive Standards and Proof', *Austrian Arbitration Yearbook*, 539

Hauser, R. (1974), *Der Zeugenbeweis im Strafprozess mit Berücksichtigung des Zivilprozesses*, Zurich

Hauser, R., E. Schweri and K. Hartmann (2005), *Schweizerisches Strafprozessrecht*, 6th edn, Basel

Heine, G. (2003), 'Part III – Comparative Analysis', in: Heine, G., B. Huber and T.O. Rose (eds.), *Private Commercial Bribery, A Comparison of National and Supranational Legal Structures*, Freiburg i.Br., 603

Heine, G., B. Huber and T.O. Rose (eds.) (2003), *Private Commercial Bribery, A Comparison of National and Supranational Legal Structures*, Freiburg i.Br.

Heiskanen, V. (2014), '*Ménage à trois?* Jurisdiction, Admissibility and Competence in Investment Treaty Arbitration', 29 *ICSID Review* 231

Hess, D. (2009), 'Corruption in the value chain: private-to-private and private-to-public corruption', in: Transparency International, *Global Corruption Report 2009, Corruption and the Private Sector*, Cambridge, 19

Hiber, D. and V. Pavić (2008), 'Arbitration and Crime', 25 *Journal of International Arbitration* 461

Higi, P. (2016), Commentary on Art. 162, in: A. Brunner, D. Gasser and I. Schwander (eds.), *Schweizerische Zivilprozessordnung (ZPO), Kommentar*, 2nd edn, Zürich and St. Gallen

Hirsch, M. (2011), 'Sources of International Investment Law', available at: http://ssrn.com/abstract=1892564

Hochstrasser, D. and S. Fuchs (2013), Introduction to ch. 12 SPILA, in: H. Honsell et al. (eds.), *Basler Kommentar, Internationales Privatrecht*, 3rd edn, Basel

Hodges, P. (2007), 'The Relevance of Article 6 of the European Convention on Human Rights in the Context of Arbitration Proceedings', 10 *International Arbitration Law Review* 163

Horder, J. (2016), *Ashworth's Principles of Criminal Law*, 8th edn, Oxford

Horvath, G.J. et al. (2013), 'Categories of Guerilla Tactics', in: G.J. Horvath and S. Wilske (eds.), *Guerilla Tactics in International Arbitration*, Alphen aan den Rijn, 3

Huguenin, C. and B. Meise (2015), Commentary on Arts. 19/20, in: H. Honsell, N.P. Vogt and W. Wiegand (eds.), *Basler Kommentar, Obligationenrecht I, Art. 1–529 OR*, 6th edn, Basel

Hunter, M. and G. Conde e Silva (2003), 'Transnational Public Policy and its Application in Investment Arbitrations', 4 *Journal of World Investment* 367

Hwang, M. and K. Lim (2012), 'Corruption in Arbitration – Law and Reality', 8 *Asian International Arbitration Journal* 1

Ibrahim, N.M. (2013), 'Proof of Corruption in International Commercial Arbitration: A Commentary on the ICC Award 12732 of February 2007', available at: http://ssrn.com/abstract=2178435 (in Arabic, with an English abstract)

Ivory, R. (2014), *Corruption, Asset Recovery, and the Protection of Property in Public International Law, The Human Rights of Bad Guys*, Cambridge

Kaiafa-Gbandi, M. (2012), 'The Commission's Proposal for a Directive on the Fight Against Fraud to the Union's Financial Interests by Means of Criminal Law (COM(2012) 363 final) – An Assessment Based on the Manifesto for a European Criminal Policy', 2 *European Criminal Law Review (EuCLR)* 319

Karrer, P.A. (2013a), 'Chapter V – Swiss Rules of International Arbitration of the Swiss Chambers' Arbitration Institution', in: Schütze, R.A. (ed.), *Institutional Arbitration, Article-by-Article Commentary*, Munich, 361

(2013b), Commentary on Art. 187, in: H. Honsell et al. (eds.), *Basler Kommentar, Internationales Privatrecht*, 3rd edn, Basel

Karsten, K. (2003), 'Money laundering: How it works and why you should be concerned', in: K. Karsten and A. Berkeley (eds.), *Arbitration: Money Laundering, Corruption and Fraud*, ICC Dossiers, Paris, 15

Karsten, K. and A. Berkeley (eds.) (2003), *Arbitration: Money Laundering, Corruption and Fraud*, ICC Dossiers, Paris

Kaufmann-Kohler, G. (2007), 'Arbitral Precedent: Dream, Necessity or Excuse?', 23 *Arbitration International* 357

Kaufmann-Kohler, G. and A. Rigozzi (2015), *International Arbitration, Law and Practice in Switzerland*, Oxford

Keane, A. and P. McKeown (2016), *The Modern Law of Evidence*, 11th edn, Oxford

Kendra, T. and A. Bonini (2014), 'Dealing with Corruption Allegations in International Investment Arbitration: Reaching a Procedural Consensus?', 31 *Journal of International Arbitration* 439

Kessedjan, C. (2007), 'Transnational Public Policy', in: A.J. van den Berg (ed.), *International Arbitration 2006: Back to Basics?*, Alphen aan den Rijn, 857

Kessler, M.A. (2015), 'Commentary on Art. 53', in: H. Honsell, N.P. Vogt and W. Wiegand (eds.), *Basler Kommentar, Obligationenrecht I, Art. 1–529 OR*, 6th edn, Basel

Khvalei, V. (2014), 'Using Red Flags to Prevent Arbitration from Becoming a Safe Harbour for Contracts that Disguise Corruption', 24 *ICC International Court of Arbitration Bulletin* (2013), Special Supplement, 'Tackling Corruption in Arbitration', 15

Kissling, C. (2015), 'Impact of Bribery on Contracts Under Swiss Civil Law', in: M.J. Bonell and O. Meyer (eds.), *The Impact of Corruption on International Commercial Contracts*, Cham et al., 351

Kjos, H.E. (2013), *Applicable Law in Investor-State Arbitration, The Interplay Between National and International Law*, Oxford

Klaw, B.W. (2015), 'State Responsibility for Bribe Solicitation and Extortion: Obligations, Obstacles, and Opportunities', 33 *Berkeley Journal of International Law* 60

Knahr, C. (2008), 'Investitionen "in Übereinstimmung mit nationalen Rechtsvorschriften"', in: C. Knahr and A. Reinisch (eds.), *Aktuelle Probleme und Entwicklungen im Internationalen Investitionsrecht*, Stuttgart et al., 125

König, V. (2013), *Präzedenzwirkung internationaler Schiedssprüche, Dogmatisch-empirische Analysen zur Handels- und Investitionsschiedsgerichtsbarkeit*, Berlin and Boston

Konrad, S. and R. Hunter (2013), 'Chapter VI – LCIA Rules', in: Schütze, R.A. (ed.), *Institutional Arbitration, Article-by-Article Commentary*, Munich, 413

Kramer, E.A. (1991), *Berner Kommentar, Obligationenrecht, Allgemeine Bestimmungen, Inhalt des Vertrages, Art. 19–22 OR*, Bern

Krauss, D. (1980), 'Das Prinzip der materiellen Wahrheit im Strafprozess', in: H. Jäger (ed.), *Kriminologie im Strafprozess, Zur Bedeutung psychologischer, soziologischer und kriminologischer Erkenntnisse für die Strafrechtspraxis*, Frankfurt a.M., 65

Kreindler, R.H. (2003a), 'Aspects of Illegality in the Formation and Performance of Contracts', 6 *International Arbitration Law Review* 1

(2003b), 'Approaches to the Application of Transnational Public Policy by Arbitrators', 4 *Journal of World Investment & Trade* 239

(2004), 'The Law Applicable to International Investment Disputes', in: S.M. Kröll and N. Horn (eds.), *Arbitrating Foreign Investment Disputes: Procedural and Substantive Legal Aspects*, The Hague, 401

(2005a), 'Arbitrators and Illegality: The Challenge of Determining the Proper Applicable Law', *The International Who's Who of Commercial Arbitration*, available at: www.shearman.com

(2005b), 'Schiedsgerichte und Rechtsverstösse der Vertragsparteien: Das für die Beurteilung von Rechtsverletzungen anzuwendende Recht', in: B. Bachmann et al. (eds.), *Grenzüberschreitungen, Beiträge zum Internationalen Verfahrensrecht und zur Schiedsgerichtsbarkeit*, Tübingen, 429

(2005c), *Strafrechtsrelevante und andere anstössige Verträge als Gegenstand von Schiedsverfahren, Zum Vorgehen von Schiedsgerichten bei Rechtsverletzungen von Vertragsparteien – ein rechtsvergleichender Beitrag zur nationalen und internationalen Schiedsgerichtsbarkeit*, Frankfurt a.M.

(2010a), 'Corruption in International Investment Arbitration: Jurisdiction and the Unclean Hands Doctrine', in: K. Hobér, A. Magnusson and M. Öhrström (eds.), *Between East and West: Essays in Honour of Ulf Franke*, Huntington NY, 309

(2010b), 'Die Internationale Investitionsschiedsgerichtsbarkeit und die Korruption: Eine alte Herausforderung mit neuen Antworten', *Zeitschrift für Schiedsverfahren (SchiedsVZ)*, 2

(2013a), 'Competence-Competence in the Face of Illegality in Contracts and Arbitration Agreements', 361 *Recueil des Cours, Collected Courses of the Hague Academy of International Law*, 131

(2013b), 'The Role of State Courts in Assisting Arbitral Tribunals Confronted With Guerilla Tactics', in: G.J. Horvath and S. Wilske (eds.), *Guerilla Tactics in International Arbitration*, Alphen aan den Rijn, 102

Kreindler, R.H. and F. Gesualdi (2015), 'The Civil Law Consequences of Corruption Under the UNIDROIT Principles of International Commercial Contracts: An Analysis in Light of International Arbitration Practice', in: M.J. Bonell and O. Meyer (eds.), *The Impact of Corruption on International Commercial Contracts*, Cham et al., 391

Kulick, A. (2012), *Global Public Interest in International Investment Law*, Cambridge

Kulick, A. and C. Wendler (2010), 'A Corrupt Way to Handle Corruption? Thoughts on the Recent ICSID Case Law on Corruption', 37 *Legal Issues of Economic Integration* 61

Kurkela, M.S. (2008), 'Criminal Laws in International Arbitration – the May, the Must, the Should and the Should Not', 26 *ASA Bulletin* 280

Lalive, P. (1987), 'Transnational (or Truly International) Public Policy and International Arbitration', in: P. Sanders (ed.), *Comparative Arbitration Practice and Public Policy in Arbitration*, Deventer, 258

(2009), 'L'ordre public transnational et l'arbitre international', in: *Nuovi strumenti del diritto internazionale privato, Liber Fausto Pocar*, Vol. 2, Milano, 599

Lamm, C.B. (2011), 'Internationalization of the Practice of Law and Important Emerging Issues for Investor-State Arbitration', The Hague Academy of International Law Opening Lecture, 25 July 2011, available at: www.law.yale.edu

Lamm, C.B., B.K. Greenwald and K.M. Young (2014), 'From *World Duty Free* to *Metal-Tech*: A Review of International Investment Treaty Arbitration Cases Involving Allegations of Corruption', 29 *ICSID Review* 328

Lamm, C.B., E.R. Hellbeck and M.I. Khan (2015), 'Pleading and Proof of Fraud and Comparable Forms of Abuse in Treaty Arbitration', in: A.J. van den Berg (ed.), *Legitimacy: Myths, Realities, Challenges*, Alphen aan den Rijn, 557

Lamm, C.B., H.T. Pham and R. Moloo (2010), 'Fraud and Corruption in International Arbitration', in: M.Á. Fernández-Ballesteros and D. Arias (eds.), *Liber Amicorum Bernardo Cremades*, Madrid, 699

Landolt, P. (2012), 'Arbitrators' Initiatives to Obtain Factual and Legal Evidence', 28 *Arbitration International* 173

Lardelli, F. (2014), 'Commentary on Art. 8', in: H. Honsell, N.P. Vogt and T. Geiser (eds.), *Basler Kommentar, Zivilgesetzbuch I, Art. 1–456 ZGB*, 5th edn, Basel

Lauterpacht, E. (2009), 'Foreword', in: C. Schreuer et al., *The ICSID Convention, A Commentary*, 2nd edn, Cambridge, ix

Leuenberger, C. (2008), 'Parteibefragung und Beweisaussage im Entwurf für eine Schweizerische Zivilprozessordnung', in: M. Leupold et al. (eds.), *Der Weg zum Recht, Festschrift für Alfred Bühler*, Zurich, 47

Leuenberger, C. and B. Uffer-Tobler (2016), *Schweizerisches Zivilprozessrecht*, 2nd edn, Bern

Levine, J. (2015), 'Can Arbitrators Choose Who to Call as Witnesses? (And What Can Be Done If They Don't Show Up?)', in: A.J. van den Berg (ed.), *Legitimacy: Myths, Realities, Challenges*, Alphen aan den Rijn, 315

Lew, J.D.M. (1978), *Applicable Law in International Commercial Arbitration*, New York

Lew, J.D.M., L.A. Mistelis and S.M. Kröll (2003), *Comparative International Commercial Arbitration*, The Hague

Lim, K. (2013), 'Upholding Corrupt Investors' Claims against Complicit or Compliant Host States – Where Angels Should Not Fear to Tread', in: K.P. Sauvant (ed.), *Yearbook on International Investment Law & Policy 2011–2012*, Oxford

Litwin, D. (2013), 'On the Divide between Investor-State Arbitration and the Global Fight against Corruption', 10(3) *Transnational Dispute Management*

Llamzon, A.P. (2014), *Corruption in International Investment Arbitration*, Oxford

Llamzon, A. (2015), '*Yukos Universal Limited (Isle of Man) v The Russian Federation*, The State of the 'Unclean Hands' Doctrine in International Investment Law: *Yukos* as both Omega and Alpha', 30 *ICSID Review* 315

Llamzon, A. and A. Sinclair (2015), 'Investor Wrongdoing in Investment Arbitration: Standards Governing Issues of Corruption, Fraud, Misrepresentation and Other Investor Misconduct', in: A.J. van den Berg (ed.), *Legitimacy: Myths, Realities, Challenges*, Alphen aan den Rijn, 451

Losco, M.A. (2014), 'Streamlining the Corruption Defense: A Proposed Framework for FCPA-ICSID Interaction', 63 *Duke Law Journal* 1201

Lüderssen, K. (1984), *Kriminologie, Einführung in die Probleme*, Baden-Baden

Mächler-Erne, M. and S. Wolf-Mettier (2013), Commentary on Art. 19, in: H. Honsell et al. (eds.), *Basler Kommentar, Internationales Privatrecht*, 3rd edn, Basel

Makinwa, A.O. (2009), 'Civil Remedies for International Corruption: The Role of International Arbitration', in: O. Meyer (ed.), *The Civil Law Consequences of Corruption*, Baden-Baden, 257

(2013), *Private Remedies for Corruption, Towards an International Framework*, The Hague

Manciaux, S. (2008), 'The Notion of Investment: New Controversies', 9 *Journal of World Investment & Trade* 443

Mantilla-Serrano, F. (2004), 'Towards a Transnational Procedural Public Policy', 20 *Arbitration International* 333

Martin, A.T. (2003), 'International Arbitration and Corruption: An Evolving Standard', available at: www.timmartin.ca

Martin, J. (2014), *English Legal System*, London and New York

Mayer, P. (1986), 'Mandatory Rules of Law in International Arbitration', 2 *Arbitration International* 274

(2006), 'Effect of International Public Policy in International Arbitration?', in: L.A. Mistelis and J.D.M. Lew (eds.), *Pervasive Problems in International Arbitration*, Alphen aan den Rijn, 61

Mbiyavanga, S. (2017), 'Improving domestic governance through international investment law: Should bilateral investment treaties learn from international anti-corruption conventions?', Research Paper, 2017 OECD Global Anti-Corruption & Integrity Forum, available at: www.oecd.org

McDougall, A. de Lotbiniére (2005), 'International Arbitration and Money Laundering', 20 *American University International Law Review* 1021

Mégevand, G. (2013), *Confiscation et corruption, L'application des articles 70 et 71 CP dans le contexte des infractions réprimées par les articles 322*[ter] *ss CP et 4a LCD*, Basel

Mehren, R.B. von (1996), 'Burden of Proof in International Arbitration', in: A.J. van den Berg (ed.), *Planning Efficient Arbitration Proceedings, the Law Applicable in International Arbitration*, 123

Menaker, A.J. (2010), 'The Determinative Impact of Fraud and Corruption on Investment Arbitrations', 25 *ICSID Review* 67

Mendes, R.O.B. (2009), 'A Private Transnational Law to Transnational Legal Regimes?', in: G.-P. Calliess et al. (eds.), *Soziologische Jurisprudenz, Festschrift für Gunther Teubner zum 65. Geburtstag*, Berlin, 827

Meshel, T. (2013), 'The Use and Misuse of the Corruption Defence in International Investment Arbitration', 30 *Journal of International Arbitration* 267

Meyer, O. (2013), 'The Formation of a Transnational *Ordre Public* against Corruption: Lessons for and from Arbitral Tribunals', in: S. Rose-Ackerman and P.D. Carrington (eds.), *Anti-Corruption Policy, Can International Actors Play a Constructive Role?*, Durham, North Carolina, 229

(2017), *Korruption im Vertrag*, Tübingen

Mills, K. (2002), 'Corruption and Other Illegality in the Formation and Performance of Contracts and in the Conduct of Arbitration Relating Thereto', 5 *International Arbitration Law Review* 126

Mirzayev, R. (2012), 'International Investment Protection Regime and Criminal Investigations', 29 *Journal of International Arbitration* 71

Mistelis, L.A. (2009), 'Legal Issues Arising Out of Disputes Involving Fraud, Bribery, Corruption and Other Illegality and Illicitness Issues', in: E. Gaillard and D. Di Pietro (eds.), *Enforcement of Arbitration Agreements and International Arbitral Awards, The New York Convention in Practice*, London, 573

Moloo, R. (2010), 'A Comment on the Clean Hands Doctrine in International Law', available at: http://ssrn.com/abstract=2358229

Moloo, R. and A. Khachaturian (2011), 'The Compliance with the Law Requirement in International Investment Law', 34 *Fordham International Law Journal* 1473

Mosk, R.M. and T. Ginsburg (2001), 'Evidentiary Privileges in International Arbitration', 50 *International and Comparative Law Quarterly* 345

Mouawad, C. and E. Silbert (2013), 'A Guide to Interim Measures in Investor-State Arbitration', 29 *Arbitration International* 381

Mourre, A. (2009), 'Arbitration and Criminal Law: Jurisdiction, Arbitrability and Duties of the Arbitral Tribunal', in: L.A. Mistelis and S.L. Brekoulakis (eds.), *Arbitrability, International and Comparative Perspectives*, Alphen aan den Rijn

Muller, W.H., C.H. Kälin and J.G. Goldsworth (eds.) (2007), *Anti-Money Laundering, International Law and Practice*, Chichester

Nadakavukaren Schefer, K. (2016), *International Investment Law, Text, Cases and Materials*, 2nd edn, Cheltenham

Nadeau-Séguin, S. (2013), 'Commercial Arbitration and Corrupt Practices: Should Arbitrators Be Bound by a Duty to Report Corrupt Practices?', 10(3) *Transnational Dispute Management*

Nasarre, C. (2013), 'International Commercial Arbitration and Corruption: The Role and Duties of the Arbitrator', 10(3) *Transnational Dispute Management*

Newcombe, A. (2011), 'Investor misconduct: Jurisdiction, admissibility or merits?', in: C. Brown and K. Miles (eds.), *Evolution in Investment Treaty Law and Arbitration*, Cambridge, 187

Newcombe, A. and J.-M. Marcoux (2015), '*Hesham Talaat M. Al-Warraq v Republic of Indonesia*, Imposing International Obligations on Foreign Investors', 30 *ICSID Review* 525

Nicholls, C. et al. (2011), *Corruption and Misuse of Public Office*, 2nd edn, Oxford

Niggli, M.A. and S. Maeder (2013), Commentary on Art. 12, in: M.A. Niggli and H. Wiprächtiger (eds.), *Basler Kommentar, Strafrecht I, Art. 1–110 StGB, Jugendstrafgesetz*, 3rd edn, Basel

Nueber, M. (2015), 'The Arbitration Agreement and Arbitrability, Corruption in International Commercial Arbitration – Selected Issues', *Austrian Arbitration Yearbook*, 3

Obersteiner, T. (2014), '"In Accordance with Domestic Law" Clauses: How International Investment Tribunals Deal with Allegations of Unlawful Conduct of Investors', 31 *Journal of International Arbitration* 265

Olaya, J. (2009), *Good Governance and International Investment Law, The Challenges of Lack of Transparency, Corruption and Legal Stability with a Particular Reference to Colombia*, Bonn

O'Malley, N.D. (2012), *Rules of Evidence in International Arbitration, An Annotated Guide*, London

Partasides, C. (2010), 'Proving Corruption in International Arbitration: A Balanced Standard for the Real World', 25 *ICSID Review* 47

Patocchi, P.M. and I.L. Meakin (1996), 'Procedure and the Taking of Evidence in International Commercial Arbitration, The Interaction of Civil Law and Common Law Procedures', 7 *International Business Law Journal* 884

Patocchi, P.M. and T. Niedermaier (2013), 'Chapter XV – UNCITRAL Rules', in: Schütze, R.A. (ed.), *Institutional Arbitration, Article-by-Article Commentary*, Munich, 1007

Paulsson, J. (2005), 'Jurisdiction and Admissibility', in: G. Aksen et al. (eds.), *Global Reflections on International Law, Commerce and Dispute Resolution, Liber amicorum in honour of Robert Briner*, Paris, 601

Peters, A. (2016), *Völkerrecht, Allgemeiner Teil*, 4th edn, Zurich

Peterson, L.E. (2002), 'All Roads Lead Out of Rome, Divergent Paths of Dispute Settlement in Bilateral Investment Treaties', available at: www.iisd.org

Petrochilos, G. (2004), *Procedural Law in International Arbitration*, Oxford

Pfisterer, S. (2013), Commentary on Art. 190, in: H. Honsell et al. (eds.), *Basler Kommentar, Internationales Privatrecht*, 3rd edn, Basel

Philip, A. (2003), 'Arbitration – money laundering, corruption and fraud: The role of the tribunals', in: K. Karsten and A. Berkeley (eds.), *Arbitration: Money Laundering, Corruption and Fraud*, ICC Dossiers, Paris, 147

Pieth, M. (1984), *Der Beweisantrag des Beschuldigten im Schweizer Strafprozessrecht*, Basel and Frankfurt a.M.

(2007), 'The Wolfsberg Process', in: W.H. Muller, C.H. Kälin and J.G. Goldsworth (eds.), *Anti-Money Laundering, International Law and Practice*, West Sussex, UK, 93

(2008), *Recovering Stolen Assets*, Bern

(2011), 'Contractual Freedom v. Public Policy Considerations in Arbitration', in: A. Büchler and M. Müller-Chen (eds.), *Private Law, national-global-comparative, Festschrift für Ingeborg Schwenzer zum 60. Geburtstag*, Band II, Bern, 1375

(2012a), *Collective Action: Innovative Strategies to Prevent Corruption*, Zurich and St. Gall

(2012b), 'Der Einfluss des internationalen Rechts auf das Schweizer Strafrecht', 131 *Zeitschrift für Schweizerisches Recht* 233

(2013), Commentary on Arts. 305bis and 322ter, in: M.A. Niggli and H. Wiprächtiger (eds.), *Basler Kommentar, Strafrecht II, Art. 111–392 StGB*, 3rd edn, Basel

(2014a), 'Introduction', in: M. Pieth, L.A. Low and N. Bonucci (eds.), *The OECD Convention on Bribery, A Commentary*, 2nd edn, Cambridge, 3

(2014b), 'Article 7 – Money Laundering', in: M. Pieth, L.A. Low and N. Bonucci (eds.), *The OECD Convention on Bribery, A Commentary*, 2nd edn, Cambridge, 422

(2014c), *Strafrecht Besonderer Teil*, Basel

(2015), *Strafrechtsgeschichte*, Basel

(2016a), *Schweizerisches Strafprozessrecht*, 3rd edn, Basel

(2016b), *Wirtschaftsstrafrecht*, Basel

Pieth, M. and G. Aiolfi (2003), 'The Private Sector becomes Active: The Wolfsberg Process', in: A. Clark and P. Burrell (eds.), *A Practitioner's Guide to International Money Laundering Law and Regulation*, Surrey, UK, 267

Polkinghorne, M. and C.B. Rosenberg (2015), 'The Adverse Inference in ICSID Practice', 30 *ICSID Review* 741

Poudret, J.-F. and S. Besson (2007), *Comparative Law of International Arbitration*, 2nd edn, London

Powles, S., L. Waine and R. May (2015), *Criminal Evidence*, 6th edn, London

Radicati di Brozolo, L. (2013), 'International arbitration and domestic law', in: G. Cordero-Moss (ed.), *International Commercial Arbitration, Different Forms and Their Features*, Cambridge, 40

Raeschke-Kessler, H. (2004), 'Corrupt Practices in the Foreign Investment Context: Contractual and Procedural Aspects', in: N. Horn (ed.), *Arbitrating Foreign Investment Disputes, Procedural and Substantive Legal Aspects*, The Hague, 471

Redfern, A. (1994), 'The Practical Distinction between the Burden of Proof and the Taking of Evidence – An English Perspective', 10 *Arbitration International* 317

Redfern, A. and M. Hunter (2004), *Law and Practice of International Commercial Arbitration*, 4th edn, London

Reed, L., J. Paulsson and N. Blackaby (2011), *Guide to ICSID Arbitration*, 2nd edn, Alphen aan den Rijn

Reiner, A. (1994), 'Burden and General Standards of Proof', 10 *Arbitration International*, 328

Reiner, A. and C. Aschauer (2013), 'Chapter II – ICC Rules', in: R.A. Schütze (ed.), *Institutional Arbitration, Article-by-Article Commentary*, Munich, 25

Reinisch, A. (2008), 'The Role of Precedent in ICSID Arbitration', *Austrian Arbitration Yearbook*, 495

Reisman, W.M. (2007), 'Law, International Public Policy (So-called) and Arbitral Choice in International Commercial Arbitration', in: A.J. van den Berg (ed.), *International Arbitration 2006: Back to Basics?*, Alphen aan den Rijn, 849

Reymond, C. (1994), 'The Practical Distinction between the Burden of Proof and Taking of Evidence – A Further Perspective', 10 *Arbitration International*, 323

Riedo, C. and B. Boner (2014), Commentary on Art. 301, in: M.A. Niggli, M. Heer and H. Wiprächtiger (eds.), *Basler Kommentar, Schweizerische Strafprozessordnung, Jugendstrafprozessordnung, Art. 196–457 StPO, Art. 1–54 JStPO*, 2nd edn, Basel

Rose, C. (2014), 'Questioning the Role of International Arbitration in the Fight against Corruption', 31 *Journal of International Arbitration* 183

Rosell, J. and H. Prager (1999), 'Illicit Commissions and International Arbitration: The Question of Proof', 15 *Arbitration International* 329

Rubins, N. (2004), 'The Notion of "Investment" in International Investment Arbitration', in: N. Horn and S.M. Kröll (eds.), *Arbitrating Foreign Investment Disputes, Procedural and Substantive Legal Aspects*, The Hague, 283

Rüedi, Y. (2009), *Materiell rechtswidrig beschaffte Beweismittel im Zivilprozess*, Zurich and St. Gallen

Sacerdoti, G. (2009), 'Corruption in Investment Transactions: Policy Initiatives, Legal Principles and Arbitral Practice', 24 *ICSID Review* 565

Safferling, C. (2009), 'Das Recht zu schweigen und seine Konsequenzen, Entwicklungen in nationalen und internationalen Strafverfahren', 4 *Zeitschrift für Internationale Strafrechtsdogmatik* 784

Sanders, A. and R. Young (2012), 'From Suspect to Trial', in: M. Maguire, R. Morgan and R. Reiner (eds.), *The Oxford Handbook of Criminology*, 5th edn, Oxford

Sandifer, D.V. (1939), *Evidence Before International Tribunals*, Chicago

Sattar, S. (2011), 'Document Production and the 2010 IBA Rules on the Taking of Evidence in International Arbitration, A Commentary', *International Arbitration Law Review* 210

Sayed, A. (2001), 'La question de la corruption dans l'arbitrage commercial international: Inventaire des solutions', 19 *ASA Bulletin* 653

(2004), *Corruption in International Trade and Commercial Arbitration*, The Hague

Scherer, M. (2002), 'Circumstantial Evidence in Corruption Cases Before International Arbitral Tribunals', 5 *International Arbitration Law Review* 29

Schill, S.W. (2012), 'Illegal Investments in International Arbitration', available at: http://ssrn.com/abstract=1979734

Schlabrendorff, F. von (2005), 'Geldwäsche in internationalen Schiedsverfahren', in: B. Bachmann et al. (eds.), *Grenzüberschreitungen, Beiträge zum Internationalen Verfahrensrecht und zur Schiedsgerichtsbarkeit, Festschrift für Peter Schlosser zum 70. Geburtstag*, 851

Schlosser, P. (1989), *Das Recht der internationalen privaten Schiedsgerichtsbarkeit*, 2nd edn, Tübingen

Schmid, H. (2000), 'Art. 8 ZGB: Überblick und Beweislast', in: C. Leuenberger (ed.), *Der Beweis im Zivilprozess*, Bern

Schmid, N. (2013), *Handbuch des schweizerischen Strafprozessrechts*, 2nd edn, Zurich and St. Gallen

Schmidlin, B. (2013), *Berner Kommentar, Obligationenrecht, Allgemeine Bestimmungen, Mängel des Vertragsabschlusses, Art. 23–31 OR*, 2nd edn, Bern

Schneider, M.E. and M. Scherer (2013), Commentary on Art. 184, in: H. Honsell et al. (eds.), *Basler Kommentar, Internationales Privatrecht*, 3rd edn, Basel

Schnyder, A.K. (1995), 'Anwendung ausländischer Eingriffsnormen durch Schiedsgerichte, Überlegungen zu einem Grundsatzentscheid des Schweizer Bundesgerichts', 59 *Rabels Zeitschrift für ausländisches und internationales Privatrecht* 293

Schreuer, C. et al. (2009), *The ICSID Convention, A Commentary*, 2nd edn, Cambridge

Schwebel, S.M. and S.G. Lahne (1987), 'Public Policy and Arbitral Procedure', in: P. Sanders (ed.), *Comparative Arbitration Practice and Public Policy in Arbitration*, Deventer, 205

Seelmann, K. and C. Geth (2016), *Strafrecht Allgemeiner Teil*, 6th edn, Basel

Segesser, G. von, E. Leimbacher and K. Bell (2014), 'Admitting illegally obtained evidence in CAS proceedings – Swiss Federal Supreme Court Shows Match-Fixing the Red Card', kluwerarbitrationblog.com, 17 October 2014

Sharpe, J.K. (2006), 'Drawing Adverse Inferences from the Non-production of Evidence', 22 *Arbitration International* 549

Sheppard, A. (2011), 'Mandatory Rules in International Commercial Arbitration: An English Law Perspective', in: G.A. Bermann and L.A. Mistelis (eds.), *Mandatory Rules in International Arbitration*, Huntington, 171

Shihata, I.F.I. and A.R. Parra (1994), 'Applicable Substantive Law in Disputes Between States and Private Foreign Parties: The Case of Arbitration Under the ICSID Convention', 9 *ICSID Review – Foreign Investment Law Journal* 183

Shore, L. (2009), 'State Courts and Document Production', in: T. Giovannini and A. Mourre (eds.), *Written Evidence and Discovery in International Arbitration*, Paris, 57

(2011), 'Applying Mandatory Rules of Law in International Commercial Arbitration', in: G.A. Bermann and L.A. Mistelis (eds.), *Mandatory Rules in International Arbitration*, Huntington, 131

Smit, H. (2011), 'Mandatory Law in Arbitration', in: G.A. Bermann and L.A. Mistelis (eds.), *Mandatory Rules in International Arbitration*, Huntington, 207

Smith, J. and S. Nadeau-Séguin (2015), 'The Illusive Standard of Proof in International Commercial Arbitration', in: A.J. van den Berg (ed.), *Legitimacy: Myths, Realities, Challenges*, Alphen aan den Rijn, 134

Spühler, K. (2004), 'Verwendung von legal und illegal beschafften Beweismitteln unter besonderer Berücksichtigung des Daten- und Geheimnisschutzes', 2 *Schweizerische Zeitschrift für Zivilprozess- und Zwangsvollstreckungsrecht* 147

Srinivasan, D. et al. (2014), 'Effect of bribery in international commercial arbitration', 4 *International Journal of Public Law and Policy* 131

Stacher, M. (2011), '"Die Nichtigkeit ist von Amtes wegen zu beachten"', Zur Regel und ihrer Bedeutung bei Korruptionsverdacht in Schiedsverfahren', in:

F. Lorandi and D. Staehelin (eds.), *Innovatives Recht, Festschrift für Ivo Schwander*, Zurich and St. Gall

(2014), 'Rechtsprechung des Bundesgerichts in Schiedssachen (2013 und 2014)', *Aktuelle Juristische Praxis*, 1545

Steinbeisser, A. (1977), *Die Bestechung von Bediensteten in obligationen-, arbeits- und wettbewerbsrechtlicher Hinsicht*, Basel

Stiglitz, J.E. and M. Pieth (2016), *Overcoming the Shadow Economy*, Berlin

Stratenwerth, G. (2011), *Schweizerisches Strafrecht, Allgemeiner Teil I, Die Straftat*, 4th edn, Bern

Stree, W. and B. Hecker (2014), Commentary on § 261, in: Schönke/Schröder, *Strafgesetzbuch, Kommentar*, 29th edn, Munich

Sutter-Somm, T. (2017), *Schweizerisches Zivilprozessrecht*, 3rd edn, Zurich

Tercier, P. (1999), 'La corruption et le droit des contrats', 121(10) *Semaine Judiciaire* 225

Tirado, J., M. Page and D. Meagher (2014), 'Corruption Investigations by Governmental Authorities and Investment Arbitration: An Uneasy Relationship', 29 *ICSID Review* 493

Tophinke, E. (2014), Commentary on Art. 10, in: M.A. Niggli, M. Heer and H. Wiprächtiger (eds.), *Basler Kommentar, Schweizerische Strafprozessordnung, Jugendstrafprozessordnung, Art. 1–195 StPO*, 2nd edn, Basel

Van den Berg, A.J. (1996), 'Argentine engineer v British Company, Award, ICC Case No. 1110, 1963', *Yearbook Commercial Arbitration* XXI, 47

Van Houtte, V. (2009), 'Adverse Inferences in International Arbitration', in: T. Giovannini and A. Mourre (eds.), *Written Evidence and Discovery in International Arbitration*, Paris, 195

Vasani, B.S. and T.L. Foden (2010), 'Burden of Proof Regarding Jurisdiction', in: K. Yannaca-Small (ed.), *Arbitration Under International Investment Agreements, A Guide to the Key Issues*, Oxford, 271

Verniory, J.-M. (2000), 'La libre appréciation de la preuve pénale et ses limites', 118 *Schweizerische Zeitschrift für Strafrecht* 378

Vervaele, J.A.E. (1992), *Fraud against the Community, The Need for European Fraud Legislation*, Deventer

Vest, H. and S. Horber (2014), Commentary Vor Art. 168–176 and on Art. 169, in: M.A. Niggli, M. Heer and H. Wiprächtiger (eds.), *Basler Kommentar, Schweizerische Strafprozessordnung, Jugendstrafprozessordnung, Art. 1–195 StPO*, 2nd edn, Basel

Vincke, F. (2014), 'Recent Anti-Corruption Initiatives and Their Impact on Arbitration', 24 *ICC International Court of Arbitration Bulletin* (2013), Special Supplement, 'Tackling Corruption in Arbitration', 5

Voser, N. (1996), 'Mandatory Rules of Law as a Limitation on the Law Applicable in International Commercial Arbitration', 7 *The American Review of International Arbitration* 319

Voser, N. and B. Moss (2014), 'Arbitral tribunal's admission of unlawfully obtained evidence did not violate procedural public policy (Swiss Supreme Court)', uk.practicallaw.com, 28 May 2014

Waincymer, J. (2012), *Procedure and Evidence in International Arbitration*, Alphen aan den Rijn

Wälde, T.W. (2010), '"Equality of Arms" in Investment Arbitration: Procedural Challenges', in: K. Yannaca-Small (ed.), *Arbitration Under International Investment Agreements, A Guide to the Key Issues*, Oxford, 161

Wehrli, D. and M. Stacher (2013), 'Arbitration Under the Swiss Rules', in: G. Cordero-Moss (ed.), *International Commercial Arbitration, Different Forms and their Features*, Cambridge, 345

Weibel, T. and C. Walz (2016), Commentary on Art. 168, in: T. Sutter-Somm, F. Hasenböhler and C. Leuenberger (eds.), *Kommentar zur Schweizerischen Zivilprozessordnung (ZPO)*, 3rd edn, Zurich

Wells, J. (2014), 'Corruption and collusion in construction: A view from the industry', in: T. Søreide and A. Wells (eds.), *Corruption, Grabbing and Development*, Cheltenham, 23

Wetter, J.G. (1994), 'Issues of Corruption Before International Arbitral Tribunals: The Authentic Text and True Meaning of Judge Gunnar Lagergren's 1963 Award in ICC Case No. 1110', 10 *Arbitration International* 277

Williams, D.A.R. and S. Foote (2011), 'Recent developments in the approach to identifying an 'investment' pursuant to Article 25(1) of the ICSID Convention', in: C. Brown and K. Miles (eds.), *Evolution in Investment Treaty Law and Arbitration*, Cambridge, 42

Wilske, S. (2010), 'Sanctions for Unethical and Illegal Behavior in International Arbitration, A Double-Edged Sword?', 3 *Contemporary Asia Arbitration Journal* 211

Wilske, S. and T.J. Fox (2011), 'Corruption in International Arbitration and Problems with Standard of Proof, Baseless Allegations or Prima Facie Evidence?', in: S. Kröll et al. (eds.), *Liber Amicorum Eric Bergsten, International Arbitration and International Commercial Law: Synergy, Convergence and Evolution*, Alphen aan den Rijn, 489

Wilske, S. and W. Obel (2013), 'The "corruption objection" to jurisdiction in investment arbitration: Does It really protect the poor?', in: K. Nadakavukaren Schefer (ed.), *Poverty and the International Economic Legal System, Duties to the World's Poor*, Cambridge, 177

Wilske, S. and M. Raible (2009), 'The Arbitrator as Guardian of International Public Policy? Should Arbitrators Go Beyond Solving Legal Issues?', in: C.A. Rogers and R.P. Alford (eds.), *The Future of Investment Arbitration*, Oxford, 249

Wilson, S. et al. (2016), *English Legal System*, 2nd edn, Oxford

Wirth, M. (2009), 'Production of Documents and Fraud in International Arbitration', in: T. Giovannini and A. Mourre (eds.), *Written Evidence and Discovery in International Arbitration*, Paris, 177

Wohlers, W. (2014), Commentary on Arts. 10 and 141, in: A. Donatsch, T. Hansjakob and V. Lieber (eds.), *Kommentar zur Schweizerischen Strafprozessordnung (StPO)*, 2nd edn, Zurich

Yackee, J.W. (2012), 'Investment Treaties & Investor Corruption: An Emerging Defense for Host States', 52 *Virginia Journal of International Law* 723

Yannaca-Small, K. (2010), 'Definition of "Investment": An Open-Ended Search for a Balanced Approach', in: K. Yannaca-Small (ed.), *Arbitration Under International Investment Agreements, A Guide to the Key Issues*, Oxford, 243

Yseult, M. (2015), 'English Judges: Little Mice in the Big Business of Corruption?', in: M.J. Bonell and O. Meyer (eds.), *The Impact of Corruption on International Commercial Contracts*, Cham et al., 141

Zadkovich, J. (2011), 'International Commercial Arbitration and the Bribery Act 2010 (United Kingdom): A Matter of Common Sense', 14 *International Arbitration Law Review* 103

Zerbes, I. (2014), 'Article 1 – The Offence of Bribery of Foreign Public Officials', in: M. Pieth, L.A. Low and N. Bonucci (eds.), *The OECD Convention on Bribery, A Commentary*, 2nd edn, Cambridge, 59

Zivkovic, V. (2012), 'Recognition of Contracts as Investments in International Investment Arbitration', 5(1) *European Journal of Legal Studies* 174

Zuberbühler, T. and A. Schregenberger (2016), 'Corruption in Arbitration – The Arbitrator's Duty to Investigate', in: C. Müller, S. Besson and A. Rigozzi (eds.), *New Developments in International Commercial Arbitration 2016*, Zurich, 1

Zuberbühler, T. et al. (2012), *IBA Rules of Evidence, Commentary on the IBA Rules on the Taking of Evidence in International Arbitration*, Zurich

Selected Documentation

AfDB 2014, Sanctions Procedures of the African Development Bank Group, 18 November 2014

AU 2003, African Union Convention on Preventing and Combating Corruption (adopted 11 July 2003; entry into force 5 August 2006)

Botschaft Korruptionsstrafrecht 2014, Botschaft über die Änderung des Strafgesetzbuchs (Korruptionsstrafrecht) vom 30. April 2014 (14.035), BBl 2014 3591

CIArb 2010, Chartered Institute of Arbitrators, Guideline 12, The Proceeds of Crime Act 2002, Guidance for arbitrators and mediators, 2010, available at: www.ciarb.org

CoE 1990, Council of Europe Convention on Laundering, Search, Seizure and Confiscation of the Proceeds from Crime, ETS No. 141 (open for signature 8 November 1990; entry into force 1 September 1993)

1999a, Council of Europe Criminal Law Convention on Corruption, ETS No. 173 (open for signature 27 January 1999; entry into force 1 July 2002)

1999b, Council of Europe Civil Law Convention on Corruption, ETS No. 174 (open for signature 4 November 1999; entry into force 1 November 2003)

2005, Council of Europe Convention on Laundering, Search, Seizure and Confiscation of the Proceeds from Crime and on the Financing of Terrorism, ETS No. 198 (open for signature 16 May 2005; entry into force 1 May 2008)

CoE ECHR 1950, Council of Europe, European Convention on Human Rights (open for signature 4 November 1950; entry into force 3 September 1953)

Collection of ICC Arbitral Awards, Vol. I (1974–1985), Vol. II (1986–1990), Vol. III (1991–1995), Vol. IV (1996–2000), Vol. V (2001–2007), Vol. VI (2008–2011)

Commentary on the Vienna Convention 1988, Commentary on the United Nations Convention against Illicit Traffic in Narcotic Drugs and Psychotropic Substances, New York 1998

EBRD 2014, Document of the European Bank for Reconstruction and Development, Enforcement Policy and Procedures, 25 April 2014

Energy Charter Treaty 1994, The Energy Charter Treaty (ECT) (signed 17 December 1994; entry into force 16 April 1998)

EU 1991, Council Directive 91/308/EEC of 10 June 1991 on prevention of the use of the financial system for the purpose of money laundering (OJ L 166, 77–82)

1995, Convention Drawn up on the basis of Article K.3 of the Treaty on European Union, on the protection of the European Communities' financial interests, 26 July 1995 (OJ C 316, 49–57)

1997a, Convention drawn up on the basis of Article K.3 (2) (c) of the Treaty on European Union on the fight against corruption involving officials of the European Communities or officials of Member States of the European Union, 26 May 1997 (OJ C 195, 2–11)

1997b, Second Protocol, drawn up on the basis of Article K.3 of the treaty on European Union, to the Convention on the protection of the European Communities' financial interests, 19 June 1997 (OJ C 221, 12–22)

2003, Council Framework Decision 2003/568/JHA of 22 July 2003 on combating corruption in the private sector (OJ L 192, 54–56)

2012, European Commission, Proposal for a Directive of the European Parliament and of the Council on the fight against fraud to the Union's financial interests by means of criminal law, 11 July 2012 (COM[2012] 363 final)

2015, Directive (EU) 2015/849 of the European Parliament and of the Council of 20 May 2015 on the prevention of the use of the financial system for the purposes of money laundering or terrorist financing (OJ L 141, 73–117)

FATF Recommendations 2012, Financial Action Task Force, International Standards on Combating Money Laundering and the Financing of Terrorism & Proliferation, The FATF Recommendations, February 2012

FCPA Resource Guide 2012, US Department of Justice and US Securities and Exchange Commission, A Resource Guide to the US Foreign Corrupt Practices Act, 14 November 2012

Geneva Convention 1927, Convention on the Execution of Foreign Arbitral Awards (signed 26 September 1927; entry into force 25 July 1929), League of Nations Treaty Series (Vol. XCII, 301)

Geneva Protocol 1923, Protocol on Arbitration Clauses (signed 24 September 1923; entry into force 28 July 1924), League of Nations Treaty Series (Vol. XXVII, 157)

IADB 2015, Sanctions Procedures of the Inter-American Development Bank, 9 June 2015

IBA 2010, International Bar Association, IBA Rules on the Taking of Evidence in International Arbitration (adopted 29 May 2010)

ICC 2012, Rules of Arbitration of the International Chamber of Commerce (in force as from 1 January 2012)

ICCPR 1966, International Covenant on Civil and Political Rights (adopted 16 December 1966; entry into force 23 March 1976)

ICJ Statute 1945, United Nations, Charter of the United Nations and Statute of the International Court of Justice (signed 26 June 1945; entry into force 24 October 1945)

ICSID Annual Report 2014, International Centre for Settlement of Investment Disputes, Annual Report, 29 August 2014

ICSID 1965, Convention on the Settlement of Investment Disputes between States and Nationals of Other States (open for signature 18 March 1965; entry into force 14 October 1966)

2006, International Centre for Settlement of Investment Disputes, Rules of Procedure for Arbitration Proceedings (Arbitration Rules) (amended and effective 10 April 2006)

2006a, International Centre for Settlement of Investment Disputes, Rules Governing the Additional Facility for the Administration of Proceedings by the Secretariat of the International Centre for Settlement of Investment Disputes (Additional Facility Rules) (amended and effective 10 April 2006)

ILA 2000, International Law Association, London Conference (2000), Committee on International Commercial Arbitration, Interim Report on Public Policy as a Bar to Enforcement of International Arbitral Awards

2002, International Law Association, New Delhi Conference (2002), Committee on International Commercial Arbitration, Final Report on Public Policy as a Bar to Enforcement of International Arbitral Awards

ILC 2001, International Law Commission, Draft Articles on Responsibility of States for Internationally Wrongful Acts (UNGA resolution 56/83 of 12 December 2001, annex)

LCIA 2014, LCIA Arbitration Rules (effective 1 October 2014)

NAFTA 1992, North American Free Trade Agreement (signed 17 December 1992; entry into force 1 January 1994)

New York Convention 1958, Convention on the Recognition and Enforcement of Foreign Arbitral Awards (adopted 10 June 1958; entry into force 7 June 1959), United Nations Treaty Series (Vol. 330, 38)

OAS 1996, Organization of American States, Inter-American Convention against Corruption, (adopted 29 March 1996; entry into force 6 March 1997)

OECD 1997, Convention on Combating Bribery of Foreign Public Officials in International Business Transactions (adopted 21 November 1997; entry into force 15 February 1999)

2009, Recommendation of the Council for Further Combating Bribery of Foreign Public Officials in International Business Transactions (adopted 26 November 2009) with Annexes I and II

2013, Bribery and Corruption Awareness Handbook for Tax Examiners and Tax Auditors, 7 November 2013

PCA 2012, Permanent Court of Arbitration, Arbitration Rules 2012 (effective 17 December 2012)

Regulation (EC) No 593/2008 of the European Parliament and of the Council of 17 June 2008 on the law applicable to contractual obligations (Rome I) (OJ L 177/6, 4 July 2008)

Rome Convention 1980, Convention on the law applicable to contractual obligations opened for signature in Rome on 19 June 1980 (OJ L 266/1, 9 October 1980)

SRIA 2012, Swiss Chambers' Arbitration Institution, the Swiss Chambers of Commerce Association for Arbitration and Mediation, Swiss Rules of International Arbitration (version in force 1 June 2012)

UK MoJ Guidance 2011, UK Ministry of Justice, The Bribery Act 2010, Guidance about procedures which relevant commercial organisations can put into place to prevent persons associated with them from bribing (section 9 of the Bribery Act 2010), March 2011

UN 1945, Charter of the United Nations and Statute of the International Court of Justice (signed 26 June 1945, entry into force 24 October 1945)

1988, United Nations Convention against Illicit Traffic in Narcotic Drugs and Psychotropic Substances (adopted 20 December 1988; entry into force 11 November 1990)

2000, United Nations Convention against Transnational Organized Crime (adopted 15 November 2000 by UNGA resolution 55/25; entry into force 29 September 2003)

UNCAC 2003, United Nations Convention against Corruption (adopted 31 October 2003 by UNGA resolution 58/4; entry into force 14 December 2005)

UNCITRAL 1985, UNCITRAL Model Law on International Commercial Arbitration (United Nations document A/40/17, annex I) (as adopted by the UNCITRAL on 21 June 1985)

2006, UNCITRAL Model Law on International Commercial Arbitration (United Nations documents A/40/17, annex I and A/61/17, annex I) (as adopted by the UNCITRAL on 21 June 1985, and as amended by the UNCITRAL on 7 July 2006)

2013a, UNCITRAL Arbitration Rules (with new article 1, paragraph 4, as adopted in 2013), UNCITRAL Rules on Transparency in Treaty-based Investor-State Arbitration

2013b, UNCITRAL Rules on Transparency in Treaty-based Investor-State Arbitration

VCLT 1969, Vienna Convention on the Law of Treaties (adopted 23 May 1969; entry into force 27 January 1980)

Wolfsberg Principles 2012, The Wolfsberg Group, Wolfsberg Anti-Money Laundering Principles for Private Banking, May 2012

Woolf Committee 2008, Woolf Committee, Business ethics, global companies and the defence industry, Ethical business conduct in BAE Systems plc – the way forward, May 2008, available at: www.baesystems.com

World Bank 2012, World Bank Sanctions Procedures, 15 April 2012

INDEX

www.ingramcontent.com/pod-product-compliance
Lightning Source LLC
LaVergne TN
LVHW011528200926
848484LV00001B/197
* 9 7 8 1 1 0 8 4 1 7 8 4 6 *